The Popes
Against the Jews

The Popes
Against
the Jews

THE VATICAN'S ROLE
IN THE RISE OF MODERN
ANTI-SEMITISM

David I. Kertzer

Alfred A. Knopf   New York   2001

THIS IS A BORZOI BOOK
PUBLISHED BY ALFRED A. KNOPF

Library of Congress Cataloging-in-Publication Data
Kertzer, David I.
The Popes against the Jews: the Vatican's role in the rise of
modern anti-Semitism /
David I. Kertzer.
p. cm.
Includes bibliographical references (p.) and index.
ISBN 0-375-40623-9
1. Judaism—Relations—Catholic Church. 2. Catholic Church—
Relations—Judaism. 3. Christianity and antisemitism.
4. Papacy—History. I. Title.
BM535 K43 2001
261.2'6'09—dc21   2001033728

Manufactured in the United States of America
First Edition

*For Seth
a father's delight*

*and for my sister Eva
one of the fortunate few*

CONTENTS

Introduction   3

PART ONE   *Keeping Jews in Their Place*

    1   A Missed Opportunity   25
    2   Forced Baptisms   38
    3   The Ghetto   60
    4   Ritual Murder Makes a Comeback   86
    5   The End of an Era   106

PART TWO   *The Church and the Rise*
            of Modern Anti-Semitism

    6   The Catholic Press   133
    7   Jewish Vampires   152
    8   France   166
    9   Austria   186
   10   Race   205
   11   Ritual Murder and the Popes
         in the Twentieth Century   213

PART THREE *On the Eve of the Holocaust*

   12   A Future Pope in Poland   239
   13   Antechamber to the Holocaust   264

         Acknowledgments   293
         Appendix: Popes and Their Secretaries of State   297
         Notes   299
         References Cited   329
         Index   345

The Popes
Against the Jews

Introduction

EDWARD CARDINAL CASSIDY, Australian head of the Vatican's
Commission for Religious Relations with the Jews, called in
reporters to announce the long-awaited results of his investigation. It was March 16, 1998—eleven years after Pope John Paul II had
asked the Commission to determine what responsibility, if any, the
Church bore for the slaughter of millions of European Jews during World
War II. For the Church, a more explosive subject could hardly be imag-
ined. It had been thirty-five years since Rolf Hochhuth's play *The Deputy*
had first raised the charge of papal complicity in the Holocaust, triggering Catholic outrage worldwide. Yet the suggestion that the Vatican bore
any responsibility for what had happened to the Jews continued to grate
on Catholic sensibilities. And so nervousness mixed with curiosity as the
report was finally released to a public sharply divided between those worried that it might criticize the Church, and those who feared it would not.

Heightening the drama and underlining the significance of the event,
the Pope himself wrote an introduction to the report. John Paul II hailed
the Commission document—"We Remember: A Reflection on the
Shoah"—as an important part of Church preparations for the upcoming
millennial celebrations. To properly observe the jubilee, the Pope wrote,
the Church's sons and daughters must purify their hearts by examining
the responsibility they bore for sins committed in the past. He voiced the
hope that by providing an accurate account of past evils, the Commission
report would help ensure that such horrors as the Holocaust would never
be repeated. The report's preamble echoed this theme, not only stressing
the Pope's commitment to repentance for past sins, but also linking the
proper understanding of the past to the building of a brighter future.[1]

At the heart of the problem, as the Vatican commissioners recognized, was the fact that the Holocaust had taken place "in countries of long-standing Christian civilization." Might there be some link, they asked, between the destruction of Europe's Jews and "the attitudes down the centuries of Christians toward the Jews"?

Those who feared that the report might criticize past popes or past Church actions were soon relieved to learn that the Commission's answer to this question was a resounding "no." True, the report admitted, Jews had for centuries been discriminated against and used as scapegoats, and, regrettably, certain misguided interpretations of Christian teachings had on occasion nurtured such behavior. But all this regarded an older history, one largely overcome by the beginning of the 1800s.

In the Commission's view, the nineteenth century was the key period for understanding the roots of the Holocaust and, in particular, the reasons why the Church bore no responsibility for it. It was in that turbulent century that new intellectual and political currents associated with extreme nationalism emerged. Amid the economic and social upheavals of the time, people started to accuse Jews of exercising a disproportionate influence. "There thus began to spread," the Commission members argued, "an anti-Judaism that was essentially more sociological and political than religious." This new form of antagonism to the Jews was further shaped by racial theories that first appeared in the latter part of the nineteenth century and reached their terrible apotheosis in the Nazis' glorification of a superior Aryan race. Far from supporting these racist ideologies, the Vatican commissioners asserted, the Church had always condemned them.

And so, according to the report, a crucial distinction must be made. What arose in the late nineteenth century, and sprouted like a poisonous weed in the twentieth, was "anti-Semitism, based on theories contrary to the constant teaching of the Church." This they contrasted with "anti-Judaism," long-standing attitudes of mistrust and hostility of which "Christians also have been guilty," but which, in the Vatican report, had nothing to do with the hatred of the Jews that led to the Holocaust.

When I read the news story of the Vatican press conference, and later read the text of the Commission report, I knew that there was something terribly wrong with the history that the Vatican was recounting. It is a history that many wish had happened, but it is not what actually happened. It is the latter story, sometimes dramatic, sometimes hard to believe, often sad, that I try to tell in the pages that follow.

. . .

JUST HOW LITTLE this history is known was driven home to me by reader reactions to my recent book *The Kidnapping of Edgardo Mortara*. The book tells of a six-year-old Jewish boy in Bologna, Italy, who, in 1858, was taken from his family on orders of the local inquisitor. Having been secretly baptized by a servant—or so it was claimed—the boy, the inquisitor argued, was now Catholic and could not remain in a Jewish household.

"You mean there was still an Inquisition in 1858?" readers asked. "I thought the Inquisition was back in the 1500s or 1600s." I also kept hearing—especially from non-Jewish readers—how amazing it was for them to learn that forcing Jews to wear yellow badges and keeping them locked in ghettoes were not inventions of the Nazis in the twentieth century, but a policy that the popes had championed for hundreds of years.

Although various histories of the fraught relations between the Roman Catholic Church and the Jews have been published, most focus on a more remote past. Others examine Church doctrine, engage in biblical exegesis, or analyze various other texts, and so do not capture the actual struggle between the Church and the Jews. Someone, I thought, needed to write a book about the Church and the Jews in modern times, one that would use original archival documents—many never before examined—to tell a story that has remained in important ways unknown.

This last point is worth emphasizing, because while recent scholarship—especially in Italy—has brought to light important new information about the Vatican and the Jews, much has remained buried in the archives. In this light, Cardinal Ratzinger's announcement in 1998 that, for the first time, the archives of the Holy Office of the Inquisition were being opened to scholars, offered a once-in-a-lifetime opportunity. Sources never before seen by scholars were now available, offering the tantalizing prospect of new insights into Church history. This book rests heavily on these newly available documents from the Inquisition archives, as well as from other Vatican archives that have become open to researchers in recent years. Together with evidence that has been reported in the specialized scholarly literature—mainly in Italy and France—over the past few years, these new sources shed light on a history that until now has remained hidden.[2]

Back in early 1998, news of the impending release of the Vatican report on the Holocaust had brought hope that the Church itself might help rectify the ignorance that surrounded the history of the Church's dealing with the Jews. Pope John Paul II had done much to foster an ecumenical spirit and warmer relations between the Catholic Church and the Jews, and he had called on the Commission to be fearless in confronting the truths of the past. The Commission did not take its task lightly, studying the question for over a decade before formulating its conclusions. Surely, thirty-six years after the Second Vatican Council opened, the time had come for the Church to face up to its own uncomfortable past.[3]

The report's key passage on the rise of modern anti-Semitism explains:

> By the end of the eighteenth century and the beginning of the nineteenth century, Jews generally had achieved an equal standing with other citizens in most states and a certain number of them held influential positions in society. But in that same historical context, notably in the nineteenth century, a false and exacerbated nationalism took hold. In a climate of eventful social change, Jews were often accused of exercising an influence disproportionate to their numbers. Thus there began to spread in varying degrees throughout most of Europe an anti-Judaism that was essentially more sociological and political than religious.

The anti-Semitism embraced by the Nazi regime, the report goes on to say, was the product of this new social and political form of anti-Judaism, which was foreign to the Church, and which mixed in new racial ideas that were similarly at odds with Church doctrine.

This argument, sadly, is not the product of a Church that wants to confront its history. If Jews acquired equal rights in Europe in the eighteenth and nineteenth centuries, it was only over the angry, loud, and indeed indignant protests of the Vatican and the Church. And if Jews in the nineteenth century began to be accused of exerting a disproportionate and dangerous influence, and if a form of anti-Judaism "that was essentially more sociological and political than religious" was taking shape, this was in no small part due to the efforts of the Roman Catholic Church itself.

As this book will show, the distinction made in the report between "anti-Judaism"—of which some unnamed and misinformed Christians were unfortunately guilty in the past—and "anti-Semitism," which led to the horrors of the Holocaust, will simply not survive historical scrutiny.

The notion that the Church fostered only negative "religious" views of the Jews, and not negative images of their harmful social, economic, cultural, and political effects—the latter identified with modern anti-Semitism—is clearly belied by the historical record. As modern anti-Semitic movements took shape at the end of the nineteenth century, the Church was a major player in them, constantly warning people of the rising "Jewish peril." What, after all, were the major tenets of this modern anti-Semitic movement if not such warnings as these: Jews are trying to take over the world; Jews have already spread their voracious tentacles around the nerve centers of Austria, Germany, France, Hungary, Poland, and Italy; Jews are rapacious and merciless, seeking at all costs to get their hands on all the world's gold, having no concern for the number of Christians they ruin in the process; Jews are unpatriotic, a foreign body ever threatening the well-being of the people among whom they live; special laws are needed to protect society, restricting the Jews' rights and isolating them. Every single one of these elements of modern anti-Semitism was not only embraced by the Church but actively promulgated by official and unofficial Church organs.

The Commission's neat distinction between anti-Judaism and anti-Semitism was not new to the 1998 document. In the wake of the Second World War, scholars and theologians close to the Church began to look for a way to defend the Church from the charge of having helped lay the groundwork for the Holocaust. The anti-Semitism/anti-Judaism distinction soon became an article of faith that relieved the Church of any responsibility for what happened. Before long, millions of people came to assume its historical reality.[4]

Given the important role played, as we shall see, by the Jesuit journal *Civiltà cattolica* in this history, I was especially struck by the use of this distinction in a recent history of the journal. Written by the well-respected Church historian and Jesuit priest Giuseppe De Rosa, the book was published on the occasion of the journal's 150th anniversary in 2000.

Father De Rosa notes with regret *Civiltà cattolica*'s century-long campaign against the Jews, observing that the journal only changed course in 1965, in the wake of the Second Vatican Council. "It is necessary, however," he adds, "to note that these [hostile articles] were not a matter of 'anti-Semitism,' the essential ingredient of which is hatred against the

Jews because of their 'race,' but rather anti-Judaism, which opposes and combats the Jews for religious and social reasons." He then lists some of the charges that were regularly made in the journal's pages: "that the Jews battled the Church, that they practiced the ritual murder of Christian children, that they had enormous political power in their hands to the point of controlling governments and, above all, that they possessed great wealth, earned by usury, and thus had incredibly strong economic influence, which they used to the detriment of Christianity and Christian peoples." Father De Rosa adds, quite correctly, that the Jesuit journal was not alone in making such accusations, for they filled the pages of many mainstream Catholic publications.

By way of illustration of *Civiltà cattolica*'s anti-Judaism (as opposed to anti-Semitism), he offers some passages from articles in the journal authored by Fathers Rondina and Ballerini in the 1890s. These tell of Jews' thirst for world domination, their hunger for gold, and their belief that Christians are no better than animals. Wherever the Jews live, in the words of these authors, they "form a *foreign* nation, and sworn *enemy* of [the people's] well-being." What should good Catholics do about this terrible threat to their livelihoods and happiness? The answer offered in the pages of *Civiltà cattolica* was clear: The Jews' *"civil equality"* must be immediately revoked, for "they have no right to it," remaining forever *"foreigners* in every country, *enemies* of the people of every country that puts up with them."[5]

There is an unsettling logic behind both Father De Rosa's use of the anti-Judaism/anti-Semitism distinction, and that of the Vatican Commission itself, for they share a disturbing subtext. They suggest that if the attitudes and actions promulgated by the Church can be labeled "religious," they can be minimized and, in any case, shown to be of a very different kind than the truly dangerous forms of anti-Semitism. Such a distinction also permits the Roman Catholic Church to argue that it played no role in spreading the hatred of the Jews in Europe that helped make the Holocaust possible.

But Father De Rosa has difficulty making this argument, for he cannot ignore Church publications that span the six decades preceding the Holocaust and that are today readily available in libraries around the world. And so along with the "religious" nature of the Church's denunciations of the Jews, he adds the "social." In doing so he is able to include what is historically obvious, and indeed apparent in the examples that he himself

gives: Much of the Church's anti-Jewish campaign involved denunciations of Jews not only as enemies of the Church but as enemies of the
nation, not only as threats to the Christian religion but to Christian people. Yet with the addition of this new category, the whole carefully con-
structed anti-Semitic / anti-Jewish distinction evaporates.

There is another uncomfortable truth that this official Church history
of relations with the Jews obscures. The legislation enacted in the 1930s
by the Nazis in their Nuremberg Laws and by the Italian Fascists with
their racial laws—which stripped the Jews of their rights as citizens—was
modeled on measures that the Church itself had enforced for as long as it
was in a position to do so. Jews in the Papal States were still being prose-
cuted in the nineteenth century when caught without the required yellow
badge on their clothes, mandated by Church councils for over six hundred years. As late as the 1850s, the Pope was busy trying to evict Jews
from most of the towns in the lands he controlled, and forcing them to
live in the few cities that had ghettoes to close them in. Jews were barred
from holding public office or teaching Christian children or even having
friendly relations with Christians. Church ideology held that any contact
with Jews was polluting to the larger society, that Jews were perpetual
foreigners, a perennial threat to Christians.[6]

When all is said and done, the Church's claim of lack of responsibility
for the kind of anti-Semitism that made the Holocaust possible comes
down to this: The Roman Catholic Church never called for, or sanctioned, the mass murder of the Jews. Yes, Jews should be stripped of their
rights as equal citizens. Yes, they should be kept from contact with the
rest of society. But Christian charity and Christian theology forbade good
Christians to round them up and murder them.

Yet if the Vatican never approved the extermination of the Jews—
indeed, the Vatican opposed it (albeit quietly)—the teachings and actions
of the Church, including those of the popes themselves, helped make it
possible. This is the sad but crucial truth that the Vatican Commission
report fails to admit—indeed strongly denies. This responsibility was a
matter, as many have observed, not only of a centuries-long condition-
ing of the Christian population to view the Jews as hateful, but of something much more recent and direct as well. The transition from the old
medieval prejudices against the Jews to the modern, political anti-Semitic
movement that developed in the half-century preceding the Holocaust
found in the Church one of its important architects.

Through the centuries, the Church conditioned people to view Jews as demonic, a threat to society. Donald Niewyk, in his study of German anti-Semitism and the road to the Final Solution, puts the matter this way: "For the vast majority of those supporters [of the Nazi regime], for whom the 'Jewish problem' was anything but central, Nazi Jew-baiting seemed nothing dramatically out of the ordinary. The old antisemitism had created a climate in which the 'new' antisemitism was, at the very least, acceptable to millions of Germans."[7]

Of course, in identifying the roots of Nazi anti-Semitism, we must recognize the fact that there were more Protestants than Catholics in Germany. But my aim here lies elsewhere, and my focus is not on the Nazis themselves. Rather, I take up Pope John Paul II's challenge to look into the role played by the Roman Catholic Church in the historical hatred and persecution of the Jews. In doing so, I focus in particular on how "traditional" Catholic forms of dealing with the Jews became transformed into modern anti-Semitism.

But I cannot resist adding a couple of brief observations here about the Holocaust itself. First, what are we to make of Austria, an overwhelmingly Catholic country that has still not come to terms with the enthusiastic role its people played in the Nazi murder of the Jews? Is there any significance in the fact that Adolf Hitler, a baptized Catholic, spent his early years in Austria, where the Vatican-supported anti-Semitic Christian Social movement was then so active? Indeed, Hitler himself admitted to being inspired by its leader, Karl Lueger. How do we account for the fact that Austrians played a disproportionately large role in the Holocaust? If Simon Wiesenthal's figures are to be credited, half of the Holocaust's crimes were committed by Austrians, despite the fact that they constituted under a tenth of the population of the Greater German Reich.[8] And, to get onto even more contested terrain, could there be any link between the efficiency of the slaughter of millions of Jews in Poland and the deep anti-Semitism inculcated in the Catholic population there? Clearly, the Final Solution in Poland was the product of the Nazis, not the Poles, who were also victims of the Nazis. But if stories of Polish Catholic collaboration in—or, at the least, indifference to—what was happening to their Jewish countrymen are to make any sense, it can only be in the context of the sad history set out in these pages.

The Vatican Commission report of 1998 offers another challenge, even if unintentionally. When writing about "anti-Judaism," those forms of discrimination against Jews that were admittedly linked to Christianity, the Commissioners never stray from the use of the passive voice and remain vague as to just who it was who was guilty of such attitudes and actions, today condemned by the Church. They tell us that sentiments of anti-Judaism in past centuries existed "in some Christian quarters," but are oddly reticent in acknowledging any institutional responsibility of the Church for such sentiments or for the actions that flowed from them. That the Vatican itself was among the primary sources of such antipathy is nowhere admitted.

Where the popes acted as temporal rulers, as they did in the Papal States until the States' absorption into a unified Italy over the period 1859–70, discrimination against Jews was public policy. Indeed, the Jews were consigned to ghettos, made to wear Jew badges on their clothes so all would know of their reviled status, and forbidden to have normal social interaction with their Christian neighbors. The popes and the Vatican worked hard to keep Jews in their subservient place—barring them from owning property, from practicing professions, from attending university, from traveling freely—and they did all this according to canon law and the centuries-old belief that in doing so they were upholding the most basic tenets of Christianity.

If this is a book about the Church and the Jews, it is also the story of the Roman Catholic Church itself and its uneasy transition into modern times. For many decades following the final demise of the Papal States, the Vatican waged a bitter struggle against what it labeled "modern" ideas. For the popes, modernity meant all the things that Church doctrine rejected: freedom of religion, of speech, of the press; the notion of separation between Church and state. In this struggle, Jews came to occupy a surprisingly important place. For it was in the face of the strong opposition of the popes—to whom Jews were divinely ordained pariahs, the murderers of Christ—that, over the course of the nineteenth century, they were emancipated in one country after another. Such admission of Jews to equal civic footing with Christians went directly counter to Church doctrine. Understandably, then, Jews, as major beneficiaries of modern times and the new ideas of freedom and equality, became in the eyes of Vatican prelates preeminent symbols of the modernity they abhorred. Revision of Church doctrine on the Jews was long in coming, the result of a painful process that would come to fruition only with the Second Vatican Council, almost two decades after the end of World War II.

Yet this is not a book about the battle of good against evil. The Church, whatever else it is, is a human institution, composed of popes, cardinals, bishops, inquisitors, monks, simple parish priests, and loyal (and not so loyal) laity. The story I tell in these pages is the story of these people. The tale includes its share of opportunism and deception, but for the most part it is the story of people who were convinced that they were doing God's own work. If I fail to bring their worldview to life, I will have failed to fully accomplish my task. It will also be clear that the Church, despite its hierarchical structure, is not monolithic. In this sense it is misleading to speak of how "the Church" acted toward the Jews. We need to look at the panoply of different players, people who had only partially overlapping perspectives and interests. Among these are important figures in the Church who struggled in vain to change Vatican policy toward the Jews, to treat Jews more humanely. In this sense, the story I tell is one of missed opportunities, of paths not taken.

WE BEGIN IN 1814, following the defeat of Napoleon's armies, with the reestablishment of the Papal States, that swath of central Italy that stretched from Rome northward to Bologna and Ferrara. The previous two decades had been devastating for the Vatican: With the march of French troops down the Italian peninsula, the Papal States had been lost, as had the Holy City of Rome itself, and two successive popes were driven into humiliating exile. In France and elsewhere on the Continent, Church property had been confiscated and religious orders suppressed. Among the many other questions confronting Pius VII on his return to Rome was what to do about the Jews, whose ghetto gates had been torn down by the French. The Pope's decision to force the Jews back into the ghettos was not a foregone conclusion. It proved to be part of a larger, historically fateful choice: Should the Church try to adapt itself to modern times, as some were urging, or should the Pope reestablish the old order, as most of the cardinals insisted was his sacred duty? The sorry saga of the popes and the Jews in the following half century is the story of the consequences of the decision to follow the latter path. It meant resuscitating the Inquisition and redoubling Church efforts to convert the Jews with the help of the police.[9]

The European monarchs restored to their thrones after Napoleon's fall in 1814 were well aware of just how tenuous their hold on power had become, and none were in a more parlous position than the popes themselves. The principles behind the French Revolution had, for influential sectors of public opinion, delegitimated the notion that one's position in life should be based on birth, and stressed instead that equal rights should be enjoyed by all. Many now rejected the divine right of rulers and the notion of a divinely ordained social and political hierarchy. In 1820 and again in 1831, popular revolts against the theocracy threatened to end papal rule. And then, in 1848, revolution broke out, briefly overthrowing the papal regime and driving the Pope from Rome. Eleven years later, the final assault began, and forces fighting for a united Italian nation quickly brought down much of the Papal States. In 1870, the last tottering remnant of papal rule collapsed when Rome itself fell.

All of a sudden, the popes were no longer in a position to keep the Jews in the place that they believed was divinely ordained for them. This proved at first to be only a minor irritant for the Vatican, given the enormity of the other changes it faced. But before long the emancipation of the Jews—which the popes had so long fought against—began to take on larger significance for the Church. Indeed, the Jews became the personification of all the ills of modern times.

Here we need to be careful not to view history backwards. While it is clear to us today that Italy's unification was permanent, and that the Church would have to adapt to the new circumstances, the popes of the time could be forgiven for not sharing this view. For them, the fact that the Papal States had fallen did not mean that they could not rise again. After all, the French had twice taken control of Rome at the turn of the nineteenth century, only to be expelled both times. And as recently as 1848 the Pope had been forced to flee the Holy City amid popular revolt, only to return to power less than two years later.

In fighting change, the popes in the latter decades of the century made use of new tools. Of these, none was more important than the Catholic press, which was given the task of combating the wicked forces of liberalism and secularism. It was in the Catholic press that the Church's battle against liberalism came for a time to focus on the Jews, who were painted as evil conspirators—in cahoots with the Masons—doing the devil's work. And it was in no small part through the press, as we shall see, that traditional Church hostility toward the Jews was transformed into modern anti-Semitism.

Perhaps the most surprising aspect of this late-nineteenth-century

Church campaign against the Jews was its reliance on one of the most medieval forms of anti-Jewish attack: the so-called "blood libel." This was the claim that Judaism commanded its adherents to capture Christian children, mutilate and torture them as painfully as possible, and then drain them of their blood. Jews' need for Christian children's blood was insatiable, thousands of Catholic newspaper accounts informed their readers. The Jewish religion, according to the papers, required such blood for many ritual purposes, from the making of Passover matzah to marriage celebrations. Nor were these charges simply a matter of idle press speculation. Not coincidentally, the closing decades of the century saw an upsurge in Europe in accusations against Jews for the murder of Christian children, charges that led to numerous trials, covered in lurid detail in the Catholic press.

Jews had faced these accusations for hundreds of years, and suffered from the periodic murderous rampages that they triggered. In defending themselves, they had often turned to Rome to ask for the Pope's help. And, indeed, from the thirteenth century on, a number of pontiffs had done what they could to protect the Jews from the blood libel. In reaction to the new outburst of ritual murder charges in the late nineteenth and early twentieth centuries, Jews similarly approached the popes, asking once again for their help—but now in vain. The hostility that greeted these modern pleas tells us much about the depths of anti-Semitism that prevailed at the highest levels of the Church as the twentieth century dawned.

The Russian Revolution in 1917 presented the Church with a new enemy, godless communism, whose spread threatened to destroy Christianity. Given the fact that some of the leaders of the Communist movement were Jewish, it was inevitable, in the context of the Vatican worldview of the time, that communism too should become associated with Judaism, the communist threat with the Jewish threat.

To understand the Vatican's reaction to the rise of Italian fascism and German National Socialism, we have to understand this fear of communism. Over the course of the nineteenth century, Vatican leaders had witnessed, with mounting horror, the rise of a mass socialist movement in Europe. The problem was not simply that the socialists opposed the existing order and displayed overt hostility toward priests and the Church. By the last two decades of the nineteenth century the socialist movement had created a dense network of associations, mutual-aid societies, recreational facilities, newspapers, and local social centers that offered an alternative world to that long provided by the Church, and by the Church alone. In place of the parish hall stood the union hall; in place of the Church's millennial vision was the vision of a workers' paradise; in the place of weekly mass where the local community came together was the weekly socialist party gathering. It was a network that enveloped with particular force that emerging proletarian class which the Church found so threatening, representing all that was new. In Italy as elsewhere, by the end of the century the socialist movement and its unions were spreading rapidly across the countryside as well, where Church influence among the people had previously been unchallenged. The threat, as the Church saw it, only got worse, much worse, with the Russian Revolution, which radicalized socialist forces throughout Europe. At the end of the First World War, amid the massive social upheavals and growing popular grievances, it seemed that the revolution might spread throughout Europe. For the Vatican, a holy struggle was under way, against a great ungodly enemy.

It was in this context that fascism in its various forms—in Italy, then Germany and Spain—came to recommend itself to the Vatican. The fascist regimes were embraced as a God-sent bulwark against the great socialist evil.[10] After having refused for sixty-eight years to recognize the legitimacy of the Italian state, in 1929 the Vatican struck a deal with Mussolini. Roman Catholicism became the official state religion in Italy, and Mussolini was praised as heaven-sent. Not that relations between the Fascists and the Vatican were free of conflict. Both the Italian Fascist and the Nazi regime placed their own ideologies above all others, and admitted no authority equal to their own, a stance the Church could only view with displeasure. Yet, as the Italian Fascist and Nazi anti-Semitic campaigns got under way, the Church's own deep anti-Semitism helped nourish popular support for them, and explains as well the Church's own weak response to their mounting horrors.

To date, the large and rapidly growing literature on Vatican responsibility for the Holocaust has concentrated almost entirely on a single question: What did Pope Pius XII do during the Second World War? Could he have done more to save Europe's Jews? I touch only briefly on this debate here, partly because the ground is already so well covered, but more importantly because I think that the single-minded focus on this question is a mistake. As the major Italian scholar on Pius XII and the Holocaust,

Giovanni Miccoli, has pointed out, by the time the war broke out, the die was in large part already cast: "The machinery of persecution and death followed a course that became increasingly hard to stop."[11]

What is most important for understanding the Church's role in making the Holocaust possible is not the discovery of what Pius XII did or did not do. Much more important is bringing to light the role his predecessors played over the previous decades in dehumanizing the Jews, in encouraging large numbers of Europeans to view them as evil and dangerous. It is only in this context that we can understand why the special legislation that in the 1930s served as the first step toward the Holocaust, making Jews second-class citizens, was greeted with indifference, if not pleasure, by large segments of the European population. Even for the more limited goal of making sense of Pius XII's behavior during the war, we need to understand this longer stretch of history. Only in its light can we understand why, as millions of Jews were being murdered, Pius XII could never bring himself to publicly utter the word "Jew."

Curiously, research on relations between the Vatican and the Jews in the nineteenth and the first four decades of the twentieth century remains skimpy. Emblematic is the fact that while publications on the Roman Inquisition's dealings with the Jews in the sixteenth and seventeenth centuries run to many thousands of pages, studies of the Inquisition and the Jews in the nineteenth century are virtually nonexistent.

The story I tell here for the first time about Achille Ratti in the years just before he became Pope Pius XI in 1922, can be seen in this light. In the literature on Pius XII's failure to speak out during the Holocaust, he is often compared unfavorably to Pius XI, the "good pope," portrayed as a firm foe of anti-Semitism. In this scenario, Pius XII's failings were personal ones, reflecting flaws in his character. Thus, in John Cornwell's recent bestseller, *Hitler's Pope,* Pius XII's "silence" is linked to his personal antipathy to the Jews along with his larger conservative political agenda which privileged maintaining good relations with the Nazi regime. But what if we find that Pius XII's benevolent predecessor shared the same stridently anti-Semitic views? The problem, we would then have to conclude, lies not in the personality or moral qualities of a single pope, but rather in a much more pervasive culture of Vatican anti-Semitism.

If I argue in these pages that the Vatican's denial of Church responsibility for anti-Semitism is belied by the facts, that the institutional Church, from the popes on down, played an important role in the development of modern anti-Semitism, I do not mean to suggest that the Roman Catholic Church is alone to blame for the Holocaust. Such a conclusion would be ludicrous. After all, as noted earlier, Germany had more Protestants than Catholics, and we know that anti-Semitism was widespread among Protestants as well. This is hardly surprising, since both Catholic and Protestant anti-Semitism have common roots in pre-Reformation Christianity.

Martin Luther's view of the Jews was no more flattering than that of the Vatican authorities against whom he rebelled. Christ, Luther wrote, viewed the Jews as "poisonous, bitter, vengeful, deceitful snakes, assassins, and the Devil's children, who . . . do harm secretly, because they dare not do it in the open." In his 1543 essay *On the Jews and Their Lies,* Luther branded the Jews a "plague of disgusting vermin" who sought world domination. He urged that their books, synagogues, schools, and houses be burned.[12]

Nor can all European anti-Semitism be attributed directly to Christianity of any sort. Many of the Church's bitterest foes during the eighteenth and nineteenth centuries professed a rather nasty brand of anti-Semitism themselves. Voltaire was not only an ardent anticleric and opponent of Church power, but a sharp-tongued critic of the Jews, whom he described as "an ignorant and barbarous people, who have combined the most sordid greed with the most detestable superstition." And it would be hard to find harsher views of the Jews in the nineteenth century than those expressed by some of the founders of the socialist movement, not least Karl Marx himself. To take but one example, Pierre-Joseph Proudhon called for the abolition of the Jewish religion, saying: "Not for nothing have the Christians called them deicides. The Jew is the enemy of mankind. That race must be sent back to Asia or exterminated."[13]

It is also true that belief in extermination as the proper solution to the "Jewish question"—the policy that produced the Holocaust—was never espoused by the Church, and, indeed, went against basic Church doctrine. Nor was the Nazi goal of a racially purified society—one of the pillars of the German drive to exterminate the Jews—ever shared by the Church; it too ran clearly contrary to Catholic theology.

Yet the physical elimination of the Jews of Europe came at the end of a long road, and, as I hope the following pages will make clear, it was a road that the Catholic Church did a great deal to help build. In many of the countries where the Holocaust unfolded—Austria, Poland, France, and Italy among them—anti-Semitism had for many decades been closely identified with Catholicism. Indeed, as the nineteenth century wore on, anti-Semitism formed an increasingly more—not less—important aspect of Catholic identity. And rather than simply being a vestige of medieval attitudes, the anti-Semitism promulgated in the name of the Church in these countries in these years was in many ways something new.

There are many aspects to this story, and only some can be discussed here. My goal is to get as direct a view as possible of the thinking and the actions of the popes themselves. This approach takes aim at one of the most common defenses offered against Church responsibility for modern anti-Semitism, which holds that, insofar as Catholic anti-Semitism existed in the past, it was the regrettable product of an assortment of renegades, reactionaries, or simply the uninformed and uneducated. In this view, the popes, embodying as they do the Church's highest ideals, always pursued a benevolent policy toward the Jews.

There is a very long history to these attempts to portray the popes as benefactors of the Jews, as their protectors against periodic outbreaks of popular violence whose roots lay outside the Church. Typical are the comments in the article "Jews and Judaism" found in the 1910 edition of the authoritative *Catholic Encyclopedia*. Far from showing any papal antipathy toward the Jews, the author argues, history "bears witness . . . to the untiring and energetic efforts of the Roman pontiffs in behalf of the Jews especially when, threatened or actually pressed by persecution, they appealed to the Holy See for protection. It chronicles the numerous protestations of the popes against mob violence against the Jewish race, and thus directs the attention of the student of history to the real cause of the Jewish persecutions, viz., the popular hatred against the children of Israel."

The article cites four main reasons for this popular hatred of the Jews: (1) "The deep and wide racial difference between Jews and Christians"; (2) "the mutual religious antipathy which prompted the Jewish masses to look upon the Christians as idolaters, and the Christians to regard the Jews as the murderers of the Divine Saviour of mankind, and to believe readily the accusation of the use of Christian blood in the celebration of the Jewish Passover, the desecration of the Holy Eucharist, etc."; (3) "the trade rivalry which caused Christians to accuse the Jews of sharp practice, and to resent their clipping of the coinage, their usury, etc."; and

(4) "the patriotic susceptibilities of the particular nations in the midst of which the Jews have usually formed a foreign element, and to the respective interests of which their devotion has not always been beyond suspicion." Given all these reasons, the *Catholic Encyclopedia* article concludes, "one can readily understand how the popular hatred of the Jews has too often defeated the beneficent efforts of the Church, and notably of its supreme pontiffs, in regard to them."[14]

There is no clearer way to discover the popes' attitudes and policies toward the Jews than seeing how the popes dealt with them when they had the power to do what they liked. This was the case in one place only, the Papal States, the lands that the popes once held as temporal rulers. For my purposes here, the most important period is the most recent, and so I focus on the popes and the Jews in the Papal States in the nineteenth century, a time when Jews were gaining equal rights elsewhere in western and central Europe, and on the following decades leading up to the Holocaust.

The rise of modern anti-Semitism began just after the collapse of the Papal States. In examining this period, I stick as close to the popes as I can get, documenting the role played by the popes and those who served them in fostering the rise of modern anti-Semitism in the late nineteenth century and into the twentieth. The resulting picture bears little relation to the Vatican's recent presentation of this same history.

"History itself," the Vatican Commission report tells us, "is *memoria futuri*," a memory of the future. But the lessons that we draw from history are a poor guide for the future if they are based on a past that we wish had happened, rather than the past that truly did.

I CAN'T RESIST concluding this introduction with some personal reflections that bear on why this book was written. When I began making my own pilgrimages to the Vatican to work in the Inquisition archives and in the Vatican Secret Archives, something from my own family past began to return slowly to me.

When I was just a year old, my father, who was a rabbi, took a new job, becoming the director of interreligious affairs for the American Jewish Committee, a position he held for the next dozen years. His mission— begun just four years after the end of the Second World War—was to work with Catholic priests and Protestant ministers to build new understanding between Jews and Christians. He threw himself into the task with great intellectual energy and sense of purpose. What gave him particular pleasure was the welcoming attitude that he encountered among the Christian clergy with whom he worked.

It soon became clear to me, even as a small child, that my father was especially fond of his Catholic colleagues. He evidently felt more at ease with the Catholic priests than he did with the Protestant ministers. Jews and Catholics, I was somehow led to believe, had more in common than did Jews and Protestants. Partly this stemmed from the common plight of Jews and Catholics as immigrants in the United States, together facing the Protestant establishment. But there was more to it as well, although just what this was is hard to say.

Of the awards my father received in his career, I recall two that were most proudly displayed in our home. One was the bronze star he had been awarded for his service as an army chaplain in Italy and France in the Second World War. The second was a large, imposing (at least to a small child) bronze medallion he had been given at the Vatican, a tribute to the contributions he had made to the promotion of greater understanding between Catholics and Jews.

I imagine some who read this book will say that if my deeper goal in writing it was to follow my father's example, I have done a poor job of it. My portrait of Church treatment of the Jews from the time of Napoleon to the time of Hitler is indeed bleak, one that some will no doubt find offensive. And, a critic might well add, if I am trying to build on my father's efforts to improve relations between Catholics and Jews, criticizing a recent Vatican commission report as a misrepresentation of history seems an odd way to go about it.

I would like to think that, despite such appearances, in digging through Church archives, and in trying to shed new light on the history of the Church and the Jews, I have been continuing my father's work. In collaboration with many brave and good Catholic priests, my father felt privileged to play a small part in a development that would have tremendous importance. With the Second Vatican Council in the early 1960s, the Church renounced its view of the Jews as the perfidious people who had crucified Jesus. It removed negative references to the Jews from the liturgy, undertook a complete revision of what was taught about the Jews in Catholic schools and catechism, and, mercifully, put an official end to the Catholic belief in Jewish ritual murder. Jews rejoiced at these changes, but they were not the only beneficiaries, for the changed attitudes proved to be a tonic for the Church as well.

Pope John Paul II's call, at the dawn of the new millennium, for the Catholic world to confront its past with clear eyes flows from a Christian belief in the need for repentance for sin. In the jubilee year of 2000, millions witnessed the sight of the ailing pontiff in Jerusalem and in Rome, his tremulous hands clutching his text, offering heartfelt apologies for the sins of the past. Throughout the world, non-Catholics as well as Catholics were moved by the Pope's sincerity and his sense of mission.

My own motives in writing this book are naturally different. It is not apologies that I seek, but a clearer understanding of the past. Thanks to Vatican archives that have only recently become available, we can now bring this past into fuller view. The true tale needs to be told, not least because it is much more than a story about the Catholic Church and the Jews. It is a more general human story, found in different forms in different places and in different times, yet often repeated. It is an age-old story of a powerful religion or powerful people that believes in its own divinely ordained position as sole possessor of the Truth and repository of all that is good, and, pitted against it, a despised minority, the Other, the agent of the devil. It should not have taken the Holocaust to teach us how dangerous such views of the world can be, but since the destruction of the Jewish millions, we owe it to the survivors and ourselves to learn its lesson.

PART ONE

Keeping Jews in Their Place

CHAPTER ONE

A Missed Opportunity

THE HISTORY of the Vatican's dealings with the Jews over the past two centuries could well have followed a different path. In many parts of the West, the late eighteenth and early nineteenth centuries marked a watershed as old ideas, products of the Middle Ages, yielded to new, modern ways of looking at the world. Jews benefited from these changes, increasingly being given the same rights as their Christian neighbors. For the Church, wedded to a medieval theocratic outlook through the eighteenth century, the crucial turning point came with the defeat of Napoleon's forces and the restoration of the Papal States in 1814.

Although Napoleon had been defeated, the impact of the Napoleonic period and, more generally, the legacy of the French Revolution, continued to shape the course of European history over the ensuing decades. In the eighteenth century, aside from a tiny number of intellectuals, rule by monarchs and nobility, in partnership with the Church, was widely accepted, although not infrequently resented. A person's position in society was determined by birth. Fatefully, the French Revolution brought with it a very different view of society and of the basis of legitimate authority. Government was to flow from the will of the people, and people's place in life was to be determined by their abilities, not the accident of their birth. People had fundamental rights, and these included the right to profess whatever religion they liked, the right to think as they pleased, and the right to a free press.

While all this had little effect at the time on the peasants, who made up the great majority, it had a profound effect on that literate segment of the population whose sympathies would shape the course of political developments. These ideological currents were further roiled by the spread of the Industrial Revolution, which was transforming social and economic life in an ever-larger part of the continent. The sense that the world was in the grip of great forces of change was widespread, shared by both the old elite, who saw these currents as harbingers of disaster, and by the new classes, who saw them as foretelling a brighter future. With aristocrats remaining in power throughout virtually all of Europe in the three decades following Napoleon's defeat, political opposition—prevented from operating in the open—took the form of plots and conspiracies, leavened with periodic popular revolts. Governments responded with repression, censorship, and increasingly ineffectual appeals to the old verities and to the divinely ordained nature of rule by aristocrats and the Church.

On Pope Pius VII's return from exile in 1814, he faced the task of rebuilding a Church whose institutions were in ruins. It was at just such a time that new directions could be considered. The Pope, however, rejected the advice of those who urged him to adapt to the new era, to abandon the old medieval ways; instead, he made a series of decisions that would prove fateful for the future of the Church, and would weigh heavily on the subsequent history of Europe's Jews.

The late eighteenth century had not been a good time to be a pope. Civil rulers, no longer willing to share power with the Church and hostile toward any foreign interference, looked for ways to limit Vatican influence. In 1773, under the weight of such pressures, Pope Clement XIV was forced to disband the Jesuit order, long viewed as the agent of papal power abroad. His successor, Pius VI, who took office two years later, faced far greater humiliation, compelled to end his quarter-century papacy outside Italy, a helpless prisoner of the French.[1]

Although Pius VI was not the strongest of popes—indeed, he was known for his nepotism, his vanity, and his love of lavish ceremony—he did have at least one strong principled belief, if we can judge by the speed with which he acted. He was angered by his predecessor's benign attitude toward the Jews. In the first decades of the eighteenth century the suffocating restrictions on the Jews put into place in the mid-sixteenth century were somewhat relaxed. Jews were allowed to travel more freely, and given the right to sell new goods, no longer limited to the sale of old clothes and rags. Of all these popes, Clement XIV was surely the most tolerant. One of his first acts on taking the papal throne in 1769 was to remove control over Rome's ghetto from the Holy Office of the Inquisition, reassigning it to the office of Rome's cardinal vicar. Jews were once again permitted to practice medicine, to work as artisans, and even to open small silk and hat factories.[2]

All of this was intolerable for Pius VI, who, immediately after his election, issued an edict that terrified the Jews of the Papal States. Its significance could hardly be overstated, for after several decades in which the Church had seemed to be moving toward more tolerant treatment of the Jews, it returned to the practices of the 1500s. And rather than representing a brief interval of backsliding on an overall course toward modernity, the edict became the blueprint followed by Pius's successors well into the nineteenth century.[3]

"Among the pastoral solicitudes that occupy the soul of the Holiness of our Lord [i.e., the Pope] at the outset of his Pontificate," the edict began, "the foremost priority is that which guards the Catholic religion from corruption among the Faithful. Considering, therefore, the need to protect the faithful from the danger of subversion that can result from excessive familiarity with the Jews, the exact observance of the measures taken by [the Pope's] glorious predecessors is absolutely necessary." Here Pius VI skipped his immediate predecessor to cite earlier examples of proper rigor directed at the Jews. Having conferred with the cardinal inquisitors of the Holy Office, the Pope announced, he was issuing this new edict and ordering its rigorous enforcement throughout the Papal States. The task of overseeing the Jews was to be returned to the inquisitors.

Jews had to be kept in social quarantine so as not to infect the Christian population. The ghetto, designed for this purpose, was over two centuries old at the time Pius VI took office. Before Pope Paul IV came to power in 1555, the Jews of the Papal States had been free to live where they wanted. But the new Pope, who had formerly headed the newly created Holy Office of the Inquisition, had strong feelings about how to deal with the Jews. One of his first acts as pope was to issue a bull that rescinded all of the Jews' previous privileges, forbade them from engaging in any occupation other than selling rags, or from owning any land or houses, and ordered that they be confined to a ghetto. Following the Pope's edict, ghettoes were set up in those towns of the Papal States where Jews resided, forcing them to live in cramped quarters surrounded by walls that closed them off from the Christian population, with gates that locked them in at night. Rome's ghetto was located in a particularly unhygienic, flood-prone part of the city along the banks of the Tiber.

So unpopular was Paul IV, whose reign of terror struck not only the Jews but many others as well, that his death in 1559 was greeted by widespread public rejoicing. The people of the Holy City plundered the palace of the Inquisition, and, before tearing down a statue of the Pope, laughed as a Jew placed atop its head the yellow hat of shame that the Pope had made him wear.[4]

But while Paul IV was gone, the ghetto remained. Indeed, life for the Jews got worse when, in 1593, Pope Clement VIII declared that Jews would only be permitted to live in the ghettoes of two cities, Rome and Ancona. Those living elsewhere were forced out. Carrying their possessions on their backs, the Jews made their way to those places where they were still permitted, whether in the Papal States or in those neighboring states that still allowed them. When the lands of the Duke of Ferrara and the Duke of Urbino were subsequently absorbed into the Papal States in the first half of the following century, the ghettoes where the Jews lived there—Ferrara, Lugo, Cento, Urbino, Senigaglia, and Pesaro—were allowed to remain. As a result, at the time Pius VI came to St. Peter's throne in 1775 and issued his order reinstating all the old restrictions, Jews lived in eight ghettoes, locked in each night behind high walls and heavy gates.[5]

Following the 1775 papal order, a Jew who wanted to spend even a single night outside the ghetto had to apply for special permission. His absence was to be allowed only for a limited period and for good reason. In the time the Jew remained outside the ghetto, he could neither live in the same house with Christians "nor speak familiarly to them."

Everyone was able to tell who was a Jew, because, in another sixteenth-century papal provision reiterated in the 1775 edict, Jews were required to wear a special badge on their clothes. "Jews of both sexes must wear a yellow-colored sign, by which they are distinguished from others, and they must always wear it at all times and places, both in the ghettoes, and when they are outside of them." The men were to wear the yellow sign on their hat, and women on their uncovered hair. To prevent the Jews from giving themselves airs, they were forbidden from riding in carriages or buggies.[6]

Jews were not allowed to keep shops or warehouses outside the ghetto and their social isolation was to be strictly enforced: "The Jews may not play, nor eat, nor drink, nor have any other familiarity or conversation with Christians, nor Christians with Jews, whether in buildings, houses, or vineyards, nor on the street, or in inns, taverns, stores, or elsewhere. And innkeepers, bartenders, and storekeepers shall not permit conversation between Christians and Jews, under the penalty for Jews of ten *scudi* and an indeterminate jail sentence, and for Christians of ten *scudi* and other, corporal punishments."[7]

To further ensure that Christians were uncontaminated by contact with the Jews, the 1775 edict brought back the earlier papal ban on the hiring of Christian domestic help. "Jews cannot keep male or female servants, nor make use of them even for the briefest moment, nor employ them to clean the ghetto, nor to light their fire, nor wash their clothes, nor to do any other task for them."[8]

Any possibility that a Christian might be subjected to the sight of a Jewish ritual was also to be zealously guarded against. Not only were Christians forbidden to set foot in a synagogue or attend any Jewish rite, but Jews were not allowed to employ any ceremony in taking their dead to the cemetery, nor were they allowed to have any inscriptions on their tombstones, which were to remain blank.

Finally, Pius VI ordered the reinstatement of the compulsory, or "forced," sermon, in which the Jews, on a rotating basis, were made to sit and listen to a priest denounce their religion. "The sermon being the most potent and efficient means to obtain the conversion of the Jews . . . we order the rabbis to take every care and due diligence to ensure that . . . the proper number of men and women attend, the number being fixed separately for each ghetto according to its size."[9]

Two decades after Pius VI assumed the papal throne and issued his edict on the Jews, the papal kingdom faced a catastrophe of its own. In 1796, French soldiers, with their doctrine of equal rights for all, invaded the Papal States. In January 1798, Napoleon ordered his troops to march on Rome itself. The following month the Pope, eighty years old, was seized. The ailing pontiff, forced to keep moving up the Italian peninsula and eventually into France, died in August 1799. The man so fond of lavish ceremony was buried in a common graveyard.[10]

It looked as though the end of the papacy might be at hand. But the French armies began suffering reverses and, just a month after the Pope's death, French soldiers retreated from the Holy City. Rome's Jews were especially vulnerable to reprisals by those trying to restore the old order, for they were resented as beneficiaries of the French, who had destroyed the ghetto gates and emancipated them. Now, with troops from Naples retaking the city for the Pope, the Jews were ordered back into the ghetto and required once more to wear the detested yellow sign on their heads.[11]

Amid the chaos of the French retreat, it took three months for the cardinals to gather for their conclave, held in Venice. There, for month after month, they fought over the choice of a new pope. Finally, at the end of March 1800, they elected the bishop of Imola, Cardinal Chiaramonti, a compromise candidate and middle-of-the-roader.

The new Pope, honoring his predecessor by taking the name Pius VII, returned to Rome that year, and briefly revived papal rule. In one of his first and most fateful actions, he named Ercole Consalvi to be a cardinal and appointed him as his secretary of state. Consalvi would prove to be one of the great statesmen of Europe and the most outstanding secretary of state that the Church has ever had.

Consalvi was born in Rome in 1757, and educated at the Academy of Noble Ecclesiastics, something of a training ground for popes and secretaries of state. In 1798, during the French occupation of Italy, he had been arrested by French troops and sent into exile. On becoming Pius VII's secretary of state, Consalvi recognized something that most of his colleagues did not: The world had changed; the Church had to adapt to modern times or face disaster.

The mission he set for himself not only required outwitting Napoleon and the Church's other adversaries, but also outmaneuvering his fellow cardinals for whom change was anathema, indeed the work of the devil. The verities of the Church, they argued, were unchanging.

Just a few months into office, Cardinal Consalvi chose to confide his frustration to his friend Annibale Cardinal della Genga, who, as it turned out, would become the next pope.

It was 3 a.m. on a night in December 1800 that the tireless secretary of state penned his letter to Della Genga. "What little has been accomplished in correcting and improving things, has caused me sweat and blood and . . . spiritual pain. I have talked myself hoarse in vain, saying that the [French] revolution has done to politics and morality what the flood did to physics, changing the entire face of the earth, and that Noah, stepping out of the ark, drank wine and ate meats and did other things that he never did before the flood. Trying to make people reflect on the fact that simply saying that this or that thing wasn't done before, and that our laws are fine as they are, and one shouldn't change anything, and the like, are errors of the most serious sort."[12]

But soon Napoleon was once more on the move, retaking the Italian peninsula. In 1809 the French once again occupied Rome, and drove Pius VII into exile in France. Again the gates of the ghetto were opened and again the Jews were given equal rights. Once more the Jews hoped that their days of living in confinement, of being marched to church for forced sermons, and wearing yellow badges were over forever. But the Jews' liberty was short-lived. Its armies defeated, Napoleon's regime collapsed in 1814, paving the way for the reestablishment of the Papal States.

Postwar peace negotiations began in Paris and then moved to Vienna. Consalvi, who represented the Papal States there, was in a weak position, for he was minister of a power that had virtually no army and that was all too obviously in disarray. Yet despite all this, he was able to win back almost all of the old papal lands, a huge victory for the talented cardinal. But, while he labored in Vienna, the news that he was getting from Rome was not good. His fellow cardinals had, he thought, learned nothing from the experiences of the past two decades. Now that the Pope was back in power, they simply wanted to return to their old ways. As he worked in Vienna to restore the Papal States, back home the reforms that Napoleon had put into place were being rapidly abandoned.

In June 1815, three days after the final peace agreement was signed, Consalvi sent a letter to Rome to Bartolomeo Cardinal Pacca, the man who was serving as secretary of state while he was abroad. "If it was difficult, and God knows it was, to get back that which was obtained," Consalvi wrote, "it will be even more difficult not to lose it. I beg you to listen to what I have to tell you. If we set out on the wrong path, if we commit some irremediable mistake, we won't keep the lands we have regained for more than six months. I wish to God that what lies in the future will not confirm this prophecy, but unfortunately it is just what will happen if we take any false steps."[13]

As it turned out, treatment of the Jews proved to be one of the issues over which this struggle between Consalvi and the hard-liners—known as the *zelanti*—was fought. When Consalvi had first returned to Italy from France in 1814, he learned of a blueprint for the restoration of papal rule prepared for the Pope by Giuseppe Sala, a monk who was close to Cardinal Pacca. Sala's "Plan for Reform Submitted to Pius VII" devoted a great deal of attention to the Jews, whose newfound freedom was a red flag for the conservatives.

"Another disorder that needs to be rectified," Sala wrote, "is the excessive freedom acquired by the Jews, who at present live in perfect communion with the Christians." All of the old restrictions must be brought back, he urged, for they were based on the centuries-old wisdom of the pontiffs. Evil new ideas were abroad in the land: "Ever since there began to be princes seated on the thrones [of Europe] who were imbued with the maxims of modern philosophy, the Jews seized on their chance to shake off their oppression and they knew how to profit from the situation to gain the grace of the Ministers and the Monarchs." The Jews' efforts had been so successful, Sala reported, "that soon they were mixed in with and placed at the same level as the Catholic subjects, and even obtained full freedom and protection for the exercise of their superstitions." It was scandalous: "These implacable enemies of Christianity and these perpetual authors of frauds and swindles found support from those same hands who were supposed to be controlling them and repressing them." The current situation had become intolerable: "In many places, having become rich and powerful, they live promiscuously among the Catholics, hiring them as servants, living together with them." Sala had learned that some Jews in Tuscany were now holding balls in their homes and inviting local Christians there. In one case, he reported, they had "even had the impudence to invite the local parish priest."[14]

When Consalvi learned of these proposals, he told the Pope that such a plan spelled disaster, that reforms had to be introduced if papal rule was to be solidified. As a result of his protests, Sala's plan, parts of which had already been published and distributed, was suppressed. But Sala's star, dimmed though it was by Consalvi, would shine again, for when Della Genga became Pope he made him a cardinal.[15]

For Consalvi, the ecclesiastical calls to have the Jews returned to their ghetto were but another sign of the cardinals' refusal to see that times had changed. This was no time to reintroduce all the old restrictions. The advanced nations of Europe had recently been granting the Jews more and more rights, and both the American and French revolutions had proclaimed the equality of all citizens. To drive the Jews back into the ghettoes was to give ammunition to those who argued that the papacy was an anachronism, a hopeless relic of medieval society.

Immediately after his return from the Congress of Vienna, as he tried to wrest control of papal policies from the hands of the *zelanti*, Consalvi began to be bombarded with requests for instructions on how to deal with the Jews. When, for example, the papal official in charge of Lugo, east of Bologna, asked what to do about the fact that Jewish children had been allowed to attend public schools there, the cardinal told him not to get in the way.

Especially significant was the letter that Consalvi wrote to the papal delegate in Ferrara, Tommaso Bernetti, a man who would later serve as secretary of state himself. In response to Bernetti's request for instruction on what to do about Ferrara's Jews, Consalvi wrote: "Putting the Jews back in their old state of servitude after they have enjoyed full freedom and all the rights of citizenship and putting them back there at a time when the Powers in restoring its states to the Holy See expected that things would be left as they had been under the former governments, would produce the most disgusting political and, indeed, economic consequences. Should the Jews see themselves treated in this way, they would leave the [Papal] States."[16]

But Consalvi was fighting a losing battle. He had higher priorities than the problem of the Jews, and knew that he could only go so far in getting the Pope to act against the advice of the great majority of the other cardinals of the Curia. Even before the Congress of Vienna had ended, the gates of Rome's ghettoes were once again closed, and in August 1814, the Inquisition, abolished by the French, was revived. Jewish students were driven out of the university, and once again the rabbis were required to take part in the humiliating Carnival ritual in which they made their offerings to the Roman authorities in front of a jeering crowd while dressed in grotesque outfits.[17]

The Roman Jews, confined in the heart of the papal kingdom, felt helpless, but the situation of the Jews living in the northern territories was very different. They had been free of Church control much longer—for the better part of two decades—and, following Napoleon's fall, with their land under Austrian control, they had reason to hope that their territories would not be returned to the Pope. When, in 1815, the Congress of Vienna did mandate the return of these territories—known as the Legations—to the Papal States, the Austrian government made clear that it opposed bringing back the old restrictions on the Jews.[18]

Indeed, the Austrian emperor's special minister in charge of coordinating the passage of the Legations from Austrian to papal control intervened on the Jews' behalf in September 1815. With his help, the Jews of Ferrara prepared a petition addressed to Cardinal Consalvi and the Pope, citing the provisions of the recent peace accords. A delegation of Jews brought the petition to Rome.

In September 1815, as they prepared for their encounter with Consalvi, the Ferrara Jews drafted some notes (in French) for the Austrian minister to review. Its key phrase read: "The Jews . . . invoking the protection of His Excellency the Imperial [Austrian] Minister, understand that the Legations have been restored to the Holy See by the House of Austria without any distinction among its inhabitants. Thus the Holy See may not, without violating the act of cession, treat the Jews differently from other citizens."[19]

The final petition they prepared, written on behalf of all the Jews of the recently ceded territories, asked that the Jews be allowed to engage freely in commerce; that they not be made to wear a yellow badge; and that they be permitted to buy property, live outside the ghettoes, and practice medicine, the law, and other professions. "It has been twenty years that the Jews of the Legations have been in possession of these rights, since the time that the Revolution brought its laws which placed the Jews on the same level as other citizens." As a result, the petition continued, "the Jews who have grown up and been educated in this period are entirely accustomed and find it almost natural to enjoy common citizenship, which they now request."[20]

The representative of Ferrara's Jewish community took the petition to Rome, joined by the rabbi of the small ghetto of Lugo, who represented not only the Lugo Jews, but those of Bologna and Cento as well. They met first with Cardinal Consalvi and then were received by Pope Pius VII.

The two men waited in Rome for the Pope's response to their petition, but weeks dragged by and they began to worry that they had been forgotten. In a note they sent to Consalvi on November 17, 1815, they reminded him of their mission, and pleaded that the Jews "not be returned to that state of political existence in which they lived at the end of the last century." Appealing to the Pope's mercy, they asked that he allow the Jews "to keep that civil status which in the previous twenty years modern civilization and the liberal sentiments of the current governments of Europe had guaranteed them."[21]

On that same date, the Austrian minister sent a new plea of his own to

Consalvi. He reminded the secretary of state that in September he had sent him a letter urging a positive response to the Jews' plea. He asked once again that the Jews be allowed to live "without fear of being sent back to that precarious, vilified state in which they found themselves near the end of the past century, leaving them instead in peace to enjoy that civil status which their civilization and the liberal sentiments of the European courts have procured for them over the past twenty years."[22]

The draft of Consalvi's response to the Austrian minister is found among the secretary of state's papers in the state archives of Rome. It is a priceless document, for not only does it reveal Consalvi's views of what should be done about the Jews, but it also makes clear that Pius VII overruled him. Although the draft carries no date, it was likely penned in late November 1815.

"The undersigned Cardinal secretary of state," the note began,

> has examined the petition presented by the Deputies of the Jews living in the lands restored to the Holy See by the Congress of Vienna. Your Excellency has seen fit to recommend the petition to the undersigned, because the requests contained therein seem in accord with the administrative measures adopted by the Great Allied Powers, and with the understandings that were reached between the governments of Rome and Vienna in the restitution of those lands.
>
> Your Excellency, in his wisdom, may know what my own feelings in this regard are, but these are separate from the duties of my office, so I believed it my duty to pass the contents of the abovementioned petition on to His Holiness. I have now obtained his response. As much as the circumstances of the time may suggest that it is not appropriate to return the Jews to that precarious state in which they were found in 1796, His Holiness does not believe it opportune to issue a solemn, public decree, as the Jewish supplicants would like, that they be put on an equal footing with the other Pontifical subjects.
>
> The pious, just heart of His Holiness permits, indeed orders, that the Jews be allowed de facto to remain in the state that they have been in over the past twenty years, although only with the modifications that can make such tolerance compatible with the doctrines of our Holy Religion. However, it is equally repug-

nant to him to make any express, public innovations, different
from what the large majority of his Holy predecessors, albeit in
other times and circumstances, believed appropriate for the good
of the Church and of the state.

Consalvi concluded: "It is therefore with the greatest displeasure that
I cannot at this time respond entirely positively to Your Excellency's
requests. . . ."[23]

Consalvi would continue to do what he could to blunt the edges of
the *zelanti*'s efforts to keep the Jews down, but his options were limited.
In a typical case, in November 1817 the Jews of Ancona pleaded with him
to do something about the archbishop of Ancona. In demanding that the
old restrictions on the Jews be reinstated, the archbishop had ordered that
all of the businesses run by Jews outside the ghetto be closed. "His Holiness [i.e., the Pope]," Cardinal Consalvi wrote the archbishop, "having
taken the matter into careful consideration, while commending Your
Excellency for the zeal you have shown . . . must, at the same time, note
that if the measure [ordered by the archbishop] were fully enforced, great
danger to commerce would result." The Pope therefore called on the
archbishop to grant the Jews special permits. The Jews were to be
allowed to keep the warehouses and stores they had outside the ghetto.
However, the secretary of state added, the law forbidding Jews to hire
female servants or wetnurses was to remain in force.[24]

Until Pius VII's death in 1823, Consalvi continued his efforts to modernize the Papal States and to prevent the *zelanti* from bringing back the
most archaic features of ecclesiastical rule.[25] But in these efforts he had
few allies among the high clergy, and the Pope would only go so far
against the overwhelming sentiment of the cardinals. While Pius VII
was a man of a kind disposition known for his benevolence, he was
not especially confident in his own judgments on matters of Church doctrine. Nicholas Cardinal Wiseman's portrait of the Pope, in attempting
to defend the pontiff against the charge that he was not too intelligent, offers faint praise: "Though not possessed of genius, nor of
over-average abilities perhaps, what he had were fully cultivated and vigorously employed."[26]

As for the Jews, Consalvi's lost battle of 1814–1815 proved fateful.
Thanks to the French invasion, the Jews had been freed, given the same
civil rights as Christians, and released from the ghettos. The Austrians,

who played a key role in the restoration of the lands of the Papal States, urged the Pope not to send the Jews back into the ghettoes, which they viewed as an archaic holdover out of keeping with enlightened administration in modern times. Pius VII was torn: He relied heavily on his secretary of state, and so Consalvi's pleadings no doubt weighed on him. Yet his own view of the pope's duty to treat the Jews as forever degraded, perpetually condemned for the killing of Christ, combined with the near-universal urgings of the cardinals around him, made him unwilling to take that fateful step. Had he acted differently, had Cardinal Consalvi prevailed, the entire history of the Church's relations with the Jews over the next century and a half might have followed a very different course.

CHAPTER TWO

Forced Baptisms

ONE DAY in late October 1815, a young man left Rome's ghetto, passed near the Coliseum, and entered the dark, narrow street where the House of the Catechumens stood. The building, although not particularly imposing in a city filled with monuments and grand palaces, inspired a peculiar kind of terror among the Jews of the city. Twenty-four-year-old Jeremiah Anticoli, seeking a new life, had conquered this fear enough to make his way to the door, but he must have been quaking as he knocked on it. Yet he was not the only Jew there at the time. Others were inside—some who had come freely, some brought in by force and imprisoned in locked rooms.

The rector, don Filippo Colonna, the priest in charge of the institution, was quickly notified of the new arrival, a cause for celebration, for it promised the saving of a soul that was otherwise damned, the winning of a new recruit for the Church. That Jeremiah was Jewish made the prospect of baptism all the more glorious, for the conversion of Jews held special meaning for the Church.

To be in this strange place, filled with crosses and religious paintings, with nuns in their habits and priests in their black gowns, made Jeremiah uneasy. But when asked by the rector whether he had come in order to receive holy grace and become a member of the Church, he replied "Sì."

"Are you married?" don Filippo asked.

"Yes," Jeremiah responded, "I have a wife."

"And what is her name?" asked the rector.

"Pazienza."

"And do you have any children?"

"Yes, a small boy, Lazzaro."

"How old is little Lazzaro?"

"About seven months," replied Jeremiah.

"You have made a momentous decision," the rector told him, "moved no doubt by the spirit of the Lord. But to be received by the Church you must demonstrate your commitment. You must share the blessing you are about to receive by offering your wife and infant son to the Church as well."

Whether Jeremiah was surprised by this request we do not know. He may not have been, for in the short time since the rector had come back from exile, following Pope Pius VII's return and the reestablishment of the papal regime, several men from the ghetto had presented themselves in these walls. Each had been asked the same question. Over the previous fifteen months, what was about to happen to Jeremiah's wife and son had already happened to four other young Roman women and their children. Among the ghetto's inhabitants these were not events that could be easily forgotten.

Once the young man signed the pledge, the rector rushed it over to the chambers of the vicegerent, Archbishop Frattini, who, as the primary deputy of the cardinal vicar of Rome, oversaw such matters. The archbishop, in turn, summoned the criminal magistrate of the vicariate, and gave him his order: He was to assemble a squad of police and extract the young woman and her baby from the ghetto that night.[1]

When the Christian attendant unlocked the ghetto gate that evening, admitting a carriage accompanied by its police escort, a sense of dread spread among the Jews. Those who did not hear the unwelcome sound of the carriage and horsemen were soon awakened by neighbors who spread word of the drama that was then unfolding. Emerging from his carriage, the magistrate demanded to see the three *fattori* of the ghetto. These officials, elected every six months by their fellow Jews, were the men through whom the papal government dealt with the people of the ghetto.

The magistrate showed them the order he had been given by the vicegerent. It called on him to locate nineteen-year-old Pazienza Picciaccio and her baby son, Lazzaro, take them from the ghetto, and deliver them to the House of the Catechumens that night.

Ominously for the magistrate, a rapidly growing crowd of Jews began to surround his carriage, undeterred by the small band of police. Enraged by the magistrate's request, they showered him with epithets, and then turned angrily on their own *fattori* as well, threatening them with dire consequences if they yielded to the magistrate's demands.

The rector, who later described these events in his diary, had his own ideas as to the object of the Jews' rage. The Jews, he thought, were trying to get at the baby, whom they would rather murder than see become a Christian. As he wrote: "Upon hearing of the order to turn over the Jewish woman and her infant, the Jews began to agitate. Some of them, armed with iron clubs, threatened to kill the baby."

With his mission slipping out of control, the distraught magistrate sent one of his men to get reinforcements. But by the time the second squad of police had made its way from the nearby Campidoglio, the crowd of Jews had swollen further. The magistrate was still unable to get hold of Pazienza and her baby. It was only when yet another set of reinforcements arrived, and they threatened to arrest the *fattori* themselves if they did not immediately produce the mother and her baby, that the magistrate succeeded in taking them into custody. Pazienza and her child were thrust into the carriage; the driver whipped the horses, and they rattled down the cobblestone streets, leaving behind the outraged Jews of the ghetto.

In a few minutes, as the bells for midnight chimed, the magistrate delivered his two wards to an impatient rector. But the magistrate was not done, for the treatment he had received in the ghetto could not go unpunished. Returning the next morning to the vicegerent's quarters, he indignantly recounted what had happened. The archbishop, displeased by this latest example of Jewish insubordination, ordered the arrest of the primary instigators of the affair; their trial and punishment would serve as a warning so that the next time a Jew was to be taken from the ghetto, proper decorum would prevail.

Every day for the next six weeks, nineteen-year-old Pazienza was visited by a succession of priests and nuns. Each tried mightily to get her to see the light and open her soul to the Holy Spirit. Hour after hour, Pazienza, whose baby had been taken away from her on her arrival, and who was kept locked in a room, was treated to heartfelt pleas that she embrace the true faith and accept baptism. The rector himself spent an hour or two with her each day, pursuing this holy mission, as did a changing constellation of his colleagues. Yet, despite their stories of the raptures of baptism and the torments that awaited the unbaptized in the Hereafter, and despite the prospect of ending these long hours of daily preaching, Pazienza kept repeating that she was born a Jew and would always be a Jew. She wanted only to be allowed to return home with her baby, she said. The rector applied to her the term that he and his colleagues always used when they encountered such determined resistance: Pazienza was *ostinata*—stubborn.[2]

And so, after thirty-nine days, following the Church law that regulated these attempted conversions, Pazienza was released to the care of the *fattori* of the ghetto to be returned home, one of the rector's failures.[3] Eight days later, on January 11, 1816, she was joined by her husband, Jeremiah, who had himself had second thoughts when he learned that his wife would not join him in converting. They would, as they knew, never see their baby again, for just a few days after Pazienza and Lazzaro had been brought to the House of the Catechumens, the boy had been baptized. In a ceremony performed by the vicegerent himself, Lazzaro the baby Jew became a Christian and was given a new name that symbolized his new identity. He was now Bernardo Maria Fortunato Andrea Cardeli.[4]

THE GHETTO and the House of the Catechumens were the two cornerstones of the Church's Jewish policy. The ghetto embodied all the restrictions that the popes believed had to be placed on the Jews, while the Catechumens was the place designed to save them, the portal through which Jews could escape the ghetto and enter into normal, Christian society.

The ghetto was necessarily a grim place, reflecting the Jews' degraded position as the people who had rejected and killed Christ and then been cast out by God. In contrast, the House of the Catechumens was a holy place, reflecting God's mercy and His saving power. Each conversion of a Jew there reflected the glory and the divinely ordained supremacy of the Roman Catholic Church. The conversion of the Jews was, indeed, one of the centerpieces of the Church's millenarian vision, for according to Christian belief, at the end of time, with the Second Coming, the Jews would be converted.[5]

Jews who entered the House of the Catechumens and prepared for baptism—which for adults usually occurred after a period of study lasting several months—thus occupied particularly hallowed ground in the Holy City. Indeed, on special occasions, popes themselves had presided over the baptism of the Cathecumens' Jews. Pope Benedict XIII marked the jubilee celebrations of the holy year 1725 by performing such a baptism, as did Benedict XIV a quarter-century later.

Baptisms of Jews were a major feature of one of Rome's most sacred annual ceremonies, the celebration of the eve of Easter Sunday in the Pope's cathedral as bishop of Rome, St. John Lateran. In the mid-nineteenth century, Ferdinand Gregorovius, a Protestant German historian who would become the world's greatest expert on medieval Rome, witnessed these rites. He left an evocative, if unflattering, description: "In 1853," he wrote,

> a Jewess was baptized [in the cathedral's baptistery] before a large gathering and with most solemn ceremonies. This daughter of Judah, not fair as Rebecca but of exquisite ugliness, stood at the baptismal font swathed in a white veil, with a burning taper, the symbol of illumination, in her hand, and after her head and the nape of her neck were thoroughly anointed . . . she was led back to the Lateran in procession. The cardinal who had baptized her blessed her before the altar, and when the ceremony was finished, pointing to the baptized woman he expressed his joy to the people that so sublime and divine a miracle had been consummated, that a person who but a moment ago was possessed of demons, and a prey of hell, had suddenly been clothed in the pure innocence of a child and in the pure light of God.[6]

Rome's House of the Catechumens was founded by Pope Paul III in 1543, and kept under close papal control. It was designed to take in both Jews and Muslims, but most of its residents were Jews.[7] In 1634, Pope Urban VIII reorganized its operations, centralizing its three branches in a single location at Madonna dei Monti, where it was still operating in the nineteenth century. In fact, the complex, with the Latin sign over its main portal, remains there today.

The first of its three sections was the House of the Catechumens proper, where the males who came to be baptized lived, and where they typically remained for a time after baptism. A separate building housed the females who entered. It was known as the Monastery of the Annunziatella, for it served as the permanent home of many of the female converts, who became nuns. The third part of the Catechumens, the Collegio, was a place where male converts could receive advanced religious instruction and, for those who chose a religious vocation, train for the priesthood. As priests, the former Jews were particularly valued by the Church for their ability to proselytize among their ex-brethren, familiar as they were with life in the ghetto and with Jewish traditions. However, Jewish converts were considered to be unsuited for pastoral duties, and not permitted to become parish priests.[8]

Although a religious institution, the House of the Catechumens had the power of the papal police behind it, and its residents were not free to come and go as they pleased. The eighteenth-century regulations under which it operated specified that no resident—whether baptized or not—could go out without the rector's permission. Those found outside at night were subject to a month in prison, in shackles, on a diet of bread and water.[9]

Throughout the seventeenth and eighteenth centuries, Rome's House of the Catechumens baptized about ten or a dozen Jews per year, many from Rome but others from lands near and far. What is most striking in looking at the lists of the baptized Jews is their peculiar age and sex distribution. From 1614 to 1798, the adults who came there to be baptized were overwhelmingly men. Indeed, there were practically four Jewish men for every woman. And these men tended to be young, most in their twenties.[10] Jews who chose to abandon the ghetto and embrace the Catholic faith came overwhelmingly in these years from the poorest families. The redoubtable Francesco Rovira Bonet, rector of Rome's Cathecumens for thirty-seven years at the end of the eighteenth century, bemoaned the poor quality of the Jews who entered. "Those who come to the House of the Catechumens to embrace the holy faith," he wrote, "come there wearing filthy rags . . . and are so disgusting that it gives one chills to see them."[11]

What prompted these Jews to take the terrifying step across the Catechumens threshold? Certainly there were cases of people whose motives were purely religious, in the sense that they had had some kind of religious inspiration and felt a spiritual need to convert. But the evidence points to the predominance of more worldly concerns. Conversion offered the poor Jew an escape from the poverty of the ghetto, and the chance to enjoy the freedoms that came with being Christian. Catechumens officials, aided not only by other clergy but also by a network of aristocratic sponsors, helped the men who converted find regular employment and a place to live.

The defeat of the French and the herding of the Jews back into the ghetto hit the men hardest, for they were the ones who had used their freedom to go off in search of a living, often leaving their wives and children back in the ghetto. For Jewish women, whose lives were lived within the Jewish community and, most of all, within the family itself, the prospect of leaving family and community behind to enter a strange institution held little allure. The future for unwed women who entered the Catechumens—either spending the rest of their lives in a convent or having a husband found for them among people they felt no kinship for—similarly had little appeal. The Jewish women who entered the Catechumens did so largely because of their husbands, and in the great majority of these cases, did so only when forced to by the police.[12]

Following the French defeat in 1814 and the restoration of the Pope in Rome, the Catechumens rector once again was able to summon the law's full force in the effort to win Jewish souls to the Church. The previous years had been trying ones for don Filippo, and he meant to do his best to make up lost ground. Two cases illustrate this in a particularly dramatic way. The first concerns the casual baptism of a small child by a Christian visitor to the ghetto; the second, a Jew who had been baptized but who then sought to return to his old faith. Both had gnawed at the rector's conscience in his years of exile during the French occupation. On his return to Rome, he hastened to set things right.

The first of these cases dates to 1809, at a time when Pope Pius VII remained precariously in Rome, at the mercy of Napoleon's army. A widow named Maddalena Pacifici, from a town not far from Rome, in the diocese of Tivoli, headed one day for Rome's ghetto to do some shopping. There, accompanied by two companions from her hometown, she met a young Jewish woman named Rachel, who offered to help her. In Rachel's arms squirmed her three-month-old daughter, Rosa.

As Maddalena would later tell the story, the young Jewish mother complained that her infant was always sick. When Rachel was about to go off to get the various goods that her Christian client had requested, Maddalena offered to hold her baby, an offer Rachel gratefully—if unwisely—accepted.

It was a rainy spring day, and the rush of water through the ghetto streets gave Maddalena an idea. Why not do a good deed and ensure that the sickly Jewish baby was saved, so that if she died, her soul would go to heaven? After a furtive glance behind her to be sure no one was looking, she took off Rosa's bonnet, scooped up a handful of water from the gutter, and dripped it over her head while pronouncing the baptismal formula.

But Maddalena was still not satisfied, for on reflection she was not sure whether water from the street was considered good enough for a baptism. Spotting a fountain nearby, she decided to make sure. Asking one of her friends to stand in such a way as to shield her from inquisitive eyes, Maddalena repeated the baptism at the fountain, uttering the words: "Rosa, I baptize you in the name of the Father, the Son, and the Holy Ghost."

The baby's mother soon returned, arms filled with the things Maddalena had ordered. The women concluded their business, Rachel oblivious to the fact that her life would never again be the same.

On her trips to Rome, Maddalena liked to go to confession and take communion, and she set off to do so the following day. To her shock, when she told the priest what she had done, expecting to be congratulated, her confessor told her that she could not receive absolution or take communion until she had gone to the Ecclesiastical Tribunal and reported what she had done. Maddalena was a devout woman, but when she left the church she was hesitant to follow the priest's injunction. She did not want to delay her return home by getting mixed up with what threatened to become a police matter. She was also fearful of what the Jews might do to her if they found out what she had done.

But no sooner had she arrived home than her conscience began bothering her. And so she went to see her own confessor, and he, too, told her that she must report the matter to her parish priest. The parish priest subsequently initiated his own judicial hearing, taking down not only Maddalena's testimony, but also that of the two friends who had been with her, and sent the whole packet of materials on to the bishop of Tivoli, who forwarded it to Rome.

When the rector, don Filippo, received these papers, he went to see the Pope. That he would go directly to the Pope reflects something of the disorder in which the papal government found itself at the time, for he would normally have gone to the vicegerent and, if doubts remained, sent a brief to the Holy Office of the Inquisition, asking authorization to take the child. Yet the Pope's willingness to meet the rector on short notice about such a matter also reflects the popes' long-standing interest in the work of Rome's House of the Catechumens.

The rector later recounted his meeting with Pius VII, which took place as French troops patrolled the streets of Rome. "Finding himself so constrained, and bereft of his forces," the rector wrote, "the Holy Father postponed the oblation of the little girl who remained in the hands of the Infidels to a more opportune time, and called on me to jealously guard the documents that I had shown him." Indeed, a month later, on June 6, 1809, French troops made their way to the papal palace, seized the Pope, and drove him off into an exile that would last five years. Not long after the Pope was taken, French soldiers arrived at the House of the Catechumens and arrested the rector as well, carting him off without allowing him to retrieve any of his papers. Don Filippo was deported to Corsica, where he remained until the French defeat in 1814.

Among the first things don Filippo did upon his return to Rome was to try to find the documents that he had shown the Pope five years earlier; but these had disappeared. He contacted the bishop of Tivoli, but the bishop's papers, too, had been lost in the Napoleonic mayhem. Fortunately—indeed, providentially, in the rector's recounting—Maddalena herself stopped by one day to ask what had happened to the little girl from the ghetto. After having Maddalena again record her recollections, don Filippo contacted the vicegerent, who sent the police into the ghetto to remove the child and deliver her to the rector.

What followed reflects a familiar pattern in these years: a zealous rector, whose only thought was to bring glory to the Church by winning perfidious Jewish souls for Christ, and a more politically cautious vicegerent. Speaking on behalf of the irate Jews of the ghetto, the *fattori* approached the vicegerent to ask on what basis the child had been taken. They also argued that, as long as the matter of whether a valid baptism had been performed remained in doubt, the child should not be kept at the House of the Catechumens. As a result, on June 1, 1815, the vicegerent sent the rector new instructions, reprimanding him for having kept the girl at the monastery of the Catechumens. He reminded him of Benedict XIV's ruling that while such cases were being decided, small children should be placed "apud honestam Matronam," with a good (Christian) woman.[13]

Don Filippo was no doubt displeased by both the tone and the substance of the note, but it did nothing to diminish his determination to see the girl won over to the Church. Indeed, he went over the vicegerent's head, sending a lengthy petition to the Holy Office of the Inquisition to ask for authorization to take the girl back to the House of the Catechumens. His petition cited various precedents and the rulings of a variety of popes. All of these agreed that a Jewish child who had been baptized—with or without the knowledge of her parents—could not be returned to them, for there she would certainly be turned away from her religion. She would be guilty of apostasy, one of the worst sins imaginable.

On July 5, 1815, with Pope Pius VII presiding, the inquisitors overruled the vicegerent and ordered that, while the case was pending, the child be returned to the House of the Catechumens and placed in its monastery. Six months later, on January 10, 1816, the Holy Office issued its final ruling. Rosa's baptism in the ghetto street was valid, and she could not be returned to her Jewish parents. She was to remain in the monastery of the House of the Catechumens. The Church had won another Jewish soul.[14]

An additional matter of unresolved business had haunted the rector in the years he spent in Corsican exile, a case that was particularly irritating because it hit so close to home. In 1804 Salvatore Tivoli, then aged twenty-four, had appeared at the door of the House of the Catechumens and told the rector that he wanted to convert. After a period of training he was brought to the baptismal font in December of that year and baptized by one of the Church's most prominent cardinals, Giuseppe Albani. In celebration of this honor, Tivoli was given the new last name of Labani, an anagram of that of his sponsor. Having nowhere to go—not being permitted to return to the ghetto, and having no job—Giuseppe (for he was given the cardinal's first name as well) was taken on by the rector himself to serve as the cook for the Catechumens.

One morning, about a year thereafter, Giuseppe vanished. Some months later the rector learned that his former cook had been seen boarding a ship bound for Turkey. The rector subsequently discovered that Giuseppe, using his old name, Salvatore, had settled in the Jewish quarter of Adrianopolis, having abandoned his new religion. The rector could not get the case of the backsliding convert out of his mind. His anger was all the greater when, following French annexation of the grand duchy of Tuscany in 1808, he heard rumors that Tivoli had moved there, living with the Jews in Livorno, confident of his safety. During don Filippo's removal to Corsica, the exiled rector had spent many months mulling this over. "In all this time," he later recalled, "while always trusting in God's mercy that the scourge [i.e., the French occupation] which He had sent to punish all mankind would end, I never stopped thinking of the need to remedy that outrage."

Indeed, as soon as he was released from custody, don Filippo set out for Livorno to arrange the arrest of the apostate. On his arrival there he was recognized and greeted by a man who came from the very parish whose church adjoined Rome's House of the Catechumens. When the rector explained why he was in Livorno, the man told him that he knew where Tivoli lived, adding something that especially piqued the rector's interest: Not only had the apostate recently married, but his wife, Rebecca, was eight months pregnant.

After failing in his initial attempts to get grand duchy officials to arrest Salvatore and his pregnant wife, don Filippo called on the Vatican for support. In reply, acting Secretary of State Pacca sent instructions to the pontifical consul in Tuscany to demand the arrest of the Tivoli couple, on the grounds that they were wanted in the Papal States for the crimes of apostasy and complicity in apostasy. When the consul's initial request to the governor of Livorno went unanswered, he turned up the diplomatic pressure. On June 6 he sent a second letter, making it clear that he was acting on behalf of the Pope himself. "I have received from His Holiness," the consul wrote, "by means of the Most Eminent Secretary of State, the most precise and authoritative orders. His Holiness informs me that the arrest of these persons is of the greatest importance to him. He calls on me to act officially, assuming the powers of the papal nuncio in the name of His Sacred Person at the Imperial and Royal Tuscan Government. Not only does he order me to ask for this arrest, but for police assistance in carrying it out as well."

Ten days later, Rebecca was tracked down in Pisa and arrested. Because she looked as though she might give birth at any minute, she was taken to a hospital rather than a jail, and, indeed, she gave birth the following day. The papal consul interrogated her as she lay in her hospital bed, for her husband was still at large. When the consul learned that, in observance of Jewish dietary laws, Rebecca was refusing her hospital food and getting meals delivered from her family, he demanded that the practice be stopped. He was afraid, he said, that the Jews would try to poison both her and her newborn baby girl.

The Jews of Livorno, who had long enjoyed rights denied Jews elsewhere in Italy, were outraged, and complained to local authorities that their rights were being trampled. As the case dragged on, Cardinal Pacca wrote again, this time addressing his letter directly to the Tuscan authorities. He now demanded the arrest not only of Salvatore Tivoli and his wife but also of Tivoli's brother, sister, and mother, and of Rebecca's parents as well. These family members, all Jews, were accused of abetting apostasy. Cardinal Pacca further demanded that the baby girl be taken from her mother and sent to the House of the Catechumens.

The Tuscan secretary of state, facing these competing pressures, reached a decision a month later: Salvatore Tivoli was to be arrested as soon as he could be found, and turned over to Vatican authorities. Similarly, the infant would be taken from her mother and sent to the House of the Catechumens in Livorno, where she would be at the disposition of the Holy See. But the baby's mother, as well as the other relatives, were in the eyes of the Tuscan government not guilty of any crime and should be released.

Cardinal Pacca made the necessary arrangements, and the baby was brought to Rome in the arms of a wetnurse. She had already been baptized in Livorno—the papal consul there having served as her godfather—and given the name Fortunata, "fortunate one." Her baptismal certificate lists her as an illegitimate child, for in the eyes of the Church her father, though an apostate, remained a Christian, and there could be no valid marriage between a Christian man and a Jewish woman.[15]

These two cases—each involving Pope Pius VII and the forced baptism of a small Jewish child—show how quickly the Church moved in 1814–1815 to take advantage of its newly reestablished police powers to enforce its program of conversion of the Jews.

The case of Maddalena, the Catholic widow who surreptitiously baptized the infant in the ghetto, reflects a practice that had gone on for centuries, and had produced an unending stream of protests from the Jews. Rather than dying out in the nineteenth century, these forced baptisms continued. In responding to the anguished pleas for mercy coming from parents whose babies had been taken by papal police, Vatican officials stuck to the same position that the popes had embraced for centuries: Christians should not go around secretly baptizing Jewish children against their parents' will. Yet a baptism, once performed, was valid, even in cases where it was illicit. The Holy Spirit had entered the child, and in the act of baptism the child's soul was regenerated by Christ's spirit. Such an act of God could not be undone by mere humans. That child was now a Catholic and could not be raised by Jewish parents, for they would undermine that holy transformation. In practice, this meant that whenever Church authorities were informed about such a baptism, they ordered the local police to remove the child from the parents' home and send it to the House of the Catechumens (whether in Rome or in the city where the parents and child lived).

Yet the Church did not always consider it a bad thing for a Christian to baptize a small child secretly, against the parents' wishes. Pope Benedict XIV's rulings on such cases in the mid-eighteenth century remained the operating canon law on the matter throughout the nineteenth century (and, in fact, into the twentieth as well). The Pope declared: "Should a Christian find a Jewish child in danger of death, he will certainly do something praiseworthy and most pleasurable to God by procuring eternal health for the child through baptismal water."[16] For this reason, Maddalena Pacifici's claim that Rachel had told her that little Rosa was in poor health, and, in Maddalena's account, "could die at any minute," was significant. It had no bearing on whether the baptism was valid or not, for the validity of the baptism depended only on whether the proper rite had been followed. But the child's health was central to the issue of whether Maddalena, in the eyes of the Church, had acted well or poorly.

For the cardinals who composed the Congregation of the Holy Office of the Inquisition, the crucial question in forced-baptism cases was to determine whether the proper baptismal rite had been followed. Two elements made such a rite valid and its effects irrevocable. The proper baptismal formula had to be pronounced while water was poured over the child's head, and the person doing the baptizing had to have the proper intent—that is, seriously intend for the child to be regenerated in the spirit of Christ. The formula was simple enough: "I baptize you in the name of the Father, the Son, and the Holy Ghost." The water could come from anywhere, even the street as in Maddalena's case, as long as it was clear. Nor did it take a priest to perform a baptism. Indeed, canon law did not even require that the person doing the baptism be a Christian. Even Jews could perform a valid baptism as long as they followed the proper rite and had the proper intent.

The question of what constituted a valid baptism was at the heart of the case of Perla Bises. The saga began outside Rome in 1814 when two Jewish girls, Perla, age eleven, and her sister Sara, six, befriended two

Christian girls, also sisters, Maria, fifteen, and Giacinta, six. One day, Maria and Giacinta came upon little Sara near her house and invited her to join them. They brought her to the local church where, stopping at the fountain of holy water at the door, Maria cupped her hand, took some water, and poured it over Sara's head, saying: "Sara, now you're a Christian too, because I've put Holy Water on your head." As the water dripped down her hair, Sara burst into tears, and ran home to tell her parents what her friends had done.

Had they heard such a story but a year earlier, Sara's parents would not have been greatly concerned, but times had changed. The Pope had just returned to Rome, the ghetto was being restored, and the Inquisition resuscitated; Jews once again lived in fear and anxiety. Afraid that word of the supposed baptism might reach Church officials at any moment, Sara's parents packed up their belongings and the four of them left Rome for Livorno, where they thought they would be beyond the reach of the Inquisition and the papal police.

There they lived, undisturbed, for three years. As it turned out, if Maria ever did tell anyone what she had done to her little Jewish friend, neither the inquisitors nor the rector of the House of the Catechumens got word of it. After three years in Livorno, confident that the danger had passed, Lazzaro Bises, his wife, and their two daughters moved back to their old home. It was August 1817.

The Bises case then took an odd turn. Sara's experience at the church continued to haunt her older sister, Perla, who became increasingly preoccupied with the idea of baptism and becoming Christian. On February 8, 1818, Perla, by then fifteen years old, sneaked away from home and made her way to the House of the Catechumens, where she told the rector her story. She not only wanted to be baptized, she said, but, believing that her sister had already been baptized, wanted the rector to have Sara brought to the Catechumens as well. Don Filippo needed no prodding, and carefully prepared a petition to the Holy Office of the Inquisition, asking that steps be taken to bring Sara in and determine if she had been baptized.

A few days later he received a response, containing unusually detailed instructions. The two Christian sisters, Maria and Giacinta, were to be interrogated, but care should be taken that they tell no one of the investigation. The Holy Office secretary added that in cases of this sort such an oath of silence was particularly important to prevent the cries of outrage that were likely to arise among the Jews, should they learn of the proceedings. If the investigation determined that Sara had been baptized, she was to be immediately seized and sent to the Catechumens.

Curiously, the Holy Office secretary showed a certain defensiveness in his instructions to the rector: "It must be presumed that the Jews will put up as much resistance as they can to prevent the little girl from being taken away from them. Thus it is advisable to prepare the Acts of the proceedings in the most precise manner, so that they clearly show the thoroughness with which the Church proceeded, and thereby remove any possible pretext that the Jews might have."

An investigation was launched, under a cardinal's direction. After interrogating the two girls, and speaking with their parents, the cardinal concluded that what had occurred had merely been "a simple game among the girls," and hence the proper intent necessary for a valid baptism was missing. Moreover, the proper baptismal formula itself had never been uttered at the time that Maria had poured the water on Sara's head. As a result, Sara remained with her family. She was the only daughter her parents had left, for Perla remained at the House of the Catechumens. On July 2, 1818, she was baptized.[17]

In a sometimes ghoulish variation on these cases of struggle over baptized Jews, several cases arose in these years in which the battle was waged over, not the living, but the dead.

In January 1820, in the grand duchy of Tuscany, where, as we have seen, the government generally afforded more protection for Jews, a Christian midwife secretly baptized the newborn daughter of Abram Castiglione.[18] When the infant died a few days later, the midwife informed the local priest what she had done, and he insisted that the girl be buried in the church cemetery. The father's protests, seconded by the influential Jewish community of Livorno, led grand duchy officials to rule that the tiny cadaver should be returned to Abram, and remain with him until such time as a final decision could be made. An ecclesiastical inquiry by a three-member board of Church theologians followed. The board concluded that the baptism was indeed valid and that the body of the little Christian had to be buried in consecrated ground. And so, six months after the baby's death, her decomposing body was dug up from the Jewish cemetery and buried beside the local church.[19]

Such cases involved the old as well as the young. In November 1851, an elderly Jewish man, Sabato Pavoncello, died in a Rome hospital. On appearing to claim his body, his family was shocked to learn that they could not have it, for he was to be given a Church burial. The ghetto's representatives rushed to the cardinal vicar to demand an explanation, and to insist on the return of Sabato's remains for Jewish burial. The cardinal, in turn, asked hospital officials what had happened. In reply, they sent a statement prepared by the hospital's Catholic chaplain.

Having been called that very morning to the hospital, he wrote, he had been directed to the bed of a dying Jew. The chaplain beseeched the man to embrace the holy faith. "Sabato," he said, "the Messiah, the Savior of the People of Israel, has sent me to you; He does not want you to wait any longer, because He has come, and He wants you to be baptized, and to become a Christian." The chaplain then asked: "If you want to be baptized, and to become a Christian, give me a sign, close your eyes"—and here the chaplain wrote in parentheses, "he had them wide open"—"and grip my hand." And, lo and behold, the chaplain went on, the dying man did give him these two signs, closing his eyes and holding his hand more firmly, so he baptized him. It turned out to be just in time. Within minutes of receiving the baptismal rites, Sabato died.

For the Church, the case was clear; the old man died a Catholic, having been validly and properly baptized, and thereby narrowly avoiding eternal damnation. It was an event to be celebrated. His body could not be returned to the Jews.[20]

But throughout these decades of the nineteenth century, for as long as the Church retained its police powers in the Papal States, the largest number of forced baptisms came not from deathbed conversions, nor from Christian women such as Maddalena, sprinkling water on children they encountered in the ghetto. In fact, the most common agents of the Jews' misfortune in Rome were not Christians, but Jews, and most commonly close family members at that. As we saw earlier, these cases involved Jewish men who came to the Catechumens voluntarily, and then "offered" their wives and children to the Church.

At the heart of the matter was the Church's policy, enforced by the police in Rome throughout the first half of the nineteenth century, that Jews entering the House of the Catechumens had to offer the Church all of their dependents. As we have seen, those who came voluntarily to the House of the Catechumens were overwhelmingly men. Because a man enjoyed legal authority over both his wife and his children, not only could he offer them to the Church, but, indeed, Church authorities required him to do so.

Church officials gave an additional rationale for seizing a man's wife from the ghetto against her will. An 1815 case in Rome led the Inquisition's theological consultant to offer the following reasoning: A man who is married has a natural right to cohabitation with his wife. "But," the theologian noted, "it is prohibited for husbands who have been converted to the [Catholic] faith to cohabit with their [Jewish] wives." In addition, "it is also prohibited in such cases for the convert to have sexual relations with a Jew." Given this situation, he concluded, "it is legitimate to make her come to the House of the Catechumens for a course of instruction for a determinate number of days, so that the impediment, which would otherwise prevent the married couple's cohabitation, can be removed."[21]

Nowhere was the force used by the Church against the Jews in this period clearer than in such cases as these. In the three and a half years from the middle of 1814 through 1818, Church authorities sent the police into the Roman ghetto on twenty-two different occasions, always at night, to extract Jews by force and take them to the House of the Catechumens. In that brief period alone, the police took seventeen married women, three fiancées, and twenty-seven children. The night hours were a time of fear for Rome's Jews.[22]

A common result of these cases was the breakup of the family. When sixty-three-year-old Sabato Rosselli entered the House of the Catechumens on January 25, 1816, he was asked to sign a statement offering his wife and three children. The rector brought the pledge to the vicegerent, Monsignor Frattini, who ordered the police to take the man's wife and children from the ghetto that night. On their arrival at the Catechumens, they were not a happy group. Fifty-year-old Preziosa told the rector that she had no intention of converting, and so was placed in one of the *stanze degl'Ostinati,* the locked rooms in which "stubborn" Jews were put. Try as they might, the rector and his colleagues got nowhere with her. "Always persisting in her Jewish wickedness," the rector recounted in his diary, "in twenty days she never gave even the slightest sign of hope for her conversion." Rather than wasting further energies on her, the vicegerent ordered that she be sent back to the ghetto.

Moses, age eighteen, like his mother, had been placed in solitary confinement on his arrival. In the first days the boy was there, the rector recalled, he remained sullen and unresponsive. This the rector blamed on the threats and bribes made by the Jews in the ghetto before the family was taken. It was partly for this reason—suspected by authorities in all cases where Jews brought in by police refused to convert—that the rector was always in such a rush to have family members extracted from the ghetto. Once it became known in the ghetto that one of their number had entered the Catechumens, family members were, the rector believed, subjected to intense pressure by the other Jews, who frightened and bribed them into holding out against the sacred enticements that they would soon encounter.

Yet eventually, the rector recalled, Moses seemed to be coming around: "Having seen through experience the falsity of what the Jews had told him, he began to respond to the interrogations, and to take some [religious] books to read. All this gave some glimmer of hope that he would see reason." But these hopes for Moses were soon dashed. "The reading of the books, the continuous discussion of the rabbis' false and capricious superstitions, persuaded him in part in favor of the Catholic Religion, but the promises that the Jews made to him steeled him in his desire to return to the Ghetto." Seeing that neither Moses nor his sixteen-year-old brother, Alessandro, would yield, the vicegerent ordered them both returned to the ghetto, just a week after their mother's departure.

The rector had more success with nine-year-old Solomon. Once the boy's recalcitrant mother was out of the way, and the rector and the other priests could spend hours each day with him, he came around. He was baptized little more than a month after his arrival, on February 27. His father was brought to the sacred font three months later.[23]

Although the rector had failed with Preziosa, he had reason not to give up too quickly on such women. Many Jewish women who, on arrival at the Catechumens, had said that they would never abandon their religion were later convinced to change their minds. Church authorities had a powerful weapon to use in this struggle for the souls of these stubborn women, at least for those who had small children. The women were told that, regardless of what either they or their husbands did, their children would soon be baptized. Under no circumstances would Church officials return baptized children to their Jewish parents. In short, the women had a simple choice. They could either accept baptism and thereby keep their children, or leave the House of the Catechumens without them.

As we have seen, despite such pressures many young women remained "obstinate" to the end, and returned to the ghetto knowing that
they would never see their children again. This proved to be the case
when another young man from the ghetto, Giuseppe Funaro, presented
himself at the House of the Catechumens in June 1815. That night, following Giuseppe's pledge, the police entered the ghetto and seized his
twenty-two-year-old wife, Fiore, and their eight-month-old son, Angelo.
Fiore was placed in a room for the *ostinati,* and, although her son was baptized just twelve days after their arrival, and she was told she would lose
him if she persisted in her obstinacy, she only grew surlier as the month
she was enclosed there wore on. At the end of July she was, in the rector's
words, "sent back to the Jews."[24]

One can only imagine the pressure faced by such women during their
weeks in the Catechumens. Take the case of Ezekiel Piatelli, a thirty-
three-year-old man from the ghetto who, in early 1818, came to the House
of the Catechumens. When asked by the rector if he was married, and
had any children, he reported that he had a wife, Regina, aged twenty-
five, and two tiny children, a three-year-old girl, Anna, and Lazzar, born
but three months before. Within four hours of Ezekiel's arrival, the
police had already been sent into the ghetto and had delivered the young
woman and her two little children to the Catechumens.

As the rector tells the story, Regina was obstinate at first but, miraculously, came to see the light. "No sooner had she arrived," he recalled,
"than she asked to be put in the room for the *ostinati,* wanting only to
return to the Ghetto. But after a few days, through the grace of the Lord,
she declared that she wanted to embrace the [true] religion." Indeed, four
months later she was baptized, and so would never return to the ghetto.
What the rector failed to mention is that her two children had been baptized just three days after the family's arrival at the Catechumens.[25]

Special problems arose when the woman offered by her husband to
the House of the Catechumens was thought to be pregnant, for in such
cases there were two souls, not one, to be saved. And while adults could
not be baptized without their consent, in the case of a fetus, and then
newborn, there was no consent to be had. The unfolding of these principles in Catechumens practice can be seen in the several accounts of such
cases recorded in the rectors' diaries in these years.

September 1823 was a memorable month in the Holy City. Pius VII,
who had sat in St. Peter's chair for over two decades, having survived the

Napoleonic invasion and exile, and then returned in triumph to Rome, had just died. The conclave of cardinals called upon to elect his replacement had opened on the second of the month. On the thirteenth, while its deliberations were still going on, a thirty-eight-year-old man from the ghetto, Pellegrino Toscano, presented himself to the Catechumens' rector. The rector could be forgiven if his attention was elsewhere, for all Rome was consumed with rumors about who the next pope would be. Don Filippo was especially interested in the latest news, for the man responsible for the Catechumens, the cardinal vicar of Rome, Annibale della Genga, although not originally regarded as a likely choice, was emerging as one of the top contenders.

That evening, however, the rector was annoyed. When he had taken Pellegrino's notarized "offer" to the vicariate to get authorization to send the police into the ghetto, he discovered that the authorities whose approval was needed were unavailable.

As it turned out, the rector only had to wait one more day for authorization to have Pellegrino's wife, Flaminia, seized and brought in. Yet, in the meantime, an unpleasant situation had developed. Shortly after telling don Filippo that he was married and had a wife who was six months pregnant, and then signing the offer of his wife and his unborn child, the Jew had changed his mind. Barely had the ink on the offer dried when Pellegrino appeared at the rector's rooms and told him that he no longer wanted to become Christian. Moreover, he informed the rector that he was withdrawing the offer he had made: His wife and the baby they were expecting should be left alone. But Pellegrino was in for an unpleasant surprise. "I told him," the rector later recorded, "that he was not in time to retract the offer he had made, that his wife had to come, and that should his child be born, he would have to be baptized."

Pellegrino was shaken by the rector's reply, but over the course of the ensuing weeks he never again changed his mind. He wanted nothing more to do with the Church and, after his obligatory forty days in the Catechumens were over, he returned to the ghetto. His wife, however, was a different story, for the baby she carried had been pledged to the Church and, and so, as long as she remained a Jew, it did not belong to her.

Despite all the rector's entreaties, and those of the other priests and nuns who each day tried to reason with her, Flaminia remained obstinate. When the forty-day period was over, she demanded to go home, as her husband had. But the procedures governing the House of the Catechumens specified that the forty-day limit for *ostinati* did not apply to pregnant women, who were to remain in the monastery until giving birth, so that their baby could be protected.

While being held there, Flaminia refused to eat the food she was given, for it was not kosher. She sobbed and wailed from morning to night, complaining about being locked in her room and about the constant harangues aimed at her by the priests and nuns.

As a result of the uproar that Flaminia caused, and the support she got from ghetto officials, the acting cardinal vicar—the previous vicar, Annibale della Genga, having in the meantime been elevated to the papacy— announced that the woman could return to the ghetto, but only under certain conditions. The ghetto's three *fattori* would be called to the Tribunal and made to sign a pledge agreeing to notify Church officials as soon as Flaminia's labor began, so that a trusted Christian midwife could be dispatched to take care of the birth. The acting vicar threatened the *fattori* with the harshest of punishments should anything "sinister" happen to the unborn child.

On December 23, Flaminia went into labor and the ghetto's representatives, as promised, notified the office of the cardinal vicar, who in turn informed don Filippo. The rector sent for the midwife, who stayed by Flaminia's side throughout the night and delivered her of a little boy the next morning. As soon as the midwife finished washing and swaddling the newborn, she bid his mother goodbye and took him to the Catechumens. Two days later the baby was baptized, with Colonel Filippo Silveni, officer of the pontifical army, serving as his godfather and giving him the name Filippo Salvini. As was customary in such cases, the Jews were sent the bill for the midwife's services.[26]

While these family dramas most commonly involved wives and children, it was another kind of "offer" that provoked the greatest uproar in the ghetto. These occurred when police came to take Jews who were not direct family dependents of the person who was making the offer. Such was the case when one day in 1816 a frail eighty-year-old Jew named David Citone made his way to via Madonna dei Monti and entered the Catechumens door. When the rector discovered that in addition to a wife he had an adult son who himself had a small child, he arranged to have both the wife and the four-year-old granddaughter seized by the police and taken to the Catechumens. The subsequent storm of protest by the Jews, who argued not only that the man was senile, but that legal authority over the girl rested with the girl's father, led to lengthy deliberations by the Holy Office. Early in these deliberations the old man died, but the Holy Office, in its ruling, determined that his offer had been valid when made, and remained so notwithstanding his death. The little girl, whose parents had petitioned in vain to have visiting rights while the case was being adjudicated, was baptized and lodged in the monastery of the Catechumens.[27]

Cases such as these could be multiplied, but the tale they tell would change little. Variations are certainly to be found: young men who offered women who they claimed were their fiancées but who, once taken by the police to the Catechumens, said they had never been engaged; women and boys who, reported by witnesses to have idly expressed an interest in becoming Christians, were pulled into the House of the Catechumens by the police, incarcerated in locked rooms, and pleaded with and cajoled by a succession of clergymen to embrace the true faith. And then there are all the cases of children—one in 1863 of a boy just nine years old—appearing at the Catechumens door and saying that they wanted to leave their parents and be taken in by the Church. The predictable protests from the ghetto followed, along with the Church officials' predictable decision in favor of Religion.

The feeling of dread that hung over the ghetto in the years after the Pope's return to power in Rome, produced by the frequent nocturnal visits of the police and the seizure of women and children, continued for as long as did the Papal States. But the first years of restoration of the papal regime were the worst for the Jews in this respect, despite the fact that, as we will see, Pius VII's successors in other ways made Pius look magnanimous in his treatment of the Jews. In the four and a half years from mid-1814—when the House of the Catechumens was reestablished—to the end of 1818, sixty women and children were extracted by force from Rome's ghetto and confined to the House of the Catechumens. Some of them came back, but for the small children it was a one-way trip.[28]

CHAPTER THREE

The Ghetto

THE 1823 ELECTION of Annibale della Genga to succeed Pius VII came as a surprise. Nicholas Wiseman, Archbishop of Westminster, later recalled the scene when the cardinals entered the Sistine Chapel to begin their deliberations. "Perhaps not a single person there present," he wrote, "noticed one in that procession, tall and emaciated, weak in his gait, and pallid in countenance, as if he had just risen from a bed of sickness, to pass within to that of death."[1] Although Della Genga was then cardinal vicar of Rome, few in either Italy or abroad knew him, partly because he spent many months each year confined to his bedroom. No one initially thought of him as a plausible candidate for the papacy, but, as often happened, this time again two major factions entered the conclave, each with its own candidate, and each failed to marshal the votes needed for election. This time, too, the last-minute search for someone else led to an unexpected choice.

The conclave that elected the bedridden vicar can only be understood in light of the resentment that many cardinals bore toward Ercole Consalvi, Pius VII's long-time secretary of state. Consalvi's efforts to modernize the Church had met with the unremitting hostility of the Church hierarchy. His attempts to limit the privileges of the nobility likewise won him no friends among the cardinals, who almost all came from noble families. While Pius VII remained alive, the other cardinals had little choice but to contain their anger, while doing all they could to thwart Consalvi's reforms. But now they were eager to see his modernizing policies—those modest steps that he had been able to take despite the *zelanti*'s opposition—overturned.

In contrast with his poor standing among his fellow cardinals, Consalvi was highly regarded by the rulers of Europe's great powers. Among

Consalvi's admirers, none was more important than Prince Klemens von Metternich, Austrian chancellor and the architect of the Vienna peace congress that had brought about the restoration following Napoleon's defeat. Fearing that the Church's modest modernizing movement would be sabotaged by the election of one of the *zelanti,* Metternich got in touch with the leaders of other Catholic nations in a futile effort to organize support for the election of Consalvi himself.

As the balloting proceeded, it appeared that Metternich's worst fears were about to be realized, for the *zelanti*'s champion, Antonio Cardinal Severoli, soon approached the two-thirds vote needed for election. At this point, the Austrian statesman intervened. The courts of Austria, France, and Spain each held the right to exclude one candidate from election, as long as it did so before that candidate received the necessary two-thirds. As Severoli neared victory, Metternich had his representative at the conclave, Giuseppe Cardinal Albani, announce the exclusion. The *zelanti* were outraged, but soon regrouped, and Severoli called on his backers to concentrate their votes on another of Consalvi's opponents, Annibale della Genga.[2]

"You have elected a cadaver!" said the sickly cardinal vicar when told of his election.

Della Genga took the name Leo XII, in tribute to Pope Leo XI, the pontiff who had conferred noble status on his ancestors two centuries earlier. A product of the Academy of Noble Ecclesiastics, Della Genga had set out on a diplomatic career that had ended badly. After serving as Pius VI's nuncio in Switzerland and Germany, he had been sent in 1814 to the Paris peace conference by Pius VII when Consalvi was not yet back from exile. He had proceeded slowly to Paris, taking twenty-two days to reach the French capital. Consalvi, having finally been contacted by the Pope, reached Paris but a few days later, and was enraged to learn that Della Genga had traveled at such a leisurely pace that he had missed the initial negotiations. A nasty scene followed, with Consalvi accusing Della Genga of incompetence. The episode had long-term consequences, for it marked a turning point in the relations between the two men. Della Genga joined the *zelanti,* those cardinals hostile to any change, and with them did what he could to thwart the secretary of state's efforts to reform the Papal States.

Despite Della Genga's ignominious return from Paris in 1814, two years later Pius VII named him a cardinal, and appointed him to head the

archdiocese of Senigaglia. The new cardinal never did make it to Senigaglia, for he claimed that the air there was bad for his health, and
two years later resigned the post without ever having set foot in his archbishopric. Two years after that, in 1820, when the prestigious post of vicar
of Rome became open, Pius VII appointed him to it.

On becoming pope, Leo XII appointed his fellow *zelante,* Giulio Cardinal della Somaglia, his predecessor as Rome's cardinal vicar, to replace
Consalvi as secretary of state. In the diplomatic community, the move
inspired little confidence in the new pope, for Della Somaglia was then
eighty-four years old, and spent much of each day resting.

Nor was the new pontiff destined to be popular among the people of
Rome. Shortly after his accession, he launched a stern morality campaign: He ordered the police to prevent taverns from serving alcohol, he
attacked the waltz as obscene, he ordered that statues of naked women
be removed from public view, and he ordered the arrest of any man found
walking too closely behind a woman. The campaign provoked popular
anger and ridicule. Popes customarily received cries of acclamation when
they appeared in the city's streets; where Leo XII passed, he was greeted
only by a stubborn silence. Sensitive to this hostility, he avoided going
out.

The *zelanti,* by contrast, were pleased. Consalvi's reforms were abandoned. Stricter press censorship was put in place, those feudal privileges
of the higher clergy that Pius VII had abolished were reinstated, and
popular opposition to the regime was squelched.

The Papal States seethed with unrest. A case in point was Ravenna,
in the north. Confronting a growing network of underground groups
dedicated to the overthrow of the theocratic state, Leo XII dispatched
the hard-nosed Agostino Cardinal Rivarola to the city. The cardinal proceeded to root out the subversives, overseeing trials in which five hundred
people were found guilty, and several were executed. When, in reaction, Rivarola's secretary was assassinated, the arrests multiplied. Papal
authorities ordered several rebels to be hanged, their bodies left in public
view to serve as a warning to others. Meanwhile, in Rome, the Pope
helped set the new tone by refusing to commute the death sentences of
two leaders of a local revolutionary cell who were seeking the overthrow
of papal rule. The two young men were beheaded in Rome in November
1825.[3]

The Jews occupied a central place in this "rechristianizing" campaign.

Embracing the virtues of the past, and purging the present of all the excrescences of modern times, meant ensuring that the Jews were confined to their divinely ordained place. As cardinal vicar of Rome, Della Genga had been outraged to discover that not all of the Holy City's Jews had returned to their ghetto following the restoration of the papal regime. One of his major projects as cardinal vicar had been to oversee a modest enlargement of the ghetto, to undermine the Jews' complaint that it was impossible for them all to fit in the densely packed space within the old ghetto walls. Now, as pope, he redoubled these efforts. In 1823, in one of his first pontifical acts, Leo XII ordered the Jews back into the ghetto, "to overcome the evil consequences of the freedom that [they] have enjoyed."[4]

Along with his campaign to tighten the seal on the ghetto, Leo XII reinstated another pillar of Church Jewish policy: forced sermons. The *predica coatta* had first been suggested to Pope Gregory XIII in 1584 by a Jewish convert, and former rabbi, Joseph Tzarphati, who had been baptized by Pope Julius III himself. The Jews had long viewed such defectors as their worst enemies, and Tzarphati was a case in point. He convinced the Pope that more converts could be won by forcing the Jews to attend conversionary sermons.

Thereafter, on Saturday afternoons, when Sabbath services at the synagogue had ended, hundreds of Jews would be paraded to a nearby church to listen to an hour-long denunciation of their rabbis, their beliefs, and their practices. The preacher assigned this duty was generally a Dominican—Dominicans being known for both their zeal and their learning—and often himself a Jewish convert. Frequently he would offer a Christian perspective on the weekly portion of the Pentateuch that had been read that day in the synagogue. Attendance was strictly enforced. Over the years, the frequency with which the Jews were required to attend these sermons varied, but with the arrival of the French in the late eighteenth century they were abolished.[5] Much to the Jews' relief, when Pius VII returned to Rome following the French occupation, he showed no interest in bringing them back. For Leo XII, however, this lapse was but another sign of his predecessor's weakness.

Among the beneficiaries of the new Pope's policies was the Holy Office of the Inquisition, which Leo XII turned to for help in his efforts.[6] In the first year of his papacy, he had the Holy Office investigate the extent to which the old restrictions on the Jews in the Papal States were still being enforced. The goal, as an internal Inquisition report expressed it, was "to contain the wickedness of the obstinate Jews so that the danger of perversion of the Catholic faithful" could be avoided. The report expressed dismay that some Jews lived outside the ghettoes, some traveled from place to place without the special permits they were required to get from the local office of the bishop or the inquisitor, and some had opened stores and businesses beyond the ghetto's walls. The list of scandals went on: Jewish men were reported to be having relationships with Christian women; Jewish families were employing Christian servants and wetnurses; and Jews could be seen hiring coachmen and riding around in carriages, an offense to Christian sensibilities. "In a word," the report concluded, "today Christians are found to be subject to the Jews, or at least put on equal footing with them, so that there hardly remains any distinction between them. We are not far, at this point, from seeing them admitted to Citizenship."[7]

The new Pope's efforts to enforce these restrictions on the Jews relied on the bureaucracy of control provided by the Inquisition and by various other agencies of the Papal States. But it also had an ideological component. One of the first signs of this new ideological offensive was the publication, in 1825, of a long treatise on the Jews in Rome's *Ecclesiastical Journal,* which was subsequently published as a separate booklet and went through four printings in 1825–26. Written by the procurator general of the Dominican order, Father Ferdinand Jabalot, it had been directly inspired by Della Genga when he was still cardinal vicar of Rome.

The booklet resurrected many of the traditional Catholic accusations against the Jews: Jews were guilty of deicide, and were crazed with the lust for lucre and the desire to bring about the ruin of Christians. So intense was their hatred of Christianity that no evil was too great for them: "They wash their hands in Christian blood, set fire to churches, trample the consecrated Host . . . kidnap children and drain them of their blood, violate virgins," and on and on.[8]

The exiguous number of Jews in Italy—they constituted less than 0.2 percent of the population—did not deter Jabalot from attributing to them a huge—and pernicious—influence. "In many parts of our land the Jews have become the richest property owners. In some cities money cannot be had, except through them, and so great has the number of mortgages they hold over Christians become, that it is only barely that the

Christians have not yet become their vassals." As for the Jews' character, the portrait could scarcely be worse: "Everywhere one hears of deceptions and frauds they have committed." Many of them are "pickpockets, thieves, swindlers, assassins," and their houses "are the general deposits for all kinds of stolen goods." The Jews are ever busy "cheating, and hoodwinking Christians," which was no surprise, since the Talmud—the Jews' sacred compilation of rabbinical commentary on the laws that governed both their religious beliefs and their social practices—called on Jews to cheat Christians at every opportunity. Christians unfortunate enough to fall into their clutches, Jabalot warned, are likely to emerge "not only without their shirt, but without their skin."[9]

Along with the traditional Catholic charges, Jabalot's text provides some of the germs of what would become the major focus of later-nineteenth-century Catholic characterizations of the Jews. Wherever they live, wrote the Dominican, the Jews "form a state within a state." Unless Christians act quickly, the Jews "will finally succeed in reducing the Christians to be their slaves. Woe to us if we close our eyes! The Jews' domination will be hard, inflexible, tyrannical. . . ."[10] The year was 1825. Jews had not yet been given equal rights in any part of Italy, nor in most of the rest of Europe.

The Pope was pleased with Jabalot's work, and not long after its publication appointed him head of the Dominican order worldwide.[11]

The Holy Office's request in 1823 that the bishops and inquisitors report on the situation of the Jews in their jurisdiction unleashed an outpouring of complaints about the Jews. Everywhere, the bishops and inquisitors wrote, the Jews were flouting the laws of the land, trying to hold on to freedoms they had won during the French occupation.

The town of Pesaro, not far from Ancona, was typical. The inquisitor there recounted that the previous fall, during the local harvest festival, Jews had danced "promiscuously" with Christians, bringing to the inquisitor's mind "a particular proclivity of the Jews for seducing Christian women." The gates of Pesaro's ghetto were no longer closed at night, and conversations between Christians and Jews had become frequent; indeed, Jews thought nothing of inviting Christians to their weddings and circumcisions. Some Jewish families now lived outside the ghetto, he reported. Others, while living within the ghetto's walls, employed female Christian servants, and these women had stopped attending mass and were ignoring the Church's fasts. The bishop of Pesaro sent in similar observations, concurring with the inquisitor on the need for strong action.[12]

Alongside these official reports, the Pope and the Holy Office received numerous unsolicited denunciations from regular citizens, complaining that the old restrictions on the Jews were no longer being enforced. Typical was an 1823 letter addressed to the Pope. It began: "The people of Pesaro, seeing the great disorders and sins that are continuously being committed owing to the excess of freedom that the evil and wicked Jewish People have been given . . . call on your Holiness to put an end to this Nation that tyrannizes Christianity." The letter went on: "The people of Pesaro beg your Holiness to shut the Jews into their Ghetto once again, to make them close the gates, and make them wear their sign, as was the custom before the invasion of the iniquitous and evil French Government."[13]

Having received the inquisitors' and bishops' reports, Leo XII conferred with the cardinals of the Holy Office. In late 1825, the Pope ordered the re-enclosure of all of the Papal States' Jews into the old ghettoes, and the reinstatement of the old restrictions on their movements and on their interaction with Christians.

The new cardinal vicar of Rome noted the new ruling on November 18, 1825. "The Jews living in Rome," he wrote, "having obtained an expansion of the ancient ghetto, by which any reasonable pretext they had of overcrowding and unhealthiness has been removed, have received the last, formal order to separate themselves totally from the Christians. They must close themselves once again in the Ghetto with all of their possessions within the fixed time of one month." The eighty-four stores and warehouses the Jews had acquired outside the ghetto were to be closed.[14]

The following year the cardinal vicar issued another edict. "His Holiness [Leo XII]," it began, "after having over the past year given the opportune orders for the return of all the Jews to the Ghetto . . . has recently prescribed the following further orders so that the Jews . . . not leave the Ghettoes and go wandering about without any license as they had been doing before." The vicar went on to warn: "Beginning this August 20 [1826], no Jew living in the Rome Ghetto will be able to leave, even for a single day, if he does not have a written permit . . . from our Criminal Tribunal which gives legitimate grounds for his absence." A Jew receiving such permission must, upon reaching his destination, show his permit to the local bishop or inquisitor. Furthermore, "while they are away from the Ghetto, the Jews shall not be allowed to live or converse in a familiar way with Christians."[15]

The Jews throughout the Papal States were devastated by these orders, having become accustomed to the freedoms they had enjoyed during Pius VII's reign. Only eight cities had ghettoes: Rome, Ancona, and Ferrara, which had the largest ones, and Cento, Lugo, Pesaro, Senigaglia, and Urbino, whose ghettoes were small. Over the years, many Jews had established homes elsewhere. Although since the restoration of the papal regime in 1814 the Jews' presence in such places was technically illegal, they had been tolerated and felt reasonably secure. Now all this changed: The Jews were ordered to leave their homes and return to the ghetto from which they had come. Many of them, especially the younger Jews, had never lived in a ghetto. Those who had lived in one of these papally mandated Jew-free towns since before 1814 were given two years to move out; those who had moved there more recently were given only five months.

In Rome, the Jews drew up a petition, which they sent both to the Pope and to the Holy Office, pleading for mercy. The order, they argued, would be disastrous for them. Because Jews were forbidden to practice professions or own real estate, they depended entirely on trade for a living. If they were made to close down their warehouses outside the ghetto, their businesses would collapse, since there was no room for their goods inside the ghetto walls. Moreover, if they could not travel freely to transact their business, the ghetto residents would be reduced to misery: "The Roman Jews who sell their goods in the rural towns live in Rome, where their wives and children live. . . . As is well known, they return to Rome for the holidays and for all those occasions on which their Religious and family duties require it . . . they labor to support the numerous families in the City. . . . Four or five hundred Romans are in one way or another supported in this way, and should thirty household heads be forced to abandon the places where, from time to time, they live, many miserable people would end up sunk in a vortex of ills. . . ."[16]

Nor was it only Jews who objected to the new measures. A number of bishops showed their concern for the Jews in their dioceses, often in the

form of complaints to the Holy Office about the local inquisitor's mal-
treatment of the Jews.

The archbishop of Senigaglia, Cardinal Testaferrata, in a letter to the
secretary of state, complained about the damage that the new restrictions
were doing to Senigaglia's big trade fair. The success of the fair depended
on the participation of Jewish merchants from the ghettoes of Ancona
and Pesaro, but the inquisitors of those cities had been making the permits required to spend time in Senigaglia more restrictive. The archbishop was angered by the inquisitors' insistence that all Jews going to
the fair return home within three days of its end. For many years, he
wrote, Jews had been allowed to stay there longer to conduct their business, benefiting the people who rented them places to stay, as well as others. Now the Jews were threatening not to come again.

The archbishop was particularly upset to learn that the inquisitors had
told the Jews that it was not enough for them to get his, the archbishop's,
validation of their permits; they also needed to have them countersigned
by the inquisitor's vicar in Senigaglia. "It is almost as if the signature of a
Bishop or Cardinal, who recognizes no superior but the Holy Father himself . . . has to be validated by a simple vicar of the Holy Office." The
insult was all the greater in his case, reported the archbishop, because the
man who had recently been appointed vicar by the inquisitor of Ancona
(who had authority over Senigaglia) was a scoundrel. He is a "troubled,
bizarre" man, wrote the archbishop, a man notorious for going about at
night in clerical garb flirting with women. And no sooner had the vicar
been appointed to his office than he began demanding that the Jews pay a
new tax. To make matters worse, the vicar had hired a bunch of repro-
bates, men with criminal records, as his aides.

The archbishop concluded by asking the secretary of state to bring the
matter to His Holiness's attention, so that such abuses could be stopped.
The secretary of state brought the letter to the Pope, who in turn took it
to the Holy Office for discussion. The cardinals came to a decision: The
archbishop was being overly indulgent toward the Jews. The new restrictions must be vigorously enforced. However, inquiries would be made
into the character of the inquisitor's vicar in Senigaglia.[17]

In a similar incident, in January 1827, Cardinal Leoni, archbishop of
Jesi, wrote the Holy Office assessor (the assessor was the prelate who
coordinated the work of the Holy Office), Cardinal Olivieri, asking for an
opinion on a matter that was troubling him. The Jews in his diocese had

always depended on Christians to come into their homes on their Sabbath to light their fires so that they could stay warm and have light, because their religion prohibited them from lighting any fire themselves on their day of rest. This employment, the archbishop wrote, benefited not only the Jews but also the Christians who obtained much-needed cash for their services.

Cardinal Olivieri was unmoved: Jews were forbidden from employing Christians in their homes. No exceptions could be made.[18]

The assessor received another such plea the following year from an even more highly placed clergyman, Tommaso Cardinal Bernetti, a former protégé of Cardinal Consalvi, and newly appointed secretary of state. In an October 1828 letter marked "confidential," datelined from the rooms of the Vatican, Cardinal Bernetti told of all the complaints he had been receiving about the new Inquisition campaign against the Jews.

It had become extremely difficult, the cardinal wrote, for these "unfortunates" to get the licenses they needed to allow them to conduct their trade outside the ghetto. The result was increased poverty among the Jews, as well as hardships for those Christians who did business with them. But, the cardinal continued, "what most moves me to commiserate with them, and indeed makes me shudder, is the abandon with which the Jews are being subjected to large fines—and, where they cannot pay them, imprisoned for several days—if they are found employing Christians in their homes."

The cardinal also mentioned the Jews' need to have Christians light their fires on the Sabbath. Hiring Christians to do such work, he pointed out, "is indispensable for them, for they cannot do it themselves without failing in the tenets of the superstition that they profess." As a result of the new Church campaign, "many of them spend long winter nights without light and without heat, with great damage to their health, and especially great danger to the young and the old." Surely Christian charity suggested that the new restrictions should be modified. "I haven't the courage," wrote the cardinal, to dispute those pleading for mercy, "because I am not persuaded myself, nor do I know how to console them."

The secretary of state ended his letter to the chief inquisitor in a way few other clergy would have dared to do. "I pray you [reply] promptly," he wrote, "whether orally or in writing, for the closer we get to the cold season, the more the pleas multiply and, with them, my own true embarrassment." Bernetti was here making a case unpopular with both Pope and Holy Office. His appeal was rejected.[19]

The resistance among some of the bishops to Leo XII's new hard line on the Jews was based not only on sympathy for the Jews' plight, but on concern about the negative economic effects that the new policy would have on the Christian population. The bishop of Foligno, in a case of this sort, sent a plea to the Holy Office in 1829, just a few months after Leo XII's death, which had occurred in February of that year. Only three Jewish families, he wrote, lived in Foligno, and had lived there for eighty years. The bishop had apparently done nothing previously to enforce the order that these families be sent packing—since Foligno had no ghetto, their presence went against Leo XII's policy—but he was now under renewed pressure from the Inquisition to take action.

The bishop explained that the Jewish families had founded a textile factory in Foligno that provided employment for many of the town's poor, especially women. Realizing, no doubt, that the image of Christians working under Jews would horrify the cardinals of the Holy Office, he hastened to add that the factory was managed by Christians, and it was they who supervised the workers, "without there being any sign of oversight by the Jews." The bishop continued: "Conscious of the damage that the departure of the above-mentioned families would cause the population, [I beg] your Most Reverend Eminences that, in your prudence, you take this plea into consideration." The inquisitors took up the matter at their weekly meeting of September 16, 1829. The bishop's request was denied. The Jews were to leave town. This was a matter of God's will, not economics.[20]

Pius VIII (Francesco Saverio Castiglioni), who ascended to the papacy in early April 1829, died after only twenty months, yet he too found time to issue an order requiring all Jews of the Papal States to be closed into one of the authorized ghettoes. But years of unpopular popes and repression were producing an explosive situation. By the time Pius VIII died, in late 1830, the signs of revolt were everywhere.

Despite the urgency of electing a new pontiff to protect the Church's rule, the cardinals who gathered in conclave once again divided into opposing factions and once more found agreement difficult. It was only after seven weeks of deliberations that the votes were gathered to elect Mauro Cappellari, a sixty-five-year-old monk, who took the name of Gregory XVI.

Cappellari had been born in the Republic of Venice to a family of minor nobility. He was a man of considerable intellectual abilities and interests, yet had a stiflingly parochial outlook. Never in his life had he traveled outside Italy—indeed, he had barely been anywhere outside Venice and Rome. As a young monk he had served as the censor of books for the Inquisition in Venice, and then, in 1795, was called to the Holy City, to the old monastery of San Gregorio. He was forced out of Rome for a time by the French, but subsequently returned to his monastery. In 1825 he was made a cardinal by Leo XII, and became the Prefect of the Congregation of Propaganda Fide, the Vatican department that was responsible for the Church and Catholics in the non-Catholic countries of the world.

Two days after Cappellari's election, and even before he had time to be formally invested as pope, the people of Bologna—the second-largest city of the Papal States—rose in revolt. They chased out the papal legate, took down the papal banner, and replaced it with the tricolored Italian flag. Within two weeks, ebullient crowds in cities throughout the Papal States had done the same. The new pope, clinging precariously to power in Rome, and helpless to stop the uprising elsewhere, appealed to the Austrian government, which promptly dispatched its army. Within a month, they had crushed the revolt, and pontifical flags were again hoisted over government palaces throughout the papal lands. Yet the Austrian army had barely withdrawn when, in late 1831, new revolts broke out. Again the Pope called on Austrian forces, and again the Austrian troops put the Pope back in power. They would remain on patrol in the Papal States for another seven years.

His regime restored, Gregory XVI responded in the only way he knew, reiterating the sacred basis of papal government, and denouncing the evil of those who espoused the new, revolutionary ideas of democracy, freedom of speech, and secular rule. It is no surprise that the new pontiff, who remained in office fifteen years, proved no more popular with the people of Rome and the Papal States than had Leo XII. At least, people said, Leo XII, sickly as he was, had looked like a pope: tall, slender, and with an aristocratic bearing. By contrast, people found Gregory XVI coarse and ugly. Nor did his old monastic lifestyle win him popular favor. He rose at 4 a.m. each day, ate only simple foods, and, following centuries-long tradition, insisted that as pope he must always take his meals alone. For many of Europe's diplomats, too, the new pope was viewed with unease. He seemed to understand nothing of international politics, and spoke no language but Italian.

Gregory XVI was committed to following his predecessors' uncompromising policies. In an 1832 encyclical, *Mirari vos*, he set out the views that would guide his papacy. He condemned the belief in freedom of the press—which he dubbed "a hateful freedom, impossible to execrate enough"—and denounced belief in the separation of Church and state, and the belief that practitioners of all religions should have the same legal rights. The encyclical branded modern times calamitous, and called for a return to an earlier era when Church verities had gone unquestioned. These views came to characterize the papacy throughout the nineteenth century: "Wickedness is exultant. Shameless science exults. Licentiousness exults. . . . Errors of every kind are spread without restraint. . . . Wicked men . . . attack the divine authority of the Church."[21]

Not all of the evils faced by the Pope had human origins. During the early decades of the nineteenth century, successive waves of cholera swept through Europe, bringing suffering and death. Now, in the face of serious new outbreaks in Rome, the Pope formed a Commission for Public Health to advise him. Among the areas of the city that most attracted the commissioners' attention was the ghetto, within whose walls the densely packed Jews lived amid filth, a breeding ground for disease of all sorts. With the Pope's approval, a special Commission for the Jewish Ghetto—whose six members included three cardinals—was established in 1835, charged with taking stock of ghetto conditions and recommending appropriate action.

Struck by the ghetto's squalor and overcrowding, the commission called for a modest expansion. The commission also suggested that, as a temporary measure to relieve the crowding, Jews with wholesale businesses be allowed to move their operations outside of the ghetto. To reduce the "moral" threat posed by this proposal, the commission specified that the Jewish wholesalers could move only to a designated neighboring area, and that they could have no doorway connecting them to the home of a Christian. The dispensation was to expire in five years' time.[22] The proposal was adopted.

The following year the Pope established a new public health commission, and disbanded the special commission on the ghetto. But among the new commission's first acts was to ask one of its members, Prince Pietro

Odescalchi, to look into conditions there. In October 1836, he submitted his report, offering a graphic view of life in the squalid Jewish quarter.

On accepting his new assignment, the prince sat down to read all the documents on the ghetto that the commission had gathered. "If," he wrote, "the reading of those materials moved me to a deep commiseration for the unhappy fate of the inhabitants of that part of Rome, that commiseration, I must confess, grew a thousand times as great when, just last week, I decided to go in person . . . to walk the ghetto streets, and to go into some of those hovels which I would be going beyond the bounds of truth to call dwellings."

In an area barely able to house 2,000 souls, the prince reported, there lived over 3,500. Of these, 1,800 or maybe more "languish in the clutches of untold misery. Tiny, fetid rooms house eight or twelve people, built in such a way that they lack any air, and light shines in only from the door . . . and only a little fireplace allows those miserable souls a glimmer of light at night." He could, he wrote, hardly believe it when he saw "with my own eyes, what seems impossible to believe, that in three miserable rooms seven families were enclosed." And while the Jewish community did what it could to provide these poor Jews with a bit of money and something to eat and to wear, he added, there was nothing they could do to enlarge their homes.

The action taken by the previous special commission, reported the prince, had had only the most modest effect. There were few wholesalers in the ghetto, and the seven who had moved their businesses out had left few rooms behind. He ended by calling for the establishment of a new commission on the ghetto, a recommendation that was approved by the government, which appointed Prince Odescalchi himself to be its chair.[23]

Ghetto residents soon inundated the new commission with denunciations of the dismal conditions in which they lived, and with cries for help. In late August 1837, in the midst of a new cholera epidemic, Giuseppe Piperno sent in one such plea. He lived, he wrote, in a single room with his wife, his four little children, and his unwed sister. Conditions were unbearable, especially now, he added, "because for a long time our four children have been afflicted by diarrhea that won't go away. Since they have to relieve themselves constantly, especially at night, the stench is overpowering, as we lack even a convenient place to keep the excrement."

In such conditions, Piperno asked, how could he hope to keep the deadly cholera away?[24]

A long plea from the Jewish community of Rome reached the Pope in the midst of the epidemic, although addressing a very different complaint, one that had produced appeals from the Jews almost every year for centuries. The problem was the annual set of rites—some sponsored by the Church and local authorities, others the product of popular enthusiasms—surrounding Carnival. With its roots in the pre-Christian Roman festival of Saturnalia, Carnival was (and still is) celebrated in the days before Lent. Marked for centuries throughout Catholic Europe by raucous, if not riotous, public celebrations, Carnival was a time dreaded by those charged with maintaining public order. Among the most common activities were the use of masks and costumes and the performance of public satires in which people of the lower classes skewered those in power. These festivities were among the high points of the year for the people of Rome. Unfortunately for the Jews, one of Carnival's most popular features was the ritual degradation of the people of the ghetto.

Among the first historical references we have to such rites is a description from 1466, when for the amusement of the Romans, in festivities sponsored by Pope Paul II, Jews were made to race naked through the streets of the city. A particularly evocative later account describes them: "Races were run on each of the eight days of the Carnival by horses, asses and buffaloes, old men, lads, children, and Jews. Before they were to run, the Jews were richly fed, so as to make the race more difficult for them and at the same time more amusing for the spectators. They ran from the Arch of Domitian to the Church of St. Mark at the end of the Corso at full tilt, amid Rome's taunting shrieks of encouragement and peals of laughter, while the Holy Father stood upon a richly ornamented balcony and laughed heartily." Two centuries later, these practices, now deemed indecorous and unbefitting the dignity of the Holy City, were stopped by Clement IX. In their place the Pope assessed a heavy tax on the Jews to help pay the costs of the city's Carnival celebrations.[25]

But various other Carnival rites continued. For many years the rabbis of the ghetto were forced to wear clownish outfits and march through the city streets to the jeers of the crowd, pelted by a variety of missiles. Such rites were not peculiar to Rome. In Pisa in the eighteenth century, for example, it was customary each year, as part of Carnival, for students to chase after the fattest Jew in the city, capture him, weigh him, and then make him give them his weight in sugar-coated almonds.[26]

In 1779, Pius VI resurrected some of the Carnival rites that had been neglected in recent years. Most prominent among them was the feudal rite of homage, in which ghetto officials, made to wear special clothes, stood before an unruly mob in a crowded piazza, making an offering to Rome's governors.

It was this practice that occasioned the formal plea from the ghetto to Pope Gregory XVI in 1836. The Jews argued that such rites should be abandoned, and cited previous popes who had ordered them halted. They asked that, in his mercy, the Pope now do the same. On November 5, the Pope met with his secretary of state to discuss the plea. A note on the secretary of state's copy of the petition, along with his signature, records the Pope's decision: "It is not opportune to make any innovation." The annual rites continued.[27]

Around this time the Pope, along with his secretary of state and the Holy Office of the Inquisition over which he presided, returned to the more general problem of what to do about the Jews. The revolts of 1831 had undermined the program of rigorous restrictions on the Jews that Leo XII and Pius VIII had championed. Reports came from throughout the papal lands that the Jews were once again traveling without permission, living in places without ghettoes, hiring Christian maids and wet-nurses, and buying real estate, all in violation of the law.

On July 18, 1838, Gregory XVI, acting through the Holy Office of the Inquisition, issued a new edict, and sent copies to the inquisitors and bishops throughout the Papal States.[28]

"The unfortunate political events that recently afflicted the Pontifical dominions," the edict began, "have produced among other disorders the failure to observe the Apostolic Constitutions and the other Edicts regarding the Jews. As His Holiness Pope Gregory XVI wishes to repair this unfortunate situation, which has produced grave and sad consequences, . . . he has with sovereign Authority ordered and prescribed the following."

The goal of Gregory XVI's new edict, as stated in its first article, was to reinstate Pius VI's edict of 1775, which even in the eighteenth century was widely viewed as an anachronism. Jews were once again confined to their ghettoes. No Jew could, for any reason, live outside the ghetto to which he had been assigned. Those currently living elsewhere must quickly move back to their ghetto, or be escorted there by police. No Jew could own property outside the ghetto.

Enforcing these and the other restrictions on the Jews was not easy. The Jews of the Papal States knew that their brethren elsewhere in Europe were increasingly being given equal rights, and the restrictions that had once been accepted with a certain amount of resignation were now viewed not only as insufferably burdensome but also as archaic and out of keeping with modern times.

Reports soon flowed in from inquisitors and bishops denouncing the Jews for flouting the new orders. The large ghetto of Ancona attracted special attention, not least because of the Jews' economic importance there. On September 29, 1842, the Pope, presiding over a Holy Office discussion on the Ancona ghetto, and on the smaller neighboring ghettoes of Senigaglia and Pesaro, ordered an inquiry into the extent to which Jews there continued to employ Christian servants and wetnurses. The resulting report found that the laws were being widely ignored, and called for their renewed enforcement. The assessor of the Holy Office responded by preparing a draft proposal, which he circulated to the other cardinals for discussion.

The proposal included a concession: The Jews could employ Christian servants, but only if they were over age forty, and, in the case of females, only if they were married. Such servants were, however, forbidden to remain in Jewish homes at night. As for Christian wetnurses, these would remain forbidden, unless the Jewish babies were taken outside the ghetto to be nursed. Finally, the ban on allowing Christians into Jewish homes on Sabbath eve to light their fires was reiterated. Any Jew caught in violation of any of these orders was to be fined the first time, then sent to jail for three months for a repeat offense.

Intriguingly, in sending the final document containing these "measures of tolerance" to the bishops and inquisitors of the three cities, the Holy Office added a caveat. In signing the permits to allow Jewish applicants to have (daytime) servants, the local ecclesiastical authorities should be careful to state that they were acting on their own authority, "without naming either the Holy Father or the Holy Congregation [of the Inquisition]." The reason for this was "so as not to prejudice the Highest"—that is, the Pope. Allowing the Jews even modest relief from the divinely ordained restrictions could not be represented as official Church policy.[29]

In June 1843, the inquisitor of Ancona informed the Holy Office of local reaction to the new policy. "The wise decisions of your Eminences," the inquisitor wrote, "have been heralded by all the good people, particularly because of the arrogance that the Jews have shown, and the most serious damage that they have caused."

Yet no sooner had he posted the new orders in the synagogues of Ancona and Senigaglia, the inquisitor reported, than the Jews and their supporters—"and there are many of them," he added—began saying that they would not obey the laws. "I have been informed," the inquisitor wrote, "that many threats are being made by people who say they want to strike back at the inquisitor and at the other people working in the Holy Office." But, he concluded, "I have no fear, and I am confident that they will obey without attacking anyone."[30]

Much, however, as the inquisitor may have disapproved, times were changing. Indeed, shortly after the inquisitor sent in his report, a scandalous booklet denouncing his new edict appeared. The anonymous author, who described himself as a former friar, began with scathing words about Leo XII, the pope who had first reintroduced the restrictions. "I happen to know intimately about the task that a certain Pope Della Genga gave to a certain friar Jabalot in Rome in the year of the Jubilee [1825] to write all the worst he could think of against the Jews. And, given [Jabalot's] ambition of being made a cardinal, he marshaled all his ingenuity not to discover, but to imagine the darkest accusations to hurl against this poor people. Then, subsidized by that same [Pope] Leo, he had the book printed, and distributed it for free even to those who did not want a copy."

The ex-friar then turned his fire on Ancona's inquisitor: "Let's amuse ourselves now by taking a close look at the friar inquisitor's edict. . . . It speaks from the beginning of the Jews living under his jurisdiction. But I don't know of what kind this vaunted jurisdiction is supposed to be, whether political or religious. The first is not in his domain, as his is a purely ecclesiastical authority. As for the second, by what right does he exercise it over people of a different religion?"

Among the other provisions of the 1843 Ancona inquisitor's edict that the ex-friar attacked was the banning of Christian wetnurses. "And if

some Jewish children die for lack of nourishment, you could care less. . . .
Having to hate these people as much as possible, it only makes sense
to deny milk to their children." The inquisitor's strictures, he wrote,
"seemed to contain the idea of the extermination of the race, rather than
trying to bring about respect for others' beliefs or the reconciliation of
Jews and Christians." The counterproductive result, concluded the ex-
friar, was minimizing the possibility that the Jews would ever want to
become Christian.

The inflammatory booklet, attributed by the authorities to the "apostate ex-friar Achille," was sent to the secretary of state, who on August 31,
1843, forwarded it to the Holy Office Commissioner for discussion by the
cardinal inquisitors.[31]

Ancona's inquisitor felt besieged, and sent long letters to the Holy
Office bemoaning his situation. He was surrounded by insolent Jews, he
said, and, most appallingly, was not being supported by the city's archbishop, who, terrified by the prospect of another revolt, had sent a series
of letters to the Holy Office asking that the new restrictions on the Jews
be abandoned.

In addition to the Jews' other misdeeds, the inquisitor reported, they
were now placing Italian inscriptions on their gravestones. The Jews
thereby sought "to show themselves equal in everything to the Christians," in contravention of the law prohibiting Jews from having any
inscriptions at all to mark their graves.

The head of the local Jewish community, the inquisitor learned, had
taken down the new edict that the inquisitor had affixed to the synagogue
wall in June, and filed it in the synagogue's archives. "Now all moral
force has been paralyzed by the certainty that the Jews have received from
their correspondents that all the orders that regard them have been
suspended."

He continued: "Now you see what a poor inquisitor is reduced to! Just
yesterday evening while I was out I had to suffer the deep mortification of
seeing the Jew Gioacchino Terni, a most insolent Jew . . . look me right in
the face and laugh."[32]

That same summer of 1843 saw a much more ominous development
for the Vatican. Prince Metternich, one of the most powerful men in all of
Europe, sent a lengthy letter protesting the Pope's repression of the Jews.
This was something that the Pope could not afford to treat lightly. It had
been Metternich who had ordered Austrian troops to retake much of the

Papal States after the rebellions that accompanied Gregory XVI's election to the papacy, and it was his armies that continued to assure some security for continued papal rule. Indeed, if the Pope ruled in the Papal States at all, it was thanks to Austria's support.[33]

And so when the Austrian emissary to the Holy See brought Metternich's letter to the secretary of state, Luigi Cardinal Lambruschini, it sent a jolt through the Vatican. What had prompted the letter was a request from Baron Salomon Rothschild in Vienna. The Jewish baron had received a plea from the Jews of Ancona, asking that he use his influence to stop the Pope's new re-ghettoization campaign.

If the Pope was not in a position to ignore a request from Metternich, neither was Metternich in a position to ignore a request from Salomon Rothschild. Indeed, later in the century the relationships between the Rothschild family and the various rulers of Europe would become one of the bases of the burgeoning anti-Semitic movement.

The development of a modern system of international banking and high finance over the course of the nineteenth century owed a great deal to Jews, and none better illustrate this than the Rothschilds themselves, although they were hardly typical in the extent of their holdings and their influence. The old aristocratic elites in Europe had long looked disdainfully on finance and banking. Indeed, in a number of lands they had for centuries turned to Jews—dubbed "court Jews" for their service to the rulers—to perform these functions. Among the Jews' other advantages was that they were not hampered by the Christian religious prohibition on lending money at interest, a major stumbling block to the development of international commerce. Prohibited by law from owning land and kept out of the trades controlled by guilds, the Jews found in finance and money-lending the only economic path to prosperity open to them.

Arising out of a small family business in Frankfurt in the late eighteenth century, the Rothschild financial empire blossomed with the 1814 Vienna peace settlement, when the family began its spectacularly successful career as financiers of Europe's governments. The Rothschilds played a key role in creating the international bond market, offering crucial loans to governments whose revenues did not meet their expenditures. Over the following decades the Rothschild banking business operated out of five main branches, in Frankfurt, London, Paris, Naples, and Vienna. Each was headed by one of the sons of the founder of the business, Mayer Amschel, who had died in 1812. Nathan, in charge of the London operation, and James, in charge of Paris, were Europe's richest men in the middle decades of the century. Together the brothers were in close contact with many of Europe's rulers, who depended heavily on them for financing. By the 1820s, the Rothschilds were already the most important source of government loans for Britain, Prussia, Austria, Russia, France, and Naples.

Metternich's relation to Salomon Rothschild was a deep and close one, lasting many decades. Indeed, so close did the Rothschilds feel to Metternich that in the letters the brothers wrote one another, they referred to him as "uncle." Metternich depended on them to provide loans not only to the Austrian government, but to other governments that he sought to influence as well. These business relations also had a more personal side, for Metternich looked to the Rothschilds when members of his own family needed financial help.[34]

Pope Gregory XVI had himself been involved in this link between Metternich and the Jewish bankers. Facing mass uprisings as he took office in 1831, the Pope was in desperate need of funds to put down the unrest and to take steps to win popular backing. Metternich, eager to ensure that the Papal States did not fall, called on Salomon Rothschild in Vienna and made a personal appeal to him to make a large loan to the Vatican. In January 1832, shortly after the loan was made, Carl Rothschild, head of the bank in Naples, was invited in for a private audience with the Pope. There Gregory XVI awarded him the ribbon and star of the newly established Order of St. George. This, plus the fact that the Jewish banker was permitted to kiss the Pope's hand, rather than his foot, as was customary, led to much malicious murmuring about a pope putting himself in the debt of a Jew.[35]

Metternich's 1843 letter, buried in the central Inquisition archives, and written in French, is an extraordinary document. Marked "Confidential," it begins by explaining that Baron Rothschild had passed the Ancona Jews' plea on to him. Normally, Metternich avowed, he would not get involved in such a matter, "not because I find the demands unjust," but rather "because it is against my custom, and my principles, to concern myself with an affair that is exclusively a matter of the internal administration of an independent State." In this case, however, the issue was of such importance, he believed, that he could not remain silent.

He would like, he went on, "to suggest to His Eminence [the secretary of state] the following reflections, which, given his rare wisdom, he may appreciate, and all of which, while granting our Holy Religion's principles their rightful preeminence, do not exclude more worldly considerations as well.

"It seems to me," Metternich continued, "that the rules about which the Jews . . . are complaining are based on an ancient Ecclesiastical discipline, which may well have been in keeping with the needs of that time, but which are no longer in harmony with the times in which we live." Metternich realized that the Vatican would likely reply that rules based on Church doctrine were divinely ordained and hence not subject to change, no matter how politically expedient such changes may be. He tried to anticipate these objections by making a distinction: "When one is dealing with principles," he argued, "no change is possible, but dealing with a matter of discipline, it seems to me to make sense to adapt, as much as one can, to the needs of the moment."

Not only were the times changed, but so too, according to Metternich, were the Jews. "The Jews are no longer today," he wrote, "what they once were; they have lost almost all of their primitive fanaticism, and we have seen reformers arise among them who, in attenuating the Mosaic faith, may be preparing the way for their conversion. That is why I think that you risk absolutely nothing by allowing the Jews to enjoy a reasonable degree of tolerance, especially at a time when the Greeks and the Protestants of all types are so intolerant with respect to the Catholics.[36] It seems to me that the Holy Pontiff has nothing to lose and everything to gain in treating his Jewish subjects with a mercy that is far from being seen as a sign of weakness. . . ."[37]

Metternich's letter was written on August 3, 1843. On the 18th, the secretary of state urgently summoned the Holy Office assessor to his rooms at the Quirinal Palace of Rome, the Pope's summer headquarters. There Cardinal Lambruschini showed the assessor Metternich's letter, and they discussed what course of action they should recommend to the Pope.[38] The Pope and the secretary of state spent several weeks preparing their reply.

On September 29, Gregory XVI himself summoned the assessor for an audience, and informed him that, on his orders, the secretary of state had just sent a confidential response to the Austrian ambassador. The Pope handed him a copy of the text of this letter to Metternich, which remains today in the Inquisition archive. Nothing provides better insight into Pope Gregory XVI's attitude toward the Jews, or his belief that the Vatican should cling fast to its age-old practices.

The Pope began by rejecting Metternich's premise. The argument that the treatment of the Jews in the Papal States should be brought into harmony with modern ideas of equality was specious. "The prohibitions on the Jews," Gregory XVI's letter began, "forbidding them from employing Christian servants or wetnurses, from owning real estate . . . from living—where there is a ghetto—outside of its walls mixed in and confused with Christians, are prohibitions founded in the sacred Canons. These, in order to guarantee Christian religion and morality, command the separation of Christians and Jews."

The Pope then went on to justify each of the restrictions he had imposed, beginning with the prohibition on owning property outside the ghetto.[39] "Aside from the fact that the Jews are forbidden such ownership by the sacred Canons as a Nation of deicides and blasphemers of Christ, and sworn enemies of the Christian name," the Pope wrote, "there is also the danger that the Jews will seduce and pervert those who rent from them or peasants who depend on them." Ancona's Jews had flouted these statutes: "The Jews of that Province care nothing for the laws of the Church regarding them, although these have been reissued many times—most notably under the Pontificate of Leo XII—commanding them to get rid of their property. Rather, they continue stubbornly to keep it, indeed to extend and increase it."

The Pope then addressed the request to allow Jews to live outside the ghetto. "Beyond the dangers for Religion and Morals from the common relations to be found among those living in the same community," he warned, "there is also the scandal of seeing the Jews pretending to be living the same as others. In thus exulting in their insolence toward Christians and the Church, they put themselves on an equal basis with the Christians and laugh at the Ecclesiastical laws that oblige them to live in the Ghetto."

The Pope then turned again to the people whose complaints to Baron Rothschild had captured Metternich's attention. "Now, the Jews of Ancona, in the face of all the prohibitions concerning Christian wetnurses and servants, and all the orders that have been repeatedly given them, have, with open scorn for Ecclesiastical laws and Canonical sanctions, continued to employ over a hundred Christian servants and wet-nurses."

Nor were the Ancona Jews in compliance with the order that they live only in their ghetto. "Ever since the last French invasion, unfortunately, Jews have not infrequently moved their families and stores to towns where there is no ghetto, and have tried to settle in among the Christians, notwithstanding the ban on it."

Having painted this picture of Jewish lawlessness, the Pope went on to address Metternich's plea directly. "Disorders such as these, while they may be illegally tolerated in secular states, cannot be tolerated in the Ecclesiastical State, because they are openly contrary to the most sacrosanct principles of the Ecclesiastical laws, which also underlie the other disciplinary provisions contained in the edict of the inquisitor of Ancona."[40]

The Pope also dismissed Metternich's argument that the Jews were now less in need of special regulation. "Nor does the loss of the Jews' primitive fanaticism render the observance of the Canonical sanctions on them any the less necessary. Indeed, it makes such observance all the more necessary, because if they lose their fanaticism regarding Jewish laws and practices, they certainly do not lose their national hatred for the Religion of Jesus Christ, and for the Christian name itself. On the contrary, these increase as they abandon themselves to philosophism and indifferentism."

The Pope's only concession came at the end of his letter. The Holy Office, he wrote, was already examining the question of whether any modifications could be made in the restrictions on the Jews, while ensuring that "the fundamental principles regarding them are upheld." No doubt he had in mind such liberalization of policy as allowing older Christian servants to work for the Jews as long as they left the ghetto by dark.[41]

Word of Rothschild's intervention—and perhaps also of Metternich's—spread among the Jews of the Ancona area. The archbishop and inquisitors reported the maddening result of recent meetings they had had with representatives of the local Jewish communities. When the Jews were admonished to obey the laws restricting them, they refused. They had learned, they said, that the Pope wanted them treated more mercifully, and did not want them locked in their ghettoes. There followed, over the next months, a tug of war between the local Church authorities who sought to enforce the papally approved restrictions, and the Jews who claimed—against all evidence—to have the Pope on their side.

Similar struggles were under way elsewhere in the Papal States. In January 1844, Ferrara's archbishop sent a letter to the assessor of the Holy Office in Rome, asking that he inform the Pope of the dire consequences for religion and morality brought about by the Jews' continued employment of Christian servants. The archbishop begged the Holy Office to reactivate all the measures promulgated by Pope Leo XII, including the locking of the ghetto gates each night.

When, at his audience with the Pope on January 31, the assessor shared this letter from Ferrara with him, it brought to the Pope's mind the continued unsettled situation in Ancona. He asked the inquisitor to write to the archbishop of Ancona and to the inquisitor of Pesaro, ordering them "with the greatest prudence and caution, to insist on the full reinstatement of the restrictions on the hiring of Christian servants and wetnurses by the Jews."

A week later the Pope instructed the assessor to follow up his earlier request with a further order. The archbishop of Ancona and the inquisitor there should "call in the Deputies of the Ghetto, and let them know how kindly and with what forbearance they have thus far been treated by His Holiness." The Jews should be told, the Pope continued, to end their illegal behavior "and stop abusing His Holiness's goodness, so as not to force the Holy Father to finally take those steps that, out of his mercy, he has up to now held in abeyance." The Pope also called on the local parish priests to do everything possible to prevent their parishioners from having any social contact with Jews. Recognizing the political volatility of the situation, the Pope added that the priests should proceed cautiously, working "with the least publicity, and privately," to impress on their parishioners the "grave spiritual dangers to which they are exposing themselves."[42]

Pope Gregory XVI meanwhile resurrected another element of Leo XII's campaign, the forced sermon in Rome. The cardinal vicar put out a new edict reiterating this obligation in the early 1840s. To be sure that no Jew shirked this duty, all Jews, male and female, twelve years of age and over, were to register with ghetto officials, who were ordered to bring the list to the tribunal of the vicariate. Any Jew who failed to attend on the day assigned him or her was to be assessed a heavy fine, with a

third of the fine going to the "secret informer" who reported the delin-
quent to the authorities.

In enforcing attendance at the sermons, the cardinal vicar realized that
he risked triggering public disorders. The problem here was not the Jews
themselves, who, while angered and humiliated at the forced sermons,
were too cowed to rebel against it. The problem lay with Rome's *popolani*
(the lower classes), who for as long as anyone could remember had
delighted in taunting the Jews as they marched out of the ghetto to the
church. To minimize the possibility of any unseemly displays, the cardinal issued an order listing the occasions on which the forced sermons
should be suspended. These included all those times following the death
of a pope, and before the election of his successor—a period historically
known for public disorders—"to remove any molestation or hindrance to
which the Christians might subject them." More surprising, at least from
a meteorological perspective, was the exemption that he ordered for "all
those Saturdays when it snows, and those when there is any snow on
the ground." He explained that the motive for this (presumably rarely
invoked) dispensation was "to avoid the problems and harassment caused
by the Christians, who throw snowballs at them."[43]

All things considered, snowballs were the least of the Jews' problems
in Rome.

CHAPTER FOUR

Ritual Murder Makes a Comeback

IN EARLY APRIL 1840, newspapers throughout Europe began reporting a hair-raising story from Damascus, Syria. Two months earlier, an Italian monk—Father Tommaso—had failed to return to his monastery one evening. His fellow Capuchins spread the word that he had last been seen heading for the city's Jewish quarter. On March 5, a month after his disappearance, one of them wrote an account of the ghastly fate that had befallen him there. First appearing in a newspaper published in the Duchy of Modena, the account of Jewish evil soon made its way throughout the continent.

Father Tommaso, by then getting on in years, had lived as a missionary in Damascus for thirty-two years. He was beloved by the people of the city for his charitable works, and especially because he had devoted himself to vaccinating thousands of children of all religions for smallpox. He had gone that fateful day—his colleagues said—into the Jewish quarter, where the city's five thousand, mainly impoverished, Jews lived. He was never seen again.

The mystery of Father Tommaso's disappearance, his colleague wrote, was soon solved. He had been called to the home of one of the city's most prominent Jews, David Harrari. There several Jewish men jumped on him, bound his arms and legs, filled his mouth with cotton, and tied a handkerchief around his mouth so that he could not make a sound. Among his assailants were several of the most prominent Jewish businessmen of the city, along with a rabbi. They summoned a young Jewish barber, Solomon, and told him to slit the monk's throat. Terrified, the barber said he couldn't, he hadn't the courage, and so David Harrari himself, according to the Capuchin's account, "took the knife, laid Father Tommaso down on a mat, and began to slit his throat. But because his hand trembled so much, his brother, Aaron, took over, while the barber Solomon held [the monk] by his beard."

What the Jews sought, above all, was his blood: "They collected the blood in a large silver bowl, because it was to serve for their holiday." They stripped the lifeless friar of his vestments, which they burned, and took his body into another room. There "they began to cut it into pieces: the large bones were crushed with an iron grinder. They put everything in a big coffee sack and threw it in a ditch filled with dirty water which ran through the Jews' part of town." They then poured the blood into bottles, which they gave to the rabbi.

On the day after Tommaso's disappearance, his fellow friars notified the French consul, Count Ratti Menton, who served as diplomatic protector of all Catholics in Damascus. The count notified the local government, and an investigation was launched. Suspicion soon fell on the barber, who was seized and put in jail. "At first, the barber denied the fact; then he said only that he had seen Father Tommaso tied up, and left. But, through the use of both persuasion and threats, and promising him a pardon, he confessed the facts that I have described to you."

The other Jews named by the barber were arrested and, although they at first denied the charges, finally they too began to talk: "The four Harraris confessed that they indeed killed him. Moses Salonicli, the rabbi, denied everything. Moses Abu el-Affieh confessed to the crime, but denied having received the blood; Joseph Leniado denied everything." The Capuchin correspondent observed: "In short, all the important Jews are guilty."

In addition to those he had named, other prominent Jews were also in jail. Meanwhile, tipped off by one of the suspects, the Damascus authorities had found the place where pieces of the friar's body had been thrown. Traces of blood and shreds of bone were discovered there, including "pieces of the cranium with hairs still attached" as well as half of a cap "that all present recognized as truly belonging to Father Tommaso."

The bone fragments were carefully collected and placed in a specially made wooden box. In a procession in which all the priests of Damascus took part, the box was carried from the French consul's house to the city's largest church. "The Muslims, both men and women, accompanied the procession up to the church, shouting against the evil Jews, and mourning the loss of Father Tommaso. Many of them got down on their knees to venerate his bones. The shouts, the sobbing, and laments of the Christians were beyond description."[1]

Shortly thereafter, the Capuchin friars placed a marble tombstone over the remains of their martyred brother. It read:[2]

HERE LIE THE BONES

OF

FATHER TOMMASO OF SARDINIA

CAPUCHIN APOSTOLIC MISSIONARY

ASSASSINATED BY THE JEWS

ON THE DAY OF 5 FEBRUARY IN THE YEAR 1840

Pope Gregory XVI, through his secretary of state for foreign affairs, Luigi Cardinal Lambruschini, followed the horrifying news from Syria closely. They had their own informants—most notably, the Tuscan consul in Egypt—but were also kept posted by Giacomo Cardinal Fransoni, Prefect of the Congregation of Propaganda Fide, a position once held by the Pope himself. The Congregation that Cardinal Fransoni headed had great influence, as it was charged with overseeing the operations of the Church wherever Catholics were in a minority, including North America, Asia, and Africa, and Protestant Northern Europe as well as Christian Orthodox Eastern Europe. Father Tommaso, and the mission he was part of, came under the authority of Propaganda Fide, whose headquarters were (and still are) in the center of Rome.[3]

Cardinal Fransoni had his own network of informants, both ecclesiastical and lay. No source was more important to him in the Damascus case than Pietro Cerruti, who, as Consul General of the Kingdom of Sardinia[4] in Alexandria, Egypt, was in a good position to get timely information from Damascus. Greater Syria—which at the time included Lebanon and Palestine—came under the rule of the Egyptian viceroy of the Ottoman Empire, Mehemet Ali, who was based in Alexandria. Ali had conquered Syria in the early 1830s, in the process dividing the Ottoman Empire in two, with Ali controlling the eastern regions. The Governor-General of Damascus, Sherif Pasha, was his adopted son.[5]

Cerruti sent the cardinal a series of letters of his own, but, more important, included with them copies of the reports he was receiving from his agents in Syria. The cardinal's—and through him the Pope's—early view of the case was heavily influenced by this correspondence.

One of the first of these reports was prepared by the Sardinian consul in Beirut, sent on February 29, 1840, to Cerruti, who forwarded it to Cardinal Fransoni. The consul told of Father Tommaso's disappearance, and revealed that suspicion had fallen immediately on the Jews. The Harrari brothers had been arrested, along with other "distinguished Jews," and their homes had been searched without, as yet, producing "any trace of this mysterious crime."

The Beirut consul's subsequent report, written a month later, and also passed on to the cardinal by Cerruti, tells of further developments. "Unfortunately," the consul wrote, "it has now been verified that the Jews, motivated by an execrable Superstition, slaughtered him, together with his servant, to get his blood, and use it . . . to bake their Passover bread. The Harrari brothers, rich merchants in that city, slit Father Tommaso's throat in their home, assisted by rabbis and others. After gathering the blood in a silver basin, and having cut his body into tiny pieces and ground them together with the bones in a mortar, they threw it all in a sewage canal, where [the remains] have, in part, been found." As for the friar's Muslim servant, he had met the same fate in the home of one of the other wealthy Jewish merchants of the city. "The principal Jewish families of Damascus," the consul reported, "have participated in this atrocious crime; a large number of people are in jail, including various rabbis. Some of the main guilty parties have been the victims of unheard-of tortures applied by the Authorities, which have forced them to confess."

The Sardinian consul general in Egypt also sent the cardinal a letter he had received from the Sardinian consul in Aleppo, Syria's second largest city, dated March 18. The letter reported that ever since the unfortunate Capuchin's bones had been found, everyone in Aleppo was talking about the case. "It has been proven," wrote the Aleppo consul, "that, as a matter of religious principle, each year the Jews slaughter victims to use their blood."[6]

The first full report that Gregory XVI himself received on the Damascus affair came from a different Alexandria source, a man named Rossetti, consul of the grand duchy of Tuscany. Over the next months, the Tuscan consul would send a series of such reports to Cardinal Lambruschini, the secretary of state. He sent the first of these on March 27, appending to it copies of letters (in French) that he had received from Damascus providing the latest details.

The first of these letters, dated February 28, told of the friar's disappearance, the Capuchins' immediate suspicions, the barber's testimony, the governor general's order to arrest the Jews whom the barber had named, and the arrest of four other rabbis, who were told they would remain in jail until Father Tommaso was found. "The following day," the letter continued, "the barber was subjected to torture," and gave more details and more names. "A large number of children have been put in prison," he added. Here the reference was to the imprisonment of sixty Jewish children; their parents had been told that they would remain in jail until the Jews brought in Father Tommaso. "Jews who try to flee," the Damascus correspondent added, "are arrested and put in prison."

The second Damascus letter that he appended, dated March 12, tells of the triumph of justice, with the discovery of what had really happened. "The authors of the assassination of poor Father Tommaso have been discovered, thanks to the full confession of the barber and of the Jewish servants of the Harrari merchants." They had revealed the story in all its gory detail. Not only had the barber held the friar by his beard while Harrari slit his throat, but the Jews had then hung the dying Tommaso by his feet the better to collect all his blood, before chopping his bloodless cadaver into little pieces.

The correspondent went on to explain what had impelled the Jews to such an inhuman deed. It could only be attributed, he wrote, to the Jews' fanaticism, as they "need a Christian victim at particular times for an anniversary or for the celebration of one of their religious mysteries (it is said that they need Christian blood for their Passover bread)." The perpetrators "form the elite of the commercial fortunes of Damascus, and pass for very respectable people," and it would be hard to believe they were capable of such a crime, but seven of the nine men accused had already confessed.

The people of Damascus, he continued, were so outraged by these atrocities that it had taken all of the efforts of the authorities "to prevent the population from wiping out the Jewish quarter and the Jewish race of Damascus."[7]

The Vatican secretary of state soon learned more details, having received French translations of two reports sent by Sherif Pasha to Mehemet Ali in Alexandria, recounting the testimony he had gathered.[8]

In the complex religious geography of Syria, where several branches of Catholicism coexisted, the Jews' putative murder of the Capuchin friar brought new ecumenical cooperation. In mid-May the Maronite arch-bishop and the Greek Melchite Catholic bishop of Aleppo, together with the Roman Catholic Antioch patriarch of Syria, jointly addressed a letter to the Pope. The Antioch patriarch sent the letter via Cardinal Fransoni, to whom he addressed a cover note, asking him to see that the plea reached the Pope.[9]

They began their letter with an expression of outrage for "the distress-ing massacre of Capuchin Father Tommaso and his assistant, committed by the Jews." They too went over the horrifying details. The friar, they wrote, had barely arrived at a Jewish merchant's home when "many Jews bound his hands and feet tightly and cut his throat in such a way as to be able to get all of his blood. They bashed his head with hammers as one does to cattle . . . then cut him into pieces."

The episode had led the local inhabitants, the bishops wrote, "to attribute many other murders to this wicked people, because so many children and adults have disappeared suddenly, never to be seen again." They explained that the Jews had been able to get away with such crimes over the years because, "in addition to their craftiness, they are protected by Jewish consuls, who are to be found in Aleppo." The Aleppo-based religious leaders then came to the point of their letter, urging the Pope to use his influence to ensure that Catholic countries, such as Austria, removed these Jewish consuls and replaced them with good Catholics.[10]

Shortly after the Aleppo leaders sent their plea to the Pope, the Greek Catholic patriarch of Alexandria sent a long letter of his own to Cardinal Fransoni, asking him to pass its contents along to the Pope. The patriarch, who had written Rome earlier about the Damascus affair, reported that he had been outraged to read letters in the recent French press. These contained lies that the Jews were promulgating in their attempt "to try to deny the horrible assassination." To set the record straight, he was send-ing along a French translation of the Damascus Jews' trial transcript.

"There remains no doubt," wrote the patriarch, "that the Jews, as an obligation of their wicked religion, have killed and continue to kill Chris-tians by draining them of their blood amidst the greatest torments." Nei-ther Christians nor Muslims, he continued, were going to put up with this any longer, "because the Jews will never stop doing what it is their reli-gious duty to do, and many of these duties require that they murder Christians to use their blood for these religious purposes."

Here the patriarch referred to a book that the cardinals and the Pope would show a great deal of interest in, and which would play a major role in the Church's ritual-murder campaign later in the century. It was said to be the work of a Moldavian Jew who had converted and become an Orthodox Christian monk at age thirty-eight. Scholars have yet to unearth the true story of the book's provenance and authorship. It contains the most preposterous fabrications, but at the same time shows familiarity with a number of Jewish ritual practices. The author claimed to be, for the first time, breaking the Jews' vow of silence and telling the horrible secrets that they had guarded so closely for centuries, the true story of why they needed Christian blood. The little book was first published in the Moldavian language in 1803, and then translated into Greek and published in Romania in 1834. On July 2, the Greek Catholic patriarch sent Cardinal Fransoni the handwritten Italian translation he had prepared. It was a rough, partial translation, filled with crossed-out words and corrections written in above them. Cardinal Fransoni read the document with mounting excitement. He thought himself lucky to have gotten even this partial copy, for at the bottom of the first page of the patriarch's translation was the note: "This work is extremely rare, because it seems that Jewish gold has made it disappear from the face of the earth."[11]

The author began dramatically. He would reveal the "mystery of the blood," a secret so closely guarded that not even most Jews knew it. This he was in a position to do because, he claimed, although now a monk, he had once been a rabbi.

There are three reasons, he wrote, why Jews practice ritual murder: (1) "Owing to their great hatred for Christians," they believe that in "murdering them they are offering a sacrifice to God"; (2) they need Christian blood for their magic; and (3) "because, suspecting that Jesus, son of Mary, may in fact be the true Messiah, the rabbis believe that by sprinkling themselves with Christian blood they are saved."

The monk then recounted all the different occasions on which Jews used the blood: The rabbis treat various illnesses by rubbing the blood of Christians on people's bodies, believing that this will heal them. Similarly, when Jews prepare for a marriage, the bride and groom must fast, but immediately after the ceremony the rabbi gives them an egg to eat. Instead of sprinkling it with salt, he sprinkles it with a concoction containing Christian blood.

The Jews' hatred of Christians, the Moldavian monk explained, was expressed in many ways. On Christmas Eve and the day before Epiphany, the Jews stay up all night playing cards and "cursing Christ, His Mother, and all the saints." Jewish children learn to hate Christians early, for before they are taught anything else, they are instructed how to curse them. In fact, "It is written in the Talmud that any Jew who passes within a distance of ten steps of a Christian church and forgets to pronounce the above-mentioned insult must return to do so."

The Jews' realization that Christ may well be the true Messiah was reflected in many of their uses of Christian blood. When a male infant is circumcised, wrote the Moldavian, the rabbis take some blood from a martyred Christian and place it on the wound. In this way, "the boy, not having been baptized with water, is saved by the blood of the martyred Christian, who was baptized by water, and whose blood was shed while suffering greatly, as was Christ's."

The author finally turned to the best-known occasion for ritual murder, linked to the Jews' preparation of their Passover matzah. Not all of their matzah requires Christian blood. Rather, their rites specify that a special piece of matzah, which they call their *Afikomen,* be made by mixing in ashes from a piece of cloth that had first been soaked in the blood of a martyred Christian and then burned. At the Passover meal, at which, the monk added, the Jews all get drunk, "it is obligatory for every Jew, even the youngest, to eat a little piece of that matzah, the size of an olive, which contains the blood of the Christian martyr."

Of special danger for Christians was the Jews' celebration of Purim, for in celebrating their liberation centuries earlier from the hands of Haman, they commit murder. The Christian takes the place of the hated Haman. "When [the Jews] have killed a Christian in Haman's place, the rabbi makes triangular fruit breads, and puts a little of the blood of the murdered Christian in them, and then sends them to all his friends."

But there was an important difference between the Jews' need for Christian blood on Passover and on Purim. For Purim, Jews simply need to kill Christians. But for Passover, murder is not enough. "Instead of tormenting Christ, they must torture a Christian, as Christ was tortured." To best imitate Christ's suffering, they are required to drain little children of their blood. Children are chosen rather than adults because as virgins they possess a purity which resembles that of Jesus himself.

This mystery of the blood, the Moldavian revealed, was explained to him one day by his father, who threatened him with the most horrible maledictions should he ever reveal it to anyone, even to his own brothers. Nor, when he got married, his father instructed him, should he reveal the secret to his wife. Indeed, no woman should ever be told of it. And even if he had ten children, he should only divulge it to a single son, the one who was most intelligent.

In now revealing this mystery, the Moldavian wrote, he was putting himself in the greatest danger. But, he wrote in conclusion, he was unafraid: "My hope is in the Father, my refuge is the Son, and my shield is the Holy Spirit. Glory to the Most Holy Trinity."[12]

News of the Moldavian document had been circulating in diplomatic and Church circles in Alexandria, and about the same time as the Greek Catholic patriarch was preparing an Italian translation for the Pope's benefit, the Tuscan consul general of Alexandria—the secretary of state's correspondent—was sending his own. Sometime in July, Cardinal Lambruschini received the translated booklet and, immediately seeing its value, sent it on July 23 to Cardinal Fransoni, along with other material dealing more directly with the Damascus case. It was up to Fransoni to find discreet ways to use the documents so that the Jews' guilt for Father Tommaso's death could become known throughout Europe without seeming to be the result of a Church-orchestrated campaign. The Moldavian's booklet, Cardinal Lambruschini wrote, would "shed much light on the motives for which the Reverend Father Tommaso . . . met his violent death at the hands of the Jews of Damascus."[13]

The prefect, on receiving the materials, was himself struck by the potency of the Moldavian document. On August 12, he sent a packet back to the secretary of state with a cover note: "The undersigned Cardinal Prefect of Propaganda returns to Your Eminence, with the most heartfelt thanks, the most interesting documents regarding the horrible assassination of the excellent Capuchin friar living in Damascus, Father Tommaso. I am keeping only the brief, but accurate extract of the Greek book printed in . . . Romania that Your Excellency deigned to send me, with the intention of returning it as soon as I can."[14]

Along with the other reports that he would circulate for unattributed publication in newspapers in Italy and France, Cardinal Fransoni selected the Moldavian document and sent it to the bishop of Modena. On August 26, the bishop returned the copy. He wrote: "I have the pleasure of informing you that I hope to have served you in two ways, first by making this notice public elsewhere [i.e., outside the Papal States], and secondly by multiplying its useful distribution, while at the same time taking certain cautions that prudence suggests." The bishop added, "Being always ready to do what you command, and to serve the sacred cause of Religion and its principles—which are so much embattled in our day—in any way I can, I have the honor to express all my respect, kissing your hand." After receiving the bishop's letter, Cardinal Fransoni's secretary added the notation: "The booklet was sent back to the Cardinal Secretary of State, September 17, 1840." Indeed, the letter and the Moldavian booklet can be found today in the Vatican Secret Archives.[15]

Why such "prudence"? Why the distance between the Pope, along with his secretary of state, Cardinal Lambruschini, and the European publication of the Moldavian's lurid account of Jewish evil? The decision to send the materials to the bishop of Modena grew from considerations of political geography. Modena was then a separate duchy, bordering the Papal States. By having the materials published in a Modena newspaper, the stories would easily circulate both within the Pope's dominions and beyond, and would be picked up by newspapers throughout Europe, yet the Vatican could avoid the appearance of having spread the story itself, an impression impossible to avoid with any publication originating in the Papal States.

The Pope and his secretary of state adopted this approach in the midst of an increasingly bitter controversy in Europe over what had happened in Damascus. In the early days after Father Tommaso's disappearance, European press accounts came largely from reports sent in from the French consul, Ratti Menton, his assistant consul, Jean-Baptiste Beaudin, and those close to them. Their role in the case has been much debated, but there is no question that they played a major part in pressing the Damascus authorities to charge the Jews. They were also actively involved in the interrogations of the Jewish prisoners, and in the door-to-door search for the missing suspects.[16]

The European press, which at first had overwhelmingly and uncritically accepted the charges against the Jews, now began to adopt a more skeptical stance. A push in this direction came when the Austrian consuls involved in the case began to make known their view that the Jews of Damascus had been framed, forced into confessing preposterous lies by the use of the most horrendous torture. These reports, as well as others, which came directly from the Jewish community of Damascus, began to appear in newspapers in France, Britain, Prussia, and Austria.

The about-face in the Austrian press coverage of the case was especially dramatic. On April 11, the whole first page of the country's foremost newspaper was devoted to the kind of diabolical portrait of the murderous Jews of Damascus that had, in these first days of coverage in Europe, been common. But on the very next day, the front page contained a jarringly different story. Official reports from Beirut, readers were told, revealed that in fact there was no evidence to show that Father Tommaso had even been murdered, let alone that he had been killed by Jews. Experts had determined not only that the bones found in the sewer were not new, but that they were not even human. The article went on to dismiss the "oft-refuted delusion that the Jews consume Christian blood at the time of their Passover" as a sad example of "how, over centuries, opinions can survive which revolt human nature." The sharp reversal in the paper's position most likely came as a result of intervention by Prince Metternich. The Austrian statesman had, from the beginning, regarded the ritual-murder charge as a preposterous fabrication.[17]

At the same time, reports of the tortures that had been used to extort the confessions also began to circulate in Europe, producing new doubts. Typical was the account that the chief rabbi of Damascus, Jacob Antabi, sent to the head of the English Jewish community, Moses Montefiore.

On March 1, the rabbi recalled, he had been brought in for questioning by the pasha, who ordered him to produce the bottle of the friar's blood that one of the other tortured Jews had claimed he had. When the rabbi said that no such bottle existed, the pasha threatened to cut his head off, and then had him thrown into a pool of frigid water. Each time he bobbed up to breathe, the soldiers clubbed him on the head. When the rabbi was finally pulled out, he was flogged until he fainted, then flogged again until he once more passed out. The interrogators paused to offer him a way out. If he would confess, he would not only be granted a pardon, but a life pension as well. When he refused, they placed a tourniquet around his forehead, and ratcheted it so tightly that twice the rope broke. Subsequently they dragged him by a rope tied to his penis and crushed his genitals. Unlike most of the other Jews subjected to these methods, the rabbi stood by his story.[18]

At the end of March, an English Protestant missionary arrived in Damascus to investigate the matter and sent back his own blood-curdling accounts of the tortures of the Jewish suspects. At one point, he wrote, the pasha told two of the Harrari brothers—who had previously confessed, under torture, to murdering the Sardinian friar—that all he wanted from them was the truth. They responded, "The truth is that we know of no murder, but if you . . . torture us again, we shall again return to our former deposition." Indeed, they were again tortured, and again they confessed to the crime.[19]

The Austrian consul in Alexandria—directly involved in the case because some of the Jewish suspects were subjects of the Austrian empire—sought an audience with the viceroy, Mehemet Ali, to protest the methods being used in Damascus. Subsequently, on April 20, the viceroy sent a letter ordering that the torture of the Jews be stopped. By this time, two of the Jewish prisoners had already been tortured to death.

With the case attracting unwanted attention from the West, the viceroy, in the midst of delicate diplomatic dealings of his own with the western powers, became wary about pursuing the case further. He ordered the suspension of the planned hanging of ten of the Jews. By the end of May, nine of the Jewish men who had been sentenced remained in jail, as did the chief rabbi. Another man was confined in the Austrian consulate, while many others were in hiding.[20] Meanwhile, the Jews of France and England were organizing protests on behalf of their Damascus brethren, and trying to exert diplomatic pressure on Mehemet Ali to put an end to the affair.

The Sardinian consul in Alexandria reported to Secretary of State Lambruschini on these diplomatic protests and their repercussions in a letter in early June. There was no doubt, he assured the cardinal, that the Jews had killed Father Tommaso. The French consul, Ratti Menton, had examined the procedures that had been employed and found them to be perfectly in order. Although "the confessions made separately by the defendants were extracted under torture," Rossetti wrote, they had been fully confirmed by other evidence.[21]

Three weeks later, Rossetti again wrote to Cardinal Lambruschini, reporting the latest worrisome developments in the case. "Your Eminence," he wrote, "must know more than I of all the intrigues that the richest and most prominent Jews are engaged in to stay the hand of justice and obstruct the punishment of their coreligionists and the discovery of the proof of such an abominable and atrocious murder." Fortunately, he continued, the matter remained in the hands of the French consul, and so "all the gold in the world will not suffice this time to silence truth and justice."[22]

In the midst of these reports, and of the Vatican's efforts to circulate its version of the murder in Damascus, the Austrian ambassador to the Holy See unexpectedly came to see Cardinal Lambruschini. It was June 30, and he had a note to deliver on behalf of his government. The letter, found in the Vatican Secret Archives, begins by expressing the Austrian court's sympathies to the Holy See on Father Tommaso's disappearance. But it soon came to the point. "The most insistent appeals are currently being made to the Imperial Court of Austria from different quarters. They are calling on the Court to interest itself, on behalf of outraged humanity, in ensuring that this [cause] is served by the strictest and most impartial justice and is not left to purely arbitrary action." Although the people behind these "insistent appeals" are nowhere identified in the letter, we know that one of them was none other than Salomon Rothschild. It was most likely Rothschild who told Metternich of an alternative explanation of Father Tommaso's disappearance, one that Metternich, through his ambassador, would pass on to the Pope.[23]

"As great as the Imperial Court's bitterness was in learning the news of the atrocious crime committed against the person of a Minister of the Church," the letter continued, "so too was its outrage in learning the circumstances that have accompanied the procedure adopted in Damascus to discover its authors. New crimes and murders are being committed— in large part at the instigation of our own coreligionists—under the pretext of unraveling the truth, allowing many of the accused to be sacrificed to the cruelty and arbitrary justice of the Muslims. And this, not as a result of any proven guilt they bear, but in reality out of private commercial interests and sectarian hatred that prevails among the different religions in that land."

The Austrian court, wrote the ambassador, desired only that the true author of the crime be found. The letter then offered an alternative explanation for the friar's disappearance, one championed by the Jews of Damascus themselves. The Austrians called on the secretary of state and the Pope to see that this other possibility was investigated as well.

"Three days before Reverend Father Tommaso's disappearance, he had a heated argument with some Arab Muslims in one of Damascus's busiest streets. On that occasion one of them publicly swore a vendetta against him. In addition, the day before his disappearance [was reported], a Jew who had a store near the gate of the city saw the friar leave the city from that gate around sunset, together with his servant. The unfortunate Jew was clubbed to death [by the police] for his testimony. The Muslim residents near his store have publicly stated that what the Jew said was entirely true, but they thought better of reporting the matter to the local authorities, fearing for their lives.

"From this," the letter concluded, "one may suppose that Father Tommaso tried to flee the vendetta of the above-mentioned Arab, heading with his servant toward Palestine and Mount Lebanon. There he may perhaps be hidden and still found in one of the convents, should Muslim Arabs not have already killed him along the road." The Austrian court emissary then got to the heart of his government's request. "In order to clarify these suppositions," he wrote, "it would be desirable for His Holiness to address circular letters to the religious heads of Palestine, the Holy Land, and Mount Lebanon. They should be ordered, most emphatically, to undertake a thorough search for Father Tommaso in those convents and in all other religious buildings and parishes. Or they should at least find out if a priest or anyone else has seen or encountered him on his way after his disappearance with his servant." The ambassador's letter to the secretary of state ended with the request, on behalf of the Austrian Imperial Court, that he bring the Austrian proposal to the Pope's attention.[24]

Ten days later, Cardinal Lambruschini sent his response. "As much as I respect the reasons that have caused the Imperial Court of Vienna to doubt whether the sudden disappearance of the Capuchin Father Tommaso . . . is really to be attributed to the Jews of Damascus," he wrote the Austrian ambassador, "it would nonetheless be out of keeping with the frankness of my character . . . if I did not tell you, with the necessary discretion, that the news that has reached both me and the Congregation for the Propaganda [of the Faith] from highly trustworthy individuals living in the Levant, and especially in Syria and Egypt, leaves not the slightest shadow of a doubt of the truth of this accusation, notwithstanding its wicked and atrocious nature."

Given this certainty, wrote Cardinal Lambruschini, the Austrians' suggestion that a search be launched in the convents of Syria, Palestine, and Lebanon was out of the question. Not only was the cardinal convinced that the friar had been cruelly murdered, but the alternative possibility that the Austrians had suggested would imply that Father Tommaso was "lacking in charity, justice, and at the least incapable of knowing his moral duties." If he were alive, wrote the secretary of state, the friar could hardly be unaware that the government in Damascus "was imprisoning, trying, and torturing such a large number of people solely to induce them to confess what they know about Father Tommaso's disappearance." Had the friar fled, he would surely have found some way to send out word that he was alive, while perhaps out of prudence concealing his exact whereabouts. "I thus would like to believe," concluded the cardinal, that "in your rare wisdom . . .Your Excellency will recognize the reasonableness of the negative decision that I have taken with respect to the inquiries requested by the Austrian Government."[25]

One of the "highly trusted individuals" alluded to in Lambruschini's reply, the Tuscan consul in Alexandria, sent the secretary of state yet another update on July 15. Appended to the letter were Italian translations of Sherif Pasha's two reports to the viceroy. The consul promised to send translations of the rest of the interrogations of the Jews as soon as possible. Reflecting on the evidence, the consul asked: "Given that the authors [of the crime] were motivated neither by a vendetta nor by material benefit—for they are the most prominent and richest men of their nation—how can the atrocious case be explained if not by attributing it to an abominable mystery and an even more abominable fanaticism?" Even more worrisome than discovering the truth about the mutilation of the friar, he added, was the realization of "the number of victims who for so many centuries must have been sacrificed to this execrable mystery." And if, he continued, people in the past had "always dismissed such stories as mere inventions stemming from lamentable prejudices that have held that the Jews sacrifice and martyr Christians, today there can no longer be any doubt."

The consul also enclosed with his letter a translation of extracts from the Talmud that the pasha had ordered as part of his investigation.[26] The supposed Talmud extracts were just one of various documents aimed at demonstrating the Jews' evil being collected by the secretary of state and the prefect of Propaganda Fide. Yet they merit special attention because the alleged link between Jewish malevolence and the Talmud had a long history in the Church and would arise again, with renewed force, later in the century.

In 1242, charging that the Talmud called on Jews to cheat and murder Christians, Church authorities ordered all copies of the Talmud burned.

In 1443, Pope Eugenius IV issued a bull prohibiting the Jews from study- ing the Talmud, and a century later, in 1553, Pope Julius III ruled that the Talmud was blasphemous and ordered all copies of the work seized and burned. On Rosh Hashanah, the Jewish New Year, of 1553 a huge pyre was built in the middle of Rome's Campo dei Fiori, the same spot where, a half century later, Giordano Bruno would himself be burned alive on orders of the Inquisition. Huge numbers of Talmuds and various Hebrew-language books seized from the homes of the Jews of Rome's ghetto were tossed into the conflagration. At the same time, the Holy Office called on civil and Church leaders throughout Italy to find all copies of the Talmud and have them likewise burned.

After the Torah—the Five Books of Moses, or Pentateuch—the Tal- mud is Judaism's most sacred text. The Torah embodies the "written law," traditionally regarded as having been revealed by God to the Hebrews. Over many centuries the written law was extended and elabo- rated into a vastly larger body of jurisprudence, the "oral law"; and the Babylonian Talmud (there is also a less important Jerusalem Talmud), written primarily in Aramaic, is an authoritative codification of that oral law. In form, it consists of the legal/philosophical teachings and discus- sions of scholars at the great rabbinical academies of Babylonia from the third to the fifth century C.E. These were edited by the sixth century into sixty-three books of exposition and commentary on Jewish law, ethics, ritual, and history.

The Talmud is notoriously difficult to read. Its two and a half million words of text reproduce the often dense and convoluted style of oral argument that characterized the ancient academies. It is written as if the many rabbis whose words it records were all alive together debating contentious issues and interpreting particular cases. Although a primary source of Jewish law, it is a rambling work, incorporating popular proverbs, parables, fables, facts, Jewish and heathen folklore, and moral maxims, all of which have become the source of endless interpretation and discussion among Jewish scholars over the centuries. The fact that interpretation and debate over the meaning of each portion of the Tal- mud is as important as the original text itself is reflected in the way the printed version of the Talmud is structured. At the center of each page is the original text, but surrounding it are sections of commentaries on the text by later scholars.[27]

For the Church, however, the Talmud was long viewed as a dangerous

and blasphemous work, which codified the Jews' rejection of Christianity
and hence embodied the evil path the Jews had pursued since rejecting
Jesus, the true Messiah. The brief document that the Tuscan consul sent
the secretary of state was typical. Representing itself as the authoritative
ninth-century Latin translation of passages from the Talmud, rendered
somewhere along the line into French, it contained such injunctions as
the following:

"The Jews must curse the Christians three times each day, and ask God
for their destruction and their extermination."

"God permits the Jews to seize the property of Christians in any way
they can, by ruse, trickery, usury, or theft."

"Jews must view Christians as wild beasts and animals, and treat them
accordingly. . . . and if one of us encounters a Christian at a precipice, he
should push him off."[28]

These, and other similar supposed extracts from the Talmud, as we
will see again later, combined blatant invention with mistranslation and
quotation out of context. At the time the Talmud was being written, the
Jews of Babylonia were surrounded by many different peoples. Among
these, Christians were not especially prominent. In discussing relations
with these other peoples, the rabbis were concerned, above all, to prevent
assimilation. They also viewed the Jews as the only people who followed
the laws handed down by the true God, and regarded all others as idolaters. Yet, while passages can certainly be found in the Talmud that present
a dim view of these others, talmudic law recognizes the sanctity of the
biblical commandments not to steal, not to murder, etc., and applies
these to all people.[29]

Ten days after sending the supposed Talmud extracts to the secretary
of state, the Tuscan consul wrote Cardinal Lambruschini again, once
more including a document, the French translation of the testimony
of Moses Abu el-Affieh, one of the accused murderers. The Jew, the consul explained, having just converted to Islam, had provided "the most
remarkable details of the atrocious crime." His testimony dated from
early March.

Moses, who had changed his name to Mohammed, asserted that it
was the chief rabbi of Damascus who had masterminded the murder.
"Jacob Antabi told me ten or fifteen days earlier that he needed blood to
carry out some of his religious duties, that he had spoken with the Harrari brothers, that the deed would take place at their house . . . and that I

should be present." Mohammed then went on to recount how, on the fateful day, the friar was brought in, his throat was cut, and he was taken into another room so that his blood could be drained.[30]

Although the Tuscan consul did not mention it, shortly before Moses's testimony, the Damascus police, assisted by the French consul and the consul's assistant, had taken him from the prison to his home. There they told him to produce the bottle of Father Tommaso's blood that they believed he had hidden. His wife later described the visit.

She had pleaded with the consul to believe her when she insisted that no such bottle existed; her husband had lied to stop the torture. And when neither she nor her husband could produce the bottle, a new round of torture began. "A cord was tied around my husband's neck; the consul and Salina [an assistant] dragged him across the courtyard." Moses' feet were already in shreds, the bone showing through, from the hundreds of lashes to his feet suffered in his earlier interrogation. The confrontation at their home lasted three hours, at the end of which Moses was flogged another two hundred times while his wife looked on. The next day he told his captors that he wanted to convert, and shortly thereafter, in exchange for his freedom, he provided the testimony that Rossetti had sent on to Cardinal Lambruschini.[31]

The dispatch from Rossetti in Alexandria no doubt further confirmed the Pope, the secretary of state, and the cardinal prefect of Propaganda Fide in their conviction of the Jews' guilt. But by the time they received it, their attention had been diverted by other news. A delegation of prominent English and French Jews had set sail for Egypt to plead their case with the viceroy himself.

Moses Montefiore, head of the English Jewish community, led the delegation, bearing a letter of support from the British foreign secretary. Adolphe Crémieux, a leading figure of the French Jewish community who had close ties to high French government circles, was co-leader.[32] Their goal was to get the viceroy's permission to open an inquiry in Damascus into the affair, and to obtain a new trial.

On August 4 the Jewish group arrived in Alexandria and, the next day, had their first meeting with Mehemet Ali. The moment seemed anything but propitious. The two countries most supportive of the Jews' demands—England and Austria—had been backing the sultan of the Ottoman Empire in his struggle with the viceroy. Over the course of the month that Montefiore and Crémieux would spend in Alexandria,

Austria and England, along with its allies Russia and Prussia, sent Ali an ultimatum. Either he returned his non-Egyptian territories to the Ottoman sultan or he would face war. By contrast, Mehemet Ali's chief European patron was France, the nation whose diplomats had been hard at work mounting the case against the Damascus Jews.

Yet by the end of August, after British naval ships had seized a number of Egyptian supply boats, the viceroy decided to back down. As part of his effort to blunt English and Austrian hostility, he agreed to issue an order freeing the imprisoned Jews in Damascus. The Jews were soon released, much to the anger of the Vatican, the Capuchins, and the French consul in Damascus.

Throughout Europe, the Catholic press greeted news of the Jews' release with outrage. The Catholic clergy of Damascus were especially irate. Together with the Church hierarchy in Rome, they were convinced that the decision to free the Jews had nothing to do with their innocence. Clearly they were guilty of the ritual murder of the kindly friar. The scandalous release of the Jewish prisoners was simply the result of the Jews' political influence and their skill in arranging well-placed bribes.

Although the legal case was now over, the Vatican continued to deal with various loose ends from the affair. On September 30, 1840, Cardinal Lambruschini received a confidential letter from the Austrian ambassador. "There has recently appeared among the Greek Catholic population of Damascus," the note began, "a written work directed against the Jewish community there, a work that propounds the crassest accusations and all of the fanaticism of centuries past." The Austrian letter charged that the author of the libelous work was none other than the Greek Catholic patriarch of Damascus.

"Given the unsettled state of mind that now prevails in Damascus," the letter continued, "publication of such arguments which are wholly in conflict with any sense of Christian charity can only have the most serious consequences in exciting sectarian strife and encouraging renewed persecutions." The Imperial Court of Vienna, the letter concluded, "thus believes it its precise duty to refer such deplorable developments to the most serious attention of His Holiness's government."[33]

There is no indication in the secretary of state's archives that he, or the Pope, took any action in response to the Austrian appeal.

The private correspondence of both the secretary of state and the cardinal prefect makes clear that they were fully convinced that the Jewish religion commanded its followers to murder Christians and consume their blood. It also shows how eager the two cardinals were to have these "facts" made known to the Christian public. Yet throughout the affair they proceeded in secrecy, keeping far from public view.

Moses Montefiore, the leader of the Jewish expedition to Alexandria, was a man of great confidence in his own political influence and powers of persuasion. Unaware of the extent of the Vatican's involvement in the case, he somehow thought that he could convince the Pope to come to the Jews' aid. And so, in late December, on his return voyage across the Mediterranean, he disembarked in Italy and went to Rome. He had two objectives. He wanted the Pope to order the removal of the offensive tombstone that the Capuchin friars had erected over Father Tommaso's grave, and he hoped that Gregory XVI would issue a statement condemning charges of ritual murder against the Jews, something other popes had done in previous centuries.

It was December 22 when Montefiore arrived in the Holy City. Once there, he did everything he could to try to arrange a papal audience. Within a week, the British representative in Rome was telling him that the Pope would never agree to his requests. "[A]ll the people about the pope were persuaded," said the British envoy, according to Montefiore, "that the Jews had murdered Father Tommaso and even if all the witnesses in the world were brought before the pope to prove the contrary, neither he nor his people would be convinced." Montefiore, not persuaded, spent another two weeks trying unsuccessfully to see the Pontiff. He left Rome, dejected, on January 11.[34]

Three months later, in what in retrospect seems a fitting postscript to the case, the secretary of state received a packet from the papal nuncio in Vienna. The nuncio was belatedly responding to Cardinal Lambruschini's search for copies of the Moldavian's booklet. He had succeeded in finding one, which he enclosed. He had read it with profit: "The new murder recently committed by the Jews in Damascus makes the revelations contained in the book all the more interesting."[35] Indeed, the importance of these revelations to the Church, as well as the importance of the murder of Father Tommaso itself, would only increase in the years ahead.

CHAPTER FIVE

The End of an Era

W HEN GREGORY XVI DIED, in June 1846, few mourned him. His grim crusade to banish modern ideas and practices from the papal kingdom, and his use of draconian police methods to root out opposition, had left him with little popular support. That he had had to rely on Austrian troops to keep him in power only made things worse. The former monk seemed a throwback to an earlier time, when absolute rule was taken for granted, when divine authority was the only authority.

The cardinals who gathered in conclave to elect a new pope were alarmed at the mounting signs of popular unrest. Things were not going well for the Holy See, not least because of the rapid rise of the movement to unify Italy, which before long would doom the Papal States.

As in the past, Italians totally dominated the Church hierarchy. Of the sixty-two cardinals in all the world, fifty-four were Italian, and none of the eight non-Italians appeared in Rome in time to cast a vote.

For those closest to Gregory XVI, one man was the obvious choice to continue his work: Luigi Cardinal Lambruschini, the secretary of state, on whom Gregory had increasingly relied. The first ballot saw Lambruschini in the lead. But most of the cardinals realized that if there was to be any hope of quelling the unrest, some things would have to change. The person they turned to, and elected on their fourth ballot, was the bishop of Imola, Giovanni Maria Mastai-Ferretti.

In some respects this was an unusual choice. Two of the main criteria for choosing popes—although not always honored—were experience in the central Vatican administration and in the Church's diplomatic service. Mastai-Ferretti had none of the former and little of the latter. Nor was he known for his intellectual abilities or deep learning: He was neither remarkably intelligent nor particularly well educated in Church theology and law. Moreover, at age fifty-four he was rather young to be pope.

What attracted the cardinals to him was his success in leading the Church in Romagna, which had been the scene of some of the fiercest opposition to papal rule. If he could only apply what had won him popularity in Imola to the task of governing the whole of the Papal States, the cardinals thought, all would be well.

Mastai-Ferretti, who took the name of Pius IX, was a friendly, gregarious man. He had no airs about him, a high cleric who remained delightfully approachable. Although conservative in his basic outlook, the new pope recognized that things were not going well for the Church and that some changes had to be made. He had another merit as well, for he was viewed as a sincerely religious person, one who believed deeply in the Church and its teachings. For many, it was his very lack of any recent diplomatic experience and his distance from Vatican intrigues that made him seem so attractive. He was no schemer.[1]

The first months of a new pope's reign were always crucial for the Jews, for it was then that the new pontiff typically reiterated the old policies regulating the Jews' lives or, in failing to do so, opened the door to new concessions. Upon Pius IX's election, a wave of optimism swept through the Papal States, as word spread of a kindly new pontiff who was eager to end the abuses of the past. Hopeful of better treatment, the Jews lost no time seeking the Pope's attention.

On September 13, 1846, just three months after Pius's election, the deputies of Rome's Jewish community sent him a lengthy plea, lamenting the restrictions imposed by his recent predecessors. The Jews called on Pius IX to imitate his namesake at the beginning of the century. Pius VII had allowed the Jews various liberties that Leo XII and then Gregory XVI had taken away, including the ability to have their shops outside the ghetto, and to live and work in other towns of the Papal States.

But the Jews had a number of other complaints. Rome's Jews were uneducated, they wrote, because there were no schools in the ghetto that taught nonreligious subjects (the only schools being religious schools for boys), and they were forbidden to attend schools outside the ghetto. Moreover, not only were they not allowed to become doctors—although in past centuries Jewish physicians had ministered to the popes themselves—but they were forbidden to practice most other skilled occupations: they could not open bookstores or print shops, nor could they become jewelers or silversmiths.

And then there were all the humiliations. As they lay dying, Jews had no hospital to go to—for there was none in the ghetto—and if they did succeed in being admitted to one outside they could not be comforted by a rabbi, for no rabbi was allowed there. No Jew could serve as a witness in a civil case, for in the Papal States their word was not trusted.

Particularly irksome was the continued practice of forcing the ghetto's leaders to present themselves, on the Saturday on which Carnival celebrations began, before the Roman Magistrate and Rome's Senator. As these dignitaries sat on their majestic thrones, the Jews genuflected and made ceremonial offerings while crowds of plebeians showered them with taunts. It was, in the petitioners' words, a "mocking feudal spectacle left over from the Middle Ages." They called for mercy from the new pontiff: "Good and holy God!' they pleaded, "Why such harshness toward people who have committed no crime?"

There was also the continuing degradation of being made to attend the sermons aimed at converting the Jews, another vestige of an earlier era. "In the sixteenth century Pope Clement VIII ordered that the Jews be preached to because, according to the Clementine Constitution, revived by the Edict of Cardinal Della Genga, who became Pope Leo XII, it was said that they were of depraved customs." The fact that the government compelled the Jews to attend these sermons, the petitioners argued, was taken by the general population as proof that the Jews were "entirely immoral, full to bursting with vices, so much so that they even needed to be preached to by a Dominican father." Rome's Jews begged the new pope to free them of these humiliations, to give them freedom of movement, and permit them to get an education and to practice the same occupations and professions as Christians.[2]

Before the end of the year, Pius IX, having learned how overcrowded and unhealthy a place the ghetto was, issued an order allowing a small number of families to live just outside the ghetto's walls. As the foremost Italian biographer of Pius IX, Father Giacomo Martina, explains, the Pope's attitude reflected his belief in the need for a more enlightened despotism, and a feeling of benevolent paternalism toward the Jews. Yet he would only go so far. "By temperament, education, and his understanding of what he took to be his duty of defending religion . . . he was completely opposed to the civil emancipation of the Jews."[3]

In February 1847, Baron Salomon Rothschild sent a long letter to the new pope from Vienna in support of the Roman Jews' pleas. Given the Vatican's reliance on Rothschild loans to keep it from bankruptcy, the Pope could not afford to ignore the request. A few days later the papal nuncio in Vienna was told to inform the baron that the Pope was looking into the matter and had, as a first step, agreed to end the degrading Carnival rites.

Pius IX then instituted a commission, headed by the cardinal vicar of Rome, to examine ghetto conditions and to recommend appropriate measures to improve the Jews' lot. Soon the Jews had further cause for rejoicing: The dreaded forced sermons were ended, never to be revived.

In 1847, popular enthusiasm for the new pope continued to grow. The contrast between the kindly pontiff, interested in the welfare of his subjects, and the severity and dogmatism of his predecessors nourished a widespread belief that Pius IX would usher in a new, golden age.

Rumors of acts of papal bounty spread through the Jewish communities of the Papal States. The Pope, it was said, had ordered the ghetto walls to be torn down, and it was rumored that an order giving the Jews equal rights would soon follow. The Jews' excitement proved trying for the local inquisitors, who found it increasingly difficult to get the Jews to obey the law. On July 10, 1847, for example, the inquisitor of Ancona sent an urgent request to the Holy Office in Rome, asking what to do about a petition he had just received. The Jews were insisting that they be allowed to live outside the ghetto.[4]

While waiting for the (negative) response from the Holy Office, the Ancona inquisitor was horrified to come across handbills from Rome that Ancona's Jews were circulating throughout the city. He hastened to write the Holy Office in Rome, enclosing two copies.

Titled "The Common People of Rome and the Jewish Community," and dated "Rome, July 6, 1847," the handbill told of events so bizarre they could scarcely be believed. The Pope's recent actions on behalf of the Jews, it proclaimed, had led to some grumbling among the residents of Rome's poorer neighborhoods, and attempts to revive old anti-Jewish superstitions. But, according to the handbill, a local hero had taken matters in hand, and called a meeting of the residents of the two neighborhoods where the murmurings were loudest. When the crowd had gathered, he announced: "Let's see if I can't persuade you to abandon your hostility for people who, when all is said and done, are neither better nor worse than we are." On the afternoon of July 4, he arranged for a dozen horse-drawn wagons to take people from the Piazza del Popolo to the grounds of the Tor di Quinto, where two thousand of them gathered. After everyone had gotten something to eat, one man after another climbed onto the impromptu stage to denounce prejudice against the Jews.

The following evening, inspired by these events, a group of men made their way into the ghetto and invited the Jews they met to join them at a nearby tavern, offering to treat them all to wine. When the leader of the expedition realized that he had forgotten to bring his money, he ostentatiously handed the key to his house to one of the Jews, a porter named Abraham, and asked him to go into his home, telling him where he kept his money. "Anyone who hasn't the heart of a cynic," the handbill proclaimed, "seeing such a civilized, praiseworthy, marvelous gesture, would have felt tears come to his eyes out of gratitude for that good man!"

The next day, another group of young workmen made their way into the ghetto. As the men entered, "the poor frightened Jews, trembling, asked themselves: What's going on? Are they going to set the ghetto on fire?" But the leader of the group reassured them. They shouldn't be afraid, he said. "We've come to show you that we're all friends, that we respect you, and that we don't listen to those who want to see harm come to you!" Catholics and Jews then embraced, and spoke fondly one to the other. The workmen invited their newfound Jewish comrades to join them for supper back in their own neighborhood. There the Jews went, and other people from the area gathered around and joined in the festivities. Illuminated by torchlight, they played music and sang songs. "As they were leaving, everyone gathered on the bank of the Tiber, where amidst the songs and the music the sweet name of Pius IX was saluted to great applause."

The dramatic account, signed simply "a spectator," concluded: "That moment had something grand, stupendous, sublime. . . . God, nourish this wonderful initiative, giving long life to that greatest Reformer [Pius IX] who is the source of all the good things that are happening."[5]

As the end of 1847, the first full year of Pius IX's papacy, approached, the Pope was at the height of his popularity. The problem for the Vatican was that much of the enthusiasm was for a pope who existed only in the public's imagination. Pius IX's position on the Jews offers a telling example. Those seeking radical changes in the Vatican's Jewish policy told all who would listen that they had the pontiff's blessings. They presented themselves as championing the wishes of the good Pope against the rearguard action of a bigoted local clergy. But, in fact, Pius IX had endorsed only modest changes. By late 1847, in addition to ending the feudal rite of Jewish submission at Carnival and the compulsory sermons, he had allowed the ghetto gates to remain open at night. But the great majority of the Jews remained confined there. He certainly had no intention of granting equal rights to the Jews.[6]

If many of the subjects of the Papal States were intoxicated with excitement about the reforming Pope and his beneficence toward the Jews, the bulk of the clergy had a very different view. Complaints from both inquisitors and bishops began to flood into the Holy Office in Rome. The situation was becoming intolerable. The Jews were getting out of control. They no longer knew their place.

On January 7, in the fateful year of 1848, Ancona's inquisitor sent an anguished plea to the cardinals of the Holy Office. "I believe it my duty," he wrote, "to inform Your Excellencies of something unprecedented in the history of the Papal States that has happened in the city of Ancona." The previous evening, members of the local elite, gathered at their club, had voted to admit Jews. "The Jews had tried other times to be admitted to this Society," the inquisitor wrote, "but they were never allowed in, not even in the era of the so-called Italian Kingdom [i.e., during Napoleonic times]." A prospect too grotesque to contemplate took shape in the inquisitor's mind. It was not uncommon, he pointed out, for the archbishop and other Church dignitaries to be invited for dinner at the club on special occasions. "It will be some sight," the inquisitor wrote, "to find a Jew and Jewess sitting next to the Bishop!" The older members, he noted with some satisfaction, had opposed letting the Jews in, but had been outvoted by the younger generation.[7]

Similar reports began to come in from other towns in the Papal States, where enthusiasm was building for a new era of progress and tolerance. On February 10, 1848, the archbishop of Ferrara wrote the Holy Office another complaint of this kind. The Casino Society, in which the local elite gathered, had just that week voted to admit seven Jews from the richest families of Ferrara's ghetto. He urged the authorities in Rome to do something to stop them. It was a sign of the times that the archbishop felt compelled to add: "Here I beg Your Excellency *to keep my name secret,* so that no one knows where you heard this news."[8]

The Holy Office had heard just a few weeks earlier from Ferrara's archbishop about another unpleasant development. He had been asked to give his permission to allow an article from Rome to be republished in Ferrara. Shocked by its content, which espoused "the most dangerous and erroneous doctrines," the archbishop had banned it. But the petitioners were up in arms. How, they wanted to know, could a bishop order the suppression of something that Rome had approved? The archbishop asked the Holy Office for instructions, and for confirmation of his suspicion that its publication had never been approved by the censors in Rome.[9]

In a later letter, the archbishop informed the Holy Office that, while he had prevented the publication of the offending article in Ferrara, it had been published in early January in Bologna. The piece was the work, he was convinced, "of the Jews, and, without my being able to stop them, they then distributed copies here as well, in the stores and cafes, provoking the indignation of all good people."

The article in question was in the form of a conversation among three men:

A cobbler runs into his friend, a storekeeper, and tells him the stupefying news that he has just heard: The Jews are now free to leave the ghetto. The storekeeper refuses to believe him, and so they call to their parish priest, just then walking by, to ask if the report is true.

"And why is it so amazing," replies the priest, "that, now that those cruel superstitions that prevailed for so many dark centuries have been lifted, your brothers are once again able to share in those goods and those rights that God has granted them as He has all other men? Yes, it is true," the kindly priest continued, "that our sovereign, Pius IX, wanted them to leave their ghetto, which was like a jail. How, after all, could his heart not go out, knowing that these men were living like animals without proper shelter." The rest of civilized Europe was already changing their laws on the Jews, granting them equal rights. The Pope, the toast of all Europe, could do no less.

But isn't it true, the cobbler asks, that the Jews crucified Jesus, and it is for this that they are despised?

"It's true," the priest responds. But all had taken place according to

God's plan. God used the Jews just as he had used the Roman soldiers. "If this were reason for hating the Jews, the Romans too should be hated."

But, replies the storekeeper, isn't it true that the Jews are a bunch of usurers, liars, and swindlers?

No doubt, the priest responds, there is much in their moral condition that could be improved. But, he adds, once they are given the same rights all other men have, "you will see that they have neither more nor fewer vices than the rest of us."[10]

As 1848 got underway, it was not only the Jews who were clamoring for more rights. In January, the people of Palermo rose up and forced the King of Naples to grant a constitution. The following month, in Paris, a rebellion erupted, overthrowing King Louis Philippe. In March, revolutionaries in Vienna drove Metternich into exile. The military pillars on which the Pope's rule rested had, almost overnight, disintegrated, and now anything seemed possible. Pius IX first tried to meet the threat by agreeing to additional reforms, but given the revolutionary temper of the times, these did little to calm the storm.[11]

By the summer of 1848, revolts erupted in the Papal States themselves, and Austrian troops were once again brought in to try to retake Bologna and other rebel strongholds. In the fall, the Pope's ever-weakening hold on Rome gave way. In mid-November, his prime minister was knifed to death in the center of Rome. Fearing the chaos and the threat of a popular uprising, Pius IX—dressed as a simple priest and concealed in the carriage of the Bavarian ambassador—fled the Holy City. He made his way to the fortress of Gaeta, in the nearby Kingdom of Naples. The following month Giuseppe Garibaldi and his troops entered Rome, soon joined by Italian nationalist leader Giuseppe Mazzini. A Roman Republic was proclaimed, and papal rule declared at an end. The Jews were freed from the ghetto and given equal rights. The Pope, from his fortress in Gaeta, near Naples, called on the Catholic powers of Europe to send troops to help him regain his temporal realm. By late spring, Austrian soldiers were once more advancing through the Papal States and French troops marched on Rome itself. In early July, the French entered the Holy City. Papal authority was restored, the revolutionary interlude was over.

When Pius IX returned to Rome in 1850, he was a changed man. Despite the image many of his subjects had had of him earlier, Pius IX had never been a true reformer, much less a liberal. He had always been deeply traditional, committed to the Church's never-changing verities, although he had recognized problems in his realm and believed it necessary to make some changes. On his return from exile, he saw the world differently. Forces of evil were arrayed against him, against the Holy Church, and they could be given no quarter or they would sweep away all that was good.

The Jews were to be put back in their place. The Roman Republic's proclamation of their civil equality was nullified, and the old restrictions were reintroduced.

All this had come despite efforts by the Rothschilds to withhold from the Vatican desperately needed loans unless the Pope agreed not to re-ghettoize Rome's Jews. The Pope found himself in a difficult situation. Although French troops had taken back Rome in July 1849, he was loath to return to the Holy City empty-handed. He first looked in France to find a different bank that would make him a large loan, but could not find any. Reluctantly, he turned to the Rothschilds. This was not his first experience in seeking a loan from them. Shortly after taking up the papacy, he had approached the Rothschild family to help finance a railway system for the Papal States.

The Pope called on his nuncio in Naples to negotiate the loan with Carl Rothschild, head of the family branch there. Carl, in the meantime, summoned the secretary of Rome's Jewish community to discuss the desperate conditions in which the Jews now found themselves, having been ordered back into the ghetto. After hearing the secretary's tale of woe, Rothschild informed the papal nuncio that he would only make the loan if the Pope agreed to abolish the ghetto and grant the Jews the freedom to live wherever they liked. When the Pope summarily rejected this request, saying that he could not sacrifice his higher duties as pope to the material needs of the moment, Carl turned him down.

But Pius IX was in dire financial straits and, swallowing his pride, he pressed on. The Pope told his nuncio in Paris to urge the government there to use its influence with James Rothschild, head of the French branch of the family, to make the loan. Contacted by the nuncio, Louis Napoleon, the new head of state, approached James on the matter in early January 1850.

James was, of course, well aware of what had happened in Naples. In fact, the whole family was buzzing with news of the Pope's request and the agony of Rome's Jews. Just a few days before Louis Napoleon's visit on behalf of the Pope, James had received a letter from his nephew, Anselm Rothschild, one of the rising stars of the family, based in Frankfurt. "The Pope who was once so liberal," he wrote, "is now not just wholly reactionary but, following the example of the Popes of the dark Middle Ages, intolerant in the highest degree, I am tempted even to say inhuman."[12]

When approached for the loan, then, James, too, raised the matter of the plight of the Jews in the Papal States, and demanded that before any loan was made, the Pope agree to free the Jews from the ghetto. In response, the Pope sent James a written assurance through his nuncio in Paris. He had the best intentions with respect to the Jews in the Papal States, he said, and he intimated that he would soon issue an edict abolishing the ghetto. But, he added, it would be unseemly—and indeed unthinkable—to directly link the making of the loan to such an edict. The nuncio delivered the letter to James on January 24, 1850, and the fifty-million-franc loan was made. On April 12, 1850, the Pope made his triumphal entrance into Rome. The edict he had hinted at was never issued.[13]

In January 1851 the Pope met with a delegation of Jews from Rome's ghetto. They presented him with a petition seeking a series of benefits ranging from the ability to sit in on university classes to removal of the heavy annual tax they paid to support the House of the Catechumens.

In response to this, as well as to the pressure that—at the urging of the Rothschild family—the Austrian government was exerting on him, the Pope appointed a special commission. It made its recommendations in October. As a result, a modest list of benefits was approved, such as the ability of some of the Jews to reside outside the ghetto—although limited to well-defined locations nearby. However, Christian contact with Jews was to be kept to a minimum, and Jews were not to be allowed in towns that had no ghettoes.[14]

Pius IX did not content himself with reimposing the old restrictions on the Jews in the Papal States. He also sought to pressure rulers of the other lands in which Jews had gained equal rights in the 1848 revolutions to return the Jews to their previous condition.

Such was the case in the grand duchy of Tuscany. Tuscany had long provoked papal displeasure for the rights that Jews enjoyed there, most notably in the city of Livorno, where they were neither confined to a ghetto nor limited to selling used goods for a living. Following his return to Rome in 1850, Pius IX was angered to learn that the grand duke, Leopold II, was considering allowing the Jews' emancipation to stand. The Pope branded such a move a "true crime"; his legate in Florence called it a "monstrosity."[15]

On February 21, 1852, Pius IX wrote directly to the grand duke to show him how important he felt the matter to be. "Your Highness is not unaware of the fact that the spirit of the Church, expressed in many dispositions and decrees . . . has always been to keep Catholics as much as possible from having any contact with the infidels." Why, the Pope asked, did the grand duke not simply abrogate the entire constitution rather than try to salvage parts of it? "Otherwise," he warned, "it will open the way to requests for other civil rights for the Jews and for other non-Catholics."[16] The Pope proved persuasive. On May 6, the constitution was abrogated and the Jews' emancipation revoked.[17]

Yet 1848 did have important long-term consequences for the Jews elsewhere on the Italian peninsula. While Tuscany resuscitated its restrictions on the Jews, as did the duchy of Modena, the kingdom of Sardinia—with its center in Piedmont and its capital in Turin—retained the statutes of 1848 which had emancipated the Jews. In the ensuing years the Jews there would rapidly gain economic and cultural influence, attending university and founding important businesses. By the time of the Mortara case, in 1858, while the Jews in the Papal States lived in their ghettoes, without any press of their own, and under the thumb of the Inquisition, the Jews of Piedmont would be in a position to rally international support for them.

On his return to Rome, Pius IX reestablished the Inquisition and directed the inquisitors to bring the old restrictions on the Jews back into force. The result was reminiscent of the actions of Pius IX's much-reviled predecessor, Gregory XVI.

In late September 1852, the inquisitor of Bologna, the Dominican friar Pier Gaetano Feletti, who would later gain fame—and notoriety—through his role in the Mortara affair, received instructions from the Holy Office. Pope Clement VIII had banished all Jews from Bologna in 1593. Their ghetto was dismantled and for two centuries no Jew was allowed to live there. But in 1797 French troops entered the city and, in proclaiming the equality of all citizens regardless of religion, led a number of Jews to move in. With the restoration of the papal regime in 1814, the ban on Jews in Bologna was technically reinstated, but temporary dispensations were given to enable some to stay. Despite occasional efforts under Leo XII, Pius VIII, and Gregory XVI to eject all Jews from the city, about a hundred continued to live there at mid-century.

The inquisitor was told to interview each Jewish household head in Bologna and determine the status of each family. Those who had permission to be there and whose conduct was good were to be given a permit to remain in the city for one more year. Others were to be evicted immediately, sent back to the ghetto from which they had come.

Bologna had long been regarded as one of the hot spots of resistance to the papal regime, and had played a leading role in all of the revolts of the nineteenth century, including 1848. With the restoration in 1849, the Pope appointed a special commissioner to oversee the reimposition of papal rule in the Legations, the northern swath of the Papal States of which Bologna was the major city. Told by the inquisitor what the Pope and the Holy Office wanted to do with Bologna's Jews, the commissioner grew alarmed. On January 28, 1853, he sent a letter directly to the Holy Office, warning the cardinals that they were charting a dangerous course.

"Asked by Father [Feletti] how to go about putting this order into effect, I could not hide from him the danger that it will trigger unhappiness among the general population of the city. It involves disturbing twenty families with a total of a hundred individuals, most of whom were born in Bologna or have lived here for thirty, forty, or more years. They are wealthy, industrious, and tied through important business relations to all of the commercial firms of the city and the state, many of which benefit from these relations."

In seeking the commissioner's advice, Father Feletti had floated the idea of reinstituting a ghetto in Bologna. That way, Jews could legally live there. But creating new ghettoes was hardly what the commissioner had in mind. Not only would it be impractical to find enough available real estate, he thought, but he believed that the Jews would protest such a move. Any action against the Jews would pose a wider danger as well, for their resistance would be "encouraged and acclaimed by a large proportion of the inhabitants."

The commissioner asked that the Jews of Bologna—whose behavior, he added, was no worse than that of the Christians there—be allowed to stay where they were. "My remarks," he explained, "are principally moti-vated by the desire to ensure that there is no disturbance to that calm that we have been able to regain after so much effort, especially in Bologna, where public order is now to be found in a satisfactory state."[18]

Indeed, the Holy Office's orders seemed overly severe even to Father Feletti, a man not suspected of harboring either any particular sympathy for the Jews or any inclination to question higher orders. Two months earlier he had received another order from the Holy Office, this one telling him to ensure the rigorous enforcement of the rules governing Jewish employment of Christian servants. Father Feletti's response to the Holy Office, read in the light of his involvement in the Mortara case six years later, has an eerie ring. "I think it rather unlikely that the Jews will want to give their infants to Christian wetnurses to keep in their own homes, for fear that they might secretly baptize them. Hence prohibiting Christian wetnurses from living with the Jews would be the same as not giving them permission at all, even in cases of true necessity."

As for trying to prevent Christian servants from spending the night in Jewish homes, wrote the inquisitor, this would likewise meet strong opposition. It was during the evening hours that servants were most needed to take care of the children and the household. Furthermore, the people attracted to such jobs were, for the most part, young, poor, unmarried women who came from outlying rural areas. They did not have the resources to rent a room of their own in the city.[19]

There is no record that these arguments were ever accepted by the Holy Office, or by Pius IX. Yet, the familiar pattern of Jewish resistance to the rules governing them continued. Pius IX was no more able to have the restrictions fully enforced than were his predecessors.

No one could have predicted that it would be Bologna, with its small Jewish population, and not a place like Rome, Ancona, or Ferrara, that would give rise to Pius IX's most momentous decision in dealing with the Jews. But it was in Bologna, in 1858, that the obscure act of an illiterate teenage servant girl triggered a series of events that helped to hasten the destruction of the Papal States.[20]

One night in June 1858, police arrived unexpectedly at the home of Momolo and Marianna Mortara, Jews who had lived in Bologna for a decade. Marianna's shock on seeing the police at her door quickly turned to panic when the chief officer asked to see her little children.

"Why do you want to see them?" she asked.

"Please, just let us see them, we mean you no harm," the policeman responded, wishing mightily he had never been sent on such a mission.

And so the Mortaras took him from room to room, pointing out their children. When they got to their six-year-old son Edgardo, the policeman turned to Momolo and Marianna.

"I'm afraid you have been betrayed," he said. "Edgardo has been baptized and must come with us."

"But there has been some terrible mistake," Momolo responded. "Edgardo was never baptized. He's Jewish. We all are. Who says someone baptized him?"

"I'm sorry," replied the policeman. "All I know is what the inquisitor told me."

After a heartrending scene that lasted until the following evening, the police finally succeeded in tearing Edgardo from his father's arms and placing him in a police carriage. Although his parents did not yet know it, little Edgardo was headed for Rome, to the House of the Catechumens.

Father Feletti had first heard the rumor that the Jewish boy had been baptized a few months earlier. Anna Morisi, a servant who had worked for the Mortara family, had told someone that several years earlier she had baptized the boy. When the inquisitor summoned Anna in, she repeated her story. When Edgardo was just a baby, she said, he had gotten sick. Fearing for his soul, she had sprinkled some water from a kitchen bucket over his head when his mother left the room for a moment, and pronounced the baptismal formula. The boy soon got better and she had thought nothing more of it.

Father Feletti wrote up his report and sent it to the Holy Office in Rome. For the Pope and the cardinals of the Holy Office, it was a familiar story and there was no doubt what needed to be done. They sent Father Feletti orders to have police take the boy from his family and bring him to the House of the Catechumens in Rome.

It is a telling commentary on Pius IX's way of looking at the world that it did not occur to him that taking such an action in 1858 raised any particular problems. He had done what his predecessors had done for centuries, acting as canon law required. The great virtue of being a temporal ruler in the Papal States was that there was at least one place in the world where there was no separation between God's laws and the laws of the state. He could do what the dictates of Religion commanded.

But he would soon learn that the world had changed. Even with

French soldiers patrolling the streets of Rome, and Austrian soldiers stationed in Bologna, the Pope's ability to act as he wanted, as he thought it was his duty as pontiff to act, was not what it once was.

When in the eighteenth century, and even in the first years after restoration of papal rule in the nineteenth, police had been sent to seize a Jewish child, the Vatican could be sure that the only protests to be heard would be from the Jews themselves. And even these protests would be couched in the most respectful language, for the Jews in the Papal States knew that they lived at the Pope's mercy, and were too frightened to do anything that might anger him.

Yet coming when it did, the abduction of Edgardo Mortara produced a reaction unlike any a pope had ever seen. The movement for the unification of Italy was gaining momentum, and the single greatest obstacle it faced was the Pope himself, who insisted on his continued rule of the Papal States as a matter of divine right. The Pope's defense of the removal of the Mortara boy from his parents proved to be manna from heaven for his enemies, for it showed in a way people everywhere could understand why the Papal States were an anachronism that had no place in modern Europe. Newspapers throughout Europe began to run stories about the case, and as far away as the United States large demonstrations were organized to demand that the Pope free the six-year-old boy.

Most important of all for the Pope, the French government soon made its displeasure known. French soldiers had returned the Pope to power in Rome nine years earlier, and French troops continued to be stationed in the Holy City to prevent any repetition of the earlier uprising. Pius IX could scarcely afford to offend the French government.

The Duke de Gramont, the French ambassador, was in almost daily contact with Giacomo Cardinal Antonelli. Antonelli, who had served as secretary of state for practically a decade, was a man known for his keen diplomatic skills, limited religious devotion, and questionable morals. The Pope depended heavily on him to compensate for his own inadequate knowledge of world politics.[21]

Gramont took it on himself to warn the secretary of state about the Church's conduct in the Mortara affair in July, even before he informed his own foreign minister, Count Walewski, of the matter.[22]

After a series of conversations with the secretary of state, Gramont went to see the Pope himself about the case at the beginning of September. He described the stormy meeting a few days later in a letter to

Walewski. "I did not hide from the Holy Father the painful impression that this sad affair is producing and how the enemies of Religion and the Holy See will know how to exploit it. His Holiness was deeply moved by the picture that I believed it my duty to give him, but . . . the Pope does not feel he is authorized to send back to Judaism a child who has become Christian."[23]

Gramont had tried to maximize his chance of success by not telling anyone at the Vatican of his plan to visit the Pope, taking advantage of the prerogatives of his position as French ambassador to simply appear uninvited at the Pope's quarters. He was concerned at the time that the Pope's advisors would persuade the Pontiff not to heed the diplomat's request. But Gramont soon learned that the problem lay not with papal advisors but with Pius IX himself.

Gramont used all his persuasive skills. He warned the Pope of the dangers of turning his back on public opinion, and offending the most natural and respected of human sentiments, those that bound together parent and child. He stressed the lack of any proof that the boy had ever been baptized, pointing out that by focusing on this issue the Pontiff could return the boy to his parents without repudiating previous papal policy on the Jews. Finally, he impressed on the Pope the seriousness with which the French emperor took the matter, and the great satisfaction that it would give the French court and the entire French people if the Pope sent Edgardo back home.

"The Pope was deeply moved," Gramont recounted. "But more important than this emotion for the Holy Father was his unshakeable commitment to stick to a decision dictated by his conscience." The Pope knew that what he was doing was unpopular—indeed, that it was turning much of the world against him—but the principle involved was just too great to ignore. "Tears fell slowly from his eyes," the French ambassador recalled. "And I must confess that I couldn't myself help feeling a certain anguish in witnessing the solemn struggle that I had provoked in him, a struggle between the absolute rigor of a Holy Pontiff's duties and the voice of nature which the tiara that Pius IX wears has not succeeded in extinguishing."

But there was another aspect to the Mortara story. The boy's parents had told the moving story—widely reported in the liberal press—of their frightened child, sobbing uncontrollably, being forced by police into their carriage and taken to Rome. When the Mortaras subsequently got to visit him at the House of the Catechumens—an unprecedented concession made as a result of the international protests—they painted a similar picture. Little Edgardo, distraught and afraid, had begged them not to leave without him, for he desperately wanted to return home to his brothers and sisters.

Yet, as the political storm over the case began to grow, a very different story began to circulate. Catholic papers throughout Europe and America reported the miraculous tale of a six-year-old boy who, no sooner freed from the grip of his Jewish family, was supernaturally transformed. Now that his earlier baptism had been allowed to take hold, the child wanted nothing so much as to be a Catholic. He begged the Catechumens rector not to let his Jewish parents come near him. Meanwhile, the Pope himself had taken a special interest in Edgardo, and was rapidly becoming a surrogate father for him.

In the midst of his anguished meeting with Duke Gramont in early September, Pius IX turned to this question of what it was that the child himself wished. The Pope told the French ambassador that he had asked little Edgardo what he really wanted. The boy, said the Pope, showing an intelligence beyond his years, "pleaded that he be allowed to remain Christian and that he not be made to leave the Church." Under such circumstances, the Pope concluded, "it is impossible for the head of this Church, for the Representative of Jesus Christ on earth, to refuse this child, for he begged me with an almost supernatural faith to let him share in the benefit of the Blood that Our Lord shed for his Redemption. It is impossible to eject from Christianity this soul who, although entering the Catholic faith through irregular means . . . does not want to leave it." The Pope added, "I have reflected at great length and with great pain about the extent of my obligations. I have asked for illumination from heaven to make my conscience clear. My decision is irrevocable."[24]

Later that month, Count Alexander Walewski, the French foreign minister—an interesting character himself, the illegitimate son of Napoleon—sent a telegram to his ambassador in Rome, complimenting him on his handling of the affair. The foreign minister could not have been any clearer in denouncing what the Vatican had done. "The Holy See's actions in this matter," he wrote, "constitute a violation of the most basic guarantees that involve respect for the domestic family and for paternal authority." Several governments, Walewski wrote, had approached the French emperor, Napoleon III, expressing this same outrage, and calling on the French government to use its influence with the Pope to have the child returned to his family. "You would do well, Duke, to let the secretary of state know how much pain the Holy See is causing the Emperor's Government. You should tell him that public sentiment has been profoundly wounded in learning that Monsieur Mortara has tried in vain to reclaim his son from the [Papal] government." He instructed Gramont to impress on the secretary of state as clearly as he could just how serious the matter was. "The feeling of unpleasant surprise felt by the faithful [in learning of the Pope's decision to keep the boy] was only equaled by the joy it has given the enemies of Catholicism."[25]

Although the French foreign minister's message spoke of the need to convince the Vatican secretary of state, Cardinal Antonelli, Gramont knew that Antonelli was already persuaded of the political expediency of having Edgardo sent back to his family. The problem was how to change the Pope's mind. On September 29, Gramont telegraphed Paris to ask the foreign minister if he could give Cardinal Antonelli a copy of Walewski's telegram, so that the cardinal could use it as ammunition in raising the issue once more with the Pope. The following day he received Walewski's encrypted reply: "It seems to me that allowing [Antonelli] to read the telegram on Mortara would suffice. However, if you have reason to think it useful, I authorize you to leave a copy of it with him."[26] No sooner had Gramont received this permission than he went to see the cardinal. As the duke had hoped, Antonelli saw the telegram's value and on October 1, 1858, gave it to the Pope. The cardinal added his own advice to that of the French diplomats: a way must be found to have the boy returned to his parents.[27]

The Pope valued his secretary of state's advice in political matters, recognizing his superior political skills and his knowledge of the larger world of governments and potentates. But Pius IX was not one to take advice on matters regarding Catholic faith, least of all from a cardinal who was not even an ordained priest.

The French ambassador soon received word that this latest attempt to change the Pope's mind had been unsuccessful. The ambassador of the kingdom of Naples to the Holy See, who had just gone to see the Pope, stopped by to see Gramont on his way back from his papal audience. Newly returned from a trip to Naples, the ambassador had told the Pope what a poor impression the Church's handling of the Mortara affair was making back home. He expressed his sovereign's worries that the Pope's action was increasing the Holy See's international isolation.

The Pope replied by assuring the ambassador that he was no less concerned about what was happening. "I have suffered and I continue to suffer true torments over it. People on all sides are pressuring me to give this Jewish child who became Christian back to his parents. Antonelli himself has opposed me and I have the misfortune of having displeased the entire world. Have you seen how the French papers are treating me?" the Pope asked. "But, by the grace of God, I have seen my duty, and I would rather cut off all my fingers than shrink from it."

The Neapolitan ambassador told Gramont something else that caught his attention. In lamenting how isolated he felt, the Pope had lashed out not only at his secretary of state for his lack of support but at the papal nuncio in Paris, Cardinal Sacconi, as well. In the midst of the crisis, what had Sacconi done to help him? "It would be useful to me, and perhaps to you as well," the Pope told the Neapolitan, "to have someone there who is more intelligent and more influential. But it is really painful to have named a simpleton like that to be a cardinal!"

For the French ambassador, this story was highly revealing of the character of the Pope. Such scathing remarks about his own emissary to Paris made clear that he was no diplomat. "His deep religion, pure from a theological viewpoint, carries with it a streak of mysticism that seems to have increased with time. In the silence of his chapel, alone in the presence of God and the lights of his conscience, the Holy Pontiff makes his decisions on the basis of what he takes to be divine inspiration. . . . The proprieties of the current century, the riling of public opinion fade before these celestial prescriptions, and the Pope, fortified in this belief, demonstrates the unshakeable firmness that he adopts on certain occasions."

As Gramont saw it, the Pope was becoming ever more removed from the real world, embracing an increasingly fatalistic attitude. "In the century in which we live," the French ambassador wrote, "this tendency can become the source of major complications and serious dangers, especially when it is combined, as in Pius IX's case, with a lively and sometimes impetuous nature."[28]

In fact, despite the roar of protests worldwide, despite the advice from his own secretary of state that he was undermining the Vatican's diplomatic position, which was already perilously weak, the Pope would not be moved. Edgardo was a Christian and could not be returned to his Jewish family. If his parents wanted to be reunited with him, the Pope thought, they could do so easily enough, for they would be welcomed with open arms at the House of the Catechumens. They, too, could bask in the glow of holy baptism. If they were so eager to have their son back, why did they not embrace the Holy Spirit themselves?

The Pope's stand cost the Mortara family dearly, for Edgardo never returned to his parents. He was raised in a seminary in Rome and later became a priest. But the cost for the Pope and the Church was also high. Just as Cardinal Antonelli had predicted, the taking of the child reinforced the widespread belief in Italy, and in Europe generally, that pontifical rule was a vestige of an earlier era, one that had no place in the second half of the nineteenth century. A year after Edgardo was taken from his parents, papal forces were driven out of Bologna. The champions of Italian unification—with French support—swept through much of the Papal States. And in one of the new government's first acts in Bologna, police entered the Dominican monastery there and arrested the inquisitor, Father Feletti. He was locked in a dank jail cell, charged with the kidnapping of Edgardo Mortara.

By 1861 all that was left of the Pope's temporal kingdom was Rome and the area immediately around it. Throughout the peninsula, a new, secular Kingdom of Italy had been proclaimed.

For the Pope, the collapse of the Papal States was but another trial sent by God. But the Papal States had fallen to impious forces before— indeed, more than once in the nineteenth century alone—and each time the Church had ultimately triumphed and the forces of darkness were defeated. This time, with God's help, thought the Pope, the same would happen again.

In the meantime, in the former Papal States, the inquisitors were being routed from their monasteries and the Jews freed from their ghettoes. Only around Rome did the Inquisition still function as before, although for the cardinals of the Holy Office it was difficult to avoid the sense that there too its days were numbered.

As if to hoist the papal flag high in these last days of their rule, the Pope and the Holy Office continued to do what they could to enforce the old restrictions on the Jews in the small area remaining under their control. In 1861, police were sent into Rome's ghetto to ensure that the rules preventing Christian servants from living with Jewish families were being respected. The following year, the bishop of Velletri, a nearby town still under papal rule, ordered all its Jewish residents out, for Velletri was not a town where Jews were permitted to live.[29]

But this rearguard action, a final desperate attempt to keep the Jews in the place that the Popes and canon law had long assigned them, would soon be replaced by a whole new way of viewing the Jews. The same forces that had struck against the power of the Church had granted the Jews equal rights. In marshaling Catholic public opinion in support of the Vatican and against these forces of secularization, it was tempting, very tempting, to make use of this fact. Vilified for centuries, the Jew could, if properly conjured up, be used to discredit the forces that had sought to create a modern, secular state.

Pius IX set the tone in 1864, when he issued the historic encyclical *Quanta cura,* and with it distributed a Syllabus of Errors, a listing of the eighty principal errors of modern times condemned by the Church. Along with rejecting modern ideas, the Pope embraced a conspiratorial view of the world. In an outlook that would shape Catholic attitudes for decades to come, he portrayed an embattled Church besieged by the forces of evil.

In his encyclical, Pius IX warned the world's bishops: "In these times the haters of truth and justice and the most bitter enemies of our religion deceive the people and lie maliciously. They disseminate . . . impious doctrines by means of pestilential books, pamphlets, and newspapers distributed over the whole world. Nor are you ignorant of the fact that in our age some men are found who, moved . . . by the spirit of Satan, have sunk to that degree of impiety in which they do not shrink from denying our Ruler and Lord Jesus Christ, or from impugning His Divinity with wicked pertinacity."[30]

Among the errors denounced in the accompanying syllabus were belief in freedom of religion, in the separation of Church and state, and in the ending of ecclesiastical control of public schools. What most captured people's attention was the eightieth error on the list: The syllabus rejected the doctrine that "the Roman Pontiff can, and ought to, reconcile himself, and come to terms with progress, liberalism, and modern civilization."

A postscript to the syllabus returned to the theme of the embattled Church: "Venerable Brothers, it is surprising that in our time such a great war is being waged against the Catholic Church." Responsibility for the war lay squarely with a conspiracy of secret sects, the Masons most notable among them. "Anyone who knows the nature, desires and intentions of the sects . . . cannot doubt that the present misfortune must mainly be imputed to the frauds and machinations of these sects." And then, in a phrase that would later be echoed by Pius IX's successor, Leo XIII, it continued: "It is from them that the *synagogue of Satan,* which gathers its troops against the Church of Christ, takes its strength."

With this phrase, the fateful papal identification of the Jews as the hidden enemies of the Church began to gain ground. "These wicked groups think that they have already become masters of the world." They seek nothing less than "to subject the Church of God to the most cruel servitude . . . and, if possible, to make it disappear completely from the earth."[31]

A decade later, Pius IX returned to the theme that it was the "synagogue of Satan" that lay behind the worldwide conspiracy. In an 1873 encyclical he employed the image to portray the web of forces conspiring to destroy the Church. In this, he had ample evangelical precedent, for the term came from the last book of the New Testament, where twice the Jews' places of worship are termed "synagogues of Satan" (Revelation 2.9 and 3.9).[32]

Having presided over the loss of most of the Papal States in 1859–61, in his later years the once affable Pius IX turned increasingly bitter. Among the objects of his anger were the Jews. They had shown him no gratitude for all he had done for them. He had, after all, put an end to both the Carnival rites of degradation and the forced sermons. No, as repayment for his kindness they had heaped abuse on him during the Mortara affair and done all they could to bring about the fall of his earthly kingdom.

In 1867, the Pope helped to give the charge of Jewish ritual murder new respectability by moving to put on a firmer footing the cult surrounding a martyred child, Lorenzino of Marostica.

The boy's story was indeed inspiring. Lorenzino was born in 1480 in a village near Vicenza in northeastern Italy. His father was a violent man and, when Lorenzino was just a newborn, threatened to kill both son and wife, believing his wife to have had the child by another man. But the ten-day-old baby is said to have miraculously stood up and cried out: "Stop, Father, my mother is innocent and I am your son."

Five years later, according to the Church's official account, on Good Friday, when Lorenzino went out to play, a bunch of Jews grabbed him, tore off his clothes, and crucified him on a nearby tree, draining him of his blood. When his mutilated body was found, and he was buried, the miracles began. Each night a ray of light shone from the grave, and his hand emerged from beneath the ground. The following year, townspeople drove the Jews out of Vicenza and the boy's remains were moved to a church where both locals and pilgrims came to venerate them.

Pius IX's decree, in 1867, affirmed the official Church status of the cult. Three years later he returned to the matter, declaring the second Sunday after Easter each year to be the sacred holiday devoted to celebrating the little martyr. In the late 1960s, Church schools in the area were still teaching children the story of the sainted child and the evil Jews who tortured him so cruelly.[33]

In 1869, there appeared the first important publication on ritual murder since the Damascus affair, a work by the French Catholic scholar Henri Gougenot des Mousseaux. Titled *The Jew: Judaism and the Judaization of Christian Peoples,* the book would have a major influence in focusing Catholic attention on the image of Jews as demons seeking Christian blood. The story was a familiar one: Jews required the blood of Christian children for their Passover bread. The death of Father Tommaso in Damascus was discussed at length. The Talmud, readers were told, "not only permits the Jew, but *commands him and urges him to cheat and to kill the Christian* whenever he finds an occasion to do so."

Pius IX praised the book and its author, offering Gougenot his benediction and awarding him the Cross of Commander of the Papal Order for his efforts. The Pope's actions were subsequently cited in later editions of Gougenot's book and in other works as well, all designed to show papal backing for the belief that Jews were required by their religion to murder Christian children. Gougenot's text inspired scores of Catholic works on the Jews over the next decades. Many years later, in 1921, as the Nazi movement began its ascent, Alfred Rosenberg, chief party ideologist, himself oversaw and edited the first German edition of Gougenot's book.[34]

At the end of 1869, the Pope convened the First Vatican Council in Rome, bringing together bishops from throughout Europe as well as Catholic dignitaries of all sorts, including those aristocrats recently deposed from power in the ongoing struggle for Italian unification. The Council represented the culmination of one of the Pope's most cherished goals: the proclamation of papal infallibility, for the first time, as official Church doctrine.[35]

The situation in which the six hundred bishops met could scarcely have been more unsettling. For several years, Rome had been under continual threat of annexation to the new Italian state, and the Romans lived amid constant rumors of imminent invasion. Then, in August 1870, with the Council still underway, the French troops who had been guarding the city were withdrawn and sent on what turned out to be the futile mission of fighting for their country in its war with Prussia.

After repeated attempts to reach an accommodation with the Pope failed, the Italian government ordered its army to march on the Holy City, long viewed as a necessary part of any Italian nation. The day before the army arrived, Pius IX, praying for God's aid, climbed the steps of the Scala Santa, the holy stairway of the papal palace, on his knees. On September 20, 1870, Italian soldiers broke through the city's poorly maintained walls and proclaimed Rome the capital of the Italian state.

The Vatican Council was suspended, but its main work was in any case already done. The Pope's rulings on matters of basic Church doctrine were henceforth to be regarded as infallible, the word of God. But although the Pope had God on his side, he no longer had any police powers at his disposal, nor armies at his command.

In an effort to generate diplomatic support for the return of the Papal States, Pius IX began projecting an image of himself as a prisoner of the Vatican. Although the Italian government did nothing to prevent him from traveling where he liked, the Pope refused to leave the confined space of the Vatican palaces, never again venturing into the streets of Rome, much less beyond them. It was an image that his successors nurtured as well. For fifty-eight years no pope would set foot outside the Vatican. Only in 1929 would the Vatican recognize the legitimacy of the Italian state.[36]

Given the siege mentality that now prevailed in the Vatican, the forces of good seemed to face the forces of the devil himself. And from Pius IX's point of view, and that of most other clergy, it was clear enough who had benefited from the revolutions that had deposed God's emissary on earth: the Jews. No longer confined to their ghettoes, no longer prevented from buying property or engaging in any professions they chose, no longer barred from befriending Christians, they appeared as the great beneficiaries of the catastrophe that had befallen the Church. From this perception it proved a small step to seeing them as the occult force responsible for that misfortune.

The fact that a handful of prominent Jews were among the wealthiest and most influential backers of the rapid changes taking place in society made the Jews an even more attractive target. What must Pius have felt when, in 1871, he learned the identities of the key financial advisers at the peace conference of Versailles which followed the Franco-Prussian War? The French leader, Louis-Adolphe Thiers, had the Jewish banker Alphonse de Rothschild at his side, while accompanying Bismarck was his financial adviser and banker, the Jew Gerson Bleichröder.[37]

One day in August of that year, members of a Catholic women's organization of Rome came for an audience with the Pope. As he addressed them, his mind turned to a topic that clearly had been preying on it, and he abruptly launched into a denunciation of the Jews of the city. In ancient times, Pius IX told them, before the time of Jesus, the Jews "had been *children* in the House of God." But, all this had changed, for "owing to their obstinacy and their failure to believe, they have become *dogs*." Speaking just months after Italian forces had freed the Jews of Rome's ghetto, the Pope bemoaned the result: "We have today in Rome unfortunately too many of these dogs, and we hear them barking in all the streets, and going around molesting people everywhere."[38]

Pius IX's anti-Jewish language here was of a traditional Christian kind, recalling that found in the New Testament itself: The Jews were responsible for killing Christ (Matthew, chapter 27; John, chapter 19); they were born of the devil (John 8:44) and constituted a "synagogue of Satan." But this ancient view of the Jews promulgated by the Church hierarchy would soon be transformed as the Jews increasingly came to be blamed for all the ills, or perceived ills, of modern times. No longer the frightened denizens of ghettoes, Jews, in the eyes of leading Churchmen, had now rapidly become insolent and evil masterminds plotting the destruction of the Church and all that was holy.

The Jews were now free. It was the Pope who was imprisoned in his ghetto.

PART TWO

The Church and the Rise of Modern Anti-Semitism

CHAPTER SIX

The Catholic Press

WITH THE DEMISE of the Papal States, the Pope and the opinion makers closest to the Vatican began to view the Jews in a different light. When the Pope had been king, the Jews presented an annoying problem, but one for which traditional remedies were at hand. Jews outside the Italian peninsula interested the popes only sporadically, often in response to pleas for papal help made by the Jews themselves.

In the last decades of the nineteenth century, daily newspapers, weeklies, biweeklies, and monthlies took on ever-increasing importance in shaping public opinion. Before the nineteenth century there had been few such publications, and not many people were literate enough to read them. Nor did the newspapers make lively reading, for everywhere the press was censored. With the rise of greater freedom of the press, the spread of literacy, and advances in print technology, all this changed. As more democratic governments evolved, and their fate began to depend on popular elections, the battle for the public's allegiance became more significant for elites of all kinds. In this battle the press proved crucial, and papers of all political stripes sprang up.

The Mortara case in 1858 showed the Church hierarchy how important the popular press was to Church fortunes. Both Pius IX and, especially, Leo XIII, who succeeded him in 1878, were well aware of the importance of having a Church-linked press as a way to influence popular opinion. By the early 1870s, 130 Catholic periodicals were being published in Italy alone, including 20 daily newspapers. Over the next decades the number swelled, so that by the beginning of the twentieth century Italy had about 500 Catholic periodicals, including 30 dailies. What almost universally marked the most important and influential of these was their fierce loyalty to the Pope and their pioneering role in developing a new, strident form of anti-Semitism.[1]

The most influential Catholic periodical anywhere in the world—founded at the request of Pope Pius IX and supervised by the popes and their secretaries of state—was the Jesuit biweekly, *Civiltà cattolica*. The Jesuit journal kicked off its long campaign against the Jews in December 1880 with a series of thirty-six fiercely anti-Semitic articles which were published over the following forty months.[2]

In one of the first of these, recent outbreaks of anti-Semitic violence in Germany were explained. The Jesuit author wrote that Jews were obligated by their religion to hate all non-Jews, and as a consequence Christians despised them. Societies had to protect themselves from the Jews, and so, he concluded, governments would be well advised to introduce "exceptional laws for a race that is so exceptionally and profoundly perverse."

Here we see one of the most common themes of Catholic writings on the Jews in the late nineteenth century. The argument goes something like this: We told you to keep the Jews in the ghettoes, to prevent them from coming into contact with Christians, and yet you ignored our warnings and gave them equal rights. Now look what's happened! Thanks to the Jews, religion is everywhere threatened and social disorder spreads. Our only hope of restoring social harmony and economic security is to bring back the special laws that kept them in their place.

These special laws, it was argued, would benefit the Jews as well, for it was only by restoring such restrictions that popular violence against the Jews could be prevented: "Every so often, as has recently happened in Germany, popular anti-Semitic exasperation erupts more or less violently. This could easily be avoided if only those few ancient laws of exception were brought back, laws which are as useful to the Jews themselves as they are to the Christians."[3]

As others were coming to terms with the changes that, since the French Revolution, were transforming European society, the Vatican was lashing out ever more indignantly against them. Pius IX had pioneered this path in the 1860s with his Syllabus of Errors, condemning modern ideas. When the elderly pontiff, having served as pope for thirty-two years—longer than any of his predecessors—died in 1878, his successor, Leo XIII, continued to portray himself as a "prisoner of the Vatican." But something happened under Leo XIII—who himself served for a quarter-century—that would transform Church views of the Jews in a dramatic and deadly way. Increasingly, it was the Jews who were portrayed by the Vatican as the masterminds of the conspiracy aimed at the Church's destruction.

In the Catholic world, *Civiltà cattolica* came to be regarded as the unofficial voice of the Pope himself. The journal had been founded in 1850, following Pius IX's restoration to Rome, with the Pope's strong backing and against the wishes of the head of the Jesuit order, who was loath to see the Jesuits intervene so publicly in the political realm.

The idea was to provide an authoritative Church voice on current issues and events, one aimed at influencing popular opinion. The priests who wrote for the journal—all Jesuits—formed a collective, under the leadership of their director, whose appointment was approved by the Pope. In this collective, all article drafts had to be read by two other members, who suggested revisions and had to give their approval for the article to be published. Most important for our purposes was the journal's close link to the Holy See. Before publication, the proofs of each new issue were sent to the secretary of state for final approval. Three principles determined his approval of the text: (1) The articles must conform to the Church's official teachings in matters of faith and morals; (2) on questions involving relations with other states, the position espoused must agree with that adopted by the Holy See; and (3) the timing of publishing the article in question must be opportune.

Five days before each issue came out, the journal director went to the Vatican and, up until Pius XII, in the mid-twentieth century, was often received by the Pope himself, who—along with the secretary of state—reviewed and approved the contents of the upcoming issue. From both the Pope's viewpoint and that of the *Civiltà cattolica* authors, the journal's main task was to defend the Pope and help spread his message.[4] Although it never had a huge circulation—reaching just over 11,000 subscribers at the turn of the century—its influence was tremendous. The network of Catholic newspapers throughout the world regarded it, along with the Vatican's daily paper, *L'Osservatore romano,* as the most authoritative source for Vatican perspectives on current events, and quoted its articles constantly.[5]

Civiltà cattolica's anti-Jewish campaign, coming when it did, proved crucial to the rise of modern anti-Semitism. The term "anti-Semitism" itself had only been coined a year earlier, in 1879, by a German, Wilhelm

Marr. One of the most influential tracts behind the rise of anti-Semitism, *The Talmud Jew,* by the Catholic priest August Rohling, had been published in Germany earlier in the decade, quickly becoming a best-seller. The *Civiltà cattolica* campaign picked up on Rohling's themes, giving them a papal imprimatur.

Although the *Civiltà cattolica* articles in this period were unsigned, following the journal's collegial practice, all of the first thirty-six articles on the Jews were drafted by Father Giuseppe Oreglia di Santo Stefano, one of the journal's founders. Oreglia, born in 1823 and director of *Civiltà cattolica* from 1865 to 1868, was from a noble northern Italian family. His younger brother, Luigi, was one of the most influential—and one of the most reactionary—cardinals in Rome.[6]

In the thousands of words that Oreglia would devote to the Jews in *Civiltà cattolica,* a few themes were endlessly repeated, and most of these were already on display in the first of the articles. The Jews, Oreglia argued, had always benefited from the kindness of the Church and, especially, of the popes. They had lived happily in their ghettoes, and Christians had also been able to live in peace, protected from the Jews. The fact that the Jews were prevented from owning property or practicing any other than the most menial occupations in the lands of the Pope prevented them from becoming wealthy, but "also prevented them from being too despised." The Jews had always been regarded as a foreign people, "and never considered to have the right of either native-born or naturalized citizens." As history had shown, the Jesuit wrote, "if this foreign Jewish race is left too free, it immediately becomes the persecutor, oppressor, tyrant, thief, and devastator of the countries where it lives." The lesson was clear: Special laws must be introduced to keep the Jews in their place and to protect Christian society from the hostility that the Jews harbored "against all human society not belonging to their race." Far from persecuting the Jews, such legislation served to prevent the Jews from persecuting the Christians.[7]

Alas, wrote Father Oreglia, people had not followed the Church's teachings and had come to regret it. "The Jews—eternal insolent children, obstinate, dirty, thieves, liars, ignoramuses, pests and the scourge of those near and far—... immediately abused [their newfound freedom] to interfere with that of others. They managed to lay their hands on ... all public wealth ... and virtually alone they took control not only of all the money ... but of the law itself in those countries where they have been allowed to hold public offices." Yet, Father Oreglia continued, despite all this the Jews had the nerve to complain that they were being persecuted "at the first shout by anyone who dares raise his voice against this barbarian invasion by an enemy race, hostile to Christianity and to society in general."

Thus, both the notion that Jews belonged to a separate race and the notion that the Jews were a festering foreign sore eating away at society made their appearance in this first 1880 article. "Oh how wrong and deluded," wrote Father Oreglia, "are those who think that Judaism is just a religion, like Catholicism, Paganism, Protestantism, and not in fact a race, a people, and a nation! While it is certain that others can be, for example, both Catholic and either Italian, French or English . . . or Protestant and a member of whatever country or nation . . . it is a great error to believe that the same is true of the Jews. For the Jews are not only Jews because of their religion . . . they are Jews also and especially because of their race." A Jew who lives in Italy or France does not love his country the way an Italian or a Frenchman does, but is only interested in "what he can get out of it."[8]

Father Oreglia also propounded the view that Jews remain Jews forever, even when they formally renounce Judaism. Here the Jesuit journal was getting into dangerous territory, for the sacred mission of converting the Jews had long been at the center of Church Jewish policy, with its origins in the New Testament itself.

But Oreglia's denunciation of Jews who had assimilated reflects a larger, and important, development in Church attitudes toward the Jews. It was no longer the religious Jew who posed the greatest threat to good Christians; the greater danger now came from the Jew who had strayed from his ancestral religion.

Throughout Europe, wrote Father Oreglia in early 1881, an ever-growing number of Jews were abandoning—or rather pretending to abandon—their religion, often becoming Protestant or simply atheists and free thinkers. "But all of them, having been moved not by God's spirit but by the devil's, have done so to further their material interests. . . . Even if we presume that they are no longer Jews in religion, neither do they become members of the Italian or French race, or of any other country. Because they are born Jews they must remain Jews." The same evil spirit that pushed them to leave their native religion, explained Father Oreglia, "makes them even more committed to that hatred for Christian society and the Christian race which they imbibed with their mother's milk."⁹

As in the case of almost all Vatican-linked publications dealing with the Jews in these years, Oreglia's denunciations of the Jews were regularly interspersed with protestations of love for them. We should love them, he wrote, yet at the same time, our love must not blind us to the sad fact of the evil that the Jews do, nor prevent us from taking the actions needed to save the Church and Christian society from them.

In theory, the belief in the Jews' salvation through conversion remained, but conversion became ever more distant—a praiseworthy yet wholly impractical goal. Father Oreglia put the matter allegorically, as he argued for a return to the old laws separating Jews from Christian society. One of the arguments that liberals had used for emancipating the Jews, he recalled, was that once freed from their ghetto and brought into contact with the larger society, increasing numbers of them would want to convert. But, he wrote, "Let's suppose that it were necessary for wolves to live alongside sheep. Would it therefore be necessary to emancipate the wolves and make them equal citizens, indeed sometimes guardians . . . of the sheep?" Yet was this not the logic, he asked, used by the liberals in emancipating the Jews? As he saw it, the liberal argument came down to this: "If wolves are now wolves, it is only due to the persecution they always had to suffer from the sheep and the shepherds."¹⁰

The notion that the Jews were secretly conspiring to achieve world domination is another of the pillars of the modern anti-Semitic movements that took shape in the late nineteenth century and would later nourish Nazism itself. But the theme of a vast Jewish conspiracy against Christian society was far from new. In the fourteenth century it surfaced during the Black Death, when throughout Europe people slaughtered Jews suspected of having spread the disease out of their hatred for Christians. But at that time the popes had defended the Jews against such allegations. Now, in the last decades of the nineteenth century, it was the Vatican itself that was spreading such theories of evil Jewish conspiracies, with *Civiltà cattolica* taking the lead.¹¹

In earlier incarnations of such conspiracy theories, people had focused on rabbis and Jewish ritual specialists. But now the greatest threat came from Jews who had become atheists and freethinkers, the secularized Jews. These, Oreglia argued, retained "all their ancient hatred of Christianity." It was they who formed "the principal nucleus of the secret sects that are now ascendant and which threaten the ruin and the extermination of all Christian society." Such sects "express that anger, that vendetta and that satanic hate that the Jew harbors against those who—unjustly, he believes—deprive him of that absolute domination over the entire universe that he Jewishly believes God gave him."[12]

Such a demonic portrait of the Jews, however, risked contradicting another Church doctrine: Jesus himself had been a Jew, or at least born of a Jewish family, as were many of the Christian patriarchs. If the Jews were by nature evil, what about Jesus? Moreover, the Jewish Bible remained one of Christianity's most sacred texts. How could the people of the Bible, the ancestors of modern Christians, be creatures of the devil?

These questions had long plagued Church dealings with the Jews. The solution to the conundrum, one that had been around a long time, involved making a distinction between the Jews of old—who followed God's commandments as handed down at Sinai and embodied in the Bible—and the later people who had rejected Jesus, the Messiah whose coming was foretold in the Bible itself. The latter were castigated as followers not of the Bible but of the Talmud, a work produced only after Christianity had been established, and long vilified by the Church. As we have seen, since the thirteenth century Church authorities had periodically called for the destruction of all copies of the Talmud, viewed as the root of Jewish evil. In 1240, Pope Gregory IX ordered all prelates and monarchs of Europe to see to it that all copies were handed over to the friars of the two new mendicant orders—the Franciscans and the Dominicans—who would burn them. The king of France, later to become St. Louis, had more than twenty wagons filled with the manuscripts, containing more than twenty thousand copies in all, and publicly put them to the torch in the Place de Grève.[13] Three centuries later, in 1553, a renewed papal campaign against the Jews was kicked off with the public burning of the Talmud throughout the Papal States.[14]

Oreglia drew heavily on this view of the Talmudic Jew. "The whole sinew of modern Judaism—that is of the antisocial, antihumanitarian, and above all anti-Christian law that the Jews now observe believing that they are obeying Mosaic law—consists essentially in that fundamental dogma according to which the Jew cannot and should not ever recognize as his fellow human being anyone other than a Jew. All others, whether Christian or non-Christian, must be considered, by every good Jew observing his law, . . . as hateful enemies, to be persecuted and, if possible, exterminated . . . from the face of the earth. And this according to the religious precept that they believe God Himself gave them through the Talmud and the Rabbis." Should a Jew ever inadvertently treat a non-Jew as a fellow human being, Father Oreglia explained, "he believes he has sinned against his religion and his conscience." The portrait of the Jew as demon could hardly be more complete: "While the Christian asks forgiveness for his sin, the Jew must ask forgiveness if he does a good deed."[15]

Oreglia's characterization of the Talmud—and of Jewish morality—was an outrageous misrepresentation, although one that would be used in countless stories in the Catholic press over the following decades. With Europe's Jews a minority in Christian societies, Jewish scholars and rabbis had, over the course of the preceding centuries, shown considerable interest in the question of what the Talmud said about how Jews should act in their relations with Christians. By the High Middle Ages, conditions in which Jews lived in Europe had altered so greatly from the conditions in which they had lived in the Babylon of talmudic times that the strict social segregation imposed on them by accepted talmudic teachings had made their reinterpretation indispensable. Earlier, a simple distinction had been made between the Jews, those who followed God's law, and all others, who were regarded with disdain as idolaters. The Talmud contained many passages that severely restricted Jewish contact with these others, including sharp limits on having any business dealings with them. Yet Europe's Jews, now living as a small minority amid a large Christian population, and dependent on having regular relations with them—if only through trade—in order to survive, began to reinterpret the Talmud. They began to view Christians as distinct from idolaters, as people who were part of the same religious tradition, albeit having strayed from the proper path. With this view, which had been accepted by the eleventh century, regular social contacts with Christians could be religiously justified.

In any case, Jewish communities, living for the most part as barely tolerated minorities in Christian societies, were at great risk when the actions of any of their members incurred the anger of the surrounding population. Consequently, Jewish community leaders had a strong interest in enforcing standards of behavior in Jewish-Christian relations, and in dealing harshly with those whose unprincipled behavior threatened the whole community's welfare. Various talmudic teachings were invoked to denounce Jews who wronged Christians. Among the most commonly cited was that forbidding the desecration of God's name. By acting deceitfully in his dealings with outsiders, a Jew brought shame on the name of the Jewish people, and hence on God, for such behavior would lead others to view the Jews—the Chosen People—as immoral and reprehensible. In addition, a Jew guilty of stealing or of murder violated the most fundamental biblical commandments, and thereby committed an act of rebellion against God.

In defending themselves from the charge that the Talmud commanded them to defraud or even murder Christians, the Jews could point to such famous passages of the Talmud as the story of Hillel's encounter with a pagan. According to the story, when the man asked Hillel to tell him in brief what the nature of the Jewish religion was, Hillel replied: "Do not do unto others what you do not wish to be done unto yourself. That is the entire Torah. The rest is commentary."[16]

By 1882, *Civiltà cattolica* was happily heralding the first eruptions of the modern anti-Semitic political movement. The newly formed groups sprang from different sources and had a variety of interests, but increasingly they were viewed as part of a common international movement of like-minded people. Anti-Semitic newspapers were being founded, as were anti-Semitic political clubs and parties; regular membership meetings were held, dues collected, and plans for anti-Semitic campaigns discussed. Although these groups differed in many respects—some were Catholic, some Protestant, others populist and leftist, others conservative but anticlerical—they were unified in identifying the Jews with the painful dislocations of late-nineteenth-century society.

For many, the anxieties they felt were rooted in economic changes linked to the spread of modern capitalism, industrialization, and urbanization. That the Jews—until a century earlier largely confined to ghettoes and in any case forbidden from owning real property or occupying any but the lowest economic positions—were now so conspicuous among the wealthy and the influential stirred widespread resentment. Old elites resented the Jewish parvenus, and small shopkeepers were apt to view successful Jewish businessmen as responsible for their declining fortunes. Throughout western and central Europe, Jews in the previous decades had been rapidly leaving their ghettoes—literal or figurative— and joining the national mainstream. Many were giving up Yiddish for the national language, abandoning their distinctive dress, adopting names typical of the country in which they lived, and even modifying—and in many cases curtailing—their religious practices to allow them to integrate into the larger community. Yet at the same time they remained, for the most part, proud of their Jewish identity, and seemed to stick to themselves socially, most notably by insisting that their children stay at least formally Jewish and only marry other Jews.[17]

In September 1882, the first international anti-Semitic congress was held in Dresden, with representatives present from Germany and the Austro-Hungarian empire. In reporting on the event, *Civiltà Cattolica* recounted that although many violent speeches had been made denouncing the Jews, the "relatively moderate" resolutions proposed by Reverend Adolf Stoecker had been approved. Stoecker, a Protestant minister, was one of the most influential pioneers in the development of German anti-Semitism.

The resolutions of the congress were described at length, and reflected what *Civiltà cattolica* itself had been advocating. The Jews were a people apart, they could never be integrated into any national society. "The Reform Jews (that is, those who no longer rigorously observe the ancient customs of their race) do not constitute a serious exception to the general rule, but rather, with their efforts to dominate and pervert the Christian populations, constitute no less of a danger." Emancipation of the Jews had been a "fatal mistake" and new restrictive legislation was urgently needed. "It is undeniable," the journal's German correspondent concluded, "that anti-Semitic agitation is making great progress among us. Meetings at which the protestors are expressing their denunciations are being held in rapid succession, and are attracting an immense crowd. Beyond that, the anti-Semitic press is gaining ground . . . I don't fear exaggeration in saying that, with the aid of the Jews' adversaries, it may be possible for the conservatives to win a good number of electoral districts from the liberals and the progressives."[18]

This linking of attacks on the Jews with electoral success for conservatives would have tremendous consequences for the growth of Catholic anti-Semitism in the years to come. Ever larger proportions of the population were being given the right to vote, and elites needed to find a way to appeal to people whose political opinions had formerly been of little interest to them.

Of special concern not only to the Catholic Church but to others who occupied privileged positions in European society was the alarming rise of the socialist movement. The origins of the movement went back to the beginning of the century, in the aftermath of the French Revolution with its calls for liberty, fraternity, and equality. Nourished by the Industrial Revolution and the creation of a growing proletariat, the movement had established its First International in 1864, which European elites viewed as an evil world conspiracy. Hundreds of local workers' organizations arose in this period, many calling for the abolition of private property. Socialist parties were proving adept at attracting an ever-growing, mass following, and membership in socialist-dominated trade unions grew rapidly as well. For preoccupied Church leaders, discrediting the "godless" socialists came to have increasing urgency, and, as we shall see, the tactic of identifying them with the Jews and a Jewish conspiracy proved irresistible.

But let us return to *Civiltà cattolica,* where, by 1890, the ailing Father Oreglia had passed on his leadership in the Jesuits' crusade against the Jews to colleagues.[19]

One of these men, Father Raffaele Ballerini, in an article that year titled "The Jews—Why They Remain Jews," introduced his subject by covering familiar ground. The Jews, he wrote, had long ago stopped observing Mosaic law and now followed only the execrable Talmud. They had rejected and murdered the Messiah, and believed that they were themselves divinely ordained to rule the world. "The whole Jewish race . . . is conspiring to achieve this reign over all the world's peoples."

The Church had always treated the Jews with compassion, Father Ballerini wrote, and the Jews of the past recognized that their most benign protectors were the popes themselves. But then, despite Church protests, the Jews were emancipated, and what happened? They began "a remorseless, constant war against the Christian religion and especially against Catholicism. And then [the Jews also began] an unbridled campaign of usury, monopolies, and thievery of every sort, to the detriment of those among whom they have enjoyed and continue to enjoy civil liberties." For the Jews, the Jesuit concluded, "brotherhood and peace were and are merely pretexts to enable them to prepare—with the destruction of Christianity, if possible, and with the undermining of the Christian nations—the messianic reign that they believe the Talmud promises them."[20]

In 1890 Father Ballerini devoted three long articles in *Civiltà cattolica* to "the Jewish Question in Europe." The following year these were bound together and published as a ninety-page book to reach a broader audience. The book expanded on the themes developed over the previous decade. The Jews "formed a foreign nation in the nations where they resided, a sworn enemy of the nation's well-being. . . . Although they may live in France, in Germany, in England, they never become French, or German, or English, but remain Jews and nothing but Jews." The Jews only pretended to be patriotic to fool people, so that they could destroy the nations that had foolishly given them citizenship.

Here Father Ballerini retold a story he had recently found in a German newspaper of a German general who, in the Franco-German war of 1870, had been given a large sum of money to hire spies. He returned to Berlin with the funds unspent, for he could find no Frenchman willing to betray his country. Yet only four years earlier, in the war against Austria, the same general had had a very different experience, for Austria was full of Jews, and the Jews fell all over themselves to spy on their own army, betraying them for a pittance. "History," Father Ballerini concluded, "is full of betrayal at the hands of the Jews."

The *Civiltà cattolica* articles and booklet quote approvingly from all of the artificers of the modern anti-Semitic movement: Edouard Drumont in France, Adolf Stoecker in Germany, Karl Lueger in Vienna. Nor does Father Ballerini neglect Italy. In the three decades since the founding of the new Italian state, he wrote, Italy had become "a kingdom of Jews."

Ballerini cautioned that while the extermination of the Jews might seem to be an appealing solution to the problem, it was contrary to Christian teachings. As the people cursed by God, the Jews' continued degradation and their ceaseless wandering throughout the earth, with no land of their own, offered a precious witness to the New Testament's prophecies. Of course, he wrote, the Jews' conversion, if sincere, was the best solution to the Jewish problem, but realistically there was no chance of this happening. Consequently, what was needed was the return of the laws of the Middle Ages. Here he noted with warm approval the fact that the Russian czar had recently imposed some laws of just this sort, forbidding Jews from owning property.[21]

In an 1893 article titled "Jewish Morality," another Jesuit author, Father Saverio Rondina, listed all the recent charges aimed against the Jews in Europe, ranging from fraudulent banking practices to charges of murder. Together with the mushrooming anti-Semitic movement, he wrote, these accusations "invite us to return to an argument that for over a decade we have treated at great length in this journal, but whose timeliness and importance. . . are now greater than ever."

A clearer statement of the themes of modern anti-Semitism would be hard to find. The Jewish nation, Father Rondina wrote, "does not work, but traffics in the property and the work of others; it does not produce, but lives and grows fat with the products of the arts and industry of the nations that give it refuge. It is the giant octopus that with its oversized tentacles envelops everything. It has its stomach in the banks . . . and its suction cups everywhere: in contracts and monopolies, . . . in postal services and telegraph companies, in shipping and in the railroads, in the town treasuries and in state finance. It represents the kingdom of capital . . . the aristocracy of gold. . . . It reigns unopposed."

Here modern anti-Semitism rises directly out of older Church views; the Jews' emancipation is the catalyst that transforms the earlier forms into the new. "With religious liberty proclaimed, and citizenship conceded even to the Jews, the Jews took advantage of it . . . to become our masters. Indeed, today it is the *stock market* that has political control, and this is in the hands of the Jews. What governs is *Masonry,* and this too is directed by the Jews. What shapes and reshapes public opinion is the *press,* and this also is in large part inspired and subsidized by the Jews."

The "ceaseless war that Judaism wages against other nations, especially those that are Christian" is, according to Father Rondina, a direct product of the Jewish religion, which calls on Jews to treat Christians as if they were animals, and to do all they can to rob and cheat them. "The cause . . . is their hatred of Christianity, a hatred that is imposed on the Jews by their law, and that goes so far as to justify every sort of crime against us."

By this time, in the 1890s, Church leaders had become sensitive about being accused of anti-Semitism. After all, the message of the Church was love and charity, and in some influential quarters around Europe anti-Semitism was regarded as a retrograde prejudice, and anti-Semitic politicians viewed as reckless demagogues. In this light we can understand why demurrals and denials continued to be sprinkled throughout practically all the contributions the Church made to the development of modern anti-Semitism.

Father Rondina's article was typical. No sooner had he warned that the Jews were conspiring to enslave all Christians than he added: "We do not write with any intention of sparking or fomenting any anti-Semitism in our country. Rather we seek to sound an alarm for Italians so that they defend themselves against those who, in order to impoverish them, dominate them, and make them their slaves, interfere with their faith, corrupt their morals, and suck their blood."[22]

In these years, the Jesuit journal continued its sympathetic reporting of the growing anti-Semitic movement. An 1893 piece, for example, told of rising anti-Semitism in Germany, where although the Jews were a small minority, "the banks and the money are for the most part in their hands, which makes them incredibly powerful." Not only were the Jews numerous among the professional classes there, but they had taken over the press. "As a result, the Jews' influence on public opinion, on political life and on intellectual work is disproportionate and, what is worse, highly corrosive. Every [Jewish] writer, in effect, defames, holds in contempt, ridicules, and tries to destroy all that we hold dear, all of our Christian principles. The Jew's greed for gain dominates everything he does."[23]

As the end of the century neared, with anti-Semitic outbreaks growing more common, Father Ballerini kept hammering on these themes. In 1897 he warned: "The Jew remains always in every place immutably a Jew. His nationality is not in the soil where he is born, nor in the language that he speaks, but in his seed." For the Jew, "the best country is the one that provides him the best means of accumulating [gold]. The Jew makes us laugh when, in Italy, France and Germany, he pretends to get mawkish over his tenderness for his nation." The Jew's emancipation had produced just what the Church had feared: "his domination, via the two most potent forces that rule the world: the press and money." From Poland through Hungary, Austria, Germany, and France the Jews had begun to put into effect their secret plan for world domination, "so that, in a short time, they have become the powerful masters, especially in Berlin, Paris, Budapest, and Vienna."[24]

Through these years, only *L'Osservatore romano* was closer to the Pope and the Vatican hierarchy than *Civiltà cattolica*. Owned by the Holy See, *L'Osservatore* had been founded in Rome in 1861. With Rome's annexation to the Italian state in 1870, it became in effect the Vatican's official daily newspaper. By the 1890s, the secretary of state regularly authored unsigned articles in its pages, making known the Holy See's opinions on matters of current concern.²⁵ *Civiltà cattolica* and *L'Osservatore romano* were the two publications viewed throughout the Catholic world as offering the clearest expressions of the Pope's own perspectives on the issues of the day.

In 1892, with the anti-Semitic movement gaining force in Europe, *L'Osservatore romano* devoted a series of articles to the Jewish question. The series began by adding a new wrinkle to the old belief in a Jewish conspiracy. Of concern to the Vatican paper was the disturbing increase in sympathy for the Jews prompted by revulsion to the violence that had been increasingly aimed at them.

Could the upsurge in sympathy for the Jews that had resulted from such violence simply be a coincidence? the *Osservatore romano* author asked. Or might the crafty Jews not themselves be behind the murderous rampages? The conclusion was clear: "Seeing itself on the verge of being seriously attacked by public opinion and by the general population, Judaism . . . provokes hostile demonstrations . . . so that people sympathize with the victims and forget who their true persecutors are."

The fact that the recent pogroms in Russia had stirred up so much sympathy for the Jews, the Vatican journalist argued, showed that they could only have been engineered by the Jews themselves. "We would not stray far from the truth if we said that the rather heavy-handed blow that the Muscovite Empire has aimed at the children of Judah has played into the hands of Judaism, for it has engendered compassion for the Jews, against whom the Christian and civil world has, for good reason, begun to rebel." The article went on to argue, on similar grounds, that much of the French, Russian, and Austrian anti-Semitic movements were the work of "cosmopolitan Judaism."

Here the Vatican paper developed another theme that would reappear regularly over the next decades in Church publications: that there is a good kind of anti-Semitism and a bad kind. "Anti-Semitism ought to be the natural, sober, thoughtful, Christian reaction against Jewish predominance." But, unfortunately, wrote the *Osservatore romano* journalist, there was a different, non-Christian form of anti-Semitism that was attracting the most attention lately, one that threatened to discredit the true, Christian anti-Semitism. This new form of anti-Semitism was indeed "nothing but an artificial form of Judaism itself, which has introduced and maintained it so that it will be impossible for the true anti-Semitism to be organized, to be put into action, and to succeed." True anti-Semitism, the Vatican daily explained, "is and can be in substance nothing other than Christianity, completed and perfected in Catholicism."[26]

The following day, in another front-page story, *L'Osservatore romano* returned to the same theme. Jews were desperately trying to ward off "the reaction that is everywhere about to explode against their rapacious tyranny." The Jews had no one to blame but themselves. Addressing himself to the Jews directly, the journalist added a warning: "As we have said on other occasions, take care what you are doing. Don't play with fire. The people's ire, although at the moment somewhat dampened by sentiments of Christian charity and by the tender influence of the Catholic clergy, may at any moment erupt like a volcano and strike like a thunderbolt." It was a warning that, read in the light of what would happen in Europe a half-century later, is chilling. The article ended with the threat: "A quarter-hour might be all it takes."[27]

Little had changed by the end of the century. The Dreyfus affair (to be discussed in chapter eight) had triggered violent disorders throughout France, and anti-Semitic parties were on the upswing throughout Europe. In 1898, the Vatican daily noted, not without satisfaction, a turning of the tide. "Masonry and Judaism, sprung up together to combat and to destroy Christianity in the world, must now together defend themselves against the Christian awakening and against the people's wrath."[28]

But Vatican officials had to keep their public distance from any expressions of hatred of the Jews. When a non-Catholic newspaper attacked *L'Osservatore romano* for fostering the most fanatical kind of anti-Semitism, its editor responded by distinguishing between Judaism and Jews. Judaism was to be reviled in every way, for it was responsible for the death of Jesus Christ, and for the murder of Christian children to extract their blood for the Passover bread. "But combating Judaism does not mean combating the Jews," the editorialist explained, because the great majority of the Jews themselves were but "the slaves, the instruments and the victims" of Judaism. Judaism, in this formulation, had created "a dispersed Jewish race, an evil sect and detestable caste." The Jews' "systematic plundering" and "their implacable hatred against the Church and against humanity" had led people to view them as "an abomination," yet, the editor argued, it was the Jews themselves who were "the first victims of Judaism."[29] Three days later the paper warned that, given their religion and their nature, Jews "cannot and must not live among others as any other people in the world . . . do."[30]

The Vatican crusade against the Jews in the last two decades of the nineteenth century involved not only the two semi-official voices of the Holy See, but a large and growing network of other Catholic newspapers, both in Italy and beyond. Many examples could be given, but we cite here only the two that were closest to the Vatican. As described in the authoritative *Enciclopedia cattolica,* published by the Vatican, "the Holy See," following the fall of Rome in 1870, "decided to flank *L'Osservatore romano* with a Milanese daily, *L'Osservatore cattolico,* and a preexisting Florentine daily, *L'Unità cattolica.*"[31] It is to these two papers that we turn.

L'Osservatore cattolico was established in 1864 with the encouragement of the vicar of the diocese of Milan to bolster the Pope's authority after the fall of the Papal States. Pius IX encouraged the initiative, and virtually all the paper's writers were priests. By the 1870s *L'Osservatore cattolico* had achieved great prestige among Italian Catholics. Its thundering condemnations of liberalism, read avidly by the lower clergy, were conveyed to the large mass of illiterate peasants through Sunday sermons throughout the Milan area and beyond.[32]

The paper's director throughout the last decades of the nineteenth century was don Davide Albertario, described by the *Enciclopedia cattolica* as "for thirty years, after 1870, the most brilliant journalist and the most efficient polemicist serving the Catholic cause in Italy."[33] The view of the Jews that he promulgated in those years was the same as that found in the other Vatican-linked papers. Only the tone differed, for Albertario was renowned for his sarcastic style.

We get a taste of this in Albertario's 1885 article titled "The World's Jews": "This fine race of people," he wrote, "currently numbers 6,377,602, of whom we have in Italy, by our good fortune and to our general pleasure, 26,289. They are truly our masters, that is, the masters of thirty million souls, as they are the masters in Austria-Hungary, in Germany, in France, and almost everywhere else." The Jew, wrote Father Albertario, "is the possessor of the gold . . . and so the Jew is the ruler of the world.

"This is why the Jews are our masters, dear readers, precisely our masters. You can find the Jews in the Senate, in Parliament, in Public Administration, in the Chamber of Commerce, in journalism, having more or less changed their first and last names, *but always Jews to the core!*"[34]

In the meantime, Florence's *L'Unità cattolica*, like *L'Osservatore cattolico* published by a group of priests with close ties to the Pope, was printing articles of much the same kind. The Jews, along with the Masons, said to be in the hands of the Jews, were blamed for all that had gone wrong in Italy (and beyond) in recent years. An 1892 article went so far as to claim that the "Synagogue" had been responsible for the Italian conquest of Rome in 1870.[35]

A typical example of *L'Unità cattolica*'s writings on the Jews is offered by a lead story later in 1892. St. Peter had warned the Jews, the author recounted, that if they wanted to become true Christians, they would have to give up their thirst for gold, their malice, and their penchant for fraud. Otherwise, they would forever remain Jews, embodying "the most odious form of degradation that one could imagine in the human species."

There then followed the familiar refrain: "Far be it from us (may the heavens be our witness) to have the least thought of wanting with our writing to reheat the boiling pot of anti-Semitism which, having already scalded Romania and Russia, and having boiled over in France, is already threatening Italy as well."

If such denials of anti-Semitism were common, they were rarely made without the kind of caveat that followed here: "But, my dear Jews, let's be clear," the *Unità cattolica* author wrote. "If the sky is stormy, whose fault is it? If a thunderbolt strikes your head, who provoked it? . . . The history of the Jews . . . has always been the same: abuse, provoke, invade!" He continued: "We repeat: anti-Semitism, cease your blind furies. Yet, at the same time, if it be true that there are some good men among the people of Israel, give us proof of it. Refuse to show any solidarity with the vampires of your caste, with those who suck human blood." The article concluded by returning to Peter. After nineteen centuries, St. Peter beckoned once again, saying: "Come to the Faith of Jesus Christ, more precious than the stock exchange listing, the only divinity you have left."[36]

In these articles, as in all the Catholic press closest to the Vatican, the battle against the liberals, against the separation of Church and state, was cast as the battle against the Jews. By branding the liberal cause a product of the Jews, the Vatican tried to discredit the forces of secularization.

Such a link was on display in the fall of 1892, when the tenth Italian Catholic Congress discussed ways of ensuring the Church's continued role in public education. *L'Unità cattolica* began its coverage with what otherwise might seem to be a wholly gratuitous remark. The congress, it reported, "had the virtue of filling the hearts of the Jews with terror."[37] The logic was clear to readers: It was the Jews who were the masterminds of the drive to eliminate the Church's influence from public education; the whole liberal movement for separation of Church and state was a Jewish, anti-Christian plot.[38]

Like the rest of the Catholic press, *L'Unità cattolica* combined the warning that Jews were taking over the world with the observation that it was the secular rather than the religious Jews who were behind this plan. An article late in 1892 explained that there were three kinds of Jews. The first, and smallest, group consisted of those who still followed the teachings of the Old Testament. These were sprinkled throughout some faraway lands. The second group was composed of those who "turn to that mass of absurdities that they call the Talmud." They included the bulk of the Jewish population outside of Western Europe. Finally, there were the "enlightened Jews" who were in the majority in Western Europe. "They believe in nothing," the *Unità cattolica* journalist reported. "The only ancestral tradition that they have maintained is that of the *Golden Calf.* And it is of these Jews . . . that it is said, not without reason, that today they rule the world."[39]

Over a brief but intense period in the last two decades of the nineteenth century the traditional Catholic attitudes toward the Jews—hostile but patronizing, and frequently emphasizing redemption through baptism—were transformed into something else. But in making the transition to a modern form of anti-Semitism, the Church made use of older means of demonizing the Jews as well. None of these was more dramatic than the charge of Jewish ritual murder.

CHAPTER SEVEN

Jewish Vampires

THE CHARGE that Jews secretly murdered Christian children for ritual purposes first began to spread in the twelfth century. Jews were accused of crucifying their innocent prey in demonic re-enactment of what their ancestors had done to Jesus. The notion that they murdered such children to get their blood only began to surface later. By the thirteenth century such accusations had become so common that the German emperor Frederick II convoked a committee of scholars and Jewish converts to Christianity to determine if Jews indeed did require Christian blood for their rites. The committee rejected the claim, pointing out that both the Old Testament and the Talmud specifically forbade the Jews from consuming blood of any kind.[1]

Local priests, however, often encouraged popular belief in Jewish ritual murder, raising suspicions when a Christian child went missing or was found dead. By contrast, the popes typically acted to protect the Jews from these charges. In one of the first such cases, in 1247, Pope Innocent IV received word that priests in Germany and France were fomenting anti-Jewish violence with such claims. He responded by issuing an encyclical, directed at the archbishops and bishops of those lands, defending the Jews. The Jews, he wrote, were being falsely accused, and he noted that Jewish law forbade the consumption of blood. Over the following centuries, other popes reiterated this message.[2]

There is no better illustration of early Vatican suspicion of such ritual murder charges than the case of Simon of Trent in 1475. There is an irony here, for this was not one of the many cases of local enthusiasm that the Vatican succeeded in suppressing. On the contrary, it is the best-known case of a Vatican-approved ritual murder charge, one that led to an officially sponsored Catholic cult. Indeed, it was this case, along with that of

Father Tommaso of Damascus, that was most often cited by Catholics in the late nineteenth century to demonstrate the uncontestable truth of Jewish ritual murder.

None were more influential in spreading charges of ritual murder in the late Middle Ages than members of the Franciscan order. Founded in the early thirteenth century, the Franciscans, together with the Dominicans, whose order was founded at the same time, were organized and approved by the Pope with the specific goal of combating heresy. In the 1230s, Gregory IX took responsibility for rooting out heretics away from local bishops and gave it to committees composed of members of these two mendicant orders, thereby creating the first inquisition. The Jews soon came to see the friars as their worst enemies, and for many centuries the Dominicans and Franciscans, in the words of the major expert on the subject, "directed and oversaw virtually all the anti-Jewish activities of the Christian clergy in the West."[3] Not only did they serve as inquisitors; they were also renowned as the Church's scholarly experts on the Jews. Famed for their sermonizing, the friars traipsed from town to town, whipping up popular hatred of the Jews.

Just why the Dominicans and, especially, the Franciscans came to be so obsessed by the evil of the Jews remains a matter of debate. Some scholars have linked the friars' anti-Jewish animus to the fact that members of the mendicant orders came disproportionately from the urban merchant classes, where resentment over competition from Jewish merchants was great. There is no doubt, however, that they were effective in turning people against the Jews and in spreading the belief—not previously widespread—that it was religiously desirable to expel Jews from Christian lands. In 1290 England became the first European country to do so, and over the next three centuries it was joined by France, Spain, Sicily, Portugal, the Kingdom of Naples, and several German territories, all of which became Jew-free.[4]

Barefooted Franciscan friars continued to wander through towns and villages spreading word of Jewish evil.[5] In early 1475, one of the best-known of these, Bernardino of Feltre, came to Trent to preach the Lenten sermons. His impassioned denunciations of the Jews' demonic nature roused the local population, and his prophecy that a great evil was about to befall the town alarmed them. At the time, Trent—now a city in northeastern Italy—was an ecclesiastical principality at the southern tip of the Holy Roman Empire, and ruled by a bishop-prince.

One day, shortly after the famed Franciscan had left, a small Christian boy, Simon, failed to come home. Suspicion of evildoing immediately turned to the town's Jews, although only three Jewish households lived there. A few days later, one of the Jews, to his horror, discovered a little body emerging from the water that flowed through his cellar. The Jews nervously debated what to do. Someone, they thought, had placed Simon's body there. While a number of them urged that they all flee before the body was discovered, the patriarch of the community, Samuel, insisted that they report the matter to the authorities and explain what had happened. Otherwise, he said, people would assume that the Jews were guilty of murdering the child.

Samuel proved to be overly optimistic. The Jewish men were arrested and tortured. Samuel had his arms tied behind his back, his hands behind his waist. A pulley was used to lift him up in the air by a rope tied to his wrists. When he denied having done any harm to Simon, weights were added to his feet. The interrogators lifted him high in the air, and then let the rope out rapidly before stopping suddenly, sending agonizing pain through his shoulders. When this failed to get him to change his story, they placed burning sulfur under his nose. After two days of this, he could endure no more. By asking questions to which he needed to answer only yes or no, the investigators finally got the confession they wanted: The Jews had killed the boy for his blood, needed for their Passover celebration. After similar tortures, a number of other Jewish men confessed as well.

The people of Trent were moved deeply by the stirring story of the child's martyrdom and the Jews' evil. Tales of miracles performed by the dead boy began to pour in from every quarter, and a cult rapidly took shape, with the strong support of the bishop, Prince Hinderbach.

The executions began in late June. Nine men had already been sentenced to death, but the community patriarch, Samuel, was singled out for special treatment. On the way to the execution grounds, the guards tore out his flesh with pincers. Once there, he joined other members of his family affixed to the stake. The fire was lit and they were all burned alive. The following day four more Jews were due to be immolated. At the last moment, two of them asked to be baptized, and so were separated from the others, who were burned at the stake. Once baptized, the two former Jews were shown mercy: The executioner beheaded them first, and only then were their bodies heaved onto the flames.

Before any further executions could be carried out, the bishop received unwelcome news. Pope Sixtus IV, in response to a petition from the Jews of Rome, had ordered the proceedings suspended and appointed a special commissioner, Bishop Baptista Dei Giudici, to go to Trent to investigate the Jews' claim that a terrible injustice was being done.

Bishop Dei Giudici, a Dominican, was a man known for both his learning and his rectitude. He had another trait that added to his credibility, especially important because the bishop and people of Trent were unsympathetic to his mission. As he himself put it, he had "often preached and written against the Jews and had never, in all his life, even once shared a meal or a drink with any Jews."[6]

On the commissioner's arrival in Trent, Prince Hinderbach took him to the church to view Simon's body, which had been lying on display for a month. The prince sifted through the child's remains to display the boy's shinbone, producing a stench that was so great, the commissioner later reported, that he almost vomited. Asked why he did not put the body in a coffin, Hinderbach responded that he had gotten used to the smell, and that in any case the people insisted that the boy remain on display. The commissioner then interrogated the witnesses to the miracles performed by Simon. He concluded that no such miracles had occurred. Rather, he wrote, the witnesses had "described [the purported miracles] in a mendacious, fraudulent, and deceitful manner."[7] Although he also wanted to interview the surviving Jewish prisoners to find out what had really happened, the bishop-prince would not allow him to see them.

The commissioner's growing suspicions were shared by the Pope, who was skeptical about the claim of ritual murder and the reports of miracles performed by the dead boy. When the Pope heard that friars were spreading stories of Simon's martyrdom in the territories of Venice, provoking violent assaults on the Jews there, he wrote to the doge of Venice, ordering him, on pain of excommunication, to put an end to the sermons.

Through the fall of 1475, Hinderbach continued to ignore the commissioner's demands that the prisoners be released. The commissioner meanwhile drafted his findings: The Jews' confessions proved nothing, for they had been extracted by torture so brutal that it went well beyond what the law allowed. Indeed, he had found evidence that the child might well have been killed by a Christian man who planted the body in a Jew's house to divert suspicion from himself.

But the bishop of Trent would triumph in the end. Popular enthusiasm for the cult in northeastern Italy, backing from the Austrian archduke, the strong support given by the Franciscans and other mendicant orders, and Hinderbach's political connections all led the Pope to terminate the commissioner's mission.

Fifteen members of the tiny Jewish community of Trent were executed in all, and Jews were banned from living in Trent. Over a century later, in 1588, Pope Sixtus V formally declared Simon a martyr and saint, establishing an official Church holiday in his honor to mark the day of his murder. It was only in 1965, in the wake of the Second Vatican Council, that the Holy See abolished the cult.[8]

Over the ensuing centuries, ritual murder charges continued to crop up periodically—especially in central and eastern Europe—and when they did, popular vengeance against the Jews often produced fatal results. Jews continued to appeal to the Holy See for protection, and on the whole received a positive response from the pontiffs. A series of ritual murder cases in mid-eighteenth-century Poland led to a particularly strong defense of the Jews by a special papal commissioner. In 1769, that commissioner, Lorenzo Ganganelli, was himself elevated to the papacy, and as Pope Clement XIV became known for his benevolence to the Jews.

Given this history, the change in papal attitude in the nineteenth century is striking. What had been a rather peripheral movement, associated with fringe elements of the Church, now became identified with the Vatican itself. It was a campaign that would have serious consequences, for the obsessive reports of Jewish ritual murder by the Catholic press— including the publications closest to the Vatican—helped demonize Europe's Jews. It did so at a time when the mass, modern anti-Semitic movement was taking shape.[9]

Back in 1840, when the Damascus case had attracted the interest of the Catholic papers, the press still reached a small audience, and, in any event, there was relatively little Catholic concern about the Jews. By contrast, when, around 1880, the Catholic press again began to raise the ritual murder charge, it did so with a vengeance. In 1887–1891 alone, at least twenty-two different ritual murder accusations were widely reported in the press.

The upsurge in tales of Jewish lust for human blood came amid a much larger resurgence of interest in vampirism in nineteenth-century Europe. Belief in evil humans who drank human blood had been around for many centuries in Europe, as was the identification of such people with the devil. Christianity played a complex role in these beliefs, in part absorbing preexisting folk beliefs and in part influencing popular opinion through its own theology. In many rural portions of the continent, folk religion incorporated belief in vampires, and these were linked to Christian beliefs about the blood of Christ. Most notable in this connection is the well-known passage from the New Testament, in which Jesus says (John 6:53–57): "Whoso eateth my flesh, and drinketh my blood, hath eternal life; and I will raise him up at the last day. For my flesh is meat indeed, and my blood is drink indeed. He that eateth my flesh, and drinketh my blood, dwelleth in me, and I in him. As the living Father hath sent me, and I live by the Father: so he that eateth me, even he shall live by me." Nothing could be more sacred to the Church than the belief in transubstantiation connected with the Eucharist, linked to these New Testament passages. Curiously, although it was the Jews who were accused of having a religious commandment to drink blood, the Old Testament specifically prohibited the practice.

The upsurge in interest in vampirism in the nineteenth century was dramatically on display in the literature of the period, where the theme of the vampire was everywhere. In France, with Maupassant, Baudelaire, and Gautier, in Russia with Alexis Tolstoy and Turgeniev, in England with poets from Coleridge and Byron to Shelley and Keats, and novelists from both Emily and Charlotte Brontë to D. H. Lawrence, the image of the sucker of human blood chilled the European imagination. As an image of pure human evil, associated with beliefs in powerful supernatural forces linked to the devil, the vampire had no peer. In this context, what otherwise seems so odd, that the Jews of Europe should be linked to the vampire, is perhaps not entirely surprising.[10]

On several occasions in the late nineteenth century, ritual murder accusations against the Jews produced murderous effects. Among the bloodiest of these was an 1881 case in Russia, which helped trigger a series of pogroms. Similarly, in 1903, in Kishinev, Moldavia, when a boy's dead body was found, the Christians turned against the Jews in their midst. Although an inquest found that the child's murder was the product of a family dispute over an inheritance, tensions kept rising. The head rabbi of the city asked the local Russian Orthodox bishop to help calm the people, but the bishop responded that he would do no such thing, as he was convinced that the Jews used Christian blood to make their Passover bread. On Easter weekend the people rose up and slaughtered forty-nine Jewish women, children, and men, going on a rampage that injured five hundred Jews and left two thousand Jewish families homeless.[11]

The new crusade began immediately after Italian forces seized Rome in 1870. In 1871, an Austrian Catholic priest, August Rohling, published *The Talmud Jew.* Among its main themes was the claim that Jews were bound by their religion to murder Christian children for their blood. In subsequent years, Father Rohling, a professor of theology, wrote and spoke widely on the "Jewish threat," and was called in as an expert witness in several ritual murder trials.

Officials of Austria's Interior Ministry saw in Father Rohling's work one of the primary causes of the anti-Semitic agitation that had begun to spread through the Austrian empire in the 1880s. In 1883, the governor of Bohemia wrote to the local archbishop, Fürst Cardinal Schwarzenberg, and asked him to do something to stop the priest from engaging in anti-Semitic agitation. The archbishop refused, replying: "It would make the worst impression on the clergy and the people if the episcopate would protect and defend the Jews by censuring a Christian priest and scholar who is a distinguished authority on the Talmud." Indeed, argued Cardinal Schwarzenberg, it was the Jews who were causing the problems, using the newspapers they controlled to defame the Church. Catholics were just defending themselves. "I believe that it is time to counteract the defamation of the Church . . . and to carefully investigate these issues involving the Talmud, the Kabbalah, and the blood ritual of the Jews, and to take appropriate measures depending on the result."[12]

Initially, the Vatican moved cautiously. In 1872, for example, *L'Unità cattolica,* the Vatican-linked paper in Florence, published one of its first articles on the subject. The Talmud, it reported, commands Jews to kill Christian children to use their blood for their matzah. When the editor of an Italian Jewish newspaper challenged *L'Unità cattolica* to prove its charges, and cited the contrary opinion of popes from earlier centuries, the paper's editor, a priest, retreated. In an article titled "The Popes and the Jews," he wrote: "It is our duty to declare that while such a calumny has been directed against the Jews from ancient times, the popes, among whom we recall Gregory IX and Innocent IV, themselves cleared the Jews of [the charge]." Such backtracking by a Vatican-linked publication, still possible in 1872, would be unthinkable in the last two decades of the century.[13]

Here again, the Jesuit journal *Civiltà cattolica* played an enormously

influential role, signaling Vatican backing for the ritual murder accusation, sketching out the themes to be used in the Catholic press elsewhere
in Europe, and providing the authoritative historical evidence used to
prove the charge.

The *Civiltà cattolica* campaign was begun by Father Oreglia himself, a
few months into his barrage of articles denouncing the Jews. The Talmud
commanded the "Jewish race," he wrote in a June 1881 article, to kill
Christians. Here by way of proof he cited the case of Father Tommaso of
Damascus. The evidence could not be clearer, for the witnesses had been
formally interrogated and their testimony had been published. Because
the Jews had stolen all the copies of that publication in a futile effort to
keep their awful secret, he added, he felt it his duty to publish the evidence himself.[14] Subsequent articles that year provided not only copious
detail from the Damascus testimony, but similarly chilling passages from
the trial of the Jewish murderers of Simon of Trent in 1475.

Father Oreglia realized that for many Western Europeans the charge
that Jews secretly attacked Christian children and drained them of their
blood was not easy to believe. For this he had a ready reply: The Jews
whom they knew, those of Western Europe, were moving away from
their traditions. "In all likelihood, these bloody rites have just about
ended in the synagogues and ghettoes and Jewish communities . . .
in those countries where the emancipated Jews have slowly been
de-Judaizing."[15]

As part of his campaign, Father Oreglia also helped publicize the writings of the Moldavian "ex-rabbi," the report of secret Jewish evil which
had so appealed to both the secretary of state and the cardinal prefect
of Propaganda Fide back in 1840. In May 1882, Father Oreglia provided
long excerpts from the book, focusing on the Jewish need for Christian
blood for both Purim and Passover. On Purim, "the Jews are busy captur-
ing all the Christians they can, especially children. On this night, however,
they only kill one (a child or adult), pretending to kill Haman." The fact
that an adult would serve as well as a child for Purim explained what
otherwise seemed so puzzling: why the Jews had chosen an elderly
Capuchin friar to kill when it was known they needed the blood of
children.

On Passover, reported Father Oreglia, the Jews required much more
blood, and then only a small child's blood would do. Indeed, he explained,
if you ever wondered why some matzah is labeled kosher for Passover,

now you know—it is because such matzah contains a Christian child's blood.[16]

Father Oreglia did, however, offer one small note of consolation. He had received a report from Port Said, Egypt, regarding events of the previous year. With Passover rapidly approaching, the Jews had grown increasingly desperate, for they could find no Christian child. Lacking a better alternative, they kidnapped a Muslim boy, baptized him, and then slit his throat. This, Father Oreglia explained, was a common occurrence in that part of the world. And it was here that he pointed out the unintended brighter side of the sordid deed: "If in fact the Jews actually know how to administer a valid baptism, at least these little Muslim boys are going to heaven, carried there, so to speak, by the devil."[17]

In his writings on Jewish ritual murder, as in his larger work in warning of the Jewish threat, Father Oreglia's work was continued in the 1890s by other members of the Jesuit editorial collective.

Typical was the two-part series—"Jewish Morality" and "Jewish Morality and the Mystery of the Blood"—authored by Father Rondina in January 1893. The first article began by trumpeting some of the charges that we now identify with the "modern" form of anti-Semitism, charges that Jews were behind various bank frauds and had taken over the economies of many countries. A vast Jewish conspiracy, Father Rondina warned, threatened the Christian world. He then turned to the old theme of the Talmud as the source of Jewish evil. According to the Talmud, which the Jews slavishly follow, he wrote, Christians are "cattle, donkeys, dogs . . . swine." The Jews' great thinker, Maimonides, he continued, taught them that "Every Jew who does not kill a non-Jew when he has the opportunity violates a basic principle." (In fact, what Maimonides actually wrote on the humanity of non-Jews was: "The righteous of all peoples have a part in the world to come."[18]) Moreover, claimed Father Rondina, according to the Talmud "even the best among the Goyim, or Christians, merits death." Given this teaching, he asked, "is it any surprise that they think it their duty to conspire constantly against us?"

He then came to the question of ritual murder. "All the veils have now been lifted, and the Judaic secret has been revealed in all its horror. Up until now, we have known from centuries-long experience that the Jew sucked Christian blood, but for the most part people did not realize that this was something they did out of principle, in obedience to their law." Father Rondina then returned to the Jewish conspiracy for world domination. The Jew, he wrote, "has already become our master." Look around Italy, he warned, "and you will see that most of the wealth, which has been robbed from the Church, is today in the hands of the Jews. . . . If you inquire a bit into the secret things that have gone on, and look into the origin of all those reverses and failures of the great Italian families, you will discover that behind them are the paws of the Jew."[19]

Father Rondina devoted the second of these articles entirely to the ritual murder charge. There was no point, he wrote by way of introduction, wasting more words on showing what everyone already knew, namely "that the Jews are constantly oppressing and robbing Christians." Rather, he promised, "we will set out to prove something of which many are unaware and that others are loath to believe and even try to deny, namely, the mystery of the blood."

Following the path pioneered by Father Oreglia, Father Rondina focused on the Trent and Damascus cases as the clearest proof of Jewish ritual murder. In both cases the Jews themselves had confessed and thorough criminal trials had determined their guilt. Like Father Oreglia, he showed considerable relish in recounting the grisly description provided by the Moldavian "ex-rabbi." Ghastly detail was piled on ghastly detail. "For the blood of a Christian child to be appropriate for the rite and good for the health of the Jewish soul," Father Rondina explained, "it is necessary for the little child to die amidst torments. This is what happened to the innocent little Simon and to so many others who were killed by needles stuck into them, or who were cut up piece by piece, or crucified." In such cases, when the Jews had drained the child's last drop of blood, Father Rondina continued, it was "kept by the local Rabbi." He, in turn, then sold it "at a high price in small quantities to the nearby synagogues, by means of itinerant Jews who are furnished with a certificate from the same Rabbi, attesting to the fact that it is true Christian blood."[20]

Among the most important contributions that *Civiltà cattolica* made to the Church ritual murder campaign were its repeated arguments that, despite what the Jews and their defenders maintained, earlier popes did indeed believe that Jews practiced ritual murder. In July 1881, for example, Father Oreglia railed against those who had incorrectly cited Innocent IV's letter to the bishops of Germany and France in the 1200s. It is true, he said, that the popes had always shown justice and charity toward the Jews. But nothing in the Pope's letter could be interpreted as denying Jewish ritual murder, which was based on Talmudic law and "not rarely put into practice (as shown by many authentic trials and testimony) by the Jewish race." In this and in other similar cases, wrote the Jesuit, what the popes, in their mercy, had been concerned about were outbreaks of popular violence against innocent Jews and cases in which the unscrupulous used the ritual murder charge as a mere pretext to seize Jewish property.[21]

Although less preoccupied with the theme than the Jesuit journal, *L'Osservatore romano* offered a similar view of Jews as ritual murderers, making the Vatican's position clear. A July 1892 article, commenting on a ritual murder trial then in progress in Germany, began: "The trial against a Jew accused of the ritual murder of a Christian boy has barely begun, and it has already been established by many unimpeachable witnesses that Jews practice ritual homicides so that they can use Christian blood in making their Passover matzah."

The fact that recent ritual murder trials had all resulted in acquittals meant nothing, the Vatican daily argued, for in every one of them Jews had bribed the judges. "It only confirms the conviction that the Jews truly do murder Christians to use their blood in their detestable Talmudic and rabbinical rites, and that to help them conceal these crimes, as well as for others no less atrocious, the judiciary is entirely in the synagogue's control."

The chief rabbi of Rome, *L'Osservatore romano* reported, had recently written a letter denouncing the ritual murder charge. It would have been a better use of his time, the editorialist continued, if he had written to his fellow Jews instead. The rabbi should have told those members of the "miserable race of Judah" to stop trying to conceal the fact that they "murder Christians to use their blood for their detestable rites."[22]

When later in the same trial an expert witness was called for the defense, and testified that there was no basis in Judaism for ritual murder, *L'Osservatore romano* reacted forcefully. "Unfortunately, although they tried to deny that the Talmud's followers commit such an atrocious act, one cannot reasonably deny its existence." The professor who argued that the Talmud does not contain any demand for human sacrifices, the article noted, "had by his own confession not read the entire Talmud."[23]

As the nineteenth century drew to a close, the Vatican daily kept up the drumbeat: The Jews were evil, and their continued murder and torture of Christian children revealed just how depraved they were. An early November 1899 article, titled "A new ritual murder," reported news from a Hungarian town where a poor seven-year-old orphan had been found, his throat slit, his blood entirely drained from his body, yet with no trace of any blood to be found anywhere. He had last been seen entering the house of a Jew. "From many areas come reports of violent disorders aimed at the co-religionists of these barbarous slaughterers of children."[24]

Later that month, in an article titled "Jewish ritual murder," the Vatican daily told of a recent case in which the Jews had been ruled innocent although everyone knew that they were guilty. It concluded with a warning: "We think it our duty to give a fraternal Christian bit of advice not to all Jews, but to certain Jews in particular: Don't throw oil on the fire. . . . Content yourselves . . . with the Christians' money, but stop shedding and sucking their blood."[25]

As vigorously as *Civiltà cattolica* and *L'Osservatore romano* pursued their campaign to identify Jews with the drinking of the blood, they were outdone in their zeal by some of the other Catholic papers. Most notable among these was *L'Osservatore cattolico,* the Milan Catholic daily which, as we have seen, was closely identified with the Holy See. By 1891, the subject of Jewish ritual murder had become such an obsession for the paper that, to gain greater publicity for the cause, it offered 10,000 francs to anyone who could demonstrate that the Jews were innocent of the charge.

By the following year, it seemed, barely a day went by without a story in *L'Osservatore cattolico* reporting the latest graphic details of the Jews' thirst for Christian blood. In March and April 1892, forty-four articles on the subject appeared, and many Catholic papers in Italy, France, Austria, and Germany reprinted extracts from them.[26]

In the midst of publishing these articles—many providing the most gruesome descriptions of how small children were butchered by the Jews—the director of *L'Osservatore cattolico,* Father Davide Albertario, had a private audience with Pope Leo XIII. The Pope's words of praise for the good work of the Milanese paper—as reported by Albertario himself—were widely trumpeted in the Catholic press. "I don't know how to tell you," wrote Albertario, "how much my soul filled with joy, comforted by His Holiness's smile, how brightened it was by the Sovereign's most beautiful expressions of satisfaction."[27]

Following this papal audience, *L'Osservatore cattolico*'s Berlin correspondent reported that the Germans had followed Albertario's trip to the Vatican with interest. "The *Osservatore cattolico*'s studies on the Jews' ritual murders," he went on to note, "are read here with great eagerness." Indeed, a German-language version of the series was about to be published in booklet form.[28]

There are other indications that Germany's emerging anti-Semitic movement recognized its debt to the Catholic newspaper. In late March 1892, *L'Osservatore cattolico* reported that one of the German parliament's most influential anti-Semitic deputies had given a memorable parliamentary address on Jewish ritual murder and that the conservative party was having 100,000 copies of it distributed. The newspaper's Berlin correspondent reported that just two days earlier the deputy "sent me a letter in which he begged me to express his gratitude to the wonderful editorial board of *L'Osservatore cattolico* for having furnished him with such good scientific material."[29]

In April, *L'Osservatore cattolico* reported that its campaign was finding fertile soil in Austria as well. In a debate in the Lower Austrian parliament, Deputy Ernst Schneider had, "to the applause of the anti-Semites, . . . unrolled a Hebrew parchment, reading a passage in Hebrew which he then explained. *It contains the command of ritual murder on Passover.*" The liberals, wrote the correspondent, made a big commotion, and tried to drown the man out with raucous laughter. "But do these cynical and petulant bursts of laughter," asked the *Osservatore cattolico* author, "do anything to detract from the truth that Schneider spoke?"[30]

Later in the month, the newspaper reported, twenty-five Austrian deputies, citing evidence they had obtained from *L'Osservatore cattolico*, called on the imperial government to appoint a special commission of scholars whose task would be to investigate the passages from the Talmud that command the Jews to murder Christian children. The president of the assembly, however, declared the motion out of order, saying that it was not within Parliament's purview. No doubt, concluded the *Osservatore cattolico* account, a combination of reasons motivated his decision: "As much as he feared retribution from the Jews, he loved their gold."[31]

The close interconnections between the *Osservatore cattolico* campaign and the development of the anti-Semitic political movement in Europe are clear from another April 1892 article as well. The story told of the birth of a new "anti-Semitic newspaper," *La Libre Parole*, "directed by that famous and indomitable adversary of the Jews, Edouard Drumont." Drumont, as we shall see, was one of the major figures in the development of political anti-Semitism in France.

The priests of *L'Osservatore cattolico* were quick to add that their negative feelings toward the Jews, like Drumont's, were not motivated by any unchristian hatred. "Drumont fights the Jews, as we fight them, not out of any caste or personal hatred, but rather because they are the vampires of humanity, monopolizers, usurers, speculators; they are dishonest, implacable, destroyers and slanderers, exploiters of Christian blood. It is a [matter of] defense . . . an act of patriotism, of charity, of religion."[32]

Alongside the Catholic newspaper accounts of the bloodthirsty Jews soon came an outpouring of books and pamphlets as well. Many of the most influential of these were written by priests and published with the approval of the Church hierarchy. In 1883, an Italian translation of the Moldavian "ex-rabbi's" book was published for the first time. In 1897, in France, the Dominican friar R. P. Constant published *The Jews Before the Church and History,* carrying the imprimatur of the Dominican authorities. The book told the by now familiar story of the treacherous Jews, disloyal to their country, rapacious, the enemies of all good people, and commanded by the Talmud to slaughter Christian children for their blood. Father Constant ended his book with words of praise for Edouard Drumont, "one of the best informed men on the [Jewish] question."[33]

With the great surge of public interest in Jewish ritual murder in general, and the Damascus case in particular, the Capuchin friars of Sardinia decided, in 1896, to publish their own book-length account of Father Tommaso's martyrdom. In the book's preface, the Capuchin compiler explained that the book was needed to ensure that the mists of time not cloud Tommaso's glorious memory. Both his fellow Capuchins and the people of his native Sardinia should feel great pride, he wrote. They had "produced an illustrious martyr," one of the many "whom the Synagogue, out of their hatred for Christ, had ordered to be drained of their blood." The Jews had once again, in murdering Tommaso, used their "Talmudic knife" so that they "could have their [Christian] blood to eat and to drink."[34]

The Capuchin author's fears that Father Tommaso's martyrdom would be soon forgotten seem oddly misplaced. No reader of the Catholic press at the end of the century could fail to know, in all its sickening detail, the story of how the Jews had butchered him.

CHAPTER EIGHT

France

A T THE TIME of Pius IX's death, in 1878, most Catholics then living had never known any other pope. He had sat on St. Peter's
throne for thirty-two years, bridging two eras. Having become
"pope-king"—that is, ruler of the Papal States—on his election to the
papacy, he later presided over the demise of the pope's earthly kingdom.
Having bolstered the spiritual power of his office by waging a successful
campaign for the doctrine of papal infallibility at the First Vatican Council, he ended his days as self-declared "prisoner of the Vatican." Revered
by conservatives in the Church hierarchy and among the faithful for
standing firm for Church principles against the heresies of modern times,
he was despised by Italian patriots, who thought him a dangerous, if not
pathetic, anachronism. Indeed, a group of anticlericals came close to
throwing Pius IX's body into the Tiber when, three years after his death, it
was transported to its final resting-place, and only last-minute police
intervention stopped them. But his supporters would ultimately have
grounds for claiming victory. On September 3, 2000, after more than a
century of campaigning to make him a saint, they (or more accurately,
their spiritual descendants) had the satisfaction of seeing another long-
serving pope, John Paul II, beatify him, placing him but one step from
sainthood.[1]

The cardinals who met in conclave to elect a new pope on Pius IX's
death were a conservative group. But as they gathered to decide the
Church's future they realized that they could not go on as they had. If
the Church was to survive and prosper, something new would have to be
tried. This sense was particularly acute among the non-Italian cardinals,
who, although still a minority, were for the first time a significant force.[2]

It took only three ballots to elect Pius IX's successor. Gioacchino Cardinal Pecci, archbishop of Perugia, had a background that in certain respects made him eminently *papabile*. Born to a minor noble family, he had attended the Academy of Noble Ecclesiastics, had some diplomatic experience, and had spent many years in a pastoral role as head of an archdiocese. Yet he had almost no experience with the Curia itself—for he had lived far from Rome for decades—and his modest diplomatic experience dated from many years earlier.

Indeed, Pecci had been abroad for only three years, in 1843–1846, when he was a young man and the Church's situation and European politics were very different. After a rapid rise—he was named bishop of Perugia at age thirty-six—his career stalled. Both Cardinal Antonelli and Pius IX were wary of him. They feared that he was too independent and they suspected, wrongly, that he harbored secret sympathies for the liberals.

On election, Pecci took the name of Leo XIII, in honor of Leo XII, who had been pope when he was a youth, and whose rigor he admired. A man of considerable intelligence, the new Pope had continued to read theology throughout his days as archbishop. Known for his prodigious memory, he liked to gather as much information as he could before he took any action.

Leo XIII bore the strong imprint of his aristocratic background. As Pope, he was more eager to win the admiration of the powerful than to elicit enthusiasm from the masses. He struck people as cold and distant, although always courteous. Highly attuned to the grandeur of his office, he cultivated an imperial presence.

The new Pope was no less suspicious of things modern than was his predecessor. Indeed, his encyclicals were full of warnings about demonic conspirators (usually linked to the Masonry) who plotted against the Church.[3] He often cited the Syllabus of Errors in support of his anti-modern stand, and notwithstanding his intellectual bent he was a firm proponent of censoring all books judged to be contrary to Church doctrine. The pope whom he most admired was Innocent III, the epitome of the medieval theocratic ruler.

Yet Leo XIII was more modern than Pius IX in one important respect, for he realized that, given the changes that had taken place in the world, the Church had to develop new approaches if it was to rebuild its influence. As the French Church historian Roger Aubert put it, the Pope had a well-developed sense of "public relations."[4] He realized that the Vatican had been losing its battle against the changes that were transforming the western world. Something had to be done to change the Church's image of being out of keeping with the times and to make it seem relevant again. With the socialist movement gaining ever greater influence, Leo XIII was also eager to find a way to appeal to the masses, to show that the Church could help them deal with their problems.[5]

Given the Pope's natural reserve, his deliberative style, and his sense of diplomacy, he avoided his predecessor's outbursts against the Jews. On those few public occasions on which he said anything specifically about them, he chose his words carefully. Although Leo XIII was pope while mass anti-Semitic political movements were taking shape in Europe, and he would play a significant role in encouraging them, he made sure to keep a certain distance. He realized that such movements could be dangerous if they spun out of control, and he was also sensitive to the fact that many government leaders whose approval he sought opposed them. Being identified too closely with such movements would carry a diplomatic price that the Pope did not want to pay.

No one came to be more identified with Leo XIII's pontificate than Mariano Rampolla, the man who served as his secretary of state from 1887 until the Pope's death in 1903. Rampolla, only forty-four years old at the time of his appointment, was from an aristocratic Sicilian family and, like the Pope, a graduate of the Academy of Noble Ecclesiastics. Having previously served as papal nuncio in Spain, he was a man of great abilities, a tireless worker, with a fierce dedication to the Pope and to the Church. Rampolla's own strong belief in the need to restore the Pope's temporal power reinforced the Pope's growing opposition to the Italian state. Elsewhere in Europe, Rampolla became the primary executor of the Pope's active diplomacy.[6]

It is through this diplomacy, most of it conducted secretly, that we can best glimpse the role played by the Vatican and the Church in the development of modern political anti-Semitism. Most important are those countries where Catholics were the large majority, for it was there that the Church had most influence, and there that the mix of Catholicism and nationalism produced an explosion of anti-Semitism.

Italy itself did not share in these developments. In contrast to other countries having a large Catholic majority, Italy produced no politically significant anti-Semitic movement in these years. It was not that Italy had no nationalist movement in the last decades of the century. But while in other Catholic countries Catholicism formed one of the major pillars of nationalism—and in so doing excluded Jews from full membership in the nation—in Italy quite the opposite was true. The Italian state had been created only through the demolition of the Papal States, and was bitterly opposed by the Church. As a result, Italy lacked a nationalist movement committed to the belief that Jews were enemies of the fatherland.

The situation in the other two most important Catholic states in Europe—France and the Austro-Hungarian Empire—was very different. There the potent combination of a simmering anti-Semitic tradition, encouraged by the Church, and a nationalist movement that identified the nation with Catholicism produced a new form of anti-Semitic organization. In this chapter, we shall take a look at how this took shape in France, and then in the next chapter shall turn to Austria.

Jews were expelled from France in 1394. For the next four centuries only a handful of Jews lived there, apart from the Avignon area in the south, which came under papal rule and had ghettoes, and Alsace and Lorraine in the east, which were initially part of the Holy Roman Empire. When, in 1791, Jews were given full French citizenship, Paris had a mere five hundred Jews.

From the time of the Revolution, France was wracked by conflict between those identified with the old regime—most notably the clergy and aristocracy and their partisans—and those identified with the Revolution. The first two-thirds of the nineteenth century saw a struggle between these two forces, often in the form of a battle between monarchists and republicans. By the time Leo XIII became Pope, in 1878, the republicans had gained the upper hand and, although the monarchists did not yet realize it, the monarchy was dead.

While politically on the defensive, the French Church had a great advantage: a massive local network of parishes, priests, monks, and nuns. In the first year of Leo XIII's papacy, France could boast of not only 55,000 parish priests but another 33,000 monks, and more than 127,000 women in religious orders. This meant that there was roughly one Catholic priest, monk, or nun for every 170 inhabitants. There were also over two million students enrolled in Church-run elementary schools, almost as many as were attending public schools. Even the public schools were subject to the local parish priest's oversight; they began and ended each school day with a prayer. About half of the secondary school students attended Catholic schools, many run by the Jesuits, while each public secondary school had a priest named by the local bishop to help oversee it.

But the French Church faced a new threat during Leo XIII's first years as pope, for a new parliamentary majority had come to power, committed to limiting the Church's influence in public life. Concerned that the Catholic clergy were nurturing monarchist sympathies in the nation's children, the legislature passed a series of laws in 1880–1886 aimed at bringing the schools wholly under state control. These, along with other moves by the government to limit Church influence, antagonized the priesthood and provoked an aggressive Catholic defense movement.[7]

A minor incident in 1881 offers a sense of the conservative climate within the French Church. A prominent Dominican preacher announced that year that he would give his Lenten sermons on the theme "The reconciliation of the Church with modern society." Alarmed by word of the proposed topic, the archbishop of Paris told him to preach about something else: "Speak about the Virgin Mary," advised the archbishop, "that would be better."[8]

On the whole, however, the bishops of France were a cautious lot when it came to taking public stands opposing the government. This is not surprising since, in keeping with the Concordat that Napoleon had signed with the Vatican at the beginning of the century, the government itself appointed all the bishops in France.

By the last two decades of the nineteenth century, there were about 75,000 Jews in France, under two-tenths of one percent of the country's population. Over the course of the century they had emerged from their previously ghettoized existence, in which they had been largely confined to peddling their wares in the streets and dealing in used goods, and taken up posts in modern commerce. Enthusiastically embracing the state that had awarded them equal rights, they made their way into the civil service and even into the officer corps of the military. By mid-century Jews had already served as ministers of finance and of justice in the national government. They were especially prominent in large banking and high finance; by century's end over 20 percent of the owners of France's major financial institutions were Jews.[9]

In the cauldron of Catholic resentment toward the republican state in the 1880s, the Jews, visible in national politics, in the civil service, and in the economy, served as a lightning rod, a painful sign of all that was wrong with modern French society. Yet, given the cautious approach followed by the Church hierarchy, it was the lower clergy that played the leading role in the development of the modern French anti-Semitic movement. And among the priests involved, by far the most influential was the small religious order of the Assumptionist fathers.

The order was new, founded in France only a few decades earlier. In 1880 the Assumptionists began publishing a review, *La Croix* (The Cross), which they turned into a daily newspaper in 1883. The success of the paper was enormous, eventually reaching hundreds of thousands of readers, with 104 separate regional and local editions produced throughout the country.[10] It was particularly popular among the clergy, 25,000 of whom were reading it regularly by the end of the century.[11]

As the Assumptionists saw it, their journalistic efforts were undertaken on behalf of the Pope. Leo XIII had lamented the woeful influence of non-Catholic newspapers on public opinion and called for a press that would "courageously defend the sacred rights of the Church, the majesty of the Holy See and of the Roman Pontiff." In an 1882 article reporting this papal plea, the editors declared: "We are proud to have our own modest place in that glorious phalanx and we take what the Pope said as a lesson and as precious encouragement to continue the struggle by means of journalism."[12] When the paper became a daily the following year, the editor explained, "With our eye fixed on the Vatican, we want to be and to remain simply Catholic, apostolic, and Roman."[13]

La Croix was something quite new in Catholic journalism. No clerical paper had ever come close to matching its national distribution or broad readership. The previous paper with pride of place among Catholics in France, *L'Univers*, was a stodgy operation by comparison. In contrast to *L'Univers*, with its long columns of verbiage and sophisticated terminology, *La Croix* provided much livelier reading and used illustrations to brighten its pages. It also differed from other Catholic papers in getting involved more directly in mass politics. No theme more dominated these calls for public action in these years than the need to defend French society from the Jews.

A January 1882 article titled "Who governs France?," for example, posed a question: "Germany, it is said, is governed by the Jews. Will the French Republic also become the servant of the Jews—whether baptized or unbaptized—of the Stock Exchange?"[14] The following month, the head of the Assumptionist order, Father François Picard, wrote his own disquisition on the Jews. "To whom do the treasuries of Prussia, of Austria, of the German provinces belong? To the Jewish bankers of Frankfurt, Vienna, and Berlin." As the "influence of the synagogue rises, so too do the financial disasters that befall so many families . . . showing us the all-powerful Jew atop his golden throne and modern societies under the yoke of this gutless king." Father Picard continued, "What do the collapse of nations, the destruction of families, people's desperation, and the raft of suicides matter to him? The Jew . . . seeks financial monopoly. He stops at nothing to obtain it."

His catalogue of evils, typical of modern anti-Semitism and familiar to us from the Vatican press as well, continued: "Except for the rare exception of those newspapers founded and managed by true Christians, all the periodical press in the world belongs to the Jews." And as for patriotism: "The Jew is everywhere a Jew and nothing but a Jew. One might be able to cite some exceptions where the Jew's faith has weakened, but these exceptions remain exceptions. In Spain, the Jew is not Spanish, in Austria he is not Austrian, in Russia and Poland he is neither Russian nor Polish, nor here is he French."

Father Picard pursued more traditional Catholic themes as well: Under the popes, he declared, "Rome became a *Jew's Paradise*. Yet what thanks did they get? [The Jews] battled Rome everywhere and always."

Finally, the head of the Assumptionist order came to the question of anti-Semitism. We hear it said, he wrote, that "people's incessant, instinctive struggles against the Synagogue" are the product of popular superstition, and have no place in modern times. "But is this true? Do you believe it? Just ask the Russian, the Pole, the Romanian, the Vlachs; follow the anti-Semitic movement in Germany. See the hatred, the desire for vengeance that has gripped certain hearts, even in France! and only then respond."[15]

At the same time, Father Vincent Bailly, the director of *La Croix*, began his own campaign against the Jews. In an article ominously titled "The Enemy," he began with the traditional theme of the Jews as agents of Satan, the murderers of Jesus Christ. "THE JEW IS THE ENEMY!" proclaimed Father Bailly. Until the Messiah returns, he wrote, "the Jews will be Satan's preferred nation and his preferred instrument. Ever since their deicide, they have been his property." The Jews form, he declared, "the *Synagogue of Satan* . . . the Church of the devil."

These were all rather traditional Catholic charges against the Jews, but Father Bailly quickly moved on to the issues that shaped the modern anti-Semitic campaign, the identification of the Jews with capitalism on the one hand, and revolution on the other. As we have seen, some Jews, most notably the Rothschilds, were prominent and highly visible at the highest levels of international finance. In Germany, Jews ran between 40 and 50 percent of the banks, and Gerson Bleichröder, Bismarck's own personal banker, said to be the richest man in the country, was also a Jew. Jews owned many of the major daily newspapers in Germany and Austria, and Jews predominated among owners of the new large department stores, which were much resented by small shopkeepers. While in France, Jews were much less visible in the press, a number of the major bankers in France were Jewish as well.[16]

In their attempts to fan flames of resentment, Father Bailly, along with his colleagues at *La Croix*—and indeed, both Catholic and non-Catholic champions of the anti-Semitic movement generally—exaggerated the extent of Jewish influence. In Russia, Bailly reported, where anticzarist plots were spreading, the revolutionaries were, he claimed, all Jews. But if the Jews were the main force behind revolution they were also the masters of capitalism. "The Jew Freemason," he wrote, "governs the world. . . . In Prussia, of 642 bankers, 550 are Jews . . . and in Germany, in Austria and in some parts of the Orient the word INVASION is no exaggeration to express their number, their audacity, and their near-irresistible power." He then quoted a German newspaper: "The Jews' lust for riches is ten times greater than that of a Christian. The cry of the Christians who have been cleaned out by the Jews is universal. . . . The whole press is in the hands of the Jews." And so, Father Bailly repeated in conclusion: *"The Jew is the enemy!"*[17]

The identification of a Jewish conspiracy with Freemasonry became a common theme of the Catholic anti-Semitic campaign in France and elsewhere, and was later picked up by the Nazis in Germany. The first Freemason lodge had been founded in London in the early eighteenth century and by 1750 lodges spread through large parts of the Continent. The Church condemned Freemasonry virtually from the beginning. In 1738, Pope Clement XII issued a bull against the organization. He, along with his successors, viewed Freemasonry as a threat for its championing of humanistic principles that were at odds with the Catholic worldview. But the popes also felt threatened by an organization that seemed to offer an alternative to the Church itself as a center of social life, ritual, and the search for a higher meaning in life. Not least of the Freemasons' sins, in the eyes of the Vatican, was its mixing of Catholics and non-Catholics as members. The Pope threatened any Catholic who joined the Masons with excommunication. Yet until the nineteenth century, the issue of Jewish involvement in the Masons did not arise. Indeed, until the Revolution, Jews in France were forbidden from joining, and, elsewhere, not yet emancipated, Jews were in no position to join these clubs of the Christian elite.

But for Jews, who in the nineteenth century sought to be accepted by the wider society, membership in the Freemasons came to be prized. Yet acceptance was not easy. In Germany throughout the nineteenth century and into the twentieth most lodges would not allow Jews to join. As a result, in some cities, special Jewish lodges were established. The fact that at least some of the Masonic lodges allowed Jews in, permitting them to mix with high-status Christians, was viewed dimly by those who believed Jews should never have been given equal rights, and should be kept segregated from Christian society.

Given the secrecy that had always surrounded Masonry, it was a short step to view these lodges as centers for secret conspiracies. Any evidence of Jews in positions of responsibility in the Freemasons was taken as proof that it was Jews who ran the organization and that they had transformed the organization into a conspiracy against the Church. Symptomatic was the reaction by Henri Roger Gougenot des Mousseaux to the news that Adolphe Crémieux, the prominent Jewish politician and Alliance Israélite Universelle leader, had become head of the Masons' Scottish rite in France. Indeed, in his pioneering 1869 Catholic anti-Semitic work, *Le Juif, le judaïsme et la judaïsation des peuples chrétiens*, Gougenot devoted a chapter to Crémieux and the Jewish-Masonic conspiracy.

Yet, in fact the Masonic lodges were far from cells of revolutionary or any other kind of plotting, either in Germany or in France. People wanted to join mainly as a way of making social contacts, meeting intellectual needs, and providing satisfying social interaction. Governments were of course suspicious of any secret organization and often sought to place the Masons under their own control. In the Austrian Empire of the nineteenth century, the Freemasons were for the most part banned altogether. In France, following the upheavals of 1848, Emperor Napoleon III oversaw the Freemasons directly, personally choosing their leaders.[18]

Making frequent use of this charge of an evil Jewish-Masonic conspiracy, *La Croix*'s anti-Semitic campaign thundered on. The Russian pogroms of the early 1880s provided the opportunity to remind readers that good Catholics could not condone the murder of Jews. But, the paper quickly added, because the Jews sought "universal domination and stop at nothing to obtain their end," violence was inevitable. We should hardly be surprised, wrote the Assumptionist journalist, that the Russian peasants, "having been ruined, . . . have struck back *en masse* against the cursed race, the cause of all their problems." The article then turned to the latest news of ritual murders, and reproduced five large illustrations showing knife-wielding Jews butchering Christian children and draining them of their blood.[19]

Meanwhile, the regional editions of *La Croix*, which were largely autonomous from the parent publication, and ran many articles not found in La *Croix* itself, were following much the same line. Of these, *La Croix du Nord*, published as a daily since 1890, was one of the most influential. As in the case of its parent publication, all of its writers were priests. The most prominent article each day was the front-page editorial, with its oversized headline, viewed by many readers as offering the authoritative Church view on current issues. Examination of the editorials for the twenty-six months running from November 1897 to the end of the century reveal 178 editorials of an anti-Semitic stamp.[20] The themes are all familiar: the secret passion of the Jews for Christian children's blood revealed by the Moldavian "ex-rabbi"; Jews as the secret conspirators behind all of the subversive movements of modern times, from socialism to capitalism; the Jew as traitor. One column reported that France's 72,000 Jews, although outnumbered five hundred to one, owned a quarter of the nation's wealth. And while in theory, the priests wrote, conversion offered the Jew a way out of the devil's clutches, in practice it did not usually work out that way. As Monsignor Jaspar put it, "Never trust a Jew who becomes Christian."[21]

It would be hard to overestimate the influence of *La Croix du Nord* in northern France at the end of the nineteenth century. Its 25,000 daily copies—rising to twice that number for special issues—were read not only by virtually all the local priests but by much of the literate population. The huge attention devoted to the threat posed by the Jews came in a region of the country that contained hardly any Jews at all.[22]

By 1890, the parent newspaper, *La Croix*, was proudly billing itself as "the most anti-Jewish newspaper in France." The paper's trumpeting of its militant anti-Judaism reflected its aggressive style, lashing out at all those deemed to be enemies of French Christian society. Not the least of its targets was the French government, accused of selling the nation out to the Jews. It was here, however, that *La Croix*'s anti-Semitic campaign began to run into problems with the Vatican. The Pope in this period was trying to reduce tensions between the Church and French authorities, an effort not helped by *La Croix*'s strident antigovernment attacks. Over the course of the 1890s, the Pope grew increasingly concerned about the way the Assumptionists were antagonizing the government, and he and his secretary of state, Cardinal Rampolla, devoted a great deal of effort to trying to rein them in. But in all of the meetings and all of the correspondence dealing with *La Croix* involving the Pope, the secretary of state, and their nuncio in Paris, the paper's anti-Semitism never occasioned any complaint.

In 1892, the Pope notified the French bishops that the French Church should sever its ties to the monarchist cause. It should come to terms with the republican form of government and cooperate with the government in power.[23] The more conservative Catholics in France resented this directive, seeing it as a capitulation to a godless enemy. While the Assumptionists were not wedded to monarchism, and so had no problem on that count, making peace with the government was another matter.[24]

The Pope's growing concern about the political damage the Assumptionists were causing can be seen in the correspondence between the head of the Assumptionist order, Father Picard, and *La Croix*'s director in these years, Father Bailly. In March 1896, Picard wrote to Bailly to report on his recent private audience with the Pope. "The Pope," he wrote, "showed extreme kindness toward the Assumption order and its Superior. It is a confidence that touches me deeply. In a first audience, on Monday March 9, he deigned to spend two hours asking me about the various works of the Assumption, both in the Orient and in France." There then followed a second meeting, which Father Picard left feeling pleased by the Pope's expressions of appreciation for all he was doing.[25] Three years later, however, in September 1899, when Father Bailly met with the Pope, the situation had changed. In a letter to his superior, Father Bailly reported that the Pope was worried about the impact that the Church's identification with the anti-Dreyfus movement was having, not only on the French government, but also abroad. The Pope particularly stressed the bad impression that Church championing of the anti-Dreyfus cause was making in England. Leo XIII called on Father Bailly to tone down the polemics against the French government. "I love *La Croix*," the Pope said. "I need a press and I am depending on you."[26]

Reading the private correspondence between the papal nuncio in Paris and the secretary of state of the Vatican in these years, we know that each had much to lament about *La Croix*, which they viewed as a loose cannon when it came to getting the Church enmeshed in French politics. The paper, in their eyes, was provoking an anti-Church backlash and had to be restrained. The secretary of state made this position clear in a letter to the Paris nuncio at the end of August 1899. While the Assumptionists of *La Croix* intended to serve the cause of religion, the secretary of state declared, "too often the paper appears to want to direct the politics of that country and uses an aggressive language, especially against the people in government. This is not only rather dangerous because it increases hostility against the religious organizations and risks provoking reprisals against them. It is destined as well to be ineffective because, as is well known, the country is unfortunately not inclined to accept the influence of members of the religious orders in politics." As a result, Rampolla instructed, "the Holy Father asks that you take advantage of the next possible occasion to offer opportune and kindly words of warning to the directors of *La Croix*."[27]

Nowhere in the many laments about the paper in these years was there ever a word of criticism regarding the paper's relentless and shrill anti-Semitic campaign. What *La Croix* had to say about the Jews was, to Pope Leo XIII and his secretary of state, Cardinal Rampolla, nothing remarkable in the least. *La Croix*'s anti-Semitic screeds reflected not only the worldview of the Pope and his secretary of state, but that of their representative in Paris as well. In the midst of the Dreyfus affair, the papal nuncio, Archbishop Benedetto Lorenzelli, told a French diplomat: "The Jewish danger is universal, it threatens all of Christianity . . . and all means necessary should be used to crush it."[28]

Yet, according to those who distinguish between a Catholic anti-Judaism and a secular, modern anti-Semitism, it was not the priests of the Assumptionist order or other clerics who helped nourish the development of modern anti-Semitism in France. Rather, it was others, outside the orbit of the Church and indeed hostile to the Church. Proponents of this distinction point, in particular, to the fact that Edouard Drumont, France's most prominent anti-Semitic writer and organizer at the end of the nineteenth century, was on poor terms with the Church hierarchy.

Drumont, a journalist, rocketed to fame in 1886 with the publication of *Jewish France (La France juive),* an anti-Semitic tract that became a bestseller and went through two hundred printings over the next three decades. The book has been termed the most influential anti-Semitic work published in nineteenth-century Europe, and the first to introduce racial anti-Semitism in France.[29]

Drumont saw himself as a good Catholic whose writings against the Jews flowed directly from his commitment to defending the Church and Christian society. His book *Jewish France* relied heavily on earlier Catholic authors, including Father Oreglia of *Civiltà cattolica,* and was only published after Drumont had a priest check the text to be sure that it contained no theological errors.[30] His themes—ritual murder, the Jewish lust for money, their immorality and hatred for Christians, their penchant for betrayal, their lack of national allegiance—were largely drawn from Catholic sources. Moreover, the response of the Catholic press to the book was overwhelmingly enthusiastic. Typical was the *Revue du Monde Catholique,* which praised Drumont for defending the Church against the Jews, who were termed "insatiable vampires." The journal concluded: "Monsieur Drumont's devoted wish to serve, and the virtue of his having served the cause of Christ, cannot be denied."[31]

L'Univers, the oldest and most respected Catholic paper in France, and the one with the closest ties to the Vatican, published its own rave review of *Jewish France.* Drumont, the priest who authored the article enthused, had the courage to tell the truth. "We French Christians are all, in effect, vanquished, conquered, expropriated from our own country and our own faith, by a race of cosmopolites, of cunning intelligence, of greedy soul. . . . The Jew is master of all."[32]

A study of the diocesan bulletins published throughout France in this period shows that they too were filled with praises for Drumont and his book.[33] Indeed, he was quoted regularly and approvingly by Church publications from *Civiltà cattolica* to *La Croix.* At the turn of the century, Drumont's daily newspaper, *La Libre Parole,* had among its subscribers as many as 30,000 priests, an enormous proportion of the French clergy. When, in 1895, the newspaper ran a contest for the best essay on how to deal with the Jewish threat, priests took both top prizes.[34]

If Drumont made enemies in the upper reaches of the Church, it was not because of his anti-Semitic sentiments, but rather because he showed little respect for the hierarchy. He repeatedly lashed out against bishops who, he charged, were too accommodating to the authorities. And in leveling such accusations, his most potent weapon was to claim that such churchmen were in the pay of the Jews.

Drumont's 1891 book, *An Anti-Semite's Legacy,* offers a good example. "The murder of Christian children by Jews," he wrote, "is a fact as clear as day." There was no doubt, he added, where the Church stood on the question. After meticulous Vatican investigations, he reported, various child martyrs had been proclaimed saints, based on their documented death at the hands of the Jews.

Earlier in the year, recalled Drumont, Father Henri Desportes, from Rouen, had published an important book on the subject of Jewish ritual murder, titled *Killed by the Jews.* But the Jews had an ally in the local archbishop of Rouen, Monseigneur Thomas. The archbishop, giving "new proof of a servility that knows no bounds," had told Father Desportes to either retract the book or leave the seminary. According to Drumont— whose account was based on Desportes'—the archbishop added: "The Jews are a most unpleasant people, but they are terribly powerful, and I don't want to provoke them." Desportes, however, refused to retract and left the seminary. Fortunately, wrote Drumont, "the bishop of Amiens did his duty and took Father Desportes in." It was another illustration of how much the Jews' power had grown, for the prefect of Rouen was a Jew, and the sycophantic archbishop was afraid to anger him. The world, concluded Drumont, had been treated to "the spectacle of a prince of the Church persecuting a young priest to satisfy the hatred of a Jew prefect."[35]

An Anti-Semite's Legacy not only lashed out at those French bishops judged to curry favor with the Jews but also had harsh words for the papal nuncio in France, who was skewered for acting more from political expediency than from commitment to the Church's teachings. This attack enraged the nuncio, who sent a copy of the book to the secretary of state. "I believe it my duty," wrote the nuncio in his cover letter, "to send you the new volume published by M. Edouard Drumont." The book, he wrote, was "disquieting, scandalous, defamatory and gravely offensive toward the Church, the Holy Father and the French Episcopate in general." Moreover, he added, it was libelous in its attack on the nuncio himself.[36]

The secretary of state interpreted the nuncio's letter as a request to have the book put on the Index so that Catholics could not read it. He replied diplomatically: "I do not have to tell you what a repugnant impression that even the few passages that you cited of such a monstrous libel made on the Holy Father. It would certainly merit condemning this work to the Index." However, Cardinal Rampolla added, two thoughts had occurred to him: Putting the book on the Index might simply give it greater notoriety and more attention. Secondly, "considering the nature of the author, a condemnation to the Index might easily induce him to publish a work that was even worse."

In his reply, the nuncio told the secretary of state that he recognized the wisdom of his advice. In none of this correspondence did the vilification of the Jews, which lay at the heart of Drumont's book, ever attract comment.[37]

Through the rest of the decade, while the Pope held Drumont at arm's length, his anti-Semitic writings were widely and enthusiastically cited in the Catholic press, including the papers and journals closest to the Vatican. That, from the Vatican viewpoint, the problem with Drumont was not his virulent anti-Semitism is clear from the way that *L'Osservatore romano* chose to attack him in 1892. Far from taking issue with his demonization of the Jews, the paper sought to discredit him by claiming that he was himself in the Jews' pocket. In the same article in which the Vatican newspaper had distinguished between the "true" anti-Semitism, which was Christian, and the illusory form of anti-Semitism, which actually benefited the Jews, Drumont was accused of belonging to the latter category. "To prevent Drumont or others from being able to produce a truly and effectively anti-Jewish newspaper, Jewish gold has intervened to have Drumont's pen and his newspaper in its exclusive power."[38]

Drumont's peculiar role in the development of Catholic anti-Semitism, and particularly in the transformation of a movement of opinion into one of political action, was on display in a six-day national Christian Democratic conference held in Lyon in 1896. The Christian Democratic movement was new then, an attempt by forces in the Church to build mass support by appealing to issues of economic justice. By trying to sever the Church's identification with the aristocracy and the rich, it sought to counteract the growing appeal of the socialist movement. In the French case, this meant embracing the republican form of government and cutting ties with monarchism.

The larger congress consisted of four separate parts, each itself termed a "congress." One was devoted to anti-Semitism, one to the struggle against Freemasonry, one to the building of a social Catholic movement, and one to the question of Catholicism and republicanism. The printed program of the congress began with a tribute to His Holiness Leo XIII, followed by a passage from Leo XIII's recent address to the French faithful. "All the children of the French homeland," the Pope's words read, "must unite in justice, mutual respect, and fraternal charity . . . to struggle together against the dangers that threaten them."

The first full day was devoted to the "anti-Semitic congress," with none other than Edouard Drumont presiding. It had two major sections. First came a discussion of principle. As described in the program, this addressed "the Jews' predominance and its danger for morals (pornography, divorce, usury, legalized theft)," public opinion (Jewish control of virtually the entire press), government ("infiltration of the Jewish element in teaching, administration . . ."), business (Jewish control of the economy, the banks), and national security ("the contradiction between the international essence of the Jew and the idea of the Homeland; the anti-patriotic role of the Jews today").

The afternoon session turned to the task of developing "practical means of defense." It called for improved distribution of newspapers and inexpensive pamphlets that told of "the Jewish peril." Jewish stores and businesses were to be boycotted, anti-Semitic leagues were to be organized, and electoral committees, dedicated to "anti-Semitic resistance," formed. Among the many official sponsors of the congress were the directors of the two most important Catholic newspapers in France, Father Bailly of *La Croix*, and Eugène Veuillot of *L'Univers*.[39]

For the benefit of those who could not attend the anti-Semitic congress, *La Croix* provided detailed coverage. If the priests of the Assumptionist order had any quarrel with Drumont, it was not evident from the adulatory tone adopted in their reporting. In his address to the 1,800 people in attendance, reported *La Croix*, Drumont proclaimed, "This Congress will mark a historic date in the history of anti-Semitism, because for the first time questions of practical organization have been addressed." At the gala dinner, *La Croix* recounted, the local host "welcomed the unchallenged head of anti-Semitism, who in turn toasted the valiant anti-Semites of Lyon."

At the end of the day, the congress passed a series of motions by acclamation. The 1791 decree that had emancipated the Jews and given them French citizenship should be revoked. Jews should be excluded from teaching in public schools, from the judiciary, from the public administration, and from the ranks of the military officer corps. *La Croix*'s account ended pithily: *"Mauvaise journée pour les juifs"* ("A bad day for the Jews").[40]

Three days later *La Croix* reported on the congress's concluding banquet. The evening began with a priest ascending the podium to read a letter sent on the congress's behalf to the Pope, "assuring him of the loyal obedience of those attending the congress to his political and social teachings."

The following morning, when Drumont arrived at the Lyon train station for his departure, he was met by a large and boisterous crowd. He was warmed by their shouts: "Vive la France! Down with the Jews!"[41]

Prior to the congress a request had been sent to the Vatican prelate responsible for relations with the French Church, asking that the Pope send a special benediction to bless the congress. Cardinal Rampolla took the matter up with the Pope. It presented a delicate question, since the Catholics meeting at Lyon were declaring their loyalty to the Pope and, in particular, were acceding to his request that French Catholics pledge loyalty to the republican government. But, to appear to give Drumont a papal blessing would be a slap in the face to the Pope's own nuncio and to the many bishops in France against whom the journalist had wielded his rapacious pen.

The secretary of state informed the French prelate of the Pope's decision. The Pope would send his benediction to the congress, but only if the text of the congress's formal request for a papal blessing were worked out in advance. Most important, Drumont could not be one of the signatories of the request, and the day devoted to anti-Semitism, which he chaired, could not be specifically blessed. As the prelate wrote to his contact in Lyon: "The anti-Semitic Congress must absolutely remain outside this Benediction. And this, because entirely aside from the question of individuals [i.e., Drumont], the Holy See has the policy of everywhere keeping its distance from this campaign."[42]

Shortly after the Lyon Christian Democratic congress, an unprecedented wave of anti-Semitic agitation began to sweep over France, linked to the notorious Dreyfus affair. The case had begun in October 1894, when a thirty-nine-year-old Jewish artillery captain, Alfred Dreyfus, was accused of selling military secrets to the Germans. Despite the captain's heated denials, he was court-martialed, convicted, and in April 1895 sent to the notorious Devil's Island prison, off the coast of French Guyana.[43]

At first, the incident was merely an embarrassment for the Jews of France, who had been led to believe that the evidence against the captain was overwhelming. While Drumont's paper, as well as *La Croix* and the rest of the Catholic press, trumpeted news of Dreyfus's guilt with relish, there was initially little public interest in the case.

A year later, the new head of French counterintelligence, Major Georges Picquart, happened to discover a letter in the wastebasket of a German military attaché. It was addressed to a major in the French army, Marie Charles Count Esterhazy. When Picquart then began an inquiry, he discovered that the handwriting on the document that had been used to convict Dreyfus and was supposed to be that of the Jewish captain was identical to Esterhazy's. He also learned that Esterhazy had been deeply in debt and in desperate need of money. But when news of Picquart's probe became known, the French military authorities did all they could to thwart it, and enlisted Esterhazy's help in forging new documents to provide further evidence of Dreyfus's guilt.

By the end of 1897, claims by Dreyfus partisans that the captain had been framed were threatening the government and, at the same time, producing a powerful weapon for the burgeoning anti-Semitic movement. The Catholic press played a large role in fanning the flames. Typical were the comments of *Civiltà cattolica*. "The Jews have invented the allegation of judicial error. . . . The real error was that of the Constituent Assembly which granted them French nationality. That law must be repealed."[44]

The Dreyfus case served an important role for the French Church, at least initially. Divided between monarchists and republicans, and disoriented by the Pope's request that they make peace with the government, French Catholics could express their solidarity by rallying together against the Jews.[45] In 1895 the General Assembly of the Catholics of the North called for a boycott of all Jewish businesses; in 1898 the Catholic National Congress, held in Paris, approved a similar proposal.[46] Earlier that year, local Catholic organizations of all kinds helped lead the anti-Semitic riots that were then sweeping through France, chanting "Death to Dreyfus! Death to the Jews!" Indeed, in the first two months of the year sixty-nine anti-Semitic riots erupted in France. Mobs destroyed Jewish shops, attacked synagogues, and set upon hapless individual Jews they came across.[47]

In early December 1897, through its daily newspaper *L'Osservatore romano,* the Vatican itself made known its view that if Dreyfus had betrayed his country, it should be no surprise, for he was a Jew. "The Jewish race," the Vatican paper explained, "the deicide people, wandering throughout the world, brings with it everywhere the pestiferous breath of treason." It continued: "And so too in the Dreyfus case . . . it is hardly surprising if we again find the Jew in the front ranks, or if we find that the betrayal of one's country has been Jewishly conspired and Jewishly executed."[48]

The Vatican paper had words of praise for the anti-Semitic demonstrations that were spreading throughout France. "The agitation that is now developing from one end of France to the other as a result of the truly detestable provocations of Judaism . . . attempting to rehabilitate a traitor . . . of the French nation, has neither the look nor the nature of those popular disorders motivated only by sentiments of disorder. . . . These demonstrations are becoming ever more anti-Semitic, as the term is now used, but they are not anti-Semitic out of any hatred for the Jewish people or things Jewish, but rather out of a natural weariness of Jewish oppression. . . . The anti-Semitism that is developing today—in Russia, in Germany, and in France—expresses a real concept and reflects a concrete fact." Anti-Semitism, the *Osservatore romano* article noted, was growing rapidly "among the masses who are being excessively oppressed by the Judaic spirit, a spirit which is the opposite of the Christian spirit."[49]

When, in 1899, a retrial was ordered and the Jewish captain was brought back to French soil, *L'Unità cattolica* reported that the "colossus of Jewry" was taking over France, using its gold to buy an acquittal for the traitor. "Israel won a victory today: Israel is the victor and France the vanquished."[50]

Pope Leo XIII, however, was growing increasingly concerned about the vehemence and antigovernment tone of the anti-Dreyfus movement. By the time of the retrial, in the summer of 1899, this attitude began to be reflected in the pages of *L'Osservatore romano,* and the tenor of its daily reports on the Dreyfus trial changed dramatically.

On September 9, the French military court reached its decision: Again Captain Dreyfus was found guilty, but this time some of the judges voted not guilty, and the sentence was reduced to ten years. A few days later, *L'Osservatore romano* ran a story titled "The oppressors of the Jews." It began by quoting Pope Innocent III, who, centuries earlier, had proclaimed, "Jews are the living witnesses of the true faith. The Christian is not permitted to exterminate the Jewish race." The popes, the article continued, had always adopted an attitude of "charity, tolerance, and love toward the Jews." It went on to note that it had not been the popes, but rather the high priest of Protestantism, Martin Luther, who had called for consigning all synagogues to the flames. "This little review, it seems to us," concluded the Vatican paper, "should suffice for the edification of those, Semites or not, who are going around saying that Dreyfus is a victim of the Catholics and the Jesuits!"[51]

Three days later, on September 19, 1899, Alfred Dreyfus was freed, pardoned by the French president. Within a few weeks the Vatican daily shifted its attention from the Jews of France to those of Hungary. In a small town there, *L'Osservatore romano* reported, the cadaver of a little boy had been discovered, his blood drained by the Jews. A story later that month, titled "Judaic ritual murder," beginning with a quote from Drumont's newspaper, *La Libre Parole,* returned once more to the theme.[52]

CHAPTER NINE

Austria

A T A T I M E when the French Church risked losing many of its privileges at the hands of an unfriendly government, Leo XIII sought to eliminate unnecessary sore points. He wanted to convince the civil authorities that the Church posed no threat to the republican state. Given the government's view of the Catholic anti-Semitic movement as a threat both to public order and to its own principles, the Vatican was torn between its own negative view of the Jews and the desire to appease the leaders of the secular state.

The situation in Austria was different, and there the Vatican pursued a different strategy, encouraging the growth of a Catholic political movement. Such a movement was needed, the Pope and his secretary of state believed, to confront a variety of hostile forces that threatened the Church's position in Austria. In fostering such a force, Vatican leaders saw in anti-Semitism a powerful tool for mobilizing the Catholic masses.

Modern Austrian anti-Semitism can be traced to the 1848 revolution, when a Catholic priest, Sebastian Brunner, began publishing a newspaper, *The Vienna Journal of the Church*. Obsessed with the Jewish threat to society, Father Brunner blamed the Jews for the de-Christianization of Austria. Over the following decades a broader conservative Catholic political movement began to take shape. Anti-Semitism figured among its central tenets, alongside the battle against liberalism and capitalism.[1]

Until the 1848 revolution, Jews were forbidden by law to live in Vienna, and only a small number of wealthy Jewish merchants were given special authorization to reside in the city. This was despite the fact that the Austrian chancellor in these years, Prince Metternich, was so close to the Rothschild family, and the Austrian government depended on the Jewish bankers' loans. In fact, although the Rothschilds were making a fortune in Vienna, as Jews they were not allowed to buy homes or land there. Following 1848, an increasing number of Jews from the Austrian provinces began to pour into the city. By 1880 Vienna had 73,000 Jews, rising to almost 150,000 by the turn of the century. Expanding rapidly, the Vienna population grew to over 2,000,000 by 1910, and 10 percent of them were Jews.[2]

Not all of the pioneers of Austrian anti-Semitism were close to the Catholic Church. Georg von Schönerer, one of the most important early leaders of the movement, was indeed notoriously hostile to the Church. A radical German nationalist, he began organizing an anti-Semitic movement around 1880. Taking advantage of widespread hostility to the Jews among Vienna's artisans, he espoused an antiliberal nationalism, taking aim along the way at both socialism and Catholicism. Elected to the parliament, he showed no qualms about injecting into its previously genteel proceedings a steady stream of denunciations of the Jews of finance, the railway Jews, the Jew peddlers, the Jews who controlled the press, the Jew swindlers, and the like. Despite his best efforts, though, his own brand of pro-German, nationalist, nonreligious anti-Semitism did not prove successful in attracting mass political party support.[3]

It was another leader, and another organization, that ignited a powerful, mass anti-Semitic political movement in Austria: the Christian Socialist Organization, founded in Vienna in 1887. The early organizers of the movement, committed to social reform inspired by Christian principles, discovered that nothing could more easily generate popular enthusiasm for their cause than attacks on the Jews. The movement found its charismatic leader in Karl Lueger, who, although having little personal animus toward the Jews, found attacks on them to be politically irresistible.[4]

When the first program of the United Christians, as the party was then known, appeared, it called for the exclusion of the Jews from the army, the civil service, the judiciary, retail trade, medicine, and the teaching of non-Jewish students. Lueger had been elected to the Vienna city council in 1875, and ten years later was elected to the parliament. There he met Louis Prince Liechtenstein, and together they became the leading forces of the Christian Social movement, forming the Christian Social party in 1891. The party preached social reform and identified the Jews as the enemy. Although Lueger enjoyed the Austrian clergy's enthusiastic support—on his fiftieth birthday in 1894, he was presented with a greeting signed by five hundred priests of the capital—the Austrian Church hierarchy viewed him with suspicion. They regarded him as a dangerous populist, suspected of harboring socialist sympathies.

Despite the Austrian Church hierarchy's qualms, Pope Leo XIII and his secretary of state, Cardinal Rampolla, supported the Christian Social movement enthusiastically, for they saw the party as an excellent way of rallying the Catholic faithful. The goal was to create a politically effective force to stem the rising tide of secularism. The need for the party was particularly pressing in light of the expansion of suffrage in Austria in the 1880s, for some way had to be found to win the political support of the masses.

The Pope's own sentiments about the Jews can be glimpsed from an odd case in 1889 involving his nuncio in Vienna, Luigi Galimberti. The episode is revealing in another way as well, for it shows the differences of opinion within the Church hierarchy about how to deal with the Jews.

On the death of the previous secretary of state two years earlier, many thought that Galimberti himself would win the post. As secretary of the Congregation of Extraordinary Ecclesiastical Affairs, he seemed well positioned. But conservatives in the hierarchy attacked him as too liberal. He was known both for favoring a rapprochement between the Vatican and the Italian state, and for his willingness to cooperate with the Protestants in Prussia. As a result he was passed over in favor of Mariano Rampolla, whose conservative credentials were impeccable, and, in the spring of 1887, was sent instead to Vienna to serve as nuncio.[5]

One day in 1889, an Austrian bishop came to see Galimberti, bringing with him a prominent Jewish landowner who, he told the nuncio, had made generous contributions to Catholic charities. Monsignor Galimberti praised the man for his generosity and good character. When news of the encounter was leaked to the papers, three Austrian bishops sent protests to the Pope, denouncing Galimberti for having publicly praised a Jew; they asked that disciplinary action be taken against him.

The Pope called on the nuncio to explain himself. In defending his behavior, Galimberti tried to convince the Pope that he shared the pontiff's dim view of the Jews. It had only been a private conversation, he explained, and the Viennese paper that reported what he had said—owned, he added, by the Jews—had, "with Judaic bad faith," completely altered the meaning of his remarks.

Monsignor Galimberti could point to his record to show that he had always hewn to the papal line. When, a few months earlier, he had reported the results of the recent Viennese municipal elections to the secretary of state, he had rejoiced in the "triumph of the Catholics . . . against the Judaic candidates," and delighted in the fact that "over thirty anti-Semitic councilors have entered City Hall." The result, he had written, showed "a strong shift in public opinion and a return to Christian principles of civil order."

Yet despite his anguished denial of wrongdoing, the reply he received from his rival, the secretary of state, offered less than a full exoneration. "What Monsignor Nuncio wrote in his letter of September 5 regarding the conversation with a Jewish gentleman . . . goes far to reduce the gravity of the fact, and to clarify the bad faith of those interested in exaggerating and misrepresenting the affair. However, this in itself shows all the more the necessity of taking care in choosing one's words and regulating one's conduct in every meeting in such a way as not to offer the least pretext for attacks by one's enemies." The secretary of state then got to the heart of his concern: "The Masonic sect's close ties to the Judaic sect to the detriment of the Catholic Church are all too well known. In view of this it would be more prudent for the representative of the Holy See to abstain from pronouncing such words of praise." What most concerned the Vatican was that the nuncio had inadvertently provided ammunition to the Jewish press. The Jews were trying to weaken the anti-Semitic movement in Austria by offering any evidence they could to prove that hatred of the Jews went contrary to Vatican teachings.[6]

The Vatican Secret Archives offer dramatic evidence of the active role played by the Pope and his secretary of state in nurturing the Christian Social party's anti-Semitic campaign. Most striking of all is evidence that they undermined efforts by the Austrian Church hierarchy to distance the Church from Lueger and his movement.

Such was the case when, in 1891, the archbishop of Vienna himself tried to take action against the Christian Social party, possibly with the encouragement of the nuncio, Monsignor Galimberti. Lueger, confident in having papal support, went over the archbishop's head, and sought the Pope's help in getting the archbishop to back off.

We get a glimpse of this in correspondence between Rampolla and Galimberti. On March 31, 1891, the Vatican secretary of state wrote a confidential letter to Monsignor Galimberti. "Complaints have been lodged," he informed the nuncio, "against the archbishop." Vienna's archbishop was accused, among other things, of "having forbidden three able priests who were feared by the liberals from entering parliament." Furthermore, Cardinal Rampolla wrote, it had been reported to him that Karl Lueger, "head of the Catholic party, had openly said that the Catholics have been hoodwinked by the choice of the archbishop, as he is in fact a liberal." The secretary of state ended his letter with a request: "Please brief me on the truth of these accusations and inform me of your view of their importance."[7]

The nuncio's lengthy reply, written just a few days later, is a remarkable document. It was a valiant attempt to prevent the Church's embrace of modern political anti-Semitism, yet one that failed, overruled by the Pope and his secretary of state. At the same time, the letter shows that even in the most sympathetic regions of the Vatican, certain negative views of the Jews had to be embraced if one were to maintain any credibility at all.

Galimberti's report, marked "confidential," is titled "On some accusations against Monsignor Gruscha," dated Vienna, April 6, 1891. "It is neither easy nor pleasant," he begins, "to offer a judgment on the attacks directed against the Monsignor Archbishop contained in Your Reverend Eminence's dispatch." The charges, wrote the nuncio, "can be summarized in the accusation [that he] opposed anti-Semitism and favored the liberals in the recent political elections." And so, he continued, "we must first of all determine the meaning of these two words. Let me then highlight what *anti-Semitism* and *liberalism* mean in Austria and especially in Vienna."

"The word *anti-Semitism*," Galimberti explained, "could only erroneously be taken as a synonym for Catholicism or clericalism." The anti-Semitism of Lueger and his chief aristocratic backer, Prince Louis of Liechtenstein, he argued, were based not on religion but rather on political and social theories. "Indeed many belong to the anti-Semitic party who are perfectly indifferent in religious matters, being non-practicing or *worse*. Thus the anti-Semites make no efforts in the religious field to encourage the *conversion* of the Jews, who amount to more than a hundred thousand." Yet, among the wealthy Jews, he reported, conversions were far from infrequent and would be even more frequent if the Catholics began channeling their efforts in that direction.

As for the anti-Semitic action underway in the political and social arena, wrote Galimberti, "the legal battle seeks to exclude the Jews' influence from public administration, from Parliament, and from municipal government. Such struggle is certainly praiseworthy and healthy. But unfortunately this struggle has degenerated into race hatred and has taken on a personal character, becoming transformed into social warfare or, as they say, into Christian socialism."

The nuncio here recalled a recent conversation that he had had with Baron Rothschild at a diplomatic reception.[8] "They will end up slitting our throats," Rothschild had said. The nuncio also noted that, "In their last collective pastoral letter, the bishops of Austria condemned race hatred, which people are seeking to foster with anti-Semitism."

Galimberti went on, with unusual courage, to correct Cardinal Rampolla's characterization of Lueger as the head of the "Catholic" party. "Lueger is in fact not the Head of the Catholic party, but of the anti-Semitic party in the sense explained above." For the nuncio, Lueger was a dangerous demagogue, "a socialist agitator of the masses." The first time that he had ever seen Lueger and heard him speak, the nuncio recounted, "Charles V's words when he first encountered Luther came to my mind: 'This monk will never succeed in convincing me.' "

In an effort to show that his defense of the archbishop did not flow from any love for the Jews, Galimberti turned to a familiar argument. Lueger "was initially in the pay of the Jews . . . he then belonged to the liberal camp, and now he is at the head of the anti-Semitic movement." Recall the date here—April 1891—for this was at the height of the polemics over Drumont's *An Anti-Semite's Legacy,* and the same time as the Vatican attack on Drumont in *L'Osservatore romano.* Indeed, the Vienna nuncio made the comparison between Lueger and Drumont directly: "Like Drumont, today he violently attacks the Jews, tomorrow he might attack the Pope, the cardinals, and the bishops, as he has already begun to do in lashing out at this archbishop."

As he neared his conclusions, Galimberti's language grew increasingly heated, bordering on criticism of the secretary of state, something that papal nuncios rarely dared. After what he had explained, wrote the nuncio, "one will easily understand that the archbishop of Vienna cannot be an acolyte of Mr. Lueger, nor an anti-Semite in the hateful personal and socialist sense of the word." He then returned to the charge that the archbishop was discouraging priests from participating in Lueger's movement. "Nor can the archbishop permit priests to spend the evening running around from tavern to tavern," he wrote, "from beer-hall to beer-hall, inflaming popular passions and stirring up hatred against a whole category of people." As for the charge that the archbishop was a liberal, this was "mere calumny denied by everything in his life, past and present."⁹

Over the next decade, as the Christian Social party took off under Lueger's charismatic leadership, Church backing for the aggressively anti-Semitic movement continued to be contested both by members of the Austrian Church hierarchy and by elements of the Austrian political elite and aristocracy. Yet time and again, the Pope and his secretary of state did everything they could to defend the movement. In this effort, they were aided by the appointment of a more cooperative nuncio in the spring of 1893. Monsignor Antonio Agliardi had risen through the ranks of the Church, from parish priest to professor of theology in Rome. He had attracted the favorable attention of Pius IX for his uncompromising conservatism and since 1885 been given a series of posts in the Secretariat of State. In the three years he served as papal nuncio to Vienna, he often met with Karl Lueger, and was an enthusiastic backer of Lueger and his Christian Social party.¹⁰

In early 1895, amid the Christian Social party's increasingly frequent and often rowdy anti-Semitic rallies, pressure on the Pope to condemn the movement mounted. The archbishops of Vienna and Prague prepared a joint plea to the Pope, members of the Austrian aristocracy made their protests heard, and the liberal press in Europe berated the Vatican for allowing the Church to be used for such purposes.

In January 1895, the archbishop of Prague traveled to the Vatican to present his plea to the Pope. Neither he nor the archbishop of Vienna was happy about the Christian Social party's championing of a radical form of anti-Semitism. But this was not their only complaint. They were also displeased to see Vatican backing for a movement that, as they saw it, embraced a socialist program, encouraged priests to buck the authority of their bishops, and fought against the conservative Catholics who supported the government.¹¹

Leo XIII assured the archbishop that he would have the matter investigated, and referred it to the cardinals of the Congregation for Extraordinary Ecclesiastical Affairs, under the authority of the secretary of state, Cardinal Rampolla. Leaders of the Christian Social party were contacted and called upon to offer evidence in their own defense. The task fell to the party's intellectual leader and theologian, Monsignor Franz Schindler, who replied that his movement had nothing to do with "that radical anti-

Semitism which is directed against the Judaic race as such." Schindler himself came to Rome to defend the movement, and met with the Pope, who received him warmly. Indeed, Leo XIII gave Schindler a letter to take back to Karl Lueger, in which the Pope expressed his strong sympathy for what the Christian Social party was doing, and added his personal blessings for Lueger himself.[12]

In discussing the matter in the Congregation, the master general of the Dominican order, Andreas Cardinal Frühwirth, agreed with the secretary of state that a Jewish problem existed in Vienna. There were indeed many Jews there and they had all too much influence politically and, especially, economically. But, he argued, the Church should deplore the extremism and racist nature of the Christian Social party's anti-Semitic program. The cardinal concluded by suggesting that a stern warning be sent to the heads of the party, urging them to tone down their campaign against the Jews.

The Dominican's advice did not prevail. Under the direction of the secretary of state, the Congregation concluded its investigation by finding that the Christian Social party was in fact not anti-Semitic at all. "Such an accusation," the Congregation ruled, "was found to be baseless, and does not appear to be anything other than a device used by their adversaries to discredit them." The Christian Social program makes clear, the Vatican body continued, that the party "does not hate the Jews as such, but only combats the economic system that oppresses the people, a system to which the Jews have dedicated themselves all too much."[13]

Following these deliberations, the Pope, acting through Rampolla, sent his instructions to the papal nuncio in Vienna. It contained no complaint of any kind about the Christian Social party's anti-Semitism. Instead, Agliardi was told to ask the heads of the party to publicly affirm their devotion to the Holy See, their submission to the bishops in religious matters, their loyalty to the Habsburg throne, and their rejection of the subversive theories of socialism.

As a result, on May 16, 1895, a rather strange ceremony took place. In the largest, most beautiful hall in Vienna, with the papal nuncio present, the heads of the Christian Social party pledged their allegiance to the Pope, to Church doctrine, and to the Church hierarchy in Austria. Confident of the Pope's implicit yet clear blessings for their anti-Semitic campaign, Karl Lueger, Prince Liechtenstein, and the other party leaders who spoke that day denounced the Jews as threats to Austrian society. The

Jews, they railed, were parasites who had to be driven out of Austria. The nuncio looked on with evident pleasure.[14]

A few days later, Agliardi wrote Rampolla to report the latest news on the Vienna city council. "The Catholics' sentiments," he wrote, "are naturally against the liberals who have governed up to now—much to the detriment of the Church—and in favor of the Christian Social party who offer better hope." The battle, wrote the nuncio, was a difficult one, for the Social Christians not only had to overcome the press, which was solidly in the liberal camp, but also defeat "the influence and the money of the Jews."[15]

A few months later, just eleven days after becoming the new Austrian prime minister, Count Casimir Badeni paid the nuncio a visit. Badeni, a favorite of Emperor Francis Joseph, was from an aristocratic Galician family. He had come to convince the nuncio to put an end to Vatican support for the Christian Social party. We have the nuncio's account of the meeting, which he sent Rampolla the following day.

The Christian Social party's goal of bringing about a more Christian society, said the count, was all well and good. But, he added, its methods were reprehensible and its leaders were men who inspired little faith. "In speaking of the means [used by the party]," the nuncio reported, "he told me various things that they had said about the Jews in their speeches."

Naturally, reported Monsignor Agliardi, "I praised the Count highly for having appreciated from the beginning the true objectives of the Christian Social party—which are truly good and aimed at Christianity's victory over pagan ideas—and I praised him for having recognized that religious and moral improvements have occurred in Vienna." Indeed, the nuncio had told the count, "the nuns in the convents have, with their prayers, cooperated in [the Christian Social party's] recent splendid victory."

As for the prime minister's criticism of the methods used by the party, Agliardi was less sympathetic. "I told Count Badeni," the nuncio recounted, "that I was the first to deplore any excessive statements (if any were indeed pronounced) by some of the heads or members of the party, because even in the holiest battles the Church wants the laws of justice and charity to be observed." As for the label of "anti-Semites," the nuncio told the count, "I confess that it does not please me either."[16]

The political situation in Vienna was growing tense. The Christian Social party had gained a large majority in the Vienna municipal council in 1895 and proposed Karl Lueger as mayor. On Badeni's advice, the emperor refused to confirm the appointment. In late November, the nuncio informed Cardinal Rampolla of the most recent developments. The veto had produced a split in the conservative party. Baron De Paoli and a group of other parliamentary deputies had founded the Catholic Popular party. Behind their move, according to the nuncio, was "the need to have a freer hand in defending the Church against all the acts of aggression aimed against it."

Agliardi was quick to reassure the secretary of state that the new party was not opposed to the Christian Social party. "On the contrary," he wrote, the new party was "its friend and will follow a parallel path." The men's decision to form the Catholic Popular party rather than join Lueger's party was, the nuncio explained, a matter of tactics. The baron did not want to unnecessarily irritate the Court, whose opposition to Lueger and his movement was well known. Moreover, "with a program in which anti-Semitism is not mentioned," the baron sought "to attract the sympathy of those bishops who, in the current situation, fear being seen to be too much in favor of Prince Liechtenstein and Lueger."

The nuncio concluded that "the greatest utility for us" in these new developments was the weakening of the "liberal Judaic party, which still predominates in Parliament." With the "revival of Catholic life, in future elections it cannot count on having, as before, an undisputed victory." Agliardi's letter makes the Vatican's view of the Austrian political situation clear. On the one hand were the liberals, committed to a secular state and in the pay of the Jews; on the other were the champions of the Church, Karl Lueger most prominent among them.[17]

Far from representing a departure from the Vatican's views on the Jews, the modern anti-Semitic program of the Christian Social party largely reflected them. No clearer sign of this could be found than an article that appeared in *Civiltà cattolica* in April of 1897, a time when Cardinal Rampolla exerted particularly tight control over all articles in the journal dealing with political topics.

"In no part of the world," wrote Father Ballerini, "have the Jews, in the roughly thirty years since they have been emancipated, risen to such power as they have in the Austro-Hungarian empire, which has practically become their own fiefdom. In Vienna—up until recently, when the vigorous counterattack of the Christian Socials began—they occupied all the public offices, city government, the ministries, and dictated the law to the Court itself." The Jews of Austria, he continued, had grown rich by exploiting others, never doing any real work themselves. The entire economy was now in their hands, as they leached all the money from the Christian population. Nor was this all, for not only did they also own all the major newspapers, he wrote, but virtually all of the university faculty positions were in their hands.

"Out of consideration for the offspring of that race," Father Ballerini reported, "Christian prayers—not excluding the *Pater noster*—had to be abolished from the schools of that city. Moreover, the images of the Crucified Christ had to be removed from the walls, for they might have offended the delicate sight of the children of his crucifiers." Unless something is done, he warned, Christians "will end up hungry, having with the sweat of their brow provided the Jews the means to amass their millions, all to be used to tyrannize them and to allow the Jews to keep their feet on the Christians' necks."

Thankfully, wrote the Jesuit author, the situation was not entirely bleak, for there was one ray of hope. "The most practical remedy, the one most readily available and most effective, is in that revolt against the Judaic yoke which the Social Christians of Vienna and Austria have mounted, a revolt that has given and that continues to give a splendid example to all Catholic towns and villages. . . . With the municipal elections of 1895, it chased the Jews and their lackeys from city hall, and now, with the latest elections taking place under universal suffrage, it has already largely cleared them out. Tyrannical Judaism has been defeated there . . . and victory won by the Catholics of Vienna and Austria. Legal means had earlier been used to lure [the Catholics] into the hydra's clutches, and legal means have now allowed them to escape and take back that civil, religious, and economic liberty that the evil invaders had usurped."

The Christian Social party, concluded Father Ballerini, had shown the way for Catholics everywhere. They had found the best means "that Providence offers to free the Christian countries from their slavery under the emancipated Jews' yoke." Once the Catholics had thus freed themselves, he wrote, "we can see to what degree the equality of rights, conceded to the dispersed people of Israel . . . is to be maintained, taken away, or altered." A more enthusiastic Vatican endorsement for the Christian Social anti-Semitic program is hard to imagine.[18]

The papal nuncio in Vienna was enmeshed in another controversy involving the Jews in these years as well. From Galicia, now part of Poland but then within the Austrian empire, reports came in that Christian mobs were attacking Jewish families and Jewish property. Stories began to reach the Vatican that a priest was leading outbreaks of violence against the large, impoverished Jewish population of the region. The publicity in the European press was becoming embarrassing, and so, in early 1894, Cardinal Rampolla sent a telegram to the Vienna nuncio asking him to look into the matter. The priest charged with rousing the people to attack the Jews, Stanisław Stojałowski, had in fact just a few years earlier visited the Vatican, where he had been given the coveted title of monsignor.

On February 2, Agliardi sent his initial report to the secretary of state by return telegram. The portrait he painted was not a comforting one, although the problems he identified had nothing to do with any mistreatment of the Jews. Monsignor Stojałowski, he wrote, was of a noble Polish family, and had formerly been a Jesuit. "A highly intelligent man, a skilled writer and an eloquent orator, he exercises a true fascination over the lower classes." Stojałowski, he continued, "has placed himself at the head of the socialist movement in Galicia. He fawns over the peasants, who adore him and give him money. He spreads unrest through the country, fomenting hatred against the rich and against the bishops, whose authority he seeks to demolish. He entices the impoverished and the young priests and encourages their insubordination. And he does all this saying (with great hypocrisy and much to the detriment of the rural population) that he is only carrying out the teaching of His Holiness regarding socialism." Although local bishops had censured him and various civil courts had brought charges against him, "he has become ever bolder." There was reason to fear that he could instigate a schism in the Church in Galicia. Indeed, reported the nuncio, he had recently received a telegram from three Galician bishops complaining about the priest.[19]

Cardinal Rampolla discussed Agliardi's letter with Leo XIII, and then sent new instructions: The Pope was disturbed by the nuncio's report, and wanted him to make further inquiries. Should they bear out the previous findings, the nuncio should summon Stojałowski in and warn him to change his behavior immediately or face "serious measures against him, among the first of which should be that he be stripped of the special titles and honors" given him by the Vatican.[20]

Despite the local bishops' hostility to the Galician priest—whom they viewed as a dangerous rabble-rouser—the more the secretary of state and Pope learned, the more reluctant they were to take action against the clerical firebrand. At a time when secular socialism and anarchism were spreading through central Europe, and the impoverished population in danger of succumbing to their lure, a man such as Stojałowski could be valuable, very valuable.

After the nuncio sent in further information, the Pope referred the matter to the Holy Office of the Inquisition. There, most likely in consultation with the Pope, the cardinals decided not to accept the advice of the Polish bishops, who had asked that Stojałowski be defrocked or banished. Instead, the cardinal inquisitors called on the priest to make a public vow to obey the authority of his superiors in the future. This he did.

But just a few years later, in 1898, renewed protests over the behavior of the silver-tongued priest forced the secretary of state to return to the matter. This time, in the wake of a series of violent attacks on the Jews in various Galician communities, it was the Austrian government that demanded that the Vatican take action.

In June of 1896 Agliardi had been recalled to Rome, where he was made a cardinal. The following month Archbishop Emidio Taliani replaced him as papal nuncio to Vienna. Taliani not only equaled his predecessor in his enthusiasm for Lueger and the Christian Social party, but he was more sympathetic to Stojałowski as well. He dismissed the troubling reports about the Galician priest that continued to come in as slanderous inventions of "the Judaic-liberal press."

In his new position as papal nuncio in Vienna, Taliani found himself fending off accusations from Austrian government ministers that the Vatican was to blame for the anti-Semitic violence in Galicia. On June 23, the nuncio wrote to inform the secretary of state of an unpleasant meeting he had just had with Count Goluchowski, the foreign minister of the Austrian empire, a man of Polish origin himself. "Great was my surprise yesterday," wrote the nuncio, "when Count Goluchowski, with unaccustomed agitation, complained bitterly about the actions of the aforementioned priest [Stojałowski], saying that he was responsible for the disorders and the killings." Taliani responded that as a Pole, Goluchowski might be better informed of such local developments than he was, but that he, Taliani, was surprised by his charges. "He replied that everyone knows that Stojałowski's followers were the instigators of the disorders," to which I had nothing to say in response. But when the count went so far

as "to attribute at least part of the blame to the Holy See, which had reha-
bilitated Stojałowski and had undermined the authority of the bishops,
I could do no less than protest vociferously against the injustice of his
accusation."

The nuncio added a postscript to this report: He had just received
news from a highly reliable source revealing the true causes of the disorders in Galicia: "The exorbitant taxes . . . and the usury of the Jews."[21]

The Austrian foreign minister's accusations against the Holy See provoked indignation in the Vatican. "I hardly need to tell you," wrote the
secretary of state in his reply to Taliani, "the most disagreeable impression that reading your report made on me. As for the Holy Father, to
whom I reported the matter, I must tell you that the language used by
Count Goluchowski—especially because it was employed by a Catholic minister in reference to the Holy See—could only cause him great
bitterness."[22]

On the same day that Cardinal Rampolla penned this letter, the
Vienna nuncio was sending in a new report. With pogroms multiplying
throughout Galicia, a sense of crisis grew in Vienna. Matters had gotten
to the point, wrote the nuncio, where the emperor himself had expressed
his unhappiness over what was going on. "It is true that one must take
into account the exaggeration found in the press, since the newspapers
are for the most part either Jewish or vassals of the Jews. But it cannot be
denied that Jews and Jewish property are being exposed to ferocious
reprisals . . . especially in Galicia." Taliani, however, tried to reassure
the cardinal: "Those who claim that Father Stojałowski and his party
are responsible for these excesses ignore—or, to be precise, pretend to
ignore—that the main cause is none other than the Jews themselves.
With their usury and their dishonest business dealings, they have created
anti-Semitism themselves."[23]

The nuncio did not limit himself to sharing his view of the Jews' own
responsibility for the Galician pogroms with the Vatican. He also tried to
convince the Austrian government that the violence was the Jews' own
fault.

At the end of June, Taliani sent in a new report to Cardinal Rampolla,
informing him that, in the wake of the proclamation of a state of emer-
gency in Galicia, calm had begun to return there. As a result, the Austrian
government's preoccupation with the violence against the Jews had
mercifully diminished. The nuncio had again spoken with Count Golu-

chowski, who, he reported, was now able to be more dispassionate about the matter. The count, wrote Taliani, "had to admit that the accusations hurled against the clergy as being anti-Semites had been exaggerated."

But the count had registered a new complaint with the nuncio. He lamented the danger posed by a new Jesuit newspaper. With its "markedly anti-Semitic tenor," he charged, it "imprudently incites hatred against the Jews."

"I replied to the Count," wrote the nuncio, "that the Jews themselves knew full well how best to attract hatred through their usury and their provocations, so truly it did not seem to me that there was anything left to be excited by the press."[24]

Yet while the nuncio saw no problem, the Vatican continued to be embarrassed by newspaper reports of priest-led violence against the Jews of Galicia. In early June the Pope ordered the Holy Office of the Inquisition to look once more into the matter of Monsignor Stojałowski, and the Vienna nuncio was again asked to gather information to help their inquiries. On July 15, Taliani sent Cardinal Rampolla an initial report of his findings, which painted the Galician priest in glowing terms. "From the time of his return from Rome," the nuncio wrote, Stojałowski "has never given any cause for censure. Indeed, on the contrary he has shown himself to be a protector of the Jews . . . and . . . not a few Jews have expressed their gratitude to Stojałowski."[25]

A few days later, the nuncio sent the secretary of state further evidence in his defense of the priest. In order to get to the bottom of the matter, Taliani reported, he had contacted an elderly, honest Polish monk who was well acquainted with Stojałowski. "The news he has provided me," wrote the nuncio, "refutes the complaints that the Government has made against him." Along with his own letter he included the monk's report. Dated Galicia, July 5, 1898, it was written in French.

"Father Stojałowski had no role in the anti-Semitic riots in Galicia," the monk declared. It was not his followers who had risen against the Jews, but rather, he claimed, people from the socialist party, who, in an attempt to discredit him, had then "spread the word that Stojałowski is to blame."

In a revealing passage, the monk went on to explain the attitudes toward the Jews found among the priests of Galicia. He did not mean to imply, the monk wrote, that Stojałowski was not anti-Semitic: "Father Stojalowski is, without any doubt, an anti-Semite in the sense that Lueger is and that every priest of good will in Galicia is. For how could a Catholic see the arrogance of the country's Jews without feeling the duty to oppose the infamous tactics of corrupting people's morals that the Jews in Galicia use?" Yet, to hate the Jews was one thing, to kill them another, and, the monk reported, Stojałowski had "never roused the people to murder the Jews."

Much of the Polish-speaking population of western Galicia, chafing under Austrian rule, saw the Vienna government not as their protector but as their oppressor. The nuncio's correspondent clearly could be counted among them. Far from the Polish priest Stojałowski's being responsible for the violence, he argued, it was most likely the Austrian government itself that was behind the disorders. The word in Galicia, he wrote, was that "this agitation against the Jews is only a ruse used to oppress the people." In quelling the riots, Austrian soldiers had killed thirty peasants, "and not a hair on the head of a Jew was touched." All this had happened, he added, despite the fact that "the priests have testified that in those places where the riots erupted it was the Jews who provoked the people."[26]

The Austrian government continued to urge the Vatican to do something about Stojałowski, but its pleas were met by more Vatican foot-dragging. On September 24, 1900, the substitute head of the papal nuncio's office in Vienna wrote to Cardinal Rampolla, telling of an unpleasant meeting he had just had with the Austrian foreign minister. The Austrian accused the nuncio's office of protecting Stojałowski from Vatican disciplinary action. The foreign minister had learned, he said, from the Austrian ambassador in Rome that if the Holy See had not taken "energetic measures" against the Galician priest, it was because of the nuncio's opposition. "I responded," wrote the substitute nuncio, "that the term 'protection' was not correct. We do not protect Father Stojałowski. But before we take any measures against him, we want to be sure of the accusations that are being made, and see if they are borne out by the facts."[27]

For the papal nuncio in Vienna at the turn of the century the problem was not anti-Semitism, the problem was the Jews. From his perspective, the anti-Semitic movement and the Catholic movement were largely one and the same. Typical was an incident in May 1899. When the Austrian Supreme Court handed down a ruling forbidding the use of public funds for renovating church buildings in the capital, the Christian Social party used the decision to whip up anti-Semitic frenzy in Vienna. In a report to Cardinal Rampolla, Taliani told him of the reaction to the court decision in the Viennese parliament. A Catholic deputy had gotten up to denounce it, "not without great animation nor without some pungent comments against the Judaic-liberal party, which employs all possible means and all occasions to oppress the Catholics of the capital. The orator rightly characterized the Judaic campaign as a provocation aimed at the Catholic majority of Vienna."

The nuncio then recounted that the most vehement denunciation in parliament had come from Monsignor Scheicher, "who may perhaps have crossed beyond the limits of legitimate vehemence." Indeed, wrote Taliani, the prelate had "proclaimed a crusade against Judaism and against the synagogues. Should Scheicher's attacks find an echo in the anti-Semitic population," he predicted, "a true uprising and a true anti-Semitic war could break out." Lueger himself also spoke, terming the court decision the work of scoundrels. "As usual," the nuncio recalled, Lueger "was alternatively very violent and very humorous. But taken altogether this extremely lively polemic is easily understood, if one reflects on the fact that, for some time now, the Jews have shown an audacity and a level of violence that are truly insufferable." The Christian Social party, Taliani went on to report, was not letting the matter rest in parliament; they were taking it to the people. The next day they were going to hold rallies in the public squares of every one of Vienna's eighteen districts.[28]

Of the Christian Social party's orators at the time, few were as popular as Lueger's lieutenant, Ernst Schneider. Not a man to mince words, in his speeches at the end of the century he proposed—presumably thinking that his audience would find the idea amusing—that the Austrian government should offer a cash prize to any good Christian who killed a Jew.[29]

From the nuncio's viewpoint, and from the Holy See's, Catholics were finally standing up to the Jewish-liberal threat in Austria. Thanks to Karl Lueger and his comrades, the Austrian Jews were now on the defensive.

The nuncio's perspective, shared by both the secretary of state and the Pope himself, was on display in the late summer of 1899 when plans were being made for a Christian Social national party congress.

"It is with great pleasure that I inform you," Taliani wrote Cardinal Rampolla on August 27, 1899, "of a grand Christian Social congress, to be held at the end of this October. The Social Christians are steadily enlarging their base of operation and spreading not only into the countryside, where they are finding favorable terrain, but also in the most important towns, where liberalism and Judaism united together still control local governments and oppress the people." The congress, wrote the nuncio, could prove crucial in lifting the Catholics' political fortunes if it succeeded, as he hoped, in overcoming the suspicion still found in some Catholic quarters toward the Christian Social party, and so got all Catholics to join the party.

For those who have argued that the Vatican bore no responsibility for the notoriously anti-Semitic Christian Social party, the nuncio's letter, found in the Secret Vatican Archives, cannot be welcome reading. "In carrying out the instructions that Your Eminence has repeatedly given me," he wrote, "I will not fail on this occasion too to give—with the necessary prudence—the appropriate suggestions to the party heads, so that they act in the sense that I have indicated above."

Taliani concluded his report with a renewed warning about the machinations of the enemy. "The revival that we see in Catholic activity," he explained, "has seriously frightened Masonic, Judaized liberalism which, in order to intimidate Catholics and prevent them from acting has, for some time now, abused them on every possible occasion."[30]

A few days later, a pleased secretary of state sent his reply: "I have shared [your report] of the 27th of the month with the Holy Father." Both he and Pope Leo XIII were delighted to learn of the progress "of the Catholic forces and the considerable ardor of those good people who, whether in the associations, or in the various congresses, are aiding us by gaining a solid position against our adversaries' attacks and invasion."[31]

Following more than a decade of strong support by the Vatican, and with the active participation of the lower clergy, the anti-Semitic movement in Austro-Hungary was gaining steam as the twentieth century began.

Nor were Austria or Galicia the only places where, from a Vatican perspective, this conflict between the good forces of Catholicism and the malevolent forces of Judaism was being played out. Hostilities against the Jews had been erupting in Hungary as well. In May 1901, freshly returned from a trip to Budapest, the Vienna nuncio wrote to Cardinal Rampolla. He was eager to set the record straight, for the papers had been full of biased stories on the recent disorders and street demonstrations that had broken out in Budapest. The demonstrations were, he wrote, "directed exclusively against the Jews, who with their provocations and with that arrogance of theirs, will ultimately provoke a violent reaction."[32] If, as the twentieth century got underway, an anti-Semitic flame was spreading across central Europe, it was one that Leo XIII and his secretary of state had done their share to fan.

CHAPTER TEN

Race

E FFORTS TO DENY Catholic Church involvement in the rise of modern anti-Semitism have made much of the presumed lack of a racial element in whatever hostility the Church had directed against the Jews in the past. As embraced in the 1998 Vatican Commission report on the Shoah, this argument consists of three parts: (1) One of the defining features of modern anti-Semitism is the view that Jews constitute a separate, and inferior, race; (2) the Church has always condemned racial thinking, for it goes against the Church's universal mission; and so (3) the Church could not have been involved in the development of modern anti-Semitism.

There is an element of truth in this argument, but it suffers from both a logical flaw and a misreading of history.

The element of truth is this: The official Church could not accept a view of Jews as irredeemable, as inalterably inferior. First of all, Jesus was born a Jew, as were many of the Church's founding fathers. If Jews were biologically inferior, what would this say about them? Secondly, the conversion of the Jews had, from the earliest Christian times, been given high priority in Church teachings. Salvation was available to Jews through baptism; any theory that the nature of the Jew was fixed at birth went against what the Church taught about regeneration in Christ through baptism.

Yet despite this basic truth, two basic problems remain.

The logical problem flows from the form of the argument, which looks like this: (1) Modern anti-Semitism entails the notion of Jewish biological inferiority; but (2) the Catholic Church has never embraced a belief in Jewish biological inferiority; and so (3) the Catholic Church can bear no responsibility for the rise of modern anti-Semitism.

But even if we identify modern anti-Semitism with racism, it does not follow that racism is the only significant feature of modern anti-Semitism. In fact, there are other, equally important components of the ideology that produced the first modern anti-Semitic political movements in the last two decades of the nineteenth century. Any list would have to include the following: There is a secret Jewish conspiracy; the Jews seek to conquer the world; Jews are an evil sect who seek to do Christians harm; Jews are by nature immoral; Jews care only for money and will do anything to get it; Jews control the press; Jews control the banks and are responsible for the economic ruination of untold numbers of Christian families; Jews are responsible for communism; Judaism commands its adherents to murder defenseless Christian children and drink their blood; Jews seek to destroy the Christian religion; Jews are unpatriotic, ever ready to sell their country out to the enemy; for the larger society to be properly protected, Jews must be segregated and their rights limited.

The Church played an important role in promulgating every one of these ideas that are central to modern anti-Semitism. Every one of them had the support of the highest Church authorities, including the popes.

The logical problem in the Vatican argument then comes down to this: If the Church bore major (although of course not exclusive) responsibility for the inculcation of a dozen of the major ideological pillars of the modern anti-Semitic political movement, but a thirteenth came from other sources, are we to conclude that the Church bears little or no responsibility for the flowering of modern anti-Semitism in those areas where the Church had great influence?

Yet the problem for the Vatican is more serious than this, because the Church was in fact involved in the development of racial thinking about Jews. Nor was this new. Views of biological differences between Jews and Christians, although contradicting other important aspects of Christian theology, have a long history in the Church. These helped prepare Catholics in the late nineteenth century and into the twentieth for further developments in racial thinking, some of which came into open conflict with Church teachings on the oneness of humankind.

In fact, conceptions of Jews as being not only religiously and culturally different but also biologically different—bearers of negative physical or spiritual traits that they passed down automatically from generation to generation regardless of their religious practice—have a very old history in the Church.

The most striking example comes from Spain, which in the fifteenth century had the largest Jewish population in Europe. There, in conjunction with the forced baptisms of the Jews, and the expulsion in 1492 of those who would not convert, a series of laws, the *estatutos de limpieza de sangre* (statutes of blood purity), were promulgated. The laws prevented anyone with Jewish ancestry from occupying positions of prestige in Spanish society. Indeed, they came to be applied by the Church itself to prevent Christians whose family tree showed Jewish members from occupying Church offices.[1]

In 1547, the archbishop of Toledo issued a new law banning any Christians who were descended from Jews from the various forms of assistance that the archdiocese provided. In 1555, this law was ratified by Pope Paul IV and came to serve as a model for the Church throughout Spain. No one could aspire to any of the honors or higher offices in Spanish society unless he could show that he was untainted by Jewish blood. Candidates for positions in the civil service or for admission to the universities were required to submit genealogies to show they were free from any such stain. In those cases where the unsuspecting candidate was discovered to have had a Jewish ancestor, he not only was denied the post in question but was humiliated publicly as well. Various monastic and other Church religious orders similarly excluded descendants of Jews. In justifying such a statute, one Church organization explained that it was a matter of purity. As the murderers of Jesus, the Jews of his time acquired an indelible blood taint that was passed on to succeeding generations, so that "all of their descendants . . . are as if born with polluted blood. Therefore they are denied all honors, offices, and titles . . . the abomination of their ancestors will cling to them forever."[2]

It was in the sixteenth century that a Spaniard, Ignatius Loyola, founded the Jesuit order. Although initially some of its most important recruits came from among the descendants of Jews who had been forcibly converted in Spain, the Jesuits soon put an end to this. In 1592 they introduced a rule forbidding the admission of men of Jewish origin, calculating ancestry to the fifth generation. The rule was only expunged in 1946, having been often cited by both the Nazis and the Italian Fascists to demonstrate that their own racial policies merely echoed those of the Church's most respected religious order.[3]

Among Catholics in general, belief in the stain of descent from a Jew was common and doubts about just how fully a Jew could be changed into a Christian by baptism were widespread. Even if the official Church did not directly promulgate such ideas—which went against official Catholic dogma—the Vatican sometimes found itself ceding to its popular grip.

A good example comes from central Europe in 1892. An archbishopric became open in one of the Czech provinces that year, and a respected Catholic scholar, Theodor Kohn, was named to the post. As the new archbishop's name suggests, he had himself been born Jewish. When news of the archbishop's ancestry spread, people were outraged. The sad climax of the affair came when, as Archbishop Kohn rose to speak at a Catholic congress in Salzburg in 1896, he was showered with catcalls and jeers. The situation had grown so intolerable that Vatican officials felt they had to act. The archbishop was asked to resign, told by Vatican officials that his name was stirring up too much trouble.[4]

While the language of race was employed incessantly by the Church and by many other sectors of society in past centuries, just what was meant by "race" is open to interpretation. Take a typical case. In the wake of the demolition of the gates of Rome's ghetto by French troops in 1798, the prelate Giuseppe Sala expressed his thoughts on Rome's Jews in his diary. "This wretched race is insolent beyond belief, and now that it has left the walls of the ghetto, it can live where it pleases and so it is beginning to infest the neighborhoods of the city."[5]

Even those few priests who were, at this time, more charitably inclined toward the Jews shared widespread views about their physical differences linked to a sense that they belonged to a different race. There is no better example of this than the case of a man viewed by many French Jews of the time as their greatest Catholic champion, Father Henri Grégoire. Born in 1750 of rural artisan parents in the Lorraine, he was among the Catholic clergy whose worldview was most affected by the ideas of the French Enlightenment. When the Royal Society of Metz decided to hold a contest for the best essay on the topic "Is there a way of making the Jews more useful and happier in France?," Father Grégoire entered and won one of the top three prizes. His winning essay was published in 1789.[6]

While Father Grégoire's motives in writing the essay were clearly charitable, and his interest in Jewish welfare sincere, the picture of the Jews that he takes for granted reveals how deeply a racial view was embedded in provincial Catholic society. He wrote of the "Jews' physical constitution . . . the pale face, the hooked nose, the sunken eyes, the prominent chin, and the highly pronounced muscles of the mouth." He added: "Most of them seem old before their time. . . . They constantly exhale a bad odor." Yet, despite this revolting picture, Father Grégoire argued that the poor behavior of which the Jews were constantly being accused, insofar as it was found at all, was the result of the restrictive laws and the hatred directed at them by Christians. Once the Jews were given the same freedom others had, he wrote, they would become productive members of society. Father Grégoire continued to defend the Jews all his life, and was mourned by Jews throughout Europe when he died in 1831.[7]

This mention of the Jews' smell recalls a theme with a long history in Church writings. The *foetor judaicus,* it was thought, would give away even the craftiest Jew seeking to insinuate himself into Christian company. The belief in the Jew's smell was closely linked to the view of the Jew as demonic, tied to the notion in the Middle Ages that while good spirits give off a pleasant fragrance, evil spirits, and most notably Satan himself, emit a horrible smell.[8]

There is a good reason why this belief in the Jewish odor is not identified with modern biological racism. According to traditional Christian belief, the Jews' stench evaporated upon baptism. Indeed, proselytizers sometimes used this as an argument to try to convince Jews to convert.

One notorious Jewish convert, Samuel Nahmias, who in the seventeenth century rose to the position of teacher of Hebrew in the college of the Congregation for the Propagation of the Faith in Rome, was obsessed with the Jews' foul smell. A thousand baths, he said, would not remove it. Indeed, in lecturing the Jews on why they needed to convert, he accused them of offending the surrounding population by stinking so much.[9]

But while the belief in the miraculous disappearance of the Jew's smell at the baptismal font was inspiring, it coexisted with another understanding of the Jewish odor, a part of a larger image of the Jewish body as foul. It involved no major change for anti-Semites of the late nineteenth and twentieth centuries to incorporate the smell into a larger picture of a degraded race. Edouard Drumont's *Jewish France* did just this, providing a long discussion of the *foetor judaicus,* adding that baptism could not wash it away. And for Catholic publications such as *La Croix du Nord,* the Jewish odor became simply another basic biological trait, to go along with the hooked nose and the nasal voice, to be used in vilifying the Jews.

With the rise of the Nazis, the old Catholic belief in the Jewish stench became incorporated into the new racial concepts. The author of a 1934 article in the Polish Catholic periodical *Pro Christo,* for example, argued that even after seven generations, the descendants of Jewish converts to Christianity in Poland continued to carry the Jews' distinctive smell. From this he concluded—here reaching well beyond anything to which the Vatican would subscribe—that the power of Jewish blood was so great that "putting a stop to the penetration of Aryan blood by Jewish blood is useful, proper, understandable, and moral."[10]

More generally, the old Christian idea of Jewish physical difference— although long preceding any modern understanding of genetics—came in the late nineteenth century to be mixed with newer ideas of national identity and biological difference. Catholic iconography, which had for centuries represented Jews through negative physical stereotypes, was simply updated for the new political battles. Typical was the Assumptionists' weekly newspaper, *Le Pèlerin,* which in the midst of the Dreyfus case published a large color illustration showing a rich Jew, hairy and with a large nose, standing with his son—also shown with a huge nose—in front of a series of portraits. One showed Judas (with large nose) selling out Jesus; one depicted Joseph being sold by his brothers; and another portrayed Dreyfus (big nose) receiving thirty coins from Kaiser Wihelm II. The father, in German-tainted French, asks his boy: "End ven you grow up, my little Iacov, vat vill you sell?"[11]

Nor were French Catholic authors of the time immune from the temptation of adding a touch of modern scientific authority to their disquisitions on the Jewish race. Father E. H. Chabouty's 1880 book *Freemasons and Jews,* one of the books on the Jews most widely and warmly cited in the Catholic press, offers a case in point. "Science," he explained, "agreeing here with everyday experience, shows us that the Jewish race— making it alone among all others an exception to the general law—is capable of living and perpetuating itself in any climate. [Science] demonstrates the existence in this people of . . . an immunity that exempts it from illnesses and plagues." Here Father Chabouty invoked the authority of modern science to repackage a thoroughly medieval belief, the charge that Jews, taking advantage of their own preternatural immunity, went around spreading plagues to kill the Christians.[12]

Readers of the Catholic press in Europe at the turn of the twentieth century were continually bombarded with references to the Jewish race and its noxious characteristics. An 1898 article on the Jews in *La Croix du*

Nord is typical: The Jews are a "race, a foreign race, camped among us, a race that has neither our blood, nor our instincts, nor our ideals; a race that is cosmopolitan by its nature, a race without a country, an intransigent, usurious race, lacking a moral sense, a race capable of selling and buying anything."[13] And, eight years later, an article in *Le Bloc Catholique*, in denouncing Freemasonry, argued that the Freemasons were "inspired and directed by the Jewish race, that parasitical and vampire race, always and everywhere scorned and shunned, that wandering race, witness over the centuries of the curse which weighs upon it. . . . The Church of Satan is incarnated in the Jewish race. . . ."[14]

Given the level of hostility against the Jews inculcated by the Church, popular commitment to the official Church position that Jews could be transformed from evil to good through the baptismal waters proved increasingly difficult to maintain. It strained credulity to imagine that a people so demonic could be so easily changed, that the person who until yesterday was Jewish could today be one of us.

A case at the beginning of the twentieth century offers a particularly chilling example of this in showing how Catholic anti-Semitism of the turn of the century could help set the stage for the later, eliminationist Nazi anti-Semitism.[15] In a parliamentary debate in 1901, Ernst Schneider, Karl Lueger's most trusted lieutenant in Austria's Christian Social party, proclaimed: "The Jewish question is a racial question, a question of blood." And then, no doubt to the laughter of his fellow Christian Social party deputies, he quipped: "I am not engaged in any discussion of Jewish baptism, but I will say this. If I had to baptize Jews, then I should follow the method of St. John, though in somewhat improved fashion. He held them under water for baptism, but I should immerse them for the duration of five minutes."[16]

Such an image of the Jew drowned in the baptismal water would not elicit any laughter in the Vatican, which remained committed to Jewish baptism as the single, divinely ordained solution to the Jewish problem. But the view of the Jew as fundamentally evil, as a constant danger to Christian society, was very much part of the Vatican's worldview in these years. In early 1898, the Vatican's newspaper, *L'Osservatore romano*, returned to its lament that the emancipation of the Jews had brought untold suffering to the Christian world. Having been given equal rights, the paper declared, "the Jew sought to lead a life that he absolutely could not, abandoning himself recklessly and heedlessly to that innate passion of his race, which is essentially usurious and pushy. This, in turn, aroused and magnified a thousandfold the natural aversion that the Christian peoples have for the deicide people."[17]

This article followed another that the Vatican paper had published on the subject of the Jews just a few days earlier. Its author followed what had become the standard pattern: Paint the Jews in the most horrific terms imaginable, but then add a disclaimer saying that violence against the Jews is unchristian. And so, after narrating the Jews' demonic thirst for Christian blood and their wicked conspiracy to destroy Christianity, the *Osservatore romano* article concluded that there was only one proper defense against the Jews: "a healthy anti-Semitism that is nonviolent."[18]

CHAPTER ELEVEN

Ritual Murder and the Popes in the Twentieth Century

IN THE LAST two decades of the nineteenth century, the Vatican began to use anti-Semitism to build mass political support for the Church. Yet anti-Semitism had to be handled with care, especially insofar as the popes themselves were concerned. The hierarchy saw the Roman Catholic Church as the divinely ordained carrier of a message of universalism, love, and charity. With pogroms spreading across eastern Europe, and with charges of Jewish ritual murder, Jewish economic crimes, and Jewish treason leading to violence in both western and central Europe, the popes and their secretaries of state tried to put some public distance between themselves and the anti-Semitic campaigns. In their public statements, no pope himself would publicly charge the Jews with ritual murder, nor—in so many words—argue that they were a foreign body destroying Christian society. The popes themselves would not publicly call for revoking the Jews' civil rights, nor for sending them back to the ghettoes.

Indeed, in their public pronouncements, the popes generally avoided any specific mention of the Jews at all, permitting the Vatican to deny that the Holy See bore any responsibility for the anti-Semitic movement in Europe. But out of the limelight, and with the assistance of their secretaries of state, the popes regulated the anti-Semitic campaigns conducted in the Church press—most notably through *L'Osservatore romano* and *Civiltà cattolica,* over which they exercised control. At the same time, through their diplomatic service, they worked quietly to shape the political use of anti-Semitism more directly, as we have seen was the case in Austria.

The Catholic campaign that, in the last two decades of the nineteenth century, identified the Jews with ritual murder offers a good example of how this worked. The Catholic newspapers of Italy, France, Austria, and Germany were, in these years, filled with the most horrific accounts of Jewish evil in murdering children. Stirring up old anti-Jewish sentiments in the Christian population, the lurid accusations proved useful for rallying the people to the Church's side in the battle against the forces of liberalism and change. Yet, Pope Leo XIII and his secretary of state, Cardinal Rampolla, realized that such a campaign had its risks, offering ammunition to those who sought to paint the Church as hopelessly mired in medieval superstitions. And, with emancipated Jews now able to take part in public life, and more Christians coming into contact with them, the ritual murder campaign seemed to a growing number of people to be a particularly nasty piece of work.

Nowhere was such a reaction stronger than in England, where the Roman Catholic Church's position was quite different than it was in the countries where Catholics were the large majority. Indeed, not only were Catholics a minority (of about 5 or 6 percent) in England, but the Catholic Church itself was the object of widespread fear and loathing. British Catholics had only been given the right to be elected to Parliament in 1829, and only in 1867 were they relieved of the necessity of making a declaration against transubstantiation before taking government office. And throughout the entire century the law forbade Catholics from holding public processions in which full Eucharistic vestments were worn and the consecrated Host carried. Hostility toward the Catholic Church and the papacy certainly contributed to the strong support given in 1858 by Anglican ministers and many prominent Protestant lay people for the return of Edgardo Mortara to his Jewish family. They charged the Catholic Church with enforcing medieval theocratic creeds at the Jews' expense. On the other hand, as members of a despised religious minority themselves, England's Catholics were unusually sensitive to the Jews' plight.[1]

In December 1889, the chief rabbi of London, Hermann Adler, wrote a letter to Henry Cardinal Manning, the elderly Archbishop of Westminster, telling the cardinal of a recent book titled *The Mystery of the Blood Among the Jews,* by the priest Henri Desportes. Published in France, it resurrected the old charges of Jewish ritual murder.

He normally tried to ignore such ignoble works, the rabbi wrote. But in this case the book's publication had taken on a much greater import, for it was being touted as carrying the approval of the Pope himself. "I would not like to believe," wrote Adler, "that the eminent head of the

Catholic Church could have expressed himself in this way." The rabbi asked for the archbishop's help: "It is hardly credible that His Holiness would have expressed himself in the sense attributed to him, but, if one lets such an allegation pass without denying it, it may have the gravest consequences. I therefore hope that Your Eminence will be able to give a formal denial to the approval announced in the newspapers."

The archbishop responded quickly: He had no idea, he replied, what Leo XIII might have said on the question, and so was writing to Rome to find out. "You certainly do me justice," added the archbishop, "in thinking that I lend no credence to such horrors."

On January 16, 1890, the archbishop wrote Rabbi Adler again, this time to inform him of the answer that he had received from Secretary of State Rampolla. What Father Desportes was trumpeting as evidence of the Pope's support for his book, Rampolla had replied, was nothing of the sort. "The letter that the Pope sent [to Desportes]," Rampolla explained, "was only a form letter, noting the reception of a book sent by its author, but without approval of its content." The letter, Rampolla asserted, was identical to "that which is always sent before the book is examined, and often even before it has been seen." To this brief reply from the secretary of state, the archbishop added his own defense of Leo XIII: "Nothing is further from the Pope's nature than wanting to gratuitously wound the sensitivities of the Jewish people."[2]

Recall that Henri Desportes was the author whom Edouard Drumont had so ardently defended, the priest who had run afoul of his archbishop. Desportes was on his way to becoming one of the main authorities in the Catholic ritual murder campaign in France, and his work would be cited approvingly in Catholic publications throughout Europe well into the twentieth century. Not only did he publish two books on the topic; in 1890 he also founded a monthly journal titled *The Anti-Jewish Alliance* (*L'Alliance antijuive*).[3]

When one digs through the Vatican archives, a rather different story emerges of the "form letter" that Cardinal Rampolla claimed to have sent Desportes. On July 26, 1889, Father Desportes sent two copies of his newly published book, *The Mystery of the Blood Among the Jews,* to Pope Leo XIII, via Secretary of State Rampolla. In his cover note to the cardinal, Desportes explained the book's thesis, although Rampolla certainly knew the nature of the book from its title alone. "This book reveals," Desportes wrote Rampolla, "one of the most monstrous instances of modern fanaticism, and I dare hope that Your Eminence, by giving me a word of approval, would want to help me combat this infamy."

Desportes' letter to the Pope went into greater detail. He eagerly sought the Pope's approval, and was convinced that the Pope would be pleased with his work. "It is my Christian heart's duty and my obligation as a devoted son of the Vicar of Jesus Christ to offer to Your Holiness the volume, *The Mystery of the Blood,* which I have just published. I wanted to praise the glory of the synagogue's unknown martyrs, and reveal to the world—which is ignorant of the true history—the news of the little innocents whose blood was shed for such hideous deeds. Is it not a shame that the Jews are everywhere honored, and that the Christian peoples kiss their hands, which are red with their brothers' blood? I wanted to bring this infamy to an end."

In his last paragraph, Father Desportes told the Pope of his recent banishment at the hands of his archbishop, and portrayed himself as a martyr. "The Jews are powerful and they react hatefully against those who unmask their villainy. As a result of my act of courage, I had to abandon the place where I was happy, to leave my native town and practically become a beggar. Under these conditions, Your Holiness, pardon me for offering you such a modest volume. Your apostolic benediction and a word of encouragement from you would do my soul and my heart good."[4]

Just a few days later Cardinal Rampolla wrote back to Desportes. "I have received the copies of the book that you have published, titled *The Mystery of the Blood,* and, following the wishes you expressed in your letter of July 26, I presented one of the copies to the Holy Father, keeping one for myself. His Holiness greatly appreciated your filial offering and he has asked me to thank you for it in His name, adding that he sends you a heartfelt apostolic benediction. Carrying out this pontifical assignment with pleasure, I send you special thanks for the special courtesy you showed with respect to my own person. . . ."[5]

The secretary of state's later claim, when news of the letter became public, that the Pope had this letter sent without having any idea what the book was about is clearly untrue. Both Cardinal Rampolla and Leo XIII knew exactly what kind of book it was, and what its purpose was. There is no question but that they approved of both. It was a book that read very much like the series of twenty-six articles on Jewish ritual murder that

Civiltà Cattolica was in the midst of publishing at the time, a series that was receiving warm praise in the pages of the Vatican daily, *L'Osservatore romano,* as well.

That Desportes believed he had the strong support of the Pope was clear the following year when he wrote Cardinal Rampolla once more, sending two copies of his latest book on ritual murder, *Killed by the Jews.* Father Desportes again asked the cardinal to give a copy to the Pope and to request the Pope's special benediction for his efforts. What was particularly notable about the papal praise that this request received is that the new book seemed particularly well designed to raise warning flags in the Vatican. Cardinal Rampolla received Desportes' letter and book just months after he had written to the archbishop of Westminster claiming ignorance about what Desportes' books were about. Making Desportes' request even more suspect was the fact that the new book carried a prominent preface written by a man who was supposed to be anathema to the Vatican, Edouard Drumont.

Following Drumont's preface—"Ritual murder," he wrote, "is a type of monomania linked more to the physiology [of the Jews] than to their religious history"—Desportes provided his own preface. He titled it: "To the Jew Isidore Cohen, Director of the *Archives israélites.*" *Archives Israélites* was then the leading Jewish newspaper in France. What had provoked Desportes was Cohen's claim that the priest lacked the Church's support for his ritual murder charges, citing as evidence the fact that the archbishop of Rouen had evicted him from the diocesan seminary.

It was true, Father Desportes responded, that the archbishop did not want him to publish *Mystery of the Blood,* but "it was not because Monsignor Thomas disapproved of my book or of the anti-Semitic campaign, but simply due to a fear and a servility that I could not appreciate." The archbishop's opposition was nothing more than pure political opportunism, the priest argued, for the prefect of Rouen—as we have seen—was a Jew and the archbishop did not want to offend him.

But it was not true, insisted Desportes, that the archbishop had thrown him out. No, he had left voluntarily, not wanting to be seen as an embarrassment. Nor was it true, he added, that *Mystery of the Blood* had been published without ecclesiastical approval. By the time it came out he was already resident in his new diocese, and "my bishop, *to whom my book was submitted,* found nothing in it to criticize." Moreover, added

Desportes, he had subsequently received effusive praise from the Vatican. "Rome blessed my book, many bishops and prelates approve of it, and all of the Catholic press defend it."[6]

How much of the book the secretary of state, or the Pope, may have read—if any—we do not know. Yet, on October 31, 1890, despite the denial that he had sent to the archbishop of Westminster just months earlier, Cardinal Rampolla wrote once again to Desportes, thanking him for the copies of *Killed by the Jews*. "I placed one copy in the venerable hands of the Holy Father," he told Desportes, "and I am happy to inform you that His Holiness received your filial gift with gratitude, and that from the bottom of his heart he sends you his Apostolic Benediction."[7]

Unease in the English Catholic Church over the Vatican's involvement in the ritual murder campaign continued to grow, until a series of events finally prompted the leading Catholics of England to take a most unusual step. The provocations included the Assumptionists' fierce anti-Semitic campaign in France; the appearance in 1897 of the virulently anti-Semitic book *The Jews Before the Church and History*, by a French Dominican friar; and, most painfully, publication in November 1899 of "Judaic ritual murder" in the Vatican's own newspaper, *L'Osservatore romano*. On November 27 and 28 of 1899, the archbishop of Westminster, Cardinal Vaughan (who had replaced Cardinal Manning), and the two most distinguished lay Catholics in Britain—Lord Russell, the Chief Justice of the Kingdom, and the Duke of Norfolk—each wrote separate letters of protest to the secretary of state. They beseeched both him and the Pope to reiterate the repudiations of the ritual murder charge that, they said, popes in earlier centuries had often issued.

In his letter, the Duke of Norfolk reminded the secretary of state of the ritual murder trial then underway in Bohemia, and lamented the fact that "the Catholic newspapers and many of the most influential clergy were promoting aggression against the Jews as the community responsible for such atrocities." The duke expressed the hope that Leo XIII would intervene, and begged him to release a general statement on the question to calm the souls, as his predecessors, Popes Innocent IV, Gregory X, Martin V, and Paul III, had done. The Pope's continued silence on the matter, he added, would have dire consequences on public opinion in England, as elsewhere.[8]

For his part, Lord Russell decided that the best way to get a hearing at the Holy See was to send his letter through the rector of the Catholic

Irish College in Rome. On December 4, the rector forwarded the lord chief justice's letter to Cardinal Rampolla.[9]

Cardinal Rampolla immediately took the English letters to the Pope. After conferring, they decided to refer the question to the cardinal inquisitors.

"By order of the Holy Father," Rampolla wrote to the Holy Office assessor that same day, "the attached letters of the Eminent Cardinal Archbishop of Westminster, of the Duke of Norfolk, and of Lord Russell of Killowen, Chief Justice of Her Majesty's Court in London, are being sent. I ask you to inform this secretary of state, in due course, of the response that this Supreme [Holy Office] believes it incumbent to give on the question of ritual murder."[10]

After receiving Cardinal Rampolla's letter informing him of the Inquisition's inquiry, the Duke of Norfolk wrote again, telling of new diplomatic developments. In his first letter, the duke had reported that the Austrian government was alarmed by outbreaks of violence prompted by ritual murder charges against the Jews. The government would appreciate, he said, a new papal declaration along the lines that the duke himself was requesting. Subsequent to his earlier letter, the duke now reported, the Austrians had sent him "a formal assurance" that they would view such an intervention by the Pope as making an important contribution to maintaining peace in the Austrian empire. Cardinal Rampolla responded to the duke's new plea with a brief note, advising him that the matter was now in the hands of the Holy Office, and so at the moment there was nothing he could do.[11]

A glimpse into how the inquisitors handled the request can be gleaned from internal documents recently found in the Holy Office archives.[12] The cardinals, we learn, decided to name a special consultant to help them with the case. The person they chose, Monsignor Rafael Merry del Val, was someone who would soon become famous worldwide, for in just three years he would succeed Rampolla as secretary of state.

An internal Holy Office note on the selection of Merry del Val tells us a great deal about the inquisitors' view of the British Catholic request:

"The Cardinal Archbishop of Westminster has thought to denounce present-day anti-Semitism, especially the matter of ritual murder, to the Holy See. It is easy to understand just how serious the matter is, if one considers the temerity of the powerful Jews of London, who, in their unchallenged rule in Europe have reached the point of such lunacy that

they would pretend to be defended by the Holy See." Why had the cardinals chosen to give the matter to Monsignor Merry del Val for investigation? The Holy Office note provides the answer: Because "he has among
his ancestors a boy crucified by the Jews and venerated on Church altars."
Thus, "he is the man most suited for the task."[13]

Indeed, among the grounds for Merry del Val's fame in the Catholic
world was his descent from the same family as Dominguito del Val, a
child worshipped in Spain as a martyr and saint. In his 1933 biography of
Cardinal Merry del Val—for which the future Pope Pius XII wrote the
preface—Monsignor Pius Cenci, director of the Vatican's Secret Archive,
reported on this connection. Dominguito, "a child of barely seven years
old," we learn, "was, on Good Friday 1250, crucified on a wall by the Jews
out of their hatred for the Catholic religion." Indeed, the first illustration
in Merry del Val's biography shows the hapless boy nailed to the cross,
with the text below explaining: "Saint Dominguito del Val, ancestor of
the Cardinal, martyr of the Eucharist."[14]

The unusual plea made jointly by the archbishop, the duke, and the
lord chief justice of England was attracting attention from diplomats and
churchmen elsewhere in Europe as well. A February 27, 1900, report to
Cardinal Rampolla from the papal nuncio in Vienna offers some evidence
of this and provides further evidence of how high Vatican authorities
viewed the British Catholics' petition.

"Following the polemics aroused for some time in these parts by the
Semitic party in Austria and in Galicia," wrote the nuncio, "one hears
many comments, motivated by . . . hatred for the Christian Social party,
or, to speak with greater precision, the anti-Semitic party." The nuncio's
identification of the Austrian Christian Social party with the "anti-
Semitic" party, at a time when he was working closely with Cardinal
Rampolla to back the party, is itself revealing.

"The Jews," he continued, "are all agitated about what they call
ritual murder," especially, the nuncio added, the recent case of Polna, in
Bohemia. "The whole Judaic clique" he wrote, was now going so far as
"even to invoke the Holy See's authority in support of the argument
against ritual murder." Few, however, actually believed the Jews' claim of
papal support, he added, yet "the violent polemic continues."[15]

Here the nuncio reported on disturbing developments in England.
Thanks to "the Jews' well-known solidarity," he wrote, people who
argued that Jews did not use Christian blood threatened to gain new

"proselytes to the Semite propaganda." His Excellency doubtless knows, he continued, that even "a Cardinal, some bishops, and some very notable Catholics have raised and continue to raise their voices against the fact of ritual murder and are provoking a demonstration of sympathy by the English Catholics."

The nuncio also reported that English Catholics, led by the Duke of Norfolk, were trying to extend their influence beyond Britain itself. "In recent days the English ambassador . . . has come repeatedly to see me. He has told me that it is also the desire of the [British Prime] Minister Salisbury that I intervene in favor of this argument of his."[16]

The inquisitors' deliberations dragged on. Finally, in July 1900, the cardinals reached their conclusions. On the last day of July the assessor of the Holy Office officially notified Cardinal Rampolla of the decision. "This Supreme [Holy Office]," he wrote, "has received repeated petitions, especially from England, some through the secretary of state, including most recently one of the 4th of this month signed by Mr. Russell of Killowen, Lord Chief Justice of England. These are aimed at obtaining a formal declaration from the Holy See, holding the accusation of so-called Ritual Murder, directed against the Jews from the most remote times, to be false and groundless." After due deliberation, the assessor reported, the inquisitors had concluded, with the Pope's approval, that no such declaration of the Jews' innocence could be made.[17]

A note accompanying the decision, found in the central Inquisition archives but never published, offers a further glimpse into the thinking that lay behind the decision. "Although nothing was found either in the Holy Office or at the Secretariat of State, where careful research was undertaken, bearing on this accusation . . . ritual murder is a historical certainty." The note continued: "Such murder furthermore was charged and punished many times by lay courts in Austria, and recently another case of such murder, which took place in Polna, in Bohemia, was tried in court and brought to light, as the Vienna nuncio has written." The conclusion was thus clear: "Given all this, the Holy See cannot issue the statement that has been requested, which, while it may please a few dupes in England, would trigger widespread protests and scandal elsewhere."[18]

Perhaps it would have been too much to hope for a change of heart on the part of Leo XIII. Over the previous two decades he had overseen a continuous assault on the Jews in the Vatican-linked press, and done his best to nourish and to defend a militantly anti-Semitic political party in

Austria. Nor was the Pope in any shape physically to undertake new initiatives. He had celebrated his ninetieth birthday in the midst of the Holy Office ritual murder deliberations, and the vibrancy that had once marked his papacy was long gone. His mind remained lucid, but he had little energy left. Any changes in the Vatican's dealings with the Jews would have to await his successor.

Pope Leo XIII died three years later, on July 20, 1903. Between them, Pius IX and Leo XIII had ruled the Church for well over half a century, a period that in earlier centuries might have seen ten or more papal reigns.[19] Together the two popes had made a deep impression on the Church. Each, in his own way, had painted the modern world as filled with evil. Each had portrayed himself as a prisoner of the Vatican, besieged by sinister forces. Each believed that the Jews' divinely ordained place was in the ghetto, and that healthy Christian society required protection from Jewish depredations.

When the conclave of cardinals met in August 1903 to elect a new pope, there was an obvious candidate. Cardinal Rampolla had served as Leo XIII's secretary of state for sixteen years and, for those seeking continuity, there could scarcely have been a better choice. But he had his detractors, both inside and outside the Church. When it looked as though Rampolla might be elected—he received twenty-four out of sixty-two first ballot votes—the Austrian government made its opposition known. The Austrians, among their other complaints, resented the strong support that Rampolla had given the Christian Social party. There was also a feeling among many of the cardinals that both Leo XIII and Rampolla had been too preoccupied with international diplomacy and not sufficiently interested in the Church's religious ministry.

With Rampolla's candidacy ended, the fortunes of Giuseppe Sarto, Patriarch of Venice, quickly rose. He was elected on August 4, and took the name of Pope Pius X.

The contrast between the new pope and his predecessor could scarcely have been greater. The sixty-eight-year-old Sarto came from a humble family in northeastern Italy, an area that until 1866 had been under Austrian control. He was the first pope in centuries to come from peasant stock, and to rise all the way from the lowliest of ecclesiastical positions to St. Peter's throne. Following ordination, Sarto had spent nine years as an assistant pastor, then another eight as a simple parish priest. In 1884 he was named bishop of Mantua and then, in 1893, made patriarch of

Venice. He had practically never been out of Italy, and indeed knew little even of Italy outside the northeast. He had neither diplomatic experience nor any experience in the Vatican.[20]

Pius X even looked different from his predecessor. While Leo XIII cut an aristocratic figure, tall, pale, delicate, and formal, Pius X was shorter, burly, red-faced, voluble, and affable, although he could also be quick-tempered. Leo XIII gave the impression of an intellectual, and in comparison with Pius X had a much broader cultural background and wider interests. While Leo XIII was attuned to the perceptions of the diplomats and the aristocracy of the world, Pius X was down-to-earth and genuinely concerned for the weak. Following an audience with the Pope in 1904, Theodore Herzl, founder of the Zionist movement, recorded in his diary that the pontiff looked like an "honest, rough-hewn village priest." Throughout the meeting, Pius X periodically took a pinch of snuff and then sneezed into a large red cotton handkerchief. "It is these peasant touches," wrote Herzl, "which I like about him best and which most of all compel my respect."[21]

The differences between the popes were particularly evident on public occasions, for as much as Leo XIII delighted in grand ceremonies, Pius X detested them. Whereas Leo XIII enjoyed traveling in a litter carried on the shoulders of his attendants, Pius X refused to be treated in this way, walking wherever he went. For 260 years popes had taken all their meals alone, for eating with others was considered to be beneath their dignity. Pius X could not stand solitude and ate regularly with his assistants and his sisters.

Yet despite all these differences in background, experience, and temperament, Pius X was no more positively inclined toward the changes identified with the modern world than was Leo XIII. In one of his most important encyclicals, *Pascendi*, in 1907, he condemned modern philosophy, which he denounced as contrary to the ancient faith of the Church. He also was a zealous believer in banning any books that might spread modern ideas opposed to the Church's teachings. Among the people he felt most comfortable with were some of the most reactionary members of the Church, including Father Giuseppe Sacchetti, the director of *L'Unità cattolica*. Like his predecessor, Pius X saw conspiracies against the Church everywhere, and like him, too, he tolerated no disobedience.

Recognizing his own lack of experience in diplomacy and in dealing with the world outside the Italian Church, the Pope named Rafael Merry del Val to be his secretary of state, an office he would hold throughout Pius X's papacy. A relatively young man—at age forty-seven—Merry del Val had devoted his whole career to the papal diplomatic service. Born of a Spanish diplomatic family residing at the time in England, he had stud-ied in both England and Belgium before, at age twenty, moving to Rome where he graduated from the Pontifical Academy of Noble Ecclesiastics. He soon came to the attention of Leo XIII, who dispatched him on diplo-matic missions of increasing responsibility in both Europe and Canada. By 1900 he had become an archbishop and president of the Academy of Noble Ecclesiastics.

In selecting Merry del Val to be his secretary of state, the Pope was choosing someone who was in many ways his opposite: a man of aris-tocratic, cosmopolitan background, who spoke several European lan-guages. But it was a collaboration that would work out well from the Pope's viewpoint, for not only did the new secretary of state have skills that the Pope lacked, he was also an indefatigable worker and wholly dedicated to serving the Pope. Moreover, while Merry del Val's outlook was less dominated by a concern for rooting out conspiracies, his own conservative views were in harmony with those of Pius X.[22]

Although, as noted, Pius X's peasant origins, and his rise through the ranks of the lower clergy, did not make him any less conservative in theo-logical matters than his predecessors who came from aristocratic families and attended special Church seminaries for noblemen, they do seem to have affected his feelings toward the Jews. Unlike any of his predecessors of the previous two centuries, the Pope had become friendly with several Jews while serving as a priest and then bishop and archbishop in north-eastern Italy. Most notable of all was his friendship with Romanin Jacur, a Jewish engineer from Padua. Pius X continued to stay in touch with Jacur, who entered the Italian parliament as a conservative in 1880 and remained in office throughout Pius X's papacy. They exchanged greetings on each New Year and on the feast of St. Joseph (the Pope's name day), and com-municated at other times as well.

A case has been made by some scholars, most notably Andrew Canepa, that, as reflected in such friendships, Pius X had a very different attitude toward the Jews than did his predecessors. In this view, his papacy represented a historic break with the past, an end to the papally backed campaign of vilification of the Jews. Various evidence has been cited in support of this thesis. In 1905, for example, in the wake of a new wave of pogroms, Pius X sent a letter to the Polish bishops in the Russian empire, reminding them that the Church condemned violence against the Jews.[23] More significantly, in contrast to the stream of anti-Semitic diatribes published in the papally linked press in the last two decades of Leo XIII's reign, the newspapers closest to the Pope were much less vocal on the Jewish question during Pius X's papacy.

And then there is the audience that the Pope had with Theodore Herzl on January 26, 1904. The very fact that he would receive Herzl, who was campaigning for a Jewish homeland in Palestine which the Church strongly opposed, was significant. The meeting did not begin well, Herzl thought, because, although he had been instructed in advance that he should kiss the Pope's hand on meeting him, he could not bring himself to do so. When asked by Herzl for his support in allowing a Jewish state to be created in Palestine, the Pope responded: "We won't be able to stop the Jews from going to Jerusalem, but we could never favor it. . . . The Jews have not recognized our Lord, and so we cannot recognize the Jewish people." The Pope continued: "The Jewish faith was the foundation of our own, but it has been superseded by the teachings of Christ, and we cannot admit that it still enjoys any validity."

Herzl asked the Pope if he knew anything about the Jews' current situation.

Yes, replied Pius X, back from the days when he was in Mantua where there was a Jewish community. "Only the other evening," the Pope added, "two Jews were here to see me." He continued: "There are other bonds than those of religion: social intercourse, for example, and philanthropy. Indeed we also pray for them, that their spirit see the light. This very day the Church is celebrating the feast of an unbeliever who became converted in a miraculous manner—on the road to Damascus. And so, if you come to Palestine and settle your people there, we will be ready with churches and priests to baptize all of you."[24]

What we see here is a reassertion of a more traditional Catholic view of the Jews. There is little doubt but that Pius X had more empathy for the Jews than his predecessors. Yet it would be easy to overstate the significance of these differences. Pius X was committed to doing battle with the forces of modernity, and part of this battle involved building up the forces of reaction within the Church, forces for whom anti-Semitism was central.

A typical example is the case of the French priest Henri Delassus, who for forty-nine years directed one of the better-known Catholic weekly papers in France, *La Semaine religieuse de Cambrai*. Delassus was well known within the Church and beyond as one of the fiercest campaigners against the Jews. In 1894, for example, he wrote in his weekly, "Anti-Semitism and Catholicism are one and the same thing." In 1911 the Pope honored Delassus by appointing him apostolic prothonotary, with the title of monsignor.[25] The following year, Pius X sent Delassus a personal, signed letter congratulating him on his golden anniversary as a priest.[26]

Most revealing of Pius X's papacy, and its relationship to the Church campaign against the Jews, is his relationship with Umberto Benigni, a tie which at a later point, albeit briefly, would threaten the Pope's canonization as a saint.[27]

Born in 1862, Umberto Benigni was ordained at age twenty-two in his native city of Perugia, in central Italy. The young priest devoted himself to scholarship—becoming a professor of theology at the diocesan seminary of Perugia—and to journalism, which soon became his passion. Like the articles found in much of the Catholic press in these end-of-century years, Benigni's writings were peppered with passionate attacks on the Jews.

Along with his rising career in Catholic journalism, Benigni began a rapid climb through the ecclesiastical hierarchy with his move to Rome in 1897. Appointed a member of the liturgical commission at the Vatican in 1902, he was also given the chair in ecclesiastical history at the Roman Pontifical Seminary and then, in 1904, at the College of Propaganda Fide.

With Pius X's ascension to the papacy, Benigni threw himself into the Pope's antimodernist campaign, devoting himself to the pontiff's effort to root out any signs of liberalism in the Church hierarchy. In 1907 Benigni founded the newspaper *Corrispondenza romana,* first published in Italian and then from 1909 to 1912 in French. It was aimed, in Benigni's words, "to combat in all countries the spread of current errors: liberalism, modernism in its various forms, and all opposition—open or concealed—to the directives of the Holy See."[28]

Most important, in 1909, with encouragement from Pius X, Benigni created an organization, the Sodality of St. Pius V, to serve as the spearhead in the battle against liberalism and modernity in the Church. The Sodality, with no more than fifty members spread through several countries, functioned as a secret espionage ring at the service of the Pope, over which Benigni presided. Benigni compiled files on clergymen and laymen whom he suspected of liberal sympathies, and he passed on evidence of their disloyalty—in the form of sermons and even of overheard conversations—to the Vatican.

Benigni's attitudes toward the Jews were well known, and in harmony with those of other highly placed conservative clerics closest to the Pope. An article he wrote in his newspaper *Piccolo Monitore,* in 1891, was typical. "If we keep up the way things have been going," he warned, "within a few years the property and the businesses of all countries will be divided among a dozen exploitative Cyclops. Of these, eleven will belong to that worthy rabbinical race that still today in 1891 slits the throats of little Christians for the Synagogue's Passover."[29]

Pius X showered Benigni with honors and, even more important, with influence. In 1906 Benigni was named second-in-command of the Congregation for Extraordinary Ecclesiastical Affairs, giving him the fifth-highest office in the entire Secretariat of State. He also had unusual access to the Pope, meeting almost daily with the Pope's closest advisor, Monsignor Giambattista Bressan, a man who had been Pius X's personal secretary in Venice and whom the Pope had brought with him to Rome. Although some, in trying to defend the Pope's reputation, later argued that he was not aware of Benigni's espionage network, subsequent research has revealed not only that the Pope approved it, and made use of its reports, but indeed that he provided an annual subsidy to fund it.[30]

Like his predecessor, Pius X too received a high-level plea for the Vatican to do something to distance itself from the ritual murder campaign against the Jews. The way he handled this plea tells us something about how little Vatican views of the Jews changed in these early years of the twentieth century.

The case prompting the new request turned out to be the most famous ritual murder trial of the twentieth century, the trial of Mendel Beilis, held in Kiev in 1913. Beilis, who worked at a Jewish-owned factory there, was arrested in 1911, charged with the ritual murder of a boy on the factory grounds. It was a case that from the very beginning had all the markings of an attempt to frame him by Russian authorities interested in keeping anti-Jewish feelings at a fevered pitch. As the case approached trial, Europe's Catholic press used it to keep popular passions about Jewish ritual murder alive. Coming as it did well into the twentieth century, the Beilis case also produced a strong reaction from the various Jewish rights organizations that had sprung up in Europe and North America over the previous decades. How was it possible, they asked, that in the twentieth century Jews could still be brought to trial on charges of ritual murder?

The Jewish leaders were particularly alarmed by the flood of articles in the Catholic press telling, in gruesome detail, of past Christian martyrdom at the hands of the Jews. It was time once more, they thought, to turn to the Pope for help. They were, of course, aware that little over a decade earlier the previous pope had refused such a request, but now a new pope, one considered more favorable to the Jews, had ascended St. Peter's throne. Jewish leaders also learned something about the Kiev trial that heightened their interest in getting Vatican support. Although Orthodox Christianity was the state religion in the Russian empire, a Catholic priest was scheduled to be a key witness at the Beilis trial. It was his role to establish that murdering Christian children and consuming their blood was a religious duty for Jews.

The Jews debated how they could best gain a sympathetic hearing from the Pope. Lucien Wolf, the head of the foreign relations committee of the main British Jewish organization, proposed an indirect approach. Rather than have a Jew send a request directly to the pontiff, it would be better to find a prominent Catholic to do so on the Jews' behalf. Wolf suggested to Lord Leopold Rothschild that he ask the Duke of Norfolk to transmit such a request to the Pope. Wolf himself would draft the letter, which would go out over Rothschild's signature.

On October 7, 1913, the day that the letter was finally sent to Norfolk, Wolf wrote to his counterpart in Berlin, Paul Nathan, who was coordinating pro-Beilis activities in Germany. Wolf explained how their tactics had evolved. Some members of their organization, Wolf recalled, had proposed that they ask the Pope himself to denounce the ritual murder charge. But, wrote Wolf, "I thought, and both Lord Rothschild and Mr. [Claude] Montefiore [president of the Anglo-Jewish Association] agreed with me, that it would be only a waste of time to ask for a further Papal declaration on the subject." Leo XIII's rebuff of little over a decade earlier was too vivid for them to have any hope that the Pope would agree to condemn the ritual murder charges himself.

In fact, the British Jewish leaders were not at first convinced that the effort to ask for Vatican help was worth it, for the cost of a second papal rebuff could be high. As Wolf explained in an earlier, undated letter to Montefiore: "I have not proceeded with it [approaching the Vatican] partly because I have been occupied with other things and partly because I found that Lord Rothschild was not very enthusiastic for it."

What subsequently convinced them to move ahead was an alternative plan proposed by A. S. Yahuda, a well-known Jewish scholar. Yahuda suggested a more modest request. Rather than call on the Pope to issue any statement himself, which they regarded as risky, they should simply ask the Vatican to authenticate certain earlier Church documents on the subject. "If the memorial were merely to ask for a pronouncement on the Blood Accusation," wrote Wolf, "I agree with Lord Rothschild in thinking that we should get no satisfactory response, but on the question of the authenticity of the Papal Bulls I do not see how in fairness the Pope could refuse to assist us."

To further increase their chances, Wolf and his colleagues decided to address their request to the secretary of state, Merry del Val, and not directly to the Pope. They would not ask for any statement from the Pope at all, but merely official certification by the secretary of state of the accuracy of selected texts containing earlier Vatican denunciations of the ritual murder charge.

But Wolf had some bad news for his German colleague. In researching earlier papal pronouncements, the British committee had made a discomfiting discovery. The "fact" that many Jewish organizations had been trumpeting—that earlier popes had denied the existence of Jewish ritual murder—was not true. "I mention this, " wrote Wolf, "in order to warn you and our German friends against repeating the statement that there have been a number of Papal Bulls denouncing the Blood Accusation, as, if the truth were known, we might be subjected to a very prejudicial attack." Earlier popes had only denounced particular ritual-murder accusations; none had ever issued a general refutation of the accusation.

The two documents that Wolf and his colleagues had found that they thought could be most helpful were a thirteenth-century encyclical of Innocent IV, and a report written in 1758 by Lorenzo Cardinal Ganganelli at the request of the Holy Office, both defending Jews from charges of ritual murder. It was their authenticity that Lord Rothschild asked the secretary of state to verify.[31]

The Rothschild letter, dated October 17, 1913, can be found today in the Vatican Secret Archives, along with the cover note from the Duke of Norfolk, in a file marked "Concerning the alleged ritual murder by the Judaic nation." "It is probably not unknown to your Eminence," Rothschild wrote the Vatican secretary of state, "that in the City of Kieff [sic] in the Empire of Russia certain evil disposed persons have recently revived against the Jews the atrocious accusation of Ritual Murder, which has more than once been denounced by the wisdom and the catholic solicitude of the Sovereign Pontiffs."

Rothschild went on to explain why Vatican testimony had become crucial in the Beilis case. At the trial, Justinus Pranaitis, a Roman Catholic priest and professor of theology, had introduced testimony that "reiterates the familiar arguments by which similar charges of ritual murder have been supported in past times." The priest also, according to Rothschild, denied that any papal documents had ever been issued that cast doubt on the ritual murder accusation, arguing on the contrary that the Vatican had determined that the Jews indeed did practice ritual murder. Father Pranaitis claimed that the documents cited by the Jews to make the contrary case were in fact forgeries. Given this situation, wrote Rothschild, it would be most helpful if the Vatican could provide official authentication of the text of the two documents in question, copies of which he appended to his letter.

The Rothschild letter had come via the Duke of Norfolk, who also included the cover note that Rothschild had sent him. "As the trial commences this week," Rothschild had written to Norfolk, "it would be a great advantage if we could have His Eminence's reply at his earliest convenience."[32]

After consulting with the Pope and with the Holy Office of the Inquisition, Cardinal Merry del Val replied to Rothschild on October 18. His letter was brief, but to the point. "My Lord," he wrote in English, "In reply to your letter of October 7th. I am in a position to certify that the type-written copy of Ganganelli's Report to the Consultors of the Holy Office is substantially accurate. I am able to give you this assurance after inquiries made at the Holy Office where the original document is kept. As to the extract of Innocent IVth's Letter, there can be no doubt of the accuracy . . . which is confirmed by the fact of Ganganelli citing it in his Report."[33]

By October 22, a copy of the secretary of state's letter, certified as authentic by the Russian Embassy in London, was in the hands of Paul Nathan in Berlin. He immediately sent it by special courier to Kiev, where it reached Beilis's lawyers on October 27. But the Jews were soon disappointed, for the Russian court refused to accept the document. It could only be admitted as evidence if Merry del Val himself sent it directly to the court.[34]

Rothschild had initially replied to the secretary of state's letter with a note of thanks, containing his own rosy interpretation of what the cardinal had said: Not only would the cardinal's letter have great weight in the Kiev trial, he wrote; it would also "prove to the world at large that the Holy See at the present moment, as in olden days, utterly repudiates this foul and unjustifiable accusation." When Rothschild subsequently learned that the Russian court had rejected the letter, he sent the secretary of state an urgent telegram. Before the letter could be used at the trial, he advised the cardinal, "it is necessary that your Eminence's signature should be legally certified, that is to say your Eminence will have to telegraph a repetition of your letter to me addressing it to Boldyro the presiding judge of the Kieff District Court of Justice."

But this was going too far. In the Vatican Secret Archives file, handwritten at the bottom of Rothschild's telegram the following note by the secretary of state, dated November 4, 1913, can be found: "I sincerely regret to have to say that it is quite impossible for me to take initiative of addressing any communication to Kieff. If questioned by qualified person I am of course ready to confirm statements contained in my letter to you. With highest esteem. Card. Merry del Val."[35]

As a result, the Vatican declaration was never officially entered into the Beilis murder trial. But it may well have helped anyway. There is evidence that the czar himself read the cardinal's statement, for the czar was following the trial closely. When the jury—despite widespread local belief in the Jew's guilt—read its verdict of not guilty, many observers—and not only those committed to the ritual murder charge—suspected that the jurors had been pressured. High government officials, it was thought, sought to spare the Russian government the unfavorable international publicity that a guilty verdict would have brought.[36]

For those who view Pius X as making a radical break with the Vatican's past attitudes toward the Jews, the Beilis case marked a historic turning point. After decades of papally approved campaigns smearing the Jews with the brush of ritual murder, a pope had stood up and defended them.

Andrew Canepa, in support of this interpretation, cites a letter that the Pope himself sent to his old Jewish friend Romanin Jacur, three weeks after Merry del Val sent his famous telegram to Lord Rothschild. In referring to the ongoing trial in Kiev, the Pope assured his friend that "the Holy See will study every means to prevent the fatal consequences of the infamous fanaticism of those populations," and he added, "I pray that the trial end without harm to the poor Jews."[37]

But if we take a step back, what exactly does the Beilis case show? First of all, the statement released by the Vatican could hardly have been more limited and circumspect. It simply acknowledged the authenticity of two Church texts whose authenticity was never in any serious doubt; indeed, one of which—a papal encyclical—was widely available in published form. Neither the Pope nor his secretary of state took advantage of the request to make a general statement repudiating all ritual murder charges against the Jews.

Most significant, by not taking this step, the Pope allowed the Catholic press, including that part of it viewed inside and outside the Church as communicating the Pope's true sentiments, to continue to tar the Jews with the ritual murder charge. *L'Unità cattolica*, in Florence, offers an excellent example. Known for reflecting papal perspectives, and enjoying close relations with Pius X, the paper ran article after article during the Beilis trial asserting Jewish guilt. When Jewish newspapers published copies of Merry del Val's message, and argued that it showed that the Pope himself rejected the ritual murder charge, *L'Unità cattolica* and much of the rest of the Catholic press closest to the Vatican ridiculed the Jews' claim. Indeed, *L'Unità cattolica* itself published the text of the secretary of state's telegram in order to show that nowhere had he made such a statement.

In its November 15, 1913, issue, the Italian Jewish newspaper *Il Vessillo israelitico* published a report from its correspondent in Florence, recounting these events and accusing "the Vatican organ in Florence *L'Unita cattolica*," of "conducting a true anti-Semitic campaign against us."[38] Later that month, local Jews wrote an impassioned letter of protest to the paper, citing the secretary of state's declaration as evidence that the Vatican opposed the ritual murder belief.

The *Unità cattolica* editor published the Jews' letter along with his response. The Jews, he wrote, were sadly mistaken. As shown by the trial of the murderers of Simon of Trent and the subsequent canonization of the little martyr, belief in Jewish ritual murder "cannot escape the conscience of Catholics." The editor continued: "As is well known, little Saint

Simon was honored on the altars not because he was murdered, but because it was proven through numerous confessions that it was a case of a crime committed for ritual ends." As for Innocent IV's letter, certified as accurate by Cardinal Merry del Val, "it proves only the magnanimity or, better still, the affection that the popes in every epoch have shown the Jews. Cardinal Merry del Val's letter attests to its authenticity, but is far from denying the existence of the Rite in question." Of course, continued the editor, he did not mean to imply that all Jews were involved in murdering Christian children for their blood. He alluded only, he said, "to those Jewish communities or to those individual Jews who were in the past or who are still today attached to the old traditions."[39]

In France, too, the press closest to the Vatican used the Beilis trial to renew the ritual murder campaign against the Jews, and again Merry del Val's letter did nothing to discourage them. There is no better example than *L'Univers,* which for decades enjoyed the reputation of being the French paper closest to the Vatican. *L'Univers* began a series of reports on the Beilis case on October 30, 1913, *after* the secretary of state's letter had been made known, with an article that began: "This Kiev affair brings clearly to mind that of Damascus. . . . Never has Jewish solidarity been so vividly on display." The paper went on to offer what it presented as overwhelming evidence of the Damascus Jews' guilt. The French consul himself revealed, the paper reported, "that the victim had his blood patiently and meticulously drained off, according to the form found in ritual crimes. The chief rabbi himself was suspected of having carried out the sacrifice, with the collaboration of several fanatics."[40]

A few days later, under the title "The Kiev Trial—Important Testimony," *L'Univers* recounted the gripping testimony of an expert witness at the Beilis trial. The witness had stated without any doubt that Jews still practice ritual murder in the twentieth century. After describing the horrifying way that Jews torture their victims, the paper concluded: "The jury was strongly impressed by the statements of the professor, who has an outstanding reputation in the scholarly world."[41]

Several days later, *L'Univers* linked the traditional Catholic theme of Jewish ritual murder to the modern theme of the Jewish drive for world domination. Referring to a witness's testimony, it reported, "He remarked that while Protestants and the other Christian churches are divided into sects, the Jews know no such divisions. They wish to possess the entire world and they understand that they can only attain this goal if they remain united." And here the article returned to the most traditional of Catholic charges against the Jews: "According to the Talmud, Christians are not human beings and, as a consequence, one has the right to sacrifice them."[42]

On November 12, the same day on which *L'Univers* reported the Kiev jury's not-guilty verdict, the French Catholic paper turned directly to the question of Merry del Val's letter to Lord Rothschild. The Jews, the paper reported, have orchestrated a press campaign aimed at showing that they have never committed ritual murder. In "an effort to establish this lie, they have gone so far as to invoke the testimony of the Holy See in their favor. Their audacity here knows no bounds." The paper went on to recount how the Jews, through Lord Rothschild, had petitioned the Vatican's secretary of state, asking that the authenticity of certain Church documents be confirmed.

"All it would have taken was a trip to the public library to find the books that would authenticate these documents," remarked the *Univers* author. "This is essentially what, in his witty way, Cardinal Merry del Val replied in his few lines of response." But what do the documents in question really say? Pope Innocent, wrote the journalist, in his apostolic letter to the bishops of Germany and France, "does not at all deny the existence of the ritual murder of Christian children." He had only called on the bishops to put an end to abuses of the charge, for some people were manufacturing cases of ritual murder as a cover for their own unsavory ends. As for Cardinal Ganganelli's report to the Holy Office, claimed the *Univers* author, it had only examined a particular case. Even if it were to be interpreted broadly, it would mean little since it was only Ganganelli's personal opinion, not a statement by the Holy See. Indeed, no pope could ever deny in principle the ritual murder charge, for the Holy See had officially recognized Jewish ritual murder by canonizing Simon of Trent and other Christian martyrs who were such victims of the Jews.[43]

By far the most important documents we have for interpreting the Vatican's position on the Beilis case are the two long articles by Father Paolo Silva that *Civiltà cattolica* devoted to the question. Published in the spring of 1914, in the last months of Pius X's reign, they were read by the Catholic world as putting an end to the polemics in the European press about the Vatican's view of Jewish ritual murder. Recall that the text of the *Civiltà cattolica* articles was sent in advance to the secretary of state for his review. That the journal could have published them without Merry del Val's approval is almost inconceivable.

"Among the authorities consulted . . . to demonstrate the nonexistence of ritual murder, there is one to which the synagogue attributes more value than to all the rallies and all the newspapers in the world," wrote Father Silva. "It is one that merits our own special attention as well, for it is the authority of the Holy See." It is rather curious, albeit readily understandable, Father Silva added, "to see the haste with which these eternal haters of the Christian name have sought to call on papal testimony to escape this capital charge."

The Jews, wrote Father Silva, not only had the nerve to approach the Holy See on this matter, but somehow thought Lord Rothschild to be the most appropriate person to write for them. "We confess," wrote the Jesuit, "that we cannot see why a man speaks on behalf of his people when, essentially, he is nothing but a rich trafficker, a banker." It is revealing, he continued, that the Jews' most esteemed authority is such a man, for it demonstrates that "the entire Jewish religion has been reduced to the cult of the golden calf." "What in fact did the Jew Lord ask?" He wanted the Pope to say whether a letter of Innocent IV and a report of a Holy Office consultant were authentic or not. "Well," Father Silva wrote, "it has been rightly observed that it certainly was not necessary to approach the Cardinal secretary of state to obtain such a verification."

Father Silva then examined the question of Father Pranaitis's testimony at the Beilis trial as an expert on Church theology. After praising Pranaitis's vast learning, Father Silva argued that the Jews had misrepresented the priest's testimony. The priest had never doubted the authenticity of the documents in question, "but he denied the meaning that the defenders of the synagogue gave them . . . and in this Pranaitis was correct a thousand times over."[44]

The *Civiltà cattolica* article then provided the text of Innocent IV's 1247 encyclical, to which Father Silva added his own commentary. "Now in all of this it is clear that there is nothing that Rothschild and his coreligionists claim to find." Silva then reprinted Merry del Val's brief letter to Rothschild to demonstrate that nowhere did the secretary of state deny the existence of Jewish ritual murder.

The *Civiltà cattolica* article went on to argue that, despite the not-guilty verdict, the Kiev case showed all the signs of a ritual murder performed by the Jews. Only Jewish bribes to the Russian authorities had gotten the Jews off.

"And let us sum things up," wrote Father Silva. "A boy goes missing on the grounds of a Jewish factory and his body is found riddled with wounds. Science has established the time and the method; it has measured the systematic blows and the agony suffered by the victim. It has indicated the goal . . . the murder was committed by people who wanted to extract the blood. Now of such people one race alone is known."

The following month, *Civiltà cattolica* offered further evidence from the Kiev case, portraying the Jews' diabolical nature in even more horrifying detail: The Jew, wrote Father Silva, drinks blood all the time, and, indeed, the Jesuit father had found texts that reveal that Jews consider blood to be "a drink like milk." The important thing the Jew must keep in mind, he wrote, is that he must not simply murder the Christian child, but make sure that the child dies in the most painful manner possible.

It is worth recalling here the year that this was published. It was 1914.[45]

PART THREE

On the Eve
of the Holocaust

CHAPTER TWELVE

A Future Pope in Poland

T HE DRAMATIC TIMING of Pius X's death, on August 20, 1914, two weeks after the outbreak of World War I, led some to say that the pontiff had died from a broken heart. Although no one yet realized how great the war's horrors would be, the cardinals who hurriedly assembled on the last day of August knew that there was no time for delay. In less than a week they elected Giacomo della Chiesa, archbishop of Bologna, as Pius X's successor.

Behind the election of Della Chiesa was the feeling among many of the cardinals that Pius X's lack of diplomatic skills had cost the Church dearly. As the Great War got under way, the Vatican seemed perilously isolated. In 1904, the growing dispute with France had led to a complete break in relations with the Vatican, followed the next year by a new French law separating Church and state. Similar conflicts plagued the Vatican's relations with other countries as well.

Born in 1854 to an aristocratic family in Genoa that already claimed one pope in its family tree, Della Chiesa was a graduate of Rome's Academy of Noble Ecclesiastics. As a young man he was the protégé of Mariano Rampolla, and in 1882, when Rampolla was appointed papal nuncio in Spain, he brought Della Chiesa with him as his secretary. When Rampolla subsequently became Leo XIII's secretary of state, in 1887, Della Chiesa was named his assistant once again, later rising to the post of undersecretary of state.

In his long years in the Secretariat of State, Della Chiesa impressed people with his good political judgment, diplomatic skills, and sense of history. He also developed a broad understanding of European politics.

In 1907, Della Chiesa was given his first major pastoral role when, at the age of fifty-three, he was named archbishop of Bologna. He now had the range of experience—diplomatic and pastoral—thought to make the ideal background for a pope. Yet Della Chiesa barely became a cardinal in time to take part in the 1914 conclave, rising to that rank only three months before Pius X's death. On winning the vote of his fellow cardinals, Della Chiesa took the name of Benedict XV.

Benedict XV differed from his predecessor not only in background and style, but also in outlook and approach to the world. Following a century of popes who, from the time of Napoleon's demise, sought to restore the old Catholic theocracy, there was finally a pope who understood that the old world could never be brought back, that the Church had to find a way to come to terms with modern times.[1]

Almost overnight the denunciations of the Masonic conspiracy against the Church, a regular feature of papal encyclicals since the time of Pius IX, ended. Another sign of the new breeze blowing through the Vatican was the nervous reaction to the Pope's election by those in the Church who were most invested in the previous papal outlook. Among these were the editors of the newspapers most closely associated with Leo XIII. They had long cast themselves as courageous clerical knights in the papal crusade against modern times. Now they worried that the new pope did not share their views. When, to his dismay, the editor of Florence's *L'Unità cattolica* learned that Della Chiesa had been elected pope, he searched desperately through the pages of past issues of his paper to find something positive they had written about the new pontiff. Although Della Chiesa had served for the previous seven years as archbishop of Bologna, not far from Florence, the editor could find only one positive mention of anything he had ever done there: his denunciation of the tango![2]

Following Benedict XV's papacy, no pope could return to the intransigence of his predecessors, nor could any aspire to a return of the Papal States, or reject out of hand all modern ideas. Yet his influence was limited, not least because he remained in office for only seven years. The new pope also lacked the charisma of some of his predecessors, and many people found him uninspiring.

In a rather unkind—and perhaps even unfair—description, the noted American journalist Anne O'Hare McCormick portrayed the Pope at a 1921 Vatican ceremony, announcing the names of newly appointed bishops, as less than impressive. "In his insignificant figure and rather expressionless face," she wrote, "there is no majesty, spiritual or secular. . . . He was lost in something impersonal, perpetual, obliterating." Shortly after the Pope's death the following year, she recalled him in similarly un-flattering terms. "One saw him at public functions in the Vatican," she wrote, "drooping under his tiara, dwindling within his embroidered state, plainly bored and burdened by his augustness. . . . He made no appeal to the imagination—a little man, awkward, tired, sallow, one shoulder slightly higher than the other, with no eloquence, no radiance, no personal charm."[3]

But however unimpressive he may have seemed to this American jour-nalist, Benedict XV did have the courage to try to chart a new course for papal relations with the Jews—though the course would be reversed at his death in January 1922. With his election to the papacy, the anti-Semitic campaign in the papally linked press was soon suppressed. This was nowhere more evident than in *Civiltà cattolica,* which, following its two blood-curdling articles on Jewish ritual murder in the last months of Pius X's papacy, waited until the first months of the papacy of Benedict XV's successor, Pius XI, before fully resuming its anti-Semitic campaign.

The concern that dominated Benedict XV's papacy was World War I and, in particular, finding a way to influence the peace agreement that fol-lowed it. As it turned out, the postwar peace conference would do much to shape the political history of the twentieth century. The problem, from the Vatican's perspective, began in April 1915, when the allies signed the secret Treaty of London. At the insistence of Italy—a state which the Holy See still, fifty-four years after its creation, refused to recognize as legitimate—the treaty contained an article excluding the Vatican from any postwar peace conference.

Among the Vatican's efforts to gain a place at the peace table, certainly one of the strangest involved secret negotiations with the Jewish commu-nities of France, England, and the United States. In its initial form, the Vatican proposal was triggered by what was happening in the Polish lands under czarist rule. Retreating in disorder from the advancing German army, Russian troops were wreaking havoc there, murdering Jews and pil-laging their homes. The Vatican secret proposal called for the Pope to denounce the anti-Jewish violence. In exchange, the Jews of France, Britain, and the United States were to try to persuade their governments to make a place for the Vatican at the postwar peace conference.

The negotiations were spearheaded by a French Catholic politician and journalist, François Deloncle, in conjunction with a French Jew, Lucien Perquel. The talks, however, quickly became enmeshed in international politics. With Russia fighting alongside the other allied armies against Germany and Austria, neither the French nor the British government welcomed a Vatican denunciation of the Russian army. Deloncle, on the other hand, was among those who believed that Christian Orthodox Russia was more of a long-term threat to western society than were Germany and Austria. This was also the view of many in the Vatican, including Eugenio Pacelli, the future Pope Pius XII, who, from his position in the Vatican diplomatic service, helped encourage the Deloncle talks.

In May 1915, Deloncle and Perquel met with the Pope, followed by an audience accorded to Deloncle alone the next month. The Pope received them warmly and suggested that he prepare an encyclical in defense of the Jews, to be released on the first anniversary of the outbreak of the war. He added, however, that for his efforts to be effective, it was important that his diplomatic position be reinforced. He called on the Jewish communities to use their influence with their governments to see that the Holy See be given a seat as a neutral power at the postwar conference. Later on, the Vatican also asked the Jews to help convince the British, French, and American governments to support an independent Polish state after the war.

Despite the initial excitement, the negotiations ended in failure. By early 1916, both the French and the British Jewish organizations had turned against the plan, and were worried that the Americans might be buying into it. In a letter dated April 28, 1916, David Alexander and Claude Montefiore, presidents of the two major organizations of British Jews, wrote to the president of the American Jewish Committee in New York to convince the Americans to reject the Vatican proposal.

"We need scarcely say," they wrote, "that had the proposals of M. Deloncle been limited to a humanitarian intervention of the Pope on behalf of our suffering brethren, we should have welcomed them without reserve and with the utmost gratitude; but, as you will see, the motives of the proposed intervention, as frankly avowed to us by M. Deloncle, were such as no British citizens could, in the present circumstances of Europe, entertain, while the intervention itself was made subject to conditions which, in our view, were calculated to involve the whole Jewish community in extremely serious dangers."

Alexander and Montefiore argued that Jews, as Jews, should not get involved in questions of international politics that did not specifically concern Jewish welfare. Were we to do what the Vatican proposed, they wrote, "we should have alienated our best friends among the Great Powers, lost the sympathy of the Russian Liberals, and extended, perpetuated and justified certain Anti-Semitic tendencies in the Orthodox Greek Church."

As for the idea that Jews should lobby their government to support a formal role for the Holy See at the postwar peace conference, "This proposal involves the whole delicate question of the sovereign status of the Pope, on which Italy feels very deeply. Italy would certainly resent the participation of His Holiness in the peace Congress . . . and she would certainly not soon forgive the Jews, if she found them ranged against her on this question." Nor was the situation much better in England, where "Protestant feeling would probably be aroused, by the revival of the Legate question, and it would certainly find an angry echo in France, in quarters where our best friends are now to be found. All this could only result in a wide and embittered extension of Anti-Semitism."

Finally, they wrote, it was inappropriate for foreign Jews to take a public position on Polish independence. "It is a question upon which the Poles, Jewish and Christian, must decide for themselves." Moreover, "international Jewish support for the Polish independence party at this moment would be everywhere regarded as an anti-Russian manifestation, and consequently as an attempt to embarrass the Allies in the war."[4]

Reluctantly, the American Jewish Committee closed ranks with its French and British counterparts, and the Deloncle mission was brought to an end.[5]

Although excluded from a formal place at the peace table, the Pope continued to be concerned about the fate of Poland, with its large Roman Catholic population. Poland had emerged from the Napoleonic era carved up, its land divided between czarist Russia, the Austro-Hungarian empire, and Prussia. A century later, it became one of the battlegrounds of the First World War. At the war's beginning, czarist troops swept into the Austrian-governed Polish territory of Galicia, leaving Russia in control of the bulk of the Polish lands. But in a 1915 counterattack German and Austrian armies defeated the Russians and brought German-Austrian control over virtually all of what had once been the Kingdom of Poland. Later, with the defeat of the Axis powers, the future of the Polish territories remained one of the principal questions before the postwar peace conference.[6]

At the war's end, the archbishop of Warsaw asked the Pope to send an emissary to Poland to take stock of the situation. In response, Benedict XV made what was arguably the most important single decision of his papacy, although he would have had no way of realizing it at the time. He appointed as his special ambassador a man who had no diplomatic experience whatsoever, a person who seemed in many ways a most unlikely choice: the Vatican librarian, Achille Ratti.[7]

Born in 1857 near Milan, Ratti had, as a young priest, shown a scholarly bent, and began working in Church libraries. His skills led him to positions of ever-increasing responsibility until, in 1910, he was appointed vice-prefect and then, four years later, prefect of the Vatican Library by Pius X. Had Benedict XV not appointed the scholarly cleric to the diplomatic post in Warsaw in 1918, the whole twentieth-century history of the Church might have been different. For it was on the basis of his three years in Warsaw that Ratti was named archbishop of Milan and made a cardinal in June 1921. Just seven months later he was elected pope, becoming Pius XI.

It is because of who Achille Ratti would soon become that his experience in Poland takes on such enormous importance. This was the man who, as pope, would guide the Church's response to the rise of fascism in Italy and nazism in Germany. It was he who would decide how the Church would react in the 1930s to the anti-Semitic laws that the Italian Fascist and German Nazi regimes put into place. During his stay in Poland, charged with investigating local conditions and communicating them to the Vatican, Ratti, for the first time in his life, confronted the "Jewish problem." It was in Poland, amid Europe's largest Jewish population, that he experienced firsthand the potent mix of Catholicism, nationalism, and anti-Semitism.

To fully appreciate the importance of Ratti's Polish reports, something else should be kept in mind. The Vatican has forbidden access to any of Ratti's papers from the time he became pope, in 1922. Rules in force at the Vatican archives prohibit the consultation of materials produced after the papacy of his predecessor, Benedict XV.[8] The papers of Ratti's years in Warsaw just make it under this deadline, and offer priceless insight into the mind of the man who, as pope, would plot the Church's reaction to the gathering clouds of the Holocaust.

Poland's importance for Europe's Jews was great indeed. King Casimir the Great, in the fourteenth century, had invited Jews into Poland to serve as intermediaries between the aristocratic rulers and the mass of peasants. Barred, as elsewhere, from owning land themselves, they became the traders, moneylenders, tax collectors, and estate administrators, even operating the royal mint. Over the next three centuries or so, almost all of Poland's doctors were Jews. But in the eighteenth century, as Russian influence over Poland continued to grow, the Jews' position worsened.

Serfdom was only abolished in Poland in 1862, and Poland's feudal legacy continued to weigh heavily throughout the nineteenth century. Most of Poland remained under Russian authority in the nineteenth century and when, in the last two decades of the century, new legal restrictions were imposed on the Jews in Russia, and violence against the Jews broke out, large numbers of Jews moved westward into Poland. By the end of the nineteenth century, three million Jews lived there, a tenth of the entire Polish population, the largest concentration of Jews in Europe. The great majority were poor, and lived in towns, where they worked as modest artisans, street vendors, or small shopkeepers, and remained socially segregated, mostly speaking Yiddish rather than Polish. The Jews' traditional role as middlemen meant that in small towns throughout the country, Jews often owned the only general store, a Jew was the only moneylender in town, and the local livestock dealer was likely to be a Jew. This meant that in hard times, which were all too frequent, it was to a Jew that the Christian peasant had to go to borrow money, often to be turned away; a Jew who came trying to collect on a debt; and a Jew to whom peasants would have to turn to sell their only cows. None of this was destined to make the Jews popular among the Christian peasantry.

Although the proportion of Jews who were economically well off was small, their impact on the modernization of Poland's economy in the early twentieth century was great. Poland entered the twentieth century without a well-developed Christian bourgeoisie. The aristocrats had long looked down on commerce, and Poland had one of the most backward economies in Europe. What modern business had developed was largely the product of Jewish enterprise. Poland's modest industrialization was due in good part to Jews, and Jews ran many, perhaps most, of the banks as well. A large presence in Poland's tiny middle class, the Jews were also numerous among the highly educated: by 1929, for example, 40 percent of all Poles with university degrees were Jewish.[9]

The development of modern nationalist movements in Poland can be dated to the 1880s, when the land was still divided between areas of Russian, Austrian, and German control. In that decade, the Russian-controlled Polish territories saw the rise of a nationalist movement under the leadership of the fiercely anti-Semitic Roman Dmowski. For Dmowski and his pro-Russian nationalist league, the Jewish problem was absolutely central, for they viewed the Jews as a foreign element, sapping the strength of Catholic Poland. At the same time, in the Austrian-controlled portion of Poland, the struggle against the pernicious influence of the Jews was similarly emerging as one of the central tenets of the new nationalist-Catholic movement. Symptomatic was the call by the Catholic Congress, held in 1893 in Cracow, for a Catholic boycott of all Jewish businesses. At this time, too, a priest, Stanisław Stojałowski—whom we have encountered earlier—was traveling from town to town in Austrian Galicia, rousing the Catholic peasants against the Jews.

Although things quieted down at the beginning of the new century, the anti-Semitic movement exploded once more with the outbreak of the war. With the defeat of czarist forces in 1915, and the German-Austrian invasion, people were looking for someone to blame and found this in the Jews, charged with welcoming the foreign invaders with open arms.

As the war dragged on, it became increasingly clear that Poland, having been temporarily unified under German-Austrian control, would likely remain a unified state after the war as well. When the war finally ended, international calls for the protection of minorities in Poland, together with attempts by some Polish Jewish organizations to win a measure of autonomy for the Jews, triggered a brutal reaction. In Cracow, Kielce, Lublin, and dozens of towns and villages in Galicia, local populations, joined by elements of the various demobilized armies in Poland, rioted, massacring Jews and burning down their homes, businesses, and synagogues. The pogroms were fueled by the nationalist press, filled with charges old and new. The Jews murdered Christian children for their blood, they cried; the Jews had betrayed Poland during the war, collaborating with the German occupiers; the Jews had profited from the war, growing rich while true Poles suffered; the Jews were behind bolshevism, the newest scourge to threaten Poland.

When the Paris Peace Conference began in January 1919, Roman

Dmowski was there, serving as one of Poland's two official representatives. The prospect that the fiercely anti-Semitic Dmowski or one of his associates from the National Democratic party might come to power heightened concerns in the diplomatic community about the fate of Poland's Jews. As a result, in restoring the Polish state, which had been eradicated in 1795, the peace treaty obligated the Polish government to offer guarantees protecting the rights of Jews and other ethnic minorities.[10]

The situation, from the Jews' viewpoint, quickly deteriorated, as war erupted that same year between Poland and the newly created Soviet Union. Polish armies surged deep into Russian territory, and along the way helped organize pogroms against the Jews. When, the following year, the Polish army retreated before an advancing Red Army, both the Polish military and the Church spread the notion that bolshevism was the work of the Jews, an instrument employed in their struggle for world conquest. Typical was the letter that the bishops of Poland sent in 1920 to their fellow bishops outside the country: "The real goal of bolshevism is the conquest of the whole world. The race that directs it came to dominate it through their gold and their banks. Today the ancestral imperialist impulse that flows through its veins drives it to crush the people under the yoke of its domination." Every Pole knew just which race the Polish bishops were referring to. A new round of pogroms followed.[11]

It was into this postwar battleground that the Vatican librarian stepped in June 1918, under the supervision of Pietro Cardinal Gasparri, Benedict XV's sixty-six-year-old secretary of state. A man from a humble background—he was called *"il contadino"* (the peasant) behind his back— and the last of nine children, Gasparri had by force of his intelligence and hard work risen through the ecclesiastical ranks. Known as one of the Church's greatest experts on canon law, he had spent the last two decades of the previous century teaching the subject at the Catholic Institute of Paris. Esteemed by Leo XIII, he was named archbishop in 1898 and sent as papal representative to Peru, returning three years later to Rome to become secretary of the Congregation for Extraordinary Ecclesiastical Affairs. Named cardinal in 1907, Gasparri was chosen by Benedict XV in 1914 to be his secretary of state, replacing Merry del Val.[12]

Achille Ratti was shocked by the news that the Pope had chosen him for the delicate diplomatic mission to Warsaw, but he quickly made preparations for his departure. The secretary of state presented him with a memo explaining his duties: "The mission entrusted to Mons. Ratti," wrote Gasparri, "is to be purely ecclesiastical, that is to identify the religious needs in those regions, which have long been subject to the oppressive regime of the Imperial Russian government, and to refer these findings to the Holy See. He is furthermore to collaborate closely with the Polish prelates in an effort to complete the work of reconstruction that they have undertaken, in the best possible way."[13]

Shortly after the secretary of state gave Ratti his instructions, the Pope himself sent a letter to all the bishops in Poland informing them of Ratti's mission and calling on them to stand united in order to defend the Church in the critically important times in which they lived. On his arrival in Warsaw in early summer, Ratti was briefed by the archbishop of Warsaw, Poland's highest-ranking clergyman. Much of the country remained in tatters, he learned. People lived in poverty and social unrest was spreading, pitting one ethnic group against another. Yet there was also great excitement, for the prospect of an independent Polish state, following over a century of foreign domination, had kindled people's spirits.

Ratti also learned that there was some dissension among the Polish bishops. Of special concern to him was the case of Augustinus Łosiński, bishop of Kielce, known for his insistence on forming a unified Catholic nationalist party. In mid-June, shortly after his arrival in Poland, Ratti went to visit the bishop in Kielce to try to convince him of the dangers of having the Church too closely identified with a single party at a time of great political uncertainty.

In an attempt to reinforce the bishops' unity, the archbishop of Warsaw called a conference of all the Polish bishops in late July. Following the meeting, Ratti described what had happened in a report he sent to Cardinal Gasparri in Rome. At the conference, Ratti recounted, he had argued strenuously against the formation of a single Catholic political party. "I made this proposal after having appropriately sounded people out and in agreement with Monsignor Archbishop, who also thought we should take advantage of the presence of the Monsignor of Kielce to deal with the subject." Ratti's arguments, viewed by the Polish bishops as reflecting those of the Pope himself, won agreement, at least for the moment.

But in his report to Gasparri, Ratti added a note of concern about the bishop of Kielce. "I must unfortunately say that I found him very much changed, and for the worse, from when I had left him in Kielce."[14]

It was no secret that Ratti was in Warsaw to inform the Pope of the current situation in Poland, and he was deluged by advice from people who sought to influence his outlook. In these conversations and letters, one theme kept coming up: Poland's problems were caused by the Jews.

On September 1, 1918, for example, on one of his fact-finding visits through the country, Ratti was presented with a report, in French, titled "Notes on the Current Polish Question Dedicated to His Excellency Monsignor Achille Ratti, Apostolic Visitor." Its author, George Count Moszyński, asked Ratti to convey his views to the Pope. "After the defeats of 1859 and 1866,"[15] the count had written, "Austria sought its salvation in Jewish and Masonic liberalism. . . . It was a great misfortune for the future of our country that the serious statesmen of Galicia let themselves be seduced by liberal teachings, championed by the Viennese Jews and through which the Jews have attached themselves to Austro-Polish politics." A long, fiercely anti-Semitic analysis of the problems of Poland followed.[16]

As his familiarity with the situation in Poland grew, Ratti began sending the secretary of state his own analyses of the role of the Jews in Polish society. These reports, together with the documents that he continued to accumulate, give us precious insight into his evolving view of the Jews.

In a letter to Cardinal Gasparri in late October 1918, Ratti reported on the unrest plaguing the country. "There were some days of great excitement, with some threats—soon dissipated or nearly so—by the extremist parties bent on disorder: the socialist-anarchists, the Bolsheviks (veterans of or influenced by the Russian revolution) and the Jews."[17]

About a week later, the future pope had what, as far as we know, was the only meeting he ever had with Polish Jews. The papal envoy was in the midst of a series of trips around Poland to carry out his mission of surveying the religious, social, and political situation of the country for the benefit of the Vatican. It was on his visit to Sandomierz that his encounter with the Jews took place.

His manner of telling the secretary of state of the Jews' request for a meeting is itself revealing. "Even the Jews (numerous here too as in almost all the cities of the Kingdom, whether small or large, they only subsist through small commerce involving contraband, fraud and usury) asked to be received." Ratti told the local bishop that he would be willing to see the Jews, and so they were ushered in. "The Rabbi came with the leaders of the Synagogue, showering me with compliments and saying how happy they were to greet the pontifical envoy in the name of all their people. I thanked them," Ratti wrote, "recalling the justice and charity that the pontiff had always shown [the Jews], including in Rome itself. I also told them that I was pleased to have them visit on the day in which the entire Church, and particularly that of Sandomierz, was celebrating and honoring the birth of Mary, who came from your people." Ratti concluded his report: "The Rabbi told me that he and his people were grateful and flattered, and it seemed to me and to all the others there that they truly were."[18]

The Jews had reason to be grateful for any attention they could get from the papal envoy, for the times were not good for Poland's Jews. Indeed, within a few days of Ratti's visit, a new series of pogroms erupted, with more killings and beatings of Jews, and more Jewish homes destroyed. In response, on November 25 the archbishop of Warsaw put out a call for an end to the anti-Jewish violence.[19]

Reports of new atrocities against the Polish Jews began to spread through Europe and North America, and an increasing number of newspapers blamed the massacres, at least in part, on the Polish Church. For Benedict XV, more favorably disposed to the Jews than his predecessors and in the midst of delicate diplomacy trying to have the Vatican's voice heard in the postwar settlement, this was not welcome news. Taking advantage of the fact that he had a special envoy on the scene, the secretary of state on December 22 sent an encrypted telegram to Monsignor Ratti: Labeled "Subject: Look into the reported killings of Jews," it read: "Following recent news concerning the killing of Jews, the Holy Father has received petitions. Your Excellency will want to obtain exact information in this regard and to take an interest in their welfare."[20]

Ratti's reaction to this request reveals a great deal. Although Jews in many parts of Poland were being murdered, their homes and synagogues burned to the ground, and the Pope himself had asked him to take an interest in the Jews' welfare, Ratti did nothing of the sort. Examination of his activities in the months that followed reveals that, on the contrary, he did everything he could to impede any Vatican action on behalf of the Jews and prevent any Vatican intervention that would discourage the violence. The secretary of state's telegram came in the midst of Ratti's first set of reports to the Vatican on the situation of the Jews of Poland, but these reports, rather than warning about the Jews' persecutors, were aimed at alerting the Vatican to the dangers posed by the Jews themselves.

In early December, before receiving the secretary of state's telegram, Ratti had sent him an overview of the Polish situation in which he warned of the Jews' disproportionate influence in Poland. "There are about 600,000 Protestants and about two million Jews, but their religious importance is negligible, outside of the fairly frequent conversions to Catholicism." Ratti continued: "But by contrast their economic, political, and social importance (especially that of the Jews) is large and indeed tremendous." Ratti promised the secretary of state that he would provide more details in his next report.[21]

That report came in early January 1919, in the wake of the pogroms and the telegram that Cardinal Gasparri had sent him. For those who see in Achille Ratti the man who, in contrast to his successor, Pius XII, would become the "good pope," the ecumenical spirit who would take the interests of Europe's persecuted Jews to heart, the report can only be disheartening.

"For my part, and as a duty that I believe my mission imposes on me, I never stop repeating to these Most Excellent Bishops and Most Reverend Priests that the more I have come to admire the goodness and the faith of their people, having gotten to see and know it close up, the more I fear that they may fall into the clutches of the evil influences that are laying a trap for them and threatening them. Unfortunately, if they are not defended by the work of good influences, they will certainly succumb."

After this vague, abstract assessment, Ratti then finally comes to the point. Just who are these enemies of Christianity, of the Church, of the Polish people? "One of the most evil and strongest influences that is felt here, perhaps the strongest and the most evil, is that of the Jews."[22]

The papal envoy, of course, did not ignore the urgent instructions that he had been given by Cardinal Gasparri to look into the reports of the violence against Poland's Jews. As we can see from his files, he devoted a considerable amount of time to the task in these months.

Among his earliest sources of information was a report that he commissioned in December on the relations between the Catholics and Jews of Poland (termed, as they universally were by Polish Catholics, relations between Poles and Jews, the assumption being that no Jew could be Polish). The author, who wrote in French and whose name was not noted, was most likely a Polish Catholic aristocrat.

"The Jews in Poland," he informed Monsignor Ratti, "are, in contrast with those who live elsewhere in the civilized world, an unproductive element. It is a race of shopkeepers par excellence," he wrote, although, he added, "the great majority of the Jewish population is sunk in the depths of poverty." Other than a relatively small number of artisans, he reported, the Jewish race "consists of small merchants, dealers, and usurers—or to be more precise all three simultaneously—who live by exploiting the Christian population." During the recent German occupation, the fact that "the jargon that the Jews speak in Poland [i.e., Yiddish] is but a German dialect," allowed the Jews to profit, and, he argued, the Germans' espionage "was carried out exclusively by the Jews." He attributed the recent pogrom in Lvov, Galicia, to popular anger with the Jews' link to the Bolsheviks, a theme that ran throughout the Polish anti-Semitic literature of the period. "We must call attention to the Jews' role in the Bolshevik movement. We do not want to claim that every Jew is, ipso facto, a Bolshevik. Far from it. Yet we cannot deny the preponderant role that the Jews play in this movement, both among the Polish communists and among the Russians where—with the exception of Lenin—all the Bolshevik leaders are either Polish Jews or Lithuanian Jews."[23]

Foreign press stories in late 1918 reporting the slaughter of Polish Jews and the burning of their homes, meanwhile, provoked outrage among many Polish Catholics. The stories were the result, they believed, of a Jewish conspiracy against the nascent Polish state. Some admitted the violence but blamed it on outside agitators. In any case, it was argued, whatever violence Polish Catholics had visited on the Jews was the Jews' own fault.

Shortly after the first articles began appearing in the foreign press, Ratti received a copy of a statement prepared by the Polish diplomatic mission in Vienna, which he filed under the heading "On the alleged Jewish pogroms in Galicia at the hands of the Poles." In response to foreign press accounts of the "so-called pogroms of the Jews in western Galicia," the document offered an alternative account. "Following the recent political subversion in Austria, different bands of deserters were formed in certain regions of western Galicia, and soon reinforced by some obscure local elements. Finding their best booty and their easiest prey in the shops, these bands began to plunder them. Because small commerce in the towns and hamlets of Galicia is largely in Jewish hands, this movement took on an anti-Semitic character." The report then, however, went on to argue that a larger, more sinister conspiracy was involved. "Certain indications show," it concluded, "that this movement was encouraged by foreign agents sent by those parties who have an interest in provoking troubles in Poland and presenting it before the civilized world as a country mired in anarchy."[24]

One of these pogroms had taken place in Kielce on November 11–12, where four Jews were killed, 250 injured, and many homes and shops destroyed. Among the documents Monsignor Ratti collected were several produced by the Kielce city council dealing with these events.

Three weeks after the violence, the fifteen Jewish members of the Kielce city council sent a letter of protest to the council president. Among their other complaints, they charged that neither the city government nor the central government had done anything to stop the violence; that the local police had remained hostile to the Jews during the attacks; and that although the city council had twice met since the pogrom, it had not seen fit to condemn the violence, nor had any of those responsible for it been arrested.

Presentation of this petition provoked an angry debate, pitting the Jewish councilors against the Catholic majority. The council president rejected the Jews' charges and blamed the Jews for the violence. What had provoked the disorder, he said, was a meeting that a group of Jews had held in a local theater. Word had leaked out that inside the theater the Jews were shouting, "Down with the Polish language! We don't want a Polish government!" Well, said the president, under such circumstances "it is hardly a surprise that the people get excited and are driven to commit excesses." Added another Catholic councilor, "I am afraid I must agree that all of this is the result of a campaign of provocation that the Jews have long been carrying out against the Poles." At this one Jewish councilor lamented, "Before there was a boycott [of Jewish stores], hatred, but not the shedding of blood."

Another Jewish councilor then rose to say that he himself had been the vice president of the meeting in the theater, and he could vouch for the fact that "all the speeches, whether in Polish or in Yiddish, ended with the shout: 'Long live a free, united democratic Poland!' " He concluded: "There was no anti-Polish speech. The pogrom was being prepared beforehand."

At the end of the meeting, the Kielce city council majority passed a motion. It condemned the violence against the Jews, but quickly added that it was the Jews themselves who were responsible for it. "The Council affirms," the motion asserted,

that the anti-Semitic movements were an instinctive reaction of
the mass of citizens. They were aroused by the ceaseless exploita-
tion on the part of the class of shopkeepers, of whom 80% consists
of Jews, and by the provocative behavior of the Jews during the
time of the war when they put themselves at the service of the
Germans and the Austrians. They were also provoked by the Jewish meeting that was held in Kielce on November 11, in which the
Jews asked not only for equal legal rights, which the Polish state
does not refuse them, but for special privileges, which they have in
no other State. They demanded national autonomy, which is an
attack on the vital interests of the Polish state and an expression of
their aspiration to form a Judaic Poland, something that the Polish
people will never permit.[25]

Monsignor Ratti was able to gain insight into the role being played by the
Church in the Kielce area by another document that he obtained and had
translated from Polish. It was a letter that the bishop of Kielce had sent on
December 29, 1918, to all the clergy in his diocese. Parliamentary elections were approaching—they would be held the next month—and he
wanted to prepare them for the role they would play.

"It is the goal of the Christian League of National Unity to improve
the people of the countryside in the religious, civil, and cultural domain.
Politics plays only a secondary role. The priests ought to promote this
League in order to prevent people—especially their own parishioners—
from joining the socialist-populist organizations. You should not get
upset if the peasants for the moment seem reluctant." Their reluctance,
the bishop went on to say, was the result of a campaign of slander that
"the members of the Polish Socialist Party and the Jews" had waged
against the priests.

In the upcoming election campaign, the priests "must take an active
part. It is not only a civic duty," he reminded them, "but a religious one,
because the nature of the deputies will determine the laws and the rights
for the Church and for Catholic life." The bishop then listed a series of
rules his priests should follow. The election campaign would pit two
groups against each other: "The first consists of the national bloc, in
which the parties that stand for the national principles are found; the
second consists of the socialist bloc, to which (aside from the Jews), the
'populists' . . . also adhere. The priests thus should coordinate their action

with that of the Committee of the national bloc, to prepare a common list. Do not enter into any contact with the socialist and 'populist' bloc."

"The pulpit," wrote the bishop, "is not the appropriate place for political propaganda." But, he quickly added, "the priest can say from the pulpit which list people should vote for." Do not get discouraged, he urged his priests. "Don't get upset when you hear 'down with the priests' shouted, and have no fear. Put [your parishioners] on guard against the socialist and populist program. They promise much, but no sooner would they come to power than they would abandon the people to the Jews and to the socialist government."[26]

At the same time as he was collecting information on the situation in Kielce, Monsignor Ratti also gathered reports on other recent violence against the Jews. In early January he received an account, in French, labeled "The truth about the 'pogrom' in Lvov, by an impartial witness." It began by recalling that the Lvov pogrom, which broke out on November 21, had been reported in newspapers throughout the world. Yet notwithstanding the claims to the contrary found in these accounts, "Polish authorities have taken all measures necessary to satisfy the needs of criminal justice." The goal of his report, Ratti's correspondent stated, was to correct overblown stories in the press and to state the facts impartially.

The press had reported that many of the murderers and pillagers were Polish soldiers, but this was a misimpression caused by the fact that many common criminals had donned military uniforms to deflect suspicion. On November 23, the report continued, Jewish homes were burned down, along with "three synagogues and several Jewish houses of prayer. In addition, one hundred Torah scrolls were burned, among them some having great historical value." Yet, insisted Ratti's informant, the reports in the Jewish press "of a dozen Jews burned alive during the fire in the synagogue were absolutely false." Everyone inside was able to escape "through a crevice that opened in its wall."

"News of the number of Jewish victims of the Lvov 'pogrom,'" he wrote, was exaggerated, although, he added, "one cannot deny that it was accompanied by certain acts of cruelty." The government had quickly swung into action and, by taking stern measures, had put an end to the pogrom on the same day it had begun. An accurate estimate of the damage, he figured, would include 73 murdered—"including some Jews burned alive," he added parenthetically—280 seriously injured, more than 500 Jewish businesses destroyed, and 54 larger homes burned down. As of mid-December, he concluded, 4,000 Jewish families had reg-istered for assistance, having been "the victims of murder, fire, pillage, and theft."[27]

On January 15, Monsignor Ratti was ready to send his report—titled "The Situation in Poland. The Anti-Semitic pogroms"—to Cardinal Gas-parri. "As for the pogroms and the massacres of the Jews, about which Your Excellency sent me the encrypted telegram number 22," Ratti wrote, "I have been looking into them and continue to do so, and I already have various documents in hand. But nothing yet is clear and definitive. Certainly nothing has occurred in Warsaw. I say nothing of any importance or gravity; the Jews there are incredibly numerous (approxi-mately three hundred thousand!) and they could not be more detested, but they are not being bothered, much less persecuted."

He had, he reported, received details on two of the pogroms, one in Kielce and one in Lvov. As for that of Kielce, he informed the secretary of state, "I have in hand the transcript of a session of that Town Council of early December." What had he concluded from this evidence? It was all very murky: "The Jews blame the Christians, and the Christians blame the Jews." He awaited, he wrote, further information before reaching any conclusion on the matter.

In the area of Lvov, Monsignor Ratti reported, the disorders had left "hundreds of dead and entire areas sacked and burned." But it was unclear, he wrote, just who was to blame for the violence. A government inquest had been launched, and he would let the secretary of state know the result just as soon as he received it.[28]

Although Monsignor Ratti continued to gather reports of periodic massacres of Jews, he never did send the secretary of state any further evaluation of the violence against them, and certainly never did anything to dispute the notion that the murders were the Jews' own fault.

While Ratti himself appeared to be unconcerned about the violence against the Jews, the diplomats of several of the countries at the Versailles peace conference were horrified by news of the new wave of pogroms. As a result, in the final treaty signed in June 1919, the victorious powers made the new Polish government agree to a series of provisions aimed at protecting its Jewish population.[29] Yet, despite these legal assurances, the Jews of Poland had reason to be worried. For the great majority of Poles, being Polish meant being Catholic. Symptomatically, when the first par-liament of the about-to-be-independent Polish state opened in February of that year, they began their first session by filing into the grand cathe-dral of Warsaw to celebrate a solemn mass.[30]

The depths of anti-Semitism among the Catholic clergy of Poland at the time could hardly be overstated, yet Monsignor Ratti saw nothing amiss. He had nothing to say, for example, about such prominent clerics as Father Józef Kruszyński who, like many of his fellow priests was a believer in a Jewish world conspiracy. Kruszyński in 1920 explained that "racial purity created what is called an anthropological type." Three years later, Kruszyński would write: "If the world is to be rid of the Jewish scourge, it would be necessary to exterminate them, down to the last one." Lest such views be thought to be regarded as less than respectable among the Catholic hierarchy in Poland of the time, it is worth recalling that two years later, in 1925, Kruszyński was named head of the Catholic University of Lublin. As Pope Pius XI, Achille Ratti would die shortly before he could have seen Father Kruszyński's scenario become reality, with the death of the overwhelming majority of Poland's three million Jews.[31]

There remains an episode of the Ratti mission to Poland that raises some other disturbing questions, reflecting the very recent attempts by the Vatican to rewrite its own history of dealings with the Jews. This involves the final report of the Ratti mission, written in July 1921, and published—in edited form—by the Vatican press in 1990.

Ratti had been placed in a difficult position as papal nuncio to Poland, for tensions were high and he was often caught in the middle of antago-nistic political forces. What eventually led him into trouble—indeed, brought about a hasty departure—was his attempt to keep the Vatican out of the battle over the borders that divided Poland from its neighbors.

In 1919, the Holy See had been among the first to recognize the legiti-macy of the new Polish state and it was at that time that Ratti's status was upgraded from apostolic visitor to papal nuncio. But the borders of the new Polish state were contested, with Polish nationalists agitating to have them expanded to incorporate lands that they considered historically part of the homeland. Monsignor Ratti did what he could to cool passions and to avoid having the Church too closely identified with any of the parties to the disputes. He was all the more cautious in cases, such as the contro-versy over Upper Silesia, which involved Roman Catholic populations on both sides of the border (Poland and Germany). But the result was that the papal nuncio began to be attacked by partisans on both sides, to the point where the Vatican judged it more prudent to recall him. Pope Benedict XV did so in a way that showed how much he appreciated his work, promoting his nuncio to the prestigious post of archbishop of Milan. In early June 1921, Ratti left Poland.[32]

Ratti departed before his work was finished, for the secretary of state wanted to get a complete, final report of the mission, which had lasted three eventful years. Fortunately, Ratti had left behind his most trusted assistant, Monsignor Ermenegildo Pellegrinetti.

Pellegrinetti was a forty-five-year-old priest of humble background. He had met Ratti in Rome shortly before the Vatican librarian had received the surprising news of his appointment to Warsaw. Ratti asked Pellegrinetti to come as his special assistant and, indeed, Pellegrinetti arrived in Warsaw even before Ratti, in early June 1918. Thanks to Ratti, Pellegrinetti was soon inserted into the Vatican diplomatic service, and accompanied him on all of his fact-finding trips through Poland.

On June 11, 1921, a week after Monsignor Ratti's departure, Pellegrinetti wrote in his diary how lonely he now felt, left behind in Warsaw. But all this changed when, on July 1, he received an encrypted telegram from Cardinal Gasparri. He was to prepare a report of the findings of Monsignor Ratti's mission, detailing the political and religious situation in Poland. "Now have I ever found something to do!" he wrote. "My head is spinning, but I will work hard."

Over the next week he worked hard indeed, drafting and redrafting a seventy-page report. He was proud of the result, as he confided in his diary: "It may seem boastful, but I think the work has been a success, written in a pleasant manner both in language and in style."[33]

In preparing the document titled "The Final Report of Achille Ratti's Mission in Poland," Pellegrinetti studied all the letters that Ratti had written to the secretary of state over the previous three years, as well as all the other materials they had collected. He wanted to prepare a report that Ratti would be proud of, and, as we shall see, there is every reason to believe that Ratti was most pleased with it.

The Jews were among the report's major concerns. Ratti and his assistant had been struck by the extent to which the Poles equated their national identity with being Catholic, and conversely how the Catholics did not consider Poland's Jews—although in many cases their ancestors had lived there many centuries—to be Poles at all. The territory of the new Polish Republic, wrote Pellegrinetti, contains "numerous Protestants among the Germans, schismatics [i.e., Christian Orthodox] among the Russians . . . and furthermore the cities are full of Jews." But, he added, "the totality of the population that is Polish by race and by language or that feels itself to be Polish, is, aside from a handful of exceptions . . . openly Catholic." Thus, he wrote, "the popular equation Pole = Catholic is formed." This could at times produce comical results. When the bishop of Minsk, he reported, asked a Jew what his nationality was, the Jew "responded that he was Catholic, that is . . . that he spoke Polish!" And so, Pellegrinetti concluded, "patriotism and Catholicism have become in many ways two aspects of the same sentiment."[34]

An entire section of the final report of the Ratti mission was titled simply "The Jews." In 1990, the Vatican Press, in a special series of books making the most important documents from the Vatican archives more accessible, published a volume dedicated to reports of the Ratti Warsaw mission, including the final report. The published version of the section of the final report that is devoted to the Jews begins with the actual opening from the original document: "Poland is the most Judaized country in the world. The Jews there may number as much as three million. They live for the most part in the cities, in many of which they constitute the absolute majority of the population. There are 350,000 of them in Warsaw alone."

Following this introduction, a reader familiar with the original document, found in the Vatican Secret Archives, discovers that something is amiss. The section on the Jews, unlike the bulk of the rest of the report, is interrupted with parenthetical insertions, in italics, providing summaries rather than the actual text.

The first of these interruptions reads as follows: "Mons. Pellegrinetti then briefly emphasizes some elements that characterized the Jews, among others, that they do not speak Polish but Yiddish (that is to say a dialect based on German with some Slavic and Hebrew words), which they use in their schools and their press, written in Hebrew characters. And after recalling that they dress differently and have different customs from all the other citizens, practicing for the most part—as is the case elsewhere—large and small commerce, he does not neglect to note that many are of the working class, and often live in great poverty." Following this paraphrase, the actual text continues.

Why was this section on the Jews paraphrased rather than published in its original form? In the original document the passage on the features that distinguish the Jews from the Poles includes some not mentioned in the published version: "Not only do they differ visibly from Poles owing to their racial characteristics (shortness of stature, large nose, prominent ears, bags under their eyes, etc.). They differ also because of their religion and the strong consciousness and pretension they have of forming a separate nationality." As for the paraphrased passage on the occupations of the Jews, the actual report reads: "They work, as elsewhere, in large and small commerce, including loan-sharking, speculation, and contraband, in which they are specialists, but the working class is also numerous and often lives in great poverty."[35]

Even the published portions of the Ratti report offer a portrait of Poland's Jews as a danger to society. The report continued, "One finds a sharp contrast between the Jewish capitalists who, unfortunately, have a large part of Poland's wealth in their hands, and the Jewish proletariat, among whom the most advanced parties find a following, including Bolshevism, of whom the Jews form the principal force in Poland."

The Russian czars, Pellegrinetti wrote, had pushed the entire "Judaic mass" onto land that had once been part of Poland. They did this, he explained, "with the double goal of removing this undesirable element from the zone that was most Russian, and at the same time weakening the Polish element, who were constantly dreaming of revolt, by mixing [the Jews] in." The report shows the clear signs of the counsel that Monsignor Ratti had been getting from his local Polish advisors, who branded the Jews traitors. "The Germans invading Russian territory favored them, using them as spies and helpers in the requisitions and sacking of the country."

With the end of the war and the creation of the new Polish state, Pellegrinetti went on to report, the Poles had been forced by the Treaty of Versailles to give the Jews the greatest freedom, including permission to continue using their "jargon" rather than Polish. This had led to sharp conflict. "There are a few Jews," the Ratti report continued, "who consider themselves to belong to the Polish nation. These are the so-called 'assimilators,' rejected by the large majority of their coreligionists. The Jewish mass believes itself to belong to another nation and, indeed, to be anti-Polish."

The report painted a picture of the Jews as an insidious foreign force eating away at the Polish nation, preventing it from realizing its national aspirations: "The foreign occupiers always had to try to protect and to favor the Jews in order to stop and to weaken the Poles. Having now become the rulers, the Poles have every interest in reinforcing their own ethnic element and weakening that which is foreign by race, by language, and by sentiment." Now that the Poles were back in charge, he added, the Jews were displeased to find that their own previously privileged place in commerce would face Polish competition.

Here the Ratti report provides a belated response to the secretary of state's urgent request that the stories in the foreign press about bloody attacks on Jews in Poland be investigated. It was all, the mission concluded, a libelous invention, a Jewish attempt to discredit the Polish nation. "Jewish hostility against the new state is on display everywhere, especially abroad, where people speak of pogroms, of boycotts, of persecution, etc., with clear exaggeration. In reality the Jews live here in peace, and what few killings occurred did so exclusively during war operations. There has been no case of premeditated pogroms occurring during normal times."

The report embraces the kind of conspiracy theory found repeatedly in the Catholic anti-Semitic movement. "It is certain that the Jews constitute a major cause of weakness in the Polish state. Having the banks, the press, and many important offices in their hands, and backed by their international organization, they seek the formation of a Judaic Poland." In this view, the Jews were a threat to Poland's integrity because they believed "that Poland is a mixed country where Poles and Jews should live with equal rights and without either part pretending to have the right to impose its own national character or to become predominant."

Pellegrinetti went on to note that while the socialists and radicals showed pro-Jewish attitudes, the Polish nationalists "accuse the Jews of almost all their problems." Here the version of the report published by the Vatican press edits out another portion, providing its own gloss instead. "Apart from certain gossip about the Jews," the editor tells us, the report here briefly describes problems connected with the conversion of the Jews. The report also, writes the editor, "recalls that the Jews made an appeal to the Warsaw nuncio at the end of 1918 but never after that, having apparently found other more efficient means."

The original passage cut out here actually begins by noting: "It is unnecessary to say what a danger [the Jews] represent from a religious point of view. Fortunately, a part of the danger is diminished by the national antipathy for them." As for conversions of Jews to Catholicism, some are for practical motives of career advancement or marriage, but others are sincere. Yet "the case of a Pole who becomes a Jew is extremely rare, for it means rejecting one's nation."

The published version of this passage also made a cut in the description of Ratti's only actual encounter with Jews in his three years in Poland. The Jews had appealed for the nuncio's aid in late 1918, but then never came back. The comment made on this in the original report was slightly different from the edited gloss later given it. The original reads: "Apparently they have other weapons of offense and defense."[36]

While the Jews were seeking to maintain their supremacy in the capitalist sphere, according to the Ratti mission report, they were also responsible for the communist attempts to undermine Poland. But as luck would have it, the Jews' identification with the communists, Pellegrinetti wrote, was something of a blessing. "Communism is less developed, thanks to the antipathy against the Russians who are its champions and against the Jews who (though not all) carry out its propaganda."[37]

IT DID NOT take long for Achille Ratti to show his appreciation for all that his former assistant had done. Barely half a year after Ratti became archbishop of Milan, and was further rewarded by being named a cardinal, Pope Benedict XV died. The conclave to elect his successor initially divided between two men who had served as secretary of state, cardinals Merry del Val and Gasparri. But when Gasparri saw that he could not get enough votes, he did what he could to drum up support for a man he believed would continue his policies. Achille Ratti subsequently showed his appreciation for this support by keeping Gasparri on as secretary of state for another eight years. On February 6, 1922, Achille Ratti, who just four years earlier had been the Vatican librarian, became pope, taking the name Pius XI.[38] A month later, on March 8, Pellegrinetti received a coded telegram in Warsaw: He had just been named papal nuncio to Serbia. In May he was awarded an archbishopric as well. Pellegrinetti's rise had scarcely been less rapid than Ratti's.[39]

Taken together, the reports on the Polish Jews that Achille Ratti himself wrote to the secretary of state, along with the final report of his mission and the reports on the Jews that he collected while in Warsaw, provide us with a precious resource. They allow us, for the first time, to understand the attitudes toward the Jews that Pius XI brought with him when he became pontiff.

There is even more direct evidence that the Polish experience shaped the view of Europe's Jews that Ratti would hold as pope. In a conversation that he had with Benito Mussolini in February 1932, the Pope himself raised the question of the Jews. Lamenting the persecution faced by the Catholic Church in various parts of the world, he turned his attention to Russia. There, Pius XI told Mussolini, the Church's problems had been caused in part by "Judaism's antipathy for Christianity." The Pope went on to say: "When I was in Warsaw I saw that the [Bolshevik] Commissioners . . . were all Jews." He hastened to add that the Italian Jews represented an exception. The Pope thought that the Jews in Italy—a few of whom he had met—were basically good. But the mass of the Continent's Jews, the hordes of Jews who lived in central and eastern Europe, were something quite different, a threat to healthy Christian society, a lesson he learned in Poland.[40]

CHAPTER THIRTEEN

Antechamber to the Holocaust

O VER THE COURSE of the seventeen years of Pius XI's papacy the seeds of modern anti-Semitism began to produce their deadly flowers. By the time the Pope died, in 1939, Jews in large parts of Europe had already been stripped of the equal rights they had won less than a century earlier, and lived in a growing climate of fear, humiliation, and violence.

The full story of the role that Catholic lay people, priests, bishops, and the popes themselves played in making the Holocaust possible is a huge and complex one. Parts of it, especially those concerning the actual war years, 1939–1945, have already been examined and debated in a large and contentious literature. But in sharp contrast with all the polemics over what the Church did and did not do as the Holocaust was underway—and especially the debate over the role of Pius XI's successor, Pius XII—the period leading up to the Holocaust has received relatively little attention. Yet it is to these years that we must turn if we want to know how the systematic murder of Europe's Jews could have become possible.

The story we tell here differs in another way from that more commonly told. For understandable reasons, much of that literature focuses on Germany itself, and on the role played there by the Catholic Church and Catholics (as well as, of course, the Protestant churches and Protestants). But too often the leap has been made from an examination of the Catholic Church in Germany to larger generalizations about the popes' attitudes toward the Jews, and the Vatican's role in promulgating modern anti-Semitism. This is a mistake, and so here, we instead focus more directly on the role of the Vatican and the Pope in the evolution of modern anti-Semitism. At the same time, we look beyond Germany to other dramas underway in Europe at the time, dramas that would ultimately all be linked to the larger one of the Holocaust.

The role played by the Vatican in the development of the policies of discrimination and harassment that set the stage for the Holocaust are most clearly on display in those places where the Church's influence was greatest. The case of Germany is complicated by the fact that Catholics composed a minority (albeit a large one). By contrast, in Italy, France, Austria, and Poland, Catholics formed the great majority of the population, and the Catholic Church enjoyed a central (although certainly not uncontested) place in society.

The case of Italy is of special importance for a number of reasons. First of all, until much later in the century (with John Paul II) the popes were all Italian, as were the large majority of the cardinals who ran the Vatican. Their attitudes were shaped by growing up in Italy, and by participating in a dense network of Catholic organizations there. Once ensconced in Rome, they continued to follow developments in Italian society and politics with special interest. Secondly, because the Vatican and the pope were in Rome, and because both the pope and most of the cardinals of his curia were Italian, the Vatican had more direct influence over popular attitudes in Italy than elsewhere.

The Protocols of the Elders of Zion offers a good place to begin in bringing to light the role of Catholic anti-Semitism in the rise of Nazi and fascist anti-Semitism in the 1920s. Its proponents presented the *Protocols* as a newly discovered document that detailed the Jews' secret plan for taking over the world.[1]

The history of the *Protocols* is a convoluted one. Its origins lie in a political pamphlet written by a Frenchman, Maurice Joly, in 1864. Attacking the outsized ambitions of French emperor Napoleon III, and having nothing to do with the Jews, it employed the imagery of a secret plot hatched in hell. A few years later, a German anti-Semite plagiarized Joly's work as part of a novel he wrote, but instead of focusing on Napoleon III, it fantasized a secret conspiratorial meeting of rabbis, held every hundred years, at which nefarious plans for the next century were hatched. By the 1890s, agents of the Russian secret police had transformed this latter version into a text labeled "Protocols of the Elders of Zion." This was first printed in Russia at the turn of the century, and used in an effort to discredit the Russian reform movement, which backers of the czar identified with the Jews. It was this edition that was translated into English, German, French, and Italian and published in central and western Europe beginning in 1919. The *Protocols* purported to be the newly found minutes of a meeting held by a secret international directorate of Jews plotting world conquest. Of course, no such directorate ever existed, nor had any such meeting ever taken place.

With the first publication of the *Protocols* in London in 1920, Lucien Wolf, one of the leaders of the British Jewish community, published a pamphlet demonstrating the nature of the hoax. In 1921 a series of articles in the London *Times* added further details to the story. Yet, notwithstanding its exposure as a crude forgery, the book quickly became the bible of the anti-Semitic movement of the 1920s throughout Europe and the United States, and was published and championed by the Nazi party itself.

It is easy to see why the book should have been so persuasive to many Catholics, for its basic theme was one that Church publications, from the Vatican down to local diocesan bulletins, had been promoting for decades. In both Italy and France, the best-known disseminators of the forgery were Catholic priests. In Italy, it was none other than Monsignor Umberto Benigni himself who used the book to help lead a renewed anti-Semitic crusade in the 1920s. Benigni, former head of Pope Pius X's secret spy service and former high-ranking member of the Vatican secretariat of state, had been publishing denunciations of Jews as ritual murderers since 1890. However, it was only in 1920 that he began to focus so heavily on the Jewish threat. From 1920 to 1921 he published his own *Bollettino antisemita* (Anti-Semitic Newsletter). He then joined the journal *Fede e Ragione* (Faith and Reason), which had been founded in late 1919 by another priest, Father Paolo De Töth, former director of the Florence daily newspaper, *L'Unità cattolica*. Initially a bimonthly, by 1923 *Fede e Ragione* was published every week and had two editorial offices, one in Florence headed by Father De Töth, and one in Rome directed by Monsignor Benigni.

Benigni published the first Italian edition of *The Protocols of the Elders of Zion* in 1921 as a series of supplements to *Fede e Ragione,* and followed these the next year with a separate small volume, with the title *The Documents of the Jewish Conquest of the World*. The other major publisher of the *Protocols* in Italy was Giovanni Preziosi, who brought out his own edition at the same time. Preziosi, who had left the priesthood in 1913, became with Benigni a ceaseless campaigner for the importance of the *Protocols*.

In keeping with the official Church position, both Benigni and Preziosi were careful to state that they had nothing against the Jews as people. As Benigni put it in a 1921 article, "We do not write to mount a campaign against the Jewish religion nor even against the Jewish race. We respect the Semitic race and its Mosaic religion. Rather, we fight against the degeneration of the Mosaic religion through the introduction of Talmudic teachings, which is responsible for the principle that the Jews should be masters of the world."[2]

As the new "evidence" of the Jewish world conspiracy began to circulate in Western Europe, the Vatican daily, *L'Osservatore romano,* turned to the question. It too was at pains to show that the problem was not with the Jews per se, but with the way the Jews acted. One must distinguish, the author argued, between "the Judaic religion and the political and social power of the world's Jews." The Jew had the right to be shown tolerance, but only so long as he renounced his "hostility toward Christianity, driven by racial hatred and by the thirst for domination."[3]

In France, the main champion of *The Protocols of the Elders of Zion,* and the best-known exponent of Catholic anti-Semitism in the 1920s, was Father Ernest Jouin, a man who had come to devote his life to alerting his fellow Catholics to the Jewish threat. In publishing the forgery in France in 1920, he was able to sign his foreword, aimed at establishing the work's authenticity, "E. Jouin, Prelate of His Holiness," for Pope Benedict XV had honored Jouin with this title in recognition of his work on behalf of the Church.[4]

Jouin's prominence in the French Catholic campaign against the Jews dated to 1912, when he began the *Revue Internationale des Sociétés Secrètes* (International Review of Secret Societies). The following year he founded the French-Catholic League, of which he remained president the rest of his life. Both journal and league were motivated by his desire to serve the Church. He sought only, he said, to follow the Pope's injunction that the clergy battle the forces that were conspiring to destroy Christianity. His special obsession was the Jewish-Masonic conspiracy, and, in a speech to the Congress of the Anti-Judeomasonic League in 1929, he proudly took credit for having been the one to coin the term "Judeomasonic" nine years earlier.[5] He proclaimed: "Israel is king, the Mason is his helper, the Bolshevik his executioner. The Jew believes in the world domination of his race."

Jouin's harping on the supposed Jewish-Masonic conspiracy was in harmony with developments in the German anti-Semitic movement. In the aftermath of World War I, the claim that German defeat had been caused by just such a conspiracy gained increasing popularity. Freemasons and Jews, each seen as part of an international network of people whose prime allegiance was not to the nation in which they found themselves but to one another, came to be jointly seen as the conspirators who plotted against the nation.

For Jouin, the "discovery" of the *Protocols* could not have been more welcome, for it provided, he thought, irrefutable evidence that the secret Jewish conspiracy of which he had been warning for almost a decade was an established fact. As Monsignor Jouin wrote in his commentary on the *Protocols*, its lesson was clear: "From the triple viewpoint of race, of nationality, and of religion, the Jew has become the enemy of humanity."[6] Boasting of his 30,000-volume personal library and his lifetime of study of the Jewish question, Jouin kept repeating his warning of the "two goals" that Jews everywhere shared: "The universal domination of the world and the destruction of Catholicism, out of hatred for Christ." In 1925 he praised Mussolini for saving Italy, rescuing it from the hands of Judeo-Masonic "sovietism." He also had words of praise for the Germans, who had, "better than we, recognized the Jewish peril."[7]

Jouin presented his work, and his journal, which was its centerpiece, as having papal blessing. The inside cover of each issue in the 1920s proclaimed, *"The International Review of Secret Societies does that which the Popes have always prescribed: it unmasks not only Freemasonry, but also . . . all the branches of the Counter-Church erected in opposition to the Church of Jesus Christ to try to destroy it."*[8]

In 1918, six years after Jouin had founded his anti-Semitic journal, Pope Benedict XV sent him a special papal brief of recognition. "We know that you have conducted your sacred ministry in an exemplary manner," the Pope pronounced. "You have the greatest solicitude for the eternal health of the faithful and you have, with determination and with courage, upheld the rights of the Catholic Church—not without danger for your own life—against the sects that are the enemies of religion. Finally, you have spared nothing, neither your labor nor expense, to spread your works on these matters among the public." A year later, Cardinal Gasparri, the secretary of state, sent Jouin a note of papal appreciation for his work in the battle against the Masonic conspiracy. It concluded with these words: "His Holiness is thus pleased to congratulate you and to encourage you in your work, whose influence is so important in warning the faithful and helping them to struggle effectively against the forces aimed at destroying not only religion but the whole social order."

Nor was this all, for when Achille Ratti became pope, he too showed the French anti-Semitic crusader unusual sympathy. In November 1923, at a time when Jouin was attracting great attention in the Catholic world as the prime French champion of *The Protocols of the Elders of Zion*, Pope Pius XI honored him with a private audience. At that audience—according to Jouin—the Pope told him: "Continue your *Review*, despite your financial difficulties, for you are combating our mortal enemy." Two months later, the Pope decided to bestow yet another honor on him. Jouin had already been made a prelate by Benedict XV and proudly carried the title monsignor. Pius XI raised him further in the ecclesiastical hierarchy, appointing him apostolic prothonotary.[9]

Yet the picture was not all bleak, for there were members of the Catholic clergy who were appalled by the continuing identification of the Church with anti-Semitism, and who were especially revolted by its cruder forms, such as the continued charges of Jewish ritual murder. Most notably, in 1926, a Dutch convert from Judaism, Francesca van Leer, persuaded Anthony van Asseldonk, the procurator general of the Canons of the Holy Cross, to found a new association in Rome called "The Friends of Israel." The aim of the organization was the conversion of the Jews to Catholicism; its members, drawn from around the world, included 3,000 priests, 278 bishops, and 19 cardinals.

The organization's leaders, it soon became clear, had in mind a more ambitious program than many of those who had signed on with it had realized. The clergymen had been approached about joining an organization dedicated to the conversion of the Jews. But the leaders believed that major changes first had to be made in how the Church treated the Jews. Their aims were set out in a booklet titled *Pax super Israel*, which argued that Jews should no longer be stigmatized as the "deicide" people. The booklet dismissed stories of Jewish ritual murder as old wives' tales, and attacked Church support for anti-Semitic movements. The best way to induce Jews to convert, the authors argued, was to treat them with respect.

The Friends of Israel did not last long. The inquisitors were horrified by the heretical doctrines contained in *Pax super Israel*, and officially condemned it. Nor did the Holy Office stop there. On March 25, 1928, it issued a decree dissolving the organization, and ordered that "no one in the future write or publish books or booklets that in any way favor these erroneous initiatives." Concerned about the impression that such a draconian move would create outside the Catholic world, the cardinals added a caveat condemning "hatred against the people whom God once chose, that hatred that today is commonly known by the name of 'anti-Semitism.'" The society had to be dissolved, the Holy Office document went on to say, because it embraced "a manner of acting and thinking contrary to the opinion and spirit of the church, to the thinking of the Holy Fathers, and to the liturgy itself."[10]

The dissolution of an international Catholic organization that counted so many priests, bishops, and even cardinals among its members could not fail to arouse great curiosity in the Church. What did it mean? Neither the Holy Office nor the Vatican offered any further official explanation. It was left to *Civiltà cattolica* to explain the message that the Vatican meant to impart. In an article whose title, "The Jewish Danger and the 'Friends of Israel,'" signaled its message, the journal supplied what was widely interpreted in the Catholic world as the definitive Church interpretation of the organization's dissolution. Enrico Rosa, author of the article, not only was the longtime director of the journal but was known in the Catholic world as particularly attuned to the Pope's wishes. As Rosa's obituary in the Jesuit journal put it, a decade later, "It is no exaggeration to say that Father Enrico Rosa remained for thirty years at the head of Italian Catholic journalism as interpreter and intrepid champion of the directives of the Holy See."[11]

No doubt, Father Rosa wrote, the organizers of the Friends of Israel had started out with a praiseworthy goal, the conversion of the Jews. Unfortunately, their efforts had quickly degenerated into something quite different.

Father Rosa examined the condemnation of anti-Semitism contained in the Holy Office statement, which some outside the Church were trumpeting as a change in the Vatican's position. What did it really mean? The answer, he explained, was that there was an unchristian brand of anti-Semitism, which the Church condemned, and a healthy recognition of the threat posed by the Jews, which the Church not only condoned but embraced. The decree condemned anti-Semitism "in its anti-Christian form and spirit, as it has been interpreted and applied by some of its ancient and modern proponents, alien from genuine Catholicism." Such people were "adversaries of the Jews for political party motivations or passions, or due to nationality, or material interests." Yet, while such an unchristian form of anti-Semitism must be rejected, Father Rosa added, the Church must protect itself "with equal diligence, from the other, no less dangerous, and indeed more seductive extreme, given its appearance of goodness." Such was the extreme represented by the Friends of Israel.

Civiltà cattolica, its director wrote, "has always taken care, in the painful struggle against the Jewish danger, to balance charity and justice, avoiding and—where they appear—explicitly combating the excesses of anti-Semitism, which have now been newly condemned." But, Father Rosa added, the danger that the Jews posed could not be ignored. Until their emancipation in the last century, the Jews had been subject to special restrictions, which confined them—"more as a preventative measure than as a punishment"—to the ghetto. But with emancipation, the Jews had become "bold and powerful, making them, under the pretext of equality, ever more predominant, and privileged, especially in the economic sphere." As a result, some people had advocated using violence against them, but, Father Rosa explained, the Catholic Church could not support such a course. The Church had always sought to protect "even its most bitter enemies and persecutors, which is what the Jews are."

The Holy Office statement condemning anti-Semitism, wrote Father Rosa, meant that Catholics should not "hate the Jews, much less oppress them unjustly, but rather one should pray for them, notwithstanding their blindness." Yet this Catholic charity, he warned, "must not make us forget or blind us to the sad reality, as it seems happened with some of the principal leaders and proponents of the Friends of Israel."

Father Rosa then went on to describe that "sad reality." The Jews were to blame for the Russian Revolution as they had been for the French Revolution. "We have tried in these pages to demonstrate how much the Jews are to blame for the Russian revolution and how prevalent the corrupted generation of Jews has been in it, as they were previously in the French Revolution, and as they have been in the more recent one in Hungary, with all of its massacres, cruelty, and savage horrors. The result has been the collapse of the Muscovite Empire and the tyranny imposed by the Bolshevik takeover, which threatens Europe."

Unfortunately, wrote the *Civiltà cattolica* director, "Judaic propaganda" has brought us to this point. The danger was great, for despite the Jews' constant efforts at subversion, governments had been inexplicably lax in taking countermeasures against them. And so in the short time that the Jews had been given equal rights, they had established their "hegemony in many sectors of public life, especially in the economy and industry, as well as in high finance, where they are indeed said to have dictatorial power. They can dictate laws to States and Governments, in political as well as financial matters, without fear of having any rivals."

This crushing Jewish power had come about, Father Rosa wrote, despite the fact that the Jews were such a small minority. In England, they composed less than one percent of the population, in France under half a percent, and in Italy only a tenth of one percent. And yet, "they are first in the large businesses, occupying the highest posts, especially in industry, in the large banks, in diplomacy, and even more predominant in the occult sects, scheming to achieve their world hegemony."[12]

Reading these words, what can we say about the recent Vatican Commission denial that the Church was extraneous from modern anti-Semitism? Or its claim that the spread of anti-Semitism in the 1920s and 1930s came in the face of strong Church opposition?

As the virulence of anti-Semitism increased in central Europe in the 1920s and 1930s, met by papal silence, Catholics looking for guidance could find no better source than *Civiltà cattolica* and *L'Osservatore romano.* A reader of the Jesuit journal in the 1920s would, for example, have learned of the frightening situation in Austria. Two stories, one from early 1921 and the other late 1922, are of special interest because they span two papacies, one appearing at the end of Benedict XV's reign and the other early in Pius XI's. Cardinal Gasparri served as secretary of state for both popes, and there is no doubt that he would have had to approve any *Civiltà cattolica* stories dealing with political events in Austria.[13]

The journal's Vienna correspondent reported in early 1921 of "the invasion, during the war, of a swarm of Polish Jews," which, when combined with an upsurge in inflation, had "dissipated all of Austria's riches." While the Catholics suffered, the Jews, "having put their millions safely away in foreign countries," cavorted in luxury. "The blame for such miseries," the correspondent reported, "falls in large part on the socialists, who, taking over the government after its collapse, formed . . . a kind of national militia subservient to the Jew capitalists." The *Civiltà cattolica* correspondent went on to report that in Vienna it was "the common opinion among Catholics . . . that behind Bolshevism and Communism is none other than Jewish Masonry which, by means of the total confiscation of Christians' wealth, is moving toward Judaism's absolute rule."[14]

At the end of the following year, 1922, with Achille Ratti now pope, the *Civiltà cattolica* Vienna correspondent sent in an even more dramatic report. If the Jews have their way, he warned, "Vienna will be nothing but a Judaic city; property and houses will all be theirs, the Jews will be the bosses and the gentlemen, the Christians their servants. This is what the Jews want for the future of Vienna, and the socialists' ceaseless violence, carried out by a credulous crowd under the Jews' cunning direction, serves this goal alone." The future was grim indeed: "Austria will be absolutely the subject, tributary, and slave of the Jews, or it will not exist at all. This, in short, is the guiding idea of our Judeo-Masonic socialist leaders."

Taking up a by now familiar Vatican theme, the Vienna correspondent sought to distinguish between two kinds of anti-Semitism. One was non-Catholic and immoral, the other—the true, original form of anti-Semitism—was Catholic and praiseworthy. "In its original form," he wrote, "anti-Semitism is nothing but the absolutely necessary and natural reaction to the Jews' arrogance. . . . Catholic anti-Semitism—while never going beyond the limits of moral law—adopts all necessary means to emancipate the Christian people from the abuse they suffer from their sworn enemy."[15]

Indeed, the seeds of Catholic anti-Semitism in Austria that had been planted with the Vatican's help in the last two decades of the nineteenth century continued to bear fruit in the years following the First World War. A widely distributed lecture by a well-known Jesuit orator, Victor Kolb, reflects the tenor of Austrian Catholic attitudes toward the Jews as the war began. At a meeting of the Catholic organization Piusverein (Pius Association), an organization devoted to promoting the Catholic press in Austria, Father Kolb warned of the dangers facing the country. "Wherever you look, you always see Judaism's work, a conscious work, backed by unlimited means, always aimed at supremacy in every form." It was well to remember the motto of the Pius Association, he thundered: "protection of the German people, internally and externally, from Jewish penetration, from the destructive work of the Jews." Kolb's speech was immediately translated into Italian and printed at the request of Father Wladimir Ledóchowski, the Polish priest soon to become head of the

Jesuit order worldwide. He had copies of the speech distributed throughout the Vatican. More than two decades later, Ledóchowski would play
an important, and still mysterious, role in thwarting Pope Pius XI's one
attempt to officially condemn Nazi persecution of the Jews, as we shall
soon see.[16]

By the 1920s and into the 1930s, it could be assumed that any Austrian
organization that considered itself Catholic was also anti-Semitic. Austrian Catholic publications in this period overflowed with denunciations
of the Jews. Emblematic was the prestigious Catholic news weekly,
Schönere Zukunft. Featuring commentaries on the day's events by bishops and by Catholic professors of theology, week after week it carried
attacks on the Jews' pernicious influence on Austrian society. Similarly,
the Catholic satirical magazine *Kikiriki* specialized in its portrayals of
"stock-market Jews," and its pages were filled with venomous caricatures
of Orthodox Jews with sidelocks. Indeed, the magazine has been described as a forerunner of Julius Streicher's infamous Nazi weekly, *Der
Stürmer*. Meanwhile, the Christian Social party devoted a whole section in
its new 1926 program to its battle against the Jewish threat.[17]

As the Nazi movement grew, some of Austria's Catholic laity, priests,
and monks were attracted by its uncompromising hostility toward the
Jews. Worried that the Nazis were winning the allegiance of the Catholic
faithful, the Austrian Church hierarchy tried to remind them of the Vatican's distinction between good and bad anti-Semitism. The best-known
and most influential example of such a plea was the pastoral letter published by Johannes Maria Gföllner, the bishop of Linz, just as Hitler was
poised to take power in Germany. Indeed, the letter had broad influence,
for it was translated and reproduced by the Catholic press throughout
Europe. The bishop sought to warn those in his diocese against the dangers posed by Nazi ideology. "To hate the Jewish people or to hold them
in contempt solely because of their descent is inhuman and unchristian."
He added: "The Church has always condemned such 'pogroms,' and has
protected the Jewish people from unjust hatred."

But no sooner had the bishop denounced such "unjust" hatred of the
Jews than he launched into his own warning: "It is beyond any doubt that
many Jews, unrelated to any religious concern, exercise an extremely
pernicious influence in almost all sectors of modern civilization. The
economy and business . . . law and medicine, society and politics are all
being infiltrated and polluted by materialistic and liberal principles that

derive primarily from Judaism. Newspapers and leaflets, the theater and cinema, are full of frivolous and immoral elements that deeply poison the people's Christian soul, and it is in fact Judaism that, for the most part, inspires them and spreads them."

After going on to link the main political-economic dangers of the day—international capitalism, socialism, and communism—to "degenerate Judaism," the bishop came to his conclusion. "Not only is it legitimate to combat and to end Judaism's pernicious influence," he advised, "it is indeed the strict duty of conscience of every informed Christian. One can only hope that Aryans and Christians will increasingly come to recognize the dangers and troubles created by the Jewish spirit and to fight them more tenaciously."[18]

The Austrian bishop's statement was, in many ways, characteristic of the Roman Catholic Church's approach to the rise of nazism in Germany and Austria. Hitler and his minions represented a threat to the Church, for they sought to replace popular loyalty to a Catholic worldview and Catholic liturgy with worship of the State, the party, and the regime. But the anti-Semitism of the Nazis was a problem for the Church in the 1930s not because of its negative portrayal of the Jews, much of which was shared by the Church itself; the problem stemmed, on the contrary, from the danger that the Nazis would exploit an appeal that had previously been identified with the Church to attract Catholics to a non-Christian cause. In denouncing nazism, Church leaders were eager to show people that they did not have to join the Nazis to be against the Jews. The old Church distinction between the good, Catholic anti-Semitism and the bad, pagan anti-Semitism was once more trotted out.

Similar developments were under way in Poland. In 1936, the country's highest-ranking churchman, August Cardinal Hlond, issued a pastoral letter warning that Jews were the "vanguard of atheism, the Bolshevik movement, and revolutionary activity." While condemning anti-Jewish violence, he encouraged the boycott of Jewish businesses and publications. The Jews, he warned, were waging a war against the Catholic Church. His letter to the faithful was a masterpiece of distinguishing between good and bad anti-Semitism, between that which was approved by the Church and that which was condemned: "One may not hate anyone. Not even Jews. It is good to prefer your own kind when shopping, to avoid Jewish stores . . . but it is forbidden to demolish a Jewish store, damage their merchandise, break windows, or throw things at their homes."[19] Cardinal Hlond, as a person especially close to the Vatican, belonged to a moderate minority of the Polish Church as far as the Jews were concerned, viewed by many as too soft on the Jews. The following year, the Synod of Polish Bishops adopted a resolution on public education calling for a prohibition on Jews teaching Catholic students, and on Jewish students being taught in the same classes as Catholic children.[20]

Identifying the Jews with subversion was a common theme of the Polish Catholic press. Except for the most extremist among the Catholic publications, they generally refrained from espousing the Nazis' racial characterization of the Jews, not least because the glorification of an "Aryan" race had unpalatable implications for Slavs like the Poles. But warnings of the dangers posed by the Jews, and calls for keeping Jews away from true Poles, permeated the Catholic press and, presumably, the sermons of parish priests as well.[21] As the Jesuit editor of one Polish Catholic publication wrote, Poland, with its large Jewish population, had a Jewish problem that was "a hundred times more severe than anywhere else." Nazi anti-Semitism, with its pagan philosophy, should be condemned, the Jesuit priest wrote, but the best thing that could happen to Catholic Poland would be for it to become "asemitic."[22]

The demand that Jews be expelled from Poland was no monopoly of the Church extremist fringe. In the late 1930s, a Polish Christian Democratic newspaper editorialized that the Jewish problem would remain as long as the Jews continued to be given equal rights, a position that other Catholic papers and organizations took up as well. A brochure published by the Polish Jesuits put it simply: "Jews should be expelled from Christian societies." The demand that Poland be Jew-free was in fact a common refrain in the Catholic press in the years preceding the Nazi invasion. But, to distinguish its own position from that of the ever more violent Nazi campaign against the Jews, the Polish Catholic press urged a more "civilized" approach. As the Polish Catholic paper *Maly Dziennik* put it in early 1939: "Jews must be compelled to emigrate, not by Nazi methods but by withdrawing their citizenship and reorganizing our national economy according to the needs of the Polish people. There is no other way."[23]

The Vatican viewed the Nazis' rise to power in Germany with concern, but once Hitler had become head of the German government in 1933, the Vatican sought to come to terms with him. Great weight was put

on formulating a new concordat that would provide government guarantees to protect the Church, and ensuring its freedom to operate without
government intervention. The agreement was negotiated by Pius XI's
secretary of state, Eugenio Pacelli, who had replaced Cardinal Gasparri
in 1930, and who, a few years later, would himself become pontiff as
Pius XII. However, no sooner had the concordat been signed, in 1933, than
the Nazis began to violate it.

Increasingly angered by these infringements of Church prerogatives
and the ever-greater restrictions placed on Church activities, the German
bishops met in 1937 and drafted a list of seventeen instances of government violations. A delegation of cardinals and bishops then went to
Rome to meet with Secretary of State Pacelli and Pius XI. The result was
a new encyclical, released in March 1937 by the Pope as *Mit brennender
Sorge* (With deep anxiety). It excoriated the German government for
breaking the terms of the concordat and accused it of "fundamental hostility to Christ and His Church." The encyclical went on to warn against
the deification of race and the state, and called for the free exercise of religion by the Church. Although it contained no explicit mention of persecution of the Jews, nor any direct attack on anti-Semitism, the encyclical
did clearly criticize the German regime, and produced an angry response
from the Nazi government.[24]

Events of the next several months, in conjunction with the Pope's
increasing infirmity, left the press closest to the Vatican unsure of what
tack to take. For the first half of 1937, *Civiltà cattolica* continued to run
its usual denunciations of the Jews. But, strikingly, Father Mario Barbera, who had authored strident attacks on the Jews earlier in the year,
dramatically—if briefly—changed course in mid-1937. Earlier, he had
praised Mussolini for recognizing "the Jews' hand" behind communism.
He had also approvingly cited a supposed claim by Marx that the workers'
movement offered "the means that the Jews could use to become masters
of the world." In another article he had told of the Jews' penchant for
pornography and their unwholesome interest in sex.[25]

Father Barbera's *Civiltà cattolica* article in the summer of that year
began on familiar ground: "In fact the Jews have had overwhelming predominance in modern life, and thus at the same time have been the ones
who have most influenced the materialistic, immoral, and irreligious conception of life." But the article then went on to issue a remarkable call for
Catholics to create an atmosphere conducive to the Jews' conversion.

This every good Catholic should do "by removing from his heart, from his tongue, and from his conduct every form of anti-Semitism; do not make common cause with the . . . promoters of anti-Semitism, and avoid anything that might reasonably offend or humiliate the Jews."[26]

Yet just a few months later, in the fateful year of 1938, on the eve of the horrors of Kristallnacht (the night of the crystals) in Germany, and with the Italian Fascist government preparing its "racial laws" against the Jews, *Civiltà cattolica* returned to its old warnings.[27]

Barbera began by revisiting the theme of the Jews' dual nationality. Whether a Jew was Italian or Austrian or German, he was basically a Jew, he wrote, committed to the goal of world domination. As evidence, Father Barbera cited a recent issue of the Italian Fascist journal, *Il Regime fascista*, which provided proof, he said, that the Jews controlled the city of Trieste, although they composed less than two-tenths of one percent of its population.

"The Judaic question," he warned, "will remain unsolved, because, as all agree—even those most kindly disposed toward the Jews—their corrupt messianism, that is, their fatal craving for worldwide financial and political domination, is the true cause that makes Judaism a font of disorders and a permanent danger for the world." The only Catholic solution to the perennial problem, Father Barbera concluded, was that which the popes had long embraced. This meant "charity, without persecutions, and, at the same time, prudence along with needed measures." Such measures were to include "a kind of segregation or discrimination that is appropriate for our time; in short, a hospitality and peaceful coexistence, in a manner similar to that employed in the case of foreigners."[28]

A few months later, Father Barbera and his colleagues at *Civiltà cattolica* turned their attention to another of the threats posed by the Jews of Europe, the alarming situation found in Hungary. "The Jews have become the masters of Hungary in every way," he wrote. But as a result of the recent wave of anti-Semitism there, he explained, the Jews had become frightened and so were making a great show of their moderation. One Jewish newspaper, Father Barbera reported, had even gone so far as to praise the Pope for his opposition to "racist neo-paganism." "It is clear," Barbera added, "that the Hungarian Catholics are not eager to have such allies for the Church."

The Hungarian Jews, wrote Father Barbera, needed no central organization: "Their nation's instinctive and insufferable solidarity is enough for them to make common cause in carrying out their messianic aim of world domination." In this light, "Hungarian Catholics' anti-Semitism is thus neither vulgar, fanatic anti-Semitism, nor racist anti-Semitism. It is a movement in defense of national traditions and for the true liberty and independence of the Magyar people." As an example of this healthy, Catholic anti-Semitism, he cited the recent program promulgated by the 250,000-member Hungarian Catholic Action, which stated: "The Jews . . . do not have the right to influence the intellectual life of the country, nor the press, nor literature, nor artistic life. This same principle should be applied against all those Hungarians who show solidarity with the Jews."

Since 1922, Father Barbera reported, a *numerus clausus* had been in effect, limiting the Jewish students in the Hungarian universities to no more than 5 percent, the proportion of Jews in the Hungarian population. A similar limitation on the presence of Jews in the professions, in the banks, the press, and other economic sectors was in the works, although initially set at 20 percent. "To tell the truth," wrote Barbera, "this number is not very restrictive . . . but for now people want to proceed gradually, without persecutions, hopefully favoring the peaceful departure of the Jews from Hungary." He concluded: "We will not enter into the particulars of the proposed laws; we note only that they are inspired by the noble Magyar traditions of chivalry and loyal hospitality, limited only by pure necessity."[29]

For those who see in Pope Pius XI a man who stood against anti-Semitism, 1938 was a crucial year, as it was a turning point for the Jews in Germany and Italy. Two events in particular have drawn the attention of defenders of Pius XI: remarks he made in September to a group of Belgian pilgrims at the Vatican, and reports that he commissioned a "secret" encyclical aimed at denouncing anti-Semitism.

By the fall of 1938, the physically weakened Pope had become increasingly upset by reports of the depredations that the Nazis were visiting on the Jews of Germany. With the Germans preparing for war, and with the Church itself under attack there, he was having deep misgivings about his previous dealings with the Nazi regime, which he was coming to regard as intrinsically evil. In September, ailing and with only months to live, Pius XI received a group of Belgians who had come for an audience. In accepting a special prayer book they had brought him, he told them:

"Anti-Semitism is not compatible with the thinking and the sublime reality that are expressed in this text. It is a hateful movement, a movement that we cannot, we Christians, take any part in." As he thought about the Jews' plight, the Pope was clearly moved and, indeed, began to cry. Through his tears he said, "Anti-Semitism is inadmissible. We are all spiritually Semites."[30]

This last phrase may be the most famous words ever uttered by Pius XI. The 1998 Vatican Commission on the Shoah cites them as evidence of the popes' constant opposition to anti-Semitism, and especially as demonstrating the benevolent attitude of the pope who sat on St. Peter's chair as preparations for the Holocaust began. Less often quoted is what the Pope interjected into the middle of these comments, immediately before warning that anti-Semitism was inadmissible. "We recognize everyone's right to defend themselves, to take measures to protect themselves against all who threaten their legitimate interests."[31] In context, the meaning of the Pope's caveat is clear: Yes, Catholics too are spiritually Semites, for they are spiritually descended from the Chosen People. But the heavy weight of his early years growing up in a Church where Jews were vilified, followed by his experience in Poland, remained with him. Murdering Jews, burning down their homes and stores, humiliating them, these were all unchristian and inhumane. But taking "legitimate" actions to defend the rest of the population from the Jews, this was something he did not oppose.

The Pope's statement to the Belgian pilgrims was never reported in the Vatican's own newspaper, although other Catholic papers in Europe carried the story. His remarks were informal and spontaneous, and so they were not recorded in any official papal document. They were heartfelt and sincere, the cry of a man who saw a dark shadow growing ever darker across Europe.[32]

Earlier in the summer of 1938, Pius XI had decided that some kind of public statement on anti-Semitism was needed, and invited an American Jesuit priest, Father John LaFarge, to meet with him. At that June 22 meeting, the Pope gave the surprised American the task of drafting an encyclical on the unity of humankind that would condemn both racism and anti-Semitism. The Pope had read a book that LaFarge had written about racial prejudice in the United States, and thought that the American priest would be a good person to prepare such an encyclical. But

LaFarge, awed by the enormity of the task given him, went to see the head of the Jesuit order, the Polish Father Wladimir Ledóchowski, to ask for help. Ledóchowski added two other Jesuits to work with LaFarge: the German Gustav Gundlach, and the Frenchman Gustave Desbuquois.

Recall that Father Ledóchowski was the same man who, in 1914, had taken the initiative to have Father Kolb's anti-Semitic diatribe in Austria translated into Italian and distributed to members of the Vatican Curia. In this context, it is hardly surprising that the Jesuit leader chose Gustav Gundlach to work with LaFarge on the draft encyclical. Gundlach was a well-known Catholic authority on anti-Semitism, having written the standard German Catholic text on the issue, the "Anti-Semitism" entry for the authoritative German Catholic theological encyclopedia, published just a few years earlier. In that text he invoked, yet again, the longstanding distinction between the two types of modern anti-Semitism, one "unchristian," based on *völkisch* and racial notions, and the other which was in harmony with Christian teachings. The latter opposed the Jews because of their "damaging influence" on society. This Catholic form of anti-Semitism, approved by the Church, had no room for racially based hatred. But, according to Gundlach, given the real threat posed by the Jews, Catholics should do all they could—within the law—to fight the negative influence that the Jews exercised in economic and political life, in the sciences, and the arts.[33]

Not surprisingly, the lengthy statement that the three Jesuits came up with was less than a ringing condemnation of anti-Semitism. The draft focused on the Church's opposition to racism and its belief in the oneness of humankind. Its section on the Jews, while condemning racist views of them, fully reflected the centuries-old Church attitudes. The Jews, "blinded by a vision of material domination and gain," had failed to recognize the Savior. Their leaders "had called down upon their own heads a Divine malediction" which doomed the Jews "to perpetually wander over the face of the earth." The Church's hopes for the Jews' ultimate conversion, the draft continued, "do not blind her to the spiritual dangers to which contact with Jews can expose souls, or make her unaware of the need to safeguard her children against spiritual contagion." Reflecting Gundlach's earlier article, the draft encyclical granted governments the right to deal with "the problems concerning the Jewish people that lie within those purely profane spheres," and so "the Church leaves to the power concerned the solution of these problems." The Church asked only that states exercise "justice and charity" in any steps they took to protect Christian society from the Jews.[34]

But, weak as it was, the encyclical condemning racist anti-Semitism was never issued. The circumstances of its fate remain somewhat mysterious. Father LaFarge and his colleagues completed the draft in late September, and LaFarge personally took it to Rome to give to Father Ledóchowski, expecting him to send it on immediately to the Pope. However, the Jesuit head was less than enthusiastic about the Pope's plan and instead of sending it to Pius XI, gave it to his fellow Jesuit, Enrico Rosa, former head of *Civiltà cattolica*. Recall that Rosa at the time was writing a regular series of articles denouncing the Jews, and in sending the draft encyclical to him it is hard to avoid the impression that Ledóchowski sought not only to delay it but to sabotage it. Father Gundlach, who was irate at seeing the months of work he had devoted to the project wasted, himself voiced this suspicion. As it happened, Father Rosa died a month and a half after receiving the draft. By the time it reached Pius XI, at the beginning of 1939, the Pope was on his deathbed and, indeed, died on February 9 without having released the encyclical. His successor, Pius XII, eager to try to repair relations with Hitler, decided it best to avoid any criticism of Nazi anti-Semitism, and so took no action. The document was buried in the Vatican archives.[35]

But it was not only in Germany that, in 1938, the Jews were being persecuted. Just a few days before Pius XI's famous meeting with the Belgian pilgrims, in early September, the Italian government announced its first wave of anti-Jewish laws. Supplemented two months later with additional provisions, the so-called "racial laws" dismissed all Jewish teachers from the public schools, expelled Jewish children from the secondary schools, and mandated the separation of Jewish children from Catholics in the elementary schools. Jews were dismissed from the civil service and banned from other realms of public life; they were thrown out of the armed forces, and prevented from owning any large businesses. Marriage between Jews and Catholics was forbidden, and Jews could no longer employ Christians in their homes.[36]

Had the racial laws in Germany and Italy not been followed in short order by the mass murder of the Jews of Europe, they would today have attracted much more attention. The Italian racial laws, in particular, have been strangely and disturbingly ignored, almost as if they should be excused in retrospect for being so mild compared with the actual massacre of the Jews. The anti-Jewish Fascist campaign is troubling for another reason as well. The racial laws have an uncannily familiar ring to them, for they differed little from those that the Church itself had employed when it was in power in Italy.

Mussolini and his underlings were keenly aware of this similarity, and used the fact that the Church had long backed such measures in support of their own action. In 1939, for example, Roberto Farinacci, a member of the Fascist Grand Council, spoke on "The Church and the Jews" at Milan's Institute for Fascist Culture. "For over twenty years," Farinacci proudly recalled, "I have been denouncing the Judaic peril and the need to free the nerve centers of our country from the Jews who, through diabolical means, had succeeded in extending their tentacles everywhere." Not only were the Jews to blame for bolshevism and the communist revolutions, but, Farinacci added, they were also behind the anti-Fascist movement in Italy. "We fascist Catholics," he said, "consider the Jewish problem from a strictly political point of view. . . . But it comforts our souls to know that if, as Catholics, we became anti-Semites, we owe it to the teachings that the Church has promulgated over the past twenty centuries."

Until the French Revolution, Farinacci recalled, all states—"their legislation inspired by that of the Church"—had excluded "Jews from public offices, from the schools, from university degrees, from exercising professional business positions. All this in harmony with the dispositions sanctioned by the Church through its councils and papal bulls."

What happened when the French Revolution emancipated the Jews? Did the Church then alter its laws, its papal decrees? he asked. "My question is ironic. The Church could not correct itself without dealing a death blow to the infallibility of its teaching; it could not, nor did it want to. On the contrary, it confirmed its anti-Jewish measures and principles."

Here Farinacci—and in this he was no different from many other Fascist leaders—acknowledged the important role played by *Civiltà cattolica,* "without doubt," he said, "the most authoritative of all the Catholic periodicals." He cited in particular an 1890 article. There "the rights of man proclaimed by the French Revolution are termed the *rights of the Jew,* and the remedies [that others had proposed] against the 'depraved race,' against this enemy of mankind—the most radical remedies including the confiscation of their property and expulsion—are judged inadequate.

Indeed, the reverend Jesuit fathers call for the annulment of all the laws that give the Jews political and civil equality." *Civiltà cattolica,* Farinacci continued, had long warned its readers of how the Jews used the Masons as a means of persecuting Christianity. In fact, just a few months ago, he recalled, the Jesuit journal had declared that "the Judaic religion was profoundly corrupted." The article had warned "that Judaism still aims for world domination." The article, the Fascist leader stressed, had been published only a few months before, "that is, after both fascism and Nazism had already begun testing these same truths out, to the Jews' detriment."

Farinacci recalled that the constitution of the Jesuit order forbade it from accepting as members "anyone descended from the Jewish race . . . up to the fifth generation," and added, "the Aryan racism of the Jesuits is thus more severe than that of Germany itself." The Fascists thus had in the Jesuits "constant precursors and masters in the Jewish question. . . . And if we can be faulted for anything, it is for not having applied all of their intransigence in our dealings with the Jews."

Nor were the Jesuits alone, said Farinacci, and here he gave the example of Monsignor Jouin in France, with his journal the *Revue Internationale des Sociétés Secrètes,* and his publication of *The Protocols of the Elders of Zion.* Farinacci then quoted at length from Pope Benedict XV's message of praise for Jouin's work.[37]

The use of Church texts by Fascist proponents of the racial laws was likewise on display in the 1939 booklet "Why We Are Anti-Semites," by Niccolò Giani, Professor of Fascist History at the University of Pavia. After recalling the familiar Church charge that the Talmud enjoins Jews to kill even the best of the Christians, and to treat all Christians as animals, he went on to cite a more recent event. Earlier in the year, as part of the celebration of the Epiphany, the bishop of Cremona had given a sermon in his cathedral that clearly supported the racial laws. Only a few weeks after the second wave of Italian racial laws was announced, the bishop told his congregation: "The Church has never denied the state's right to limit or to impede the economic, social, and moral influence of the Jews, when this has been harmful to the nation's tranquillity and welfare. The Church has never said or done anything to defend the Jews, the Judaics, or Judaism."[38] The sermon received broad attention, and was quoted in the Vatican's own *Osservatore romano.*[39]

The bishop of Cremona was by no means atypical of the Italian Church hierarchy in giving Church blessings to the racial laws. A month after the bishop's sermon, one of the most prominent cardinals in Italy, the archbishop of Florence, used the archdiocesan bulletin to advise his priests and the faithful how to react to the recent developments. "The Church," he wrote, "teaches absolute respect and perfect obedience to the law and to the civil authority, when they do not command that which is against divine law." He then went on: "As for the Jews, no one can forget the ruinous work that they have often undertaken not only against the spirit of the Church, but also to the detriment of civil coexistence. One only needs to recall that, with the outbreak of the First World War, Italian Jewry succeeded in seeing that the Vicar of the Prince of Peace, the Holy Father, was excluded from the future peace conference." The archbishop continued: "Above all, however, the Church has in every epoch judged living together with the Jews to be dangerous to the Faith and to the tranquility of Christian people. Hence the laws promulgated by the Church for centuries aimed at isolating the Jews." The Church, he wrote, had never changed its policy of forbidding Christians from working in Jewish homes, or forbidding Christian children from being taught by Jews. This was not a matter of race, he added, it was a matter of religion.[40]

Needless to say, Farinacci and the other Fascist leaders who cited the Church to justify the new anti-Semitic laws were doing so for their own political reasons, and there is abundant reason to question their sincerity. But they could only exploit the Church in this fashion because the Church had indeed helped lay the groundwork for the Fascist racial laws. Decade after decade, forces close to the Vatican had denounced the Jews as evil conspirators against the public good. Decade after decade saw the Vatican-linked press lament the baleful effects of the emancipation of the Jews. For decades, Church authorities had warned of the harm done by giving the Jews equal rights. For decades, the Italian Catholic press had denounced the Jews' disproportionate influence in Italy. After all this, it should be hardly surprising that Mussolini's anti-Jewish campaign met with little resistance from Italian Catholics.

Neither the Pope nor any other Church authority opposed the Fascist efforts to strip the Jews of their rights. The Pope's complaints about the racial laws, insofar as they were voiced at all, regarded only those marginal elements that affected Catholics.[41]

This is reflected in the fall 1938 article in which *Civiltà cattolica* first told of the new laws. On September 1, the journal reported, Italy's Council of Ministers had issued an edict revoking the citizenship of anyone "of

Jewish race" who had acquired Italian citizenship after 1918, and moreover ordered all Jews who were not citizens to leave Italy within six months. The *Civiltà cattolica* account continued: "The Council of Ministers inflicted a no less vigorous blow to the Jews in its session of September 2." The journal then provided the full text of the expulsion of Jewish children and teachers from the schools, and the expulsion of Jewish members from all scholarly, scientific, and artistic institutes and academies. The journal added, without comment, a further government clarification. In all these measures, "for the purposes of this law all those who are born to parents both of whom are of Jewish race are considered to be of Jewish race, even if they profess a religion different from that of Judaism."

Immediately following this item, *Civiltà cattolica* turned to the Fascist regime's recent use of the Jesuit journal in its efforts to justify the new racial laws. The Fascist press had focused special attention on the three-part series the journal had published in 1890 on "the Jewish question in Europe." In recalling the Fascist use of this earlier work, the Jesuits of *Civiltà cattolica* were eager to distinguish between their own, Catholic approach to the Jewish problem and the Fascist approach. "We must note that one cannot recognize in that vigorous [1890] campaign, inspired as it was by the spectacle of the Judaic invasion and of Judaic arrogance, the merit of having 'known how to fascistically pose the racial problem' before it had such a name [i.e., Fascist], as *Il Regime fascista* of August 28 would have it."

The difference of approach had little to do with any judgment regarding the depravity of the Jews or the danger they represented, for in this there was little to separate the Church and the Fascists. Rather, the difference lay in the use of biology to justify discrimination against the Jews. Here the journal reiterated the message contained in its original 1890 text: "The Jewish question of our time does not differ significantly from that which affected the Christian peoples in medieval times." In those articles from 1890, Father Ballerini had made clear that the problem had arisen only after the Jews had rejected Jesus, abandoned Mosaic law, and embraced the Talmud. It was the Talmud that "the Christian nations detest—not its theological part, which has been virtually reduced to nothing—but its moral aspect, which contradicts the most elementary principles of natural ethics." And so, the Jesuit journal concluded, in remarks published only days after the racial laws were introduced in Italy, the Catholic battle against the Jews "is to be understood as a struggle inspired solely by the need for the legitimate defense of Christian people against a *foreign* nation in the nations where they live and against the sworn *enemy* of their well-being. This suggests [the need for] measures to render such people harmless."[42]

With all of the attention given to what Pius XII did or did not say about the Nazi-led campaign against the Jews—over which his influence was at best limited—it is striking how little attention has been given to what Pius XI had to say about the racial laws promulgated in Italy in 1938. These laws were conceived, approved, and announced in the Holy City itself, where his influence—less than a decade after the Italian government's recognition of the Roman Catholic Church as the official state religion—was great indeed. From September to November 1938, the Italian government had declared Jews undesirables, thrown Jewish children out of school, and fired large numbers of Jewish adults from their jobs. It had called on Catholics to avoid the Jews, to treat them as a source of pollution.

Anyone who has gotten this far in this book should not find it surprising that in response to these measures against the Jews neither the Pope nor the Vatican hierarchy uttered a single word of protest. The explanation for this fact is simple: Mussolini's new laws embodied measures and views long championed by the Church itself.

There was, however, one aspect of the Italian racial laws that did draw papal protest and, indeed, clearly angered the aging Pope. The new laws treated a Jew who had been converted to Catholicism as a Jew, and hence forbade marriages between Catholics who had been born Jewish and other Catholics. Those who were already in such marriages were to be treated as fornicators.

In contrast to his silence on all the provisions of the racial laws aimed at the Jews, Pius XI objected energetically to this clause. On October 10, 1938, the Italian government's representative to the Holy See sent Mussolini a report regarding Vatican reaction to the second batch of racial laws, then being drafted. "The recent deliberations of the Grand Council regarding the defense of the race," he wrote, "have not, on the whole, found an unfavorable reception in the Vatican." He went on to report that the only concern that Vatican officials had expressed was that the new laws intruded on questions of marriage, which—according to the concordat—were supposed to be regulated by the Church, not the state.

The Italian government emissary concluded: "I have had confirmation of these impressions from Monsignor Montini [of the Vatican Secretariat of State]. . . . The major, indeed only, concerns of the Holy See [with regard to the new racial laws] involve the case of marriages with converted Jews."[43]

The Pope felt so strongly about this one point that, when his efforts to expunge the proposed provision governing marriage encountered resistance, he took the unusual step of writing directly to King Victor Emmanuel III himself. The Pope's note, calling the king's attention to the proposed law "for the oversight of the Italian race," makes absolutely no mention of, much less voices any protest against, the laws' anti-Jewish measures, which lie at their core. The Pope asked the king only to do something about the provision regarding the marriage of Catholics who were born Jewish.[44]

This same attitude was communicated more generally to the Catholic faithful in Italy in the months when the new measures against the Italian Jews were going into effect. In mid-November the Vatican newspaper, L'Osservatore romano, ran an article on the racial laws, focusing on the Church's objection to the provisions preventing marriage between Catholics and Jewish converts to Catholicism. As Jewish children were being driven from the nation's schools, Jewish scientists from the nation's scientific organizations, Jewish government employees and teachers from their jobs, the message was clear: The Church had no objection.[45]

When Pius XI died in early 1939, he was succeeded by Eugenio Pacelli, his secretary of state, who took the name of Pius XII. A year later, with the Second World War already well under way, Italy joined the German side, declaring war on France and Britain. The Holocaust too was beginning to run its deadly course, its atrocities soon to be chronicled in a stream of horrifying reports pouring into the Holy See from Nazi-occupied Europe.[46]

The war that Mussolini believed would be short and glorious turned out to be neither. By 1943 the tide had turned, and on July 10, 1943, the first Anglo-American divisions landed in Sicily. Two days later, the Allied Military Government, although it as yet controlled little Italian territory, announced the abrogation of any laws that discriminated against people on the basis of their religion or race.[47]

The reversal in the war's fortunes produced a palace coup that toppled

Mussolini two weeks later, and led to frantic Italian attempts to negotiate an armistice with the rapidly advancing allied forces in the south. Amid the chaos, on August 10, 1943, two weeks after Mussolini's fall, the Vatican's unofficial representative to the Italian government, Father Tacchi Venturi, wrote to the Holy See's secretary of state, Luigi Cardinal Maglione, suggesting that they take advantage of the overthrow of the old regime to effect a change in the Italian racial laws. But what the Vatican emissary had in mind was not a general revocation of the anti-Jewish laws. Rather—mirroring Pius XI's concerns of five years earlier—he proposed that the Vatican take action to expunge those provisions that discriminated against Christian converts from Judaism.[48]

On August 18, Cardinal Maglione responded with enthusiasm to this proposal, presumably after discussing it with Pope Pius XII. He told Father Tacchi Venturi to do all that he could to see that three changes be made in the Italian racial laws: (1) Families formed by couples consisting of a Catholic from birth and a Jewish convert to Catholicism should henceforth be considered to be fully "Aryan"; (2) individuals who had been in the process of becoming a Catholic at the time that the racial laws went into effect (1938) and who were subsequently baptized should be considered to be Catholic and not Jewish; and (3) marriages celebrated since 1938 by a person born Catholic and a Catholic who had been born a Jew should be considered legally valid.[49]

On August 29, Father Tacchi Venturi reported back to the secretary of state. Since his last note he had been contacted by a group of Italian Jews, then living in great fear of the approaching Nazi sweep through Italy. They had pleaded, he wrote, for "the complete return to the legislation that had been introduced by the liberal regimes and which had remained in effect until November 1938." In short, they asked that the laws granting Jews equal rights be restored. But, as the Vatican emissary reported, he rejected their pleas. In preparing his petition to the new Italian Minister of Interior Affairs, "I limited myself, as I was supposed to, to only the three points specified in Your Eminence's praiseworthy message of 18 August. . . . I took care not to call for the total abrogation of a law [i.e., the racial laws] which, according to the principles and the traditions of the Catholic Church, certainly has some clauses that should be abolished, but which clearly contains others that have merit and should be confirmed."[50]

Shortly thereafter, German soldiers marched down the peninsula and entered Rome, where, on October 16, they surrounded the old ghetto and rounded up over a thousand Jews.

Agitated by news of the roundup, Cardinal Maglione at once summoned the German ambassador, Ernst von Weizsäcker. Immediately after the historic meeting, the cardinal himself wrote down what had happened.

"Excellency," the cardinal pleaded with von Weizsäcker, "you have a kindly, good heart; try to save all these innocents. It is painful for the Holy Father, painful beyond all measure that right here in Rome, under the Pontiff's eyes, so many people are made to suffer solely because they are of a particular ancestry.

"The Ambassador, after a few moments of reflection, then asked me: 'What would the Holy See do if things were to continue?'

"I replied: 'The Holy See would not like to be constrained to have to pronounce its words of disapproval.'

"The Ambassador observed: 'I have followed and admired the attitude of the Holy See for more than four years now. It has succeeded in steering a boat through rocky shoals without foundering on them, and, although it has no doubt had greater faith in the allies, it has known how to maintain a perfect balance.' "

If Cardinal Maglione had ever intended this summons to the German ambassador to be a means of protesting the roundup of Rome's Jews to the Nazi high command, he soon changed his mind. Von Weizsäcker advised him that the order to seize the Jews had come "from the highest place" (that is, from Hitler himself) and suggested that the cardinal might not want to upset the Nazi high command by forcing him to report the Holy See's words of disapproval to his government.

"I responded," recalled Cardinal Maglione, "that I had sought to intervene by appealing to his sentiments of humanity. I left to his judgment whether to mention our conversation, which was so friendly."[51]

The secretary of state continued: "I wanted to remind him that the Holy See was, as he himself had noted, most prudent in not giving the German people the impression of having done or wanting to do the least thing against Germany during a terrible war.[52]

"I had, however, to tell him that the Holy See must not be placed in the position of having to protest. As for the consequences, should the Holy See be forced to do so, we would simply have to trust in divine Providence."

But Pius XII's secretary of state concluded his encounter with the German ambassador on that grim day on a note of reassurance: "I repeat," said Cardinal Maglione, "Your Excellency has told me that he will try to do something for the poor Jews. I thank you for it. As for the rest, I leave it to your judgment. If you think it more opportune not to mention this conversation, so be it."[53]

Two days later, over a thousand of the Jews rounded up in Rome by the Germans were placed on a train bound for Auschwitz. Only a handful would leave there alive.

ACKNOWLEDGMENTS

HAD THE VATICAN not made such a treasure trove of documents regarding its past available to the scholarly world, this book could not have been written. The opening in early 1998 of the central archives of the Inquisition was only the most recent and dramatic event in this move to allow researchers to dig into the Church's history. Given that the materials I worked with there dealt with sensitive topics, and the nature of my project was not one that all in the Vatican were enthusiastic about, I would first of all like to thank all those in the Church who have made such research as this possible.

The final year of work on this book in 1999–2000 could hardly have been more pleasant, or more conducive to the completion of this project. Supported by a sabbatical leave from Brown University, I was hosted for three months in the fall by the American Academy of Rome as the Department of Education Professor. The Academy is a marvelous environment for a project such as this, perched atop Rome, a beautiful half-hour walk to the Vatican archives. Special thanks there go to Lester Little, the director, who helped make the place so welcoming and at the same time so supportive of historical research.

I spent December in Paris, at the Maison Suger, while I worked in various archives and libraries. Special thanks are due to Maurice Aymard, chair of the Maison Suger board.

A Fulbright professorship at the Faculty of Political Sciences at the University of Bologna offered me a familiar environment as the writing of this book gathered steam. The faculty and staff there were most hospitable, and gave me all the resources that I needed for my work. Thanks go particularly to my colleague and friend Tiziano Bonazzi.

The final month of a year that went from one delight to the next was spent, in June, at the Rockefeller Foundation Conference and Study Center at Bellagio, on Lake Como in Italy. There could not have been a better place to work on this manuscript, nor have I ever lived in a more beautiful place in my life. Gianna Celli, the resident director, truly works wonders. My thanks to the Rockefeller Foundation for its support, and to Susan Garfield, director of the Bellagio program.

Research for this book was also underwritten by research funds from the Paul Dupee University Professorship at Brown University and from a Lucius Littauer Foundation grant. I also benefited from supplementary support provided by Brown, for which I would like to thank Provost Kathryn Spoehr.

Research for the book took place in a number of archives, mostly in Rome. I would like to thank all the archivists who facilitated my work. These include those at the Archivio Segreto Vaticano; the Archivio della Congregazione per la Dottrina della Fede; the Archivio della Congregazione di Propaganda Fide; the Archivio di Stato di Roma (special thanks to Elvira Grantaliano); the Archivio del Vicariato di Roma (and its director, Domenico Rocciolo); the Archivio degli Agostiniani dell'Assunzione (especially Jean Paul Perier-Muzet); and the Archivio Storico della Comunità Ebraica di Roma (and its director, Simona Foà). In Paris, I would like to thank the archivists at the Alliance Israélite Universelle and at the Ministère des Affaires Étrangères.

Thanks go as well to the librarians who gave of their time and expertise. Among those who were particularly helpful with the research for this book were those, in Rome, at the Biblioteca della Civiltà Cattolica; the Biblioteca di Storia Moderna e Contemporanea; and the Biblioteca Apostolica Vaticana. In Paris, the librarians at the Institut Catholique and the Alliance Israélite Universelle were most helpful, as were Otello Sangiorgi and Mirtide Gavelli at the Biblioteca del Museo del Risorgimento in Bologna. Finally, many thanks to the librarians at Brown University.

Taking on a subject as vast as the one in this book, covering 125 years, several countries, and topics ranging from Church to Jewish to political history, I had much to learn. Among those who helped me along the way I can here mention only a few. Giovanni Pizzorusso, Tomasso Caliò, and Marina Caffiero provided their expert advice in Rome. I would especially like to thank Tomasso for guiding me to the documents of the Damascus case found at the Propaganda Fide archives, with which he had already begun to work. I would also like to thank Giovanni Miccoli for his kindness. Miccoli has done pioneering work in the Vatican archives on papal policy toward the Jews, especially in the period from Leo XIII to Pius XII. In doing the work that I have for this book, I stand on his shoulders. In Bologna, I was fortunate, as always, to be able to rely on the expertise in Church history of both Pier Cesare Bori and Mauro Pesce.

Several students at Brown University assisted me with this research, including Frank Biess (now a faculty member at the University of California, San Diego), Erick Castellanos, Sara Colangelo, and Roberto Ludovico. In Rome, I was fortunate to have the aid of a young Italian scholar, Sara Messinger, and a recent Brown graduate, Annabel Briger. Throughout the project I was also ably assisted by Katherine Grimaldi and Deborah Healey at Brown.

For comments on all or parts of an earlier draft of the book, I would like to thank Giovanni Pizzorusso, Frank Biess, Thomas Row, Przemyslaw Urbanczyk, and my daughter, Molly Kertzer. None of these (except maybe Molly) should be held responsible for any of its content or for any remaining errors. Thanks too to Tracy Kidder for his helpful suggestions in Rome as I was figuring out how to write the book.

My literary agent, Ted Chichak, has been a font of encouragement, support, and good advice. Thanks to Paolo Zaninoni, my editor at Rizzoli, for his enthusiasm for the project from early on, and for his advice as the manuscript developed. Carol Brown Janeway, my editor at Knopf, bears a good part of the responsibility for my tackling this book in this way at this time, for which I thank her. I'd also like to thank her assistant, Stephanie Koven Katz, for all her good work, and Melvin Rosenthal, the production editor for the book.

For all the hardships she had to face—going from Rome to Paris to Bologna to Capri to Bellagio—as I wrote this book, my wife, Susan, is unlikely to get too much sympathy. But I don't know what I would have done without her.

I dedicate this book to my son, Seth Kertzer, and to my foster sister, Eva Paul. A better son than Seth I can't imagine. For Eva—who pushed me in my baby carriage down the streets of Manhattan, less than three years after the war in Europe ended—I have great fondness, and tremendous admiration.

APPENDIX

Popes and Their Secretaries of State

POPES (1740–1958)*

Benedict XIV (Prospero Lambertini): August 17, 1740, to May 3, 1758

Clement XIII (Carlo Rezzonico): July 6, 1758, to February 2, 1769

Clement XIV (Lorenzo Ganganelli): May 19, 1769, to September 4, 1774

Pius VI (Giovanni Braschi): February 15, 1775, to August 29, 1799

Pius VII (Luigi Barnaba Chiaramonti): March 14, 1800, to August 20, 1823

Leo XII (Annibale della Genga): September 28, 1823, to February 10, 1829

Pius VIII (Francesco Saverio Castiglioni): March 31, 1829, to November 30, 1830

Gregory XVI (Mauro Cappellari): February 2, 1831, to June 1, 1846

Pius IX (Giovanni Maria Mastai-Ferretti): June 16, 1846, to February 7, 1878

Leo XIII (Gioacchino Pecci): February 20, 1878, to July 20, 1903

Pius X (Giuseppe Sarto): August 4, 1903, to August 20, 1914

Benedict XV (Giacomo della Chiesa): September 3, 1914, to January 22, 1922

Pius XI (Achille Ratti): February 6, 1922, to February 10, 1939

Pius XII (Eugenio Pacelli): March 2, 1939, to October 9, 1958

SELECTED SECRETARIES OF STATE†

Ercole Consalvi (under Pius VII 1800–6; 1814–23)

Bartolomeo Pacca (under Pius VII, protosegretario di stato 1808–9)

Giulio Maria della Somaglia (under Leo XII 1823–28)

Tommaso Bernetti (under Leo XII 1828–29; under Gregory XVI 1831–36)

---

*Dates of papal reigns are given from date of election.

†Only those secretaries of state mentioned in this book are listed here.

Giuseppe Albani (under Pius VIII 1829–30)

Luigi Lambruschini (under Gregory XVI 1836–46)

Giacomo Antonelli (under Pius IX, 1848–76)

Lodovico Jacobini (under Leo XIII 1880–87)

Mariano Rampolla del Tindaro (under Leo XIII 1887–1903)

Rafael Merry del Val (under Pius X 1903–14)

Pietro Gasparri (under Benedict XV 1914–22, under Pius XI 1922–30)

Eugenio Pacelli (under Pius XI 1930–39)

Luigi Maglione (under Pius XII 1939–44)

NOTES

GUIDE TO CITATION OF ARCHIVAL SOURCES

Archivio della Congregazione per la Dottrina della Fede (ACDF); Santum Officiium (S.O.), Stanza Storica (St.St.). This is the newly opened archive of the Inquisition at the Vatican.
Archivio Segreto Vaticano (ASV)
    Epoca Moderna (EM), Segreteria di Stato (SS)
    Archivio della Nunziatura di Versavia (ANV)
Archivio del Vicariato di Roma (AVR)
Pia casa dei catecumeni e neofiti (PCCN)
Archivio della Congregazione di Propaganda Fide, Rome (ACPF)
Archivio Storico della Comunità Ebraica di Roma (ASCER)
Archivio di Stato di Roma (ASR)
Archivio degli Agostiniani dell'Assunzione, Rome (AAAR)
Archives, Alliance Israélite Universelle, Paris (AAIU)
Archives, Ministère des Affaires Étrangères, Paris (AMAE)

Introduction

1. The English text of the Pope's letter and the Commission report is from *First Things* 83 (May 1998), pp. 39–43.

2. On the opening of the central archives of the Inquisition in early 1998, see Prosperi 1998a and Prosperi 1998b, along with the other essays in that volume.

3. The Commission statement came only months following the statement of the French Church on Christian responsibility for the Holocaust, similarly motivated by Pope John Paul II's call for the Church to come to terms with its role in making the Holocaust possible. The French Church statement is far better than the Vatican's, accepting responsibility for promulgating anti-Jewish images that helped lead to the Holocaust (Église de France 1997).

4. Although it is interesting that immediately after the war, when the Vatican published the first volume of the new *Enciclopedia cattolica,* the entry on "anti-

Semitism" (Romeo 1948, pp. 1494–1505) called the term "very inappropriate . . . not least because the Jews have traditionally been hated by the major modern Semitic people, the Arabs." As a result, the author called for replacing the term with "anti-Judaism."

5. De Rosa 1999, pp. 93–94. Emphasis in original.

6. Raul Hilberg's *The Destruction of the European Jews* (vol. 1, pp. 11–12) provides a double-columned chart, titled "Canonical and Nazi Anti-Jewish Measures," which shows Nazi anti-Jewish laws on one side and gives the counterpart of each in canon law on the other. The chart does not, however, note the extent to which the Church provisions, many dating to medieval times, were still being enforced in the nineteenth century. See also Nicholls 1993.

7. Niewyk 1990, p. 369. On popular indifference toward anti-Semitism in Germany and its role in preparing the way for the Holocaust, see Kaplan 1998. The strong tradition of Catholic anti-Semitism in Germany, and its continuity with the political anti-Semitism that flowered in Germany after World War I, are made clear in Harris's (1994) study of the history of anti-Semitism in Bavaria.

8. Pauley 1992, p. xix.

9. The literature on the history of anti-Semitism is huge. Among notable general works dealing with the period examined in this book are the classics by Isaac 1964; Poliakov 1975, 1990; and Katz 1980. Lindemann (1997) has recently provided a general overview as well, but it is more controversial, linking the extent of anti-Semitism to the size and influence of the Jewish population in each country. For an overview of the theological roots of anti-Semitism, see Rüther (1974). Rubin (1999) provides an examination of some of the main themes of the Church's anti-Jewish activities in the late medieval period, and Chazan (1997) links these to modern anti-Semitism. For a recent overview of Christian anti-Semitism from the time of Jesus to the present, see Carroll 2001.

10. Needless to say, the Vatican view of each of these three was very different, from the Spanish regime, which from the beginning leaned heavily on the Church, to the Nazi regime, whose ideology was most distant from the Church.

11. Miccoli 2000, p. 322.

12. Luther's comments are taken from passages reproduced in Hsia (1988, p. 133) and Steiman (1998, p. 57).

13. These quotes are taken from Holmes (1978, p. 231).

14. Gigot (1910, p. 404).

Chapter One: A Missed Opportunity

1. Coppa 1998, p. 19.
2. Rosa 1989, p. 94.

3. On the Church and the Jews in the eighteenth century, see Caffiero 1997a and Rosa 1997. On Clement XIV see Rosa 1982.

4. Gregorovius 1966, pp. 67–70.

5. Moroni 1843, p. 20.

6. ACDF, S.O., St.St. TT2,0,2, Editto, xx, xxxiv. On the history of the Jews' yellow badge, see Kisch 1957.

7. ACDF, S.O. St.St. TT2,0,2, Editto, xxxii.

8. Ibid., xxxi.

9. Ibid., xliii.

10. Coppa 1998, p. 31.

11. Cecchi 1975.

12. Quoted in Colapietra 1963, pp. 18–19.

13. Quoted in Leflon 1977, p. 549.

14. Quoted in Roveri 1974, p. 143.

15. Colapietra 1963, p. 34.

16. Quoted in Roveri 1974, p. 144. Bernetti served as secretary of state under two popes, in 1828–29 under Leo XII, and 1831–36 under Gregory XVI. Here Consalvi refers to the important role played by some of the Jews in Ferrara in international trade and economic modernization.

17. Blustein 1921, p. 215.

18. On the relations between the papal government and the Austrian government in these years, see Reinerman 1979. Prince Metternich, the Austrian chancellor and architect of the Vienna conference, saw Consalvi as an ally in the effort to reform the Papal States and, with Consalvi, saw the *zelanti* as a great threat to the survival of the Papal States.

19. "Copie de note demandé par S. E. le Ministre d'Autriche le 28. 7bre 1815, redigée et consignée le même jour." ASR, Camerale II, Ebrei, b. 10.

20. ASR, Ministero dell'Interno, tit. 66, v. 486.

21. ASR, Camerale II, Ebrei, b. 10.

22. "Dal Palazzo Imperiale e Reale, Lì 17. Novembre 1815." ASR, Ministero dell'-Interno, tit. 66, v. 486, fasc. 1843.

23. "Progetto di nota: Il Sottoscritto Cardinale Segretario di Stato . . ." ASR, Camerale II, Ebrei, b. 10.

24. Num. 3. Lettera di Segreteria di Stato, Rome, November 15, 1817. ACDF, S.O., St.St. TT3, b, 6.

25. On the efforts of Consalvi and Pius VII to reform the Papal States, see Convegno Internazionale 1981.

26. Wiseman 1858, p. 44.

Chapter Two: Forced Baptisms

1. On the history of the position of vicegerent of Rome, see Del Re 1976.

2. The best account we have of what life was like for such "stubborn" Jewish women in the Catechumens is the published diary of Anna Del Monte (1989), recounting the thirteen days she was forced to stay there in 1749. It paints a dramatic portrait of the psychological pressure that such women faced.

3. The regulations governing the House of the Catechumens in the first half of the nineteenth century differed little from those in force over a century before. The basic policy was codified in a 1703 document: "If a catechumen should have a wife, or be betrothed though not wed, or have children, whether adult or youngsters, or any grandchildren or descendants who are under her care and are found in Rome, the notary of the House of the Catechumens should be immediately called and by public document make out a statement declaring his renunciation of the rites of his sect, and his desire to embrace the holy Christian religion, and . . . make the offer of his wife, or betrothed, or children and descendants to the holy Catholic faith, and by which offer it be ordered that they be extracted from the ghetto, or wherever they be found, and brought to the House of the Catechumens so that the children—whether male or female—be made Christians, and so that the will of the adults can be explored over a period of at least forty days. During this period one must preach the evangelical word to them, and open their minds so that they know the falsity of their sect, so that they be converted to the holy faith. Those who agree shall become catechumens, while those who do not, once the above-mentioned time is up, shall be returned to the synagogue, which must pay the usual expenses. But their extraction [from the ghetto] must be done immediately, so that the Jews do not discover the fact, thus avoiding many dangers and [attempted] dissuasions, and other disturbances. All this should be done with a license from the superiors, and if [the kin] are outside Rome, one should write to the Holy Office, and have them held in a safe place [so that they can be taken to the House of the Catechumens]." Source: *Istruzione e vita dei catecumeni, 1703,* reproduced in Rocciolo 1999a, pp. 420–22. For a description of the archives of Rome's House of the Catechumens, see Rocciolo 1999b.

4. This description of the Anticoli case is based on the rector's account in AVR, PCCN, n. 183 "Libro dei battesimi 1814–1824," p. 32.

5. The classic New Testament text is Paul (Romans 9–11). For more on this element of Christian theology, see Caffiero 1991.

6. Gregorovius 1966, p. 81.

7. A series of detailed analyses of the Jews and Muslims admitted to Rome's House of the Catechumens can be found in Rudt de Collenberg 1986, 1987, 1988.

8. See Rudt de Collenberg 1988, p. 149 and Rocciolo 1999a on the organization of the House of the Catechumens. Rocciolo 1999a, p. 399, also discusses the prohibition on Jewish converts taking on pastoral duties.

9. These regulations are reproduced in Fiorani 1999, p. 179. The rector of the Catechumens in the last decades of the eighteenth century, Francesco Rovira Bonet, played an important role in Pius VI's Jewish policy. In addition to his work as rector, he authored two influential works, one on the Jews' ritual murder of Simon of Trent (Rovira Bonet 1775) and another directly addressed to the conversion of the Jews (Rovira Bonet 1794). See also Caffiero 1993.

10. Rudt de Collenberg (1988, p. 144) examined the baptismal books of Rome's House of the Catechumens for this period and found that, of the 894 Jews aged twenty-one or greater who were baptized there from 1614 to 1798, 702 were men. Even among the older children the strong gender difference is evident: of the 488 Jews aged eleven to twenty baptized there in this period, 314 (64 percent) were males.

11. Cited in Fiorani 1999. p. 185n. Rocciolo (1999a, p. 406n65) comes to the same conclusion about the destitute state in which most of the Jews who came freely to the House of the Catechumens found themselves.

12. Canonici 1999, pp. 258–59.

13. AVR, PCCN, b. 28, ff. 9–10.

14. The rector's account of the Pacifici case is found in AVR, PCCN, n. 183 "Libro dei battesimi 1814–1824," pp. 21, 159–162; the Inquisition documents on the affair are found in ACDF, S.O., St.St. TT.3.g.3 fasc. 8.

15. The rector's documentation on the Tivoli case is found in AVR, PCCN, n. 183 "Libro dei battesimi 1814–1824," pp. 148–50. The Tuscan diplomatic correspondence is reported in Salvadori 1993, pp. 121–26.

16. Ruch 1905, p. 344.

17. This case is based on materials found in AVR, PCCN, n. 183 "Libro dei battesimi 1814–1824," ff. 61–64.

18. The mother's name is not reported.

19. Salvadori 1993, pp. 133–34.

20. AVR, Atti della Segreteria del Vicariato—Ebrei, b. 1, fasc. 19.

21. ACDF, S.O., St.St., CC-4.e, "Destribuita: Pro Feria IV die 6 7bre 1817."

22. This analysis is based on the examination of the Catechumens baptismal register for this period. With two exceptions, all of the Jews taken in by force listed here were seized because their husband, fiancé, or father had entered the Catechumens voluntarily and "offered" them. Twenty-five were children of men who had voluntarily come for baptism. The two exceptions are boys, aged thirteen and fourteen, who were reported to have said they wanted to become Christian, and hence were taken in by the police.

23. AVR, PCCN, n. 183 "Libro dei battesimi 1814–1824," f. 44.

24. Ibid.

25. Ibid., f. 98.

26. Ibid., ff. 156–58, 159–60. These policies remained unchanged over the next decades. Indeed, to take just one example, two decades after don Filippo gave way to his successor, Consilio Terracino entered the House of the Catechumens. It was

early December 1845, and he was required to offer his wife, Perla, who was then four or five months pregnant. The cardinal vicar himself issued the order for the papal police to seize the woman from the ghetto. After the woman had spent forty days there, never weakening in her resolve to return to the ghetto, the cardinal vicar called in the rector and proposed a solution identical to the one that had been followed in Flaminia's case twenty-two years earlier. The woman was entrusted to the responsibility of the ghetto's *fattori,* she was visited by a midwife attached to the vicariate, and the *fattori* were warned of the dire fate that would befall them if anything "sinister" (remarkably, the same word appears again) were to befall the fetus. The woman went into labor, the baby was born, and no sooner taken from her mother's womb than rushed to the Catechumens. The following day the little girl had the honor of being baptized by an overseer of the institution, Cardinal Mezzofanti (AVR, PCCN, n. 185, "Libro di battesimi 1828–78").

27. The Citone case is a particularly interesting one, not least because the Jews of the ghetto succeeded in gaining a meeting with Secretary of State Consalvi, who did what he could to help them. The inquisition documents on the case are found in ACDF, S.O., St.St. TT.3.g.3, fasc. 6,7,9. The rector's accounts of the case are found in AVR, PCCN, n. 183 "Libro dei battesimi 1814–1824," ff. 65–74.

28. Men and women were affected differently by this. In the years from the reopening of the Catechumens in mid–1814 through 1824, ninety-one Jewish men (aged twenty or more) freely entered it, but only nine women did so. Of the twenty-five adults forced by police into the institution, all were women, for the Church required Jewish husbands to offer their wives, but wives could not offer their husbands.

As we have seen, not all who entered the House of the Catechumens, even those who entered by choice, went on to be baptized. Of those women who were forced in by police, most in fact did return to the ghetto, although those who had come with small children had to leave them behind. Indeed, every one of the twenty-seven children under age ten brought by police to the Catechumens was baptized. Of the twenty-five women aged twenty or above who were forced by police to the House of the Catechumens in this period, sixteen were returned to the ghetto unbaptized. Of the eleven children aged ten to fourteen who were forced into the institution, only two were returned to the ghetto, while among the nine older teenagers forced in, five returned unbaptized. The large preponderance among the Jews of men who voluntarily presented themselves for baptism continued a much older pattern. My calculations are based on the entries found in the baptismal registers of the Pia Casa.

Canonici (1999, p. 253) calculates that in the years from 1614 to 1788, 417 men and 204 women from Rome's ghetto were baptized. However, he does not distinguish between women who came freely to the House of the Catechumens and those who (along with their small children in many cases) were forced there, so the figure underestimates the magnitude of this difference between Jewish men and women.

Chapter Three: The Ghetto

1. Wiseman 1858, p. 213. At the time, Wiseman was a student in Rome. He would receive a doctorate the following year from the English College in Rome.

2. On Metternich's relations with the Holy See in the years of the Restoration, see Reinerman 1979, 1989; and Nada 1957. A biographical sketch of Leo XII can be found in Fonzi 1951.

3. On Pope Leo XII and the executions in Rome, see Boutry 1997, pp. 356–7. On other aspects of the campaign of repression, see Leflon 1977, pp. 671–97, 742; and Coppa 1998, pp. 60–61.

4. Quote found in Caffiero 1997b, p. 378.

5. On the history of the forced sermons, see Rodocanachi 1891, pp. 277–80; Stow 1977; Gregorovius 1966, pp. 76–79; Martano 1987; Satta 1987; and Foa 1997, pp. 58–68.

6. The Sacred Roman and Universal Inquisition was the oldest of the permanent Congregations composed of cardinals and based at the Vatican. It was established in 1542 as a means of combating the spreading heresies of the Protestant Reformation. Although theoretically universal in scope (with the exception of Spain and Portugal, which had their own inquisitions), its ability to act outside of the territories directly under papal rule depended on relations with local civil authorities.

7. ACDF, S.O., St.St., TT.3.b.6. "Relazione sopra gli Ebrei."

8. Jabalot 1825. See Caffiero's (1997b) analysis of the significance of Jabalot's work.

9. Jabalot 1825, p. 17.

10. Ibid., p. 20.

11. Miccoli 1997a, p. 1385.

12. "Relazione sopra gli Ebrei," cap. III: "Circa la familiarità degli Ebrei con i Cristiani, e disordini accaduti." ACDF, S.O., St.St., TT 3—b, 6.

13. ACDF, S.O., St.St., TT.3.b.9, Pesaro 1823.

14. AVR, Atti della Segreteria del Vicariato, Ebrei, b. 1, n. 8. The same document is also to be found in the Inquisition archives at St.St., TT.3.c.10. See also the discussion in Boutry 1997, p. 359. As he points out, the fact that the Jews still owned so many businesses outside the ghetto over a decade after the restoration of papal power reflects the lack of enforcement of restrictions on Jews' ownership of property on the part of Consalvi's government. For a general history of the Jews of Rome, perhaps the best work remains Berliner 1992. On Leo XII's expansion of the Rome ghetto, see Colzi 1994.

15. ACDF, S.O., St.St., TT.3.c.10.

16. ACDF, S.O., St.St., TT.3.c.10.3; ASR, Camerale II, Ebrei, 67.

17. ACDF, S.O., St.St., CC.2.h. "Ghetto di Senigaglia."

18. ACDF, S.O., St.St., TT.3.c.5.

19. ACDF, S.O., St.St., TT.3.b.1.

20. ACDF, S.O., St.St., CC.2.f: "Ristretti e Documenti: Ebrei sparsi in Luoghi senza Ghetto."

21. Chadwick 1998, p. 23. My portrait of Gregory XVI is also indebted to Chadwick 1998, pp. 2–6. On Gregory XVI's papacy, also see Demarco 1949.

22. ASR, Camerale II, Ebrei, b. 11, ff. 104–7. 22 Nov. 1835. "Commissione speciale pel claustro israelitico"; ASR, Camerale II, Ebrei, b. 11, ff. 379–82. "Rapporto all'Emo, e Remo Principe Il Seg Card Gamberini, Seg per gli A. di Stato interni, e Presidente della Congne. Specle di Sanità. 26 Aprile 1836."

23. ASR Camerale II—Ebrei b.12. "Rapporto I per la Suprema Commissione d'Incolumità a dì 14 di Ottobre 1836."

24. ASR, Camerale II, Ebrei, b. 15, n. 1421.

25. Gregorovius 1966, pp. 49–50; Boiteux 1976, pp. 750–53.

26. Fischer 1998, p. 109.

27. ASR, Misc. Carte Ris., ff. 111–23 (n. 59755); ASR, Ministero dell'Interno, tit. 66, vol. 486, fasc. 1836.

28. ACDF, S.O., St.St., TT.3, b. 13.

29. ACDF, S.O., St.St., TT.3.f.4.

30. ACDF, S.O., St.St., TT.3.f.5.

31. ACDF, S.O., St.St., TT.3.f.4: "Editto del Governo Papale d'Ancona contro gli Ebrei e pochi cenni sullo stesso."

32. ACDF, S.O., St.St., TT.3.g, fasc. 5.

33. As Reinerman (1989, p. 323) has put it, referring to this period, "The dependence of the Papal regime upon Austrian protection was now absolute."

34. The relationship of Metternich to the Rothschilds is explored in several works, notably Ferguson 1998 and Corti 1928 and 1929.

35. Corti 1928, pp. 42–46; Ferguson 1998, p. 254.

36. This was a familiar argument for those calling on the Vatican to grant more rights to the Jews. It held that the Church could not expect other countries in which Catholics were a minority to grant Catholics rights there if these same rights were denied to minorities in the Papal States.

37. ACDF, S.O., St.St., TT.3.f., fasc. 5. Reinerman (1989) has provided an excellent analysis of the relations between Metternich and both Pope Gregory XVI and secretary of state Lambruschini, although his book ends with 1838, and hence before the events described here.

38. ACDF, S.O., St.St., TT.3.f., fasc. 5.

39. The letter indicates that, at this time, Jews could own real estate in the ghetto, which in fact had not been the case earlier.

40. ACDF, S.O., St.St., TT.3.g, fasc. 5.

41. Ibid. Metternich's failure in this case reflected a larger failure of his efforts to get the popes to modernize their government and thereby establish a more stable regime that would not depend on foreign military support to prop it up. Reinerman (1989, p. 324) has written of Metternich's growing pessimism about the survivability

of the Papal States, given the unwillingness to reform. "Austrian diplomacy," Reinerman wrote, "had done its best to breathe new life into the Temporal Power, and its best had not been good enough."

42. ACDF, S.O., St.St., TT.3.d, fasc. 6.

43. AVR, Atti della Segreteria del Vicariato, Ebrei, fasc. 21: "Editto per gli Ebrei che devono andare ogni Sabbato alla Predica . . ." and "Vacanze della Predica," both undated. According to Moroni (1843, pp. 24–26), these forced sermons were held only five times per year during Gregory XVI's reign. If so, it would mean that each Jew over age twelve would attend about once per year.

Chapter Four: Ritual Murder Makes a Comeback

1. ACPF, SRC, Siri, vol. 13, Dal 1838 al 1840; ff. 592–93. "Ragguagli intorno all'assassinio del P. Tommaso da Sardegna e d'Ibraimo suo servo in Damasco," *La Voce della Verità*, 30 aprile 1840, signed Fr. Francesco da Sardegna, Capp.

2. *Aceldama ossia processo celebre* 1896, p. 18.

3. Metzler 1973. On Cardinal Lambruschini, see Giampaolo 1931; Manzini 1960.

4. The Savoyard Kingdom of Sardinia had its capital in Turin.

5. For information on the diplomatic context of the Damascus case, see Jonathan Frankel's (1997) excellent book.

6. ACPF, SRC, Siri, v. 13, ff. 490–493.

7. ASV, EM, Esteri 1839–40, b. 536, fasc. "Uccisione in Damasco," f. 9.

8. Ibid. ff. 35–43.

9. These various Christian groups had their origins in early Christian churches; indeed, the Patriarchate of Antioch is regarded by tradition as having been founded by St. Peter himself. After centuries of separation, they rejoined the Roman church in the eighteenth century, though retaining some autonomy.

10. "We warmly call on Your Holiness's mercifulness, as the father of all the faithful, to see to it that—although it may not be easy to do for all—at least the consulates of the Catholic Powers, such as Austria, Tuscany, and the Kingdom of the Two Sicilies, are given to Catholic individuals, who may be able to help the Faithful in these parts, and to remove the support provided by the Jewish consuls, who dishonor the name of Christ, and are the secret enemies of their Sovereigns." ACPF, SRC, Siri, v. 13, f. 520.

11. ACPF, SRC, Siri, v. 13, ff. 553–54. A lengthy section (fifteen printed pages) of selections from the Moldavian "ex-rabbi's" work was also introduced into the record in Damascus at some point, and is reproduced in the version of the documents of the case published by Laurent 1846, pp. 378–93.

12. ACPF, SRC, Siri, v. 13, ff. 547–58.

13. ASV, EM, Esteri 1839–40, b. 536, fasc. "Uccisione in Damasco," ff. 47–48.

14. Ibid. ff. 50–53.

15. ACPF, SRC, Siri, v. 13, ff. 632–33.

16. What I find especially intriguing is the fact that Beaudin, the assistant to the French consul, was called upon by the French foreign ministry to send in a series of documents detailing his business dealings with many of the Jews whom he had denounced as murderers of Father Tommaso and his servant. He had fourteen such documents certified on July 10, 1840, and sent to the Foreign Ministry in Paris. These reveal that as a local Damascus businessman himself he had been the primary agent in Damascus for European-based businessmen making claims on Jewish merchants in Damascus who, they argued, owed them money. From at least 1828 and up to the time of the friar's disappearance, Beaudin was involved in extracting money from these prominent Jewish businessmen of Damascus, and in some cases brought suit against them in court. One of the most striking elements of the Damascus case has always been that those accused of the hideous murder constituted much of the Jewish community's business elite. That Beaudin could have played a key role in directing the accusations against them is an intriguing possibility, especially because the French consul, Ratti Menton, had only recently arrived in Damascus, did not speak the language, and knew little about the city. For copies of Beaudin's documents, see Laurent 1846, pp. 226–48.

17. The quote, from the April 12 issue of *Oesterreichischer Beobachter*, is taken from Frankel (1997, pp. 137–38), whose account of this instance, as well as of the diplomatic reactions to the affair more generally, has been most helpful.

18. Frankel 1997, pp. 42–43.

19. Ibid., p. 43.

20. Ibid., pp. 150–55.

21. ASV, EM, Esteri 1839–40, b. 536, fasc. "Uccisione in Damasco," ff. 12–14.

22. Ibid., ff. 15–16.

23. Ferguson 1998, p. 397.

24. ASV, EM, Esteri 1839–40, b. 536, fasc. "Uccisione in Damasco," ff. 17–20.

25. Ibid., ff. 23–25.

26. Ibid., ff. 26–29.

27. See the entries "Talmud, Babylonian," and "Talmud, Burning of" in the *Encyclopaedia Judaica* (1971, vol. 15), and Kertzer and Hoffman 1993, pp. 47–50. Steinsaltz 1976 offers a good brief introduction to the Talmud.

28. ASV, EM, Esteri 1839–40, b. 536, fasc. "Uccisione in Damasco," f. 44.

29. On the talmudic law regarding the behavior Jews should exhibit in dealing with Christians, and the evolution in its interpretation, see Katz 1961.

30. ASV, EM, Esteri 1839–40, b. 536, fasc. "Uccisione in Damasco," ff. 30–35.

31. On Moses Abu el Afieh's conversion and torture, see Frankel 1997, pp. 44–47 et passim.

32. On Crémieux, see Posener 1940.

33. ASV, EM, Esteri 1839–40, b. 536, fasc. "Uccisione in Damasco," f. 157.

34. Montefiore 1890, p. 287.

35. ACPF, SRC, Siri, v. 14, n. 1199.

Chapter Five: The End of an Era

1. On the election of Pius IX, see Chadwick 1998, pp. 60–63; and Martina 1974. The foremost biographies of Pius IX are by Aubert 1990e and Martina 1974, 1986, 1990.

Before ascending St. Peter's throne, Pius IX had had little contact with Jews. Falconi's (1981) exhaustive biography of his first thirty-five years makes no mention of any such experience, and it is unlikely that in his first bishopric, at Spoleto, he had any either. In Imola, which was his second bishopric, his only responsibility for Jews involved the small town of Lugo, which fell within his archdiocese and had a small ghetto. Just two years before his election to the papacy, as the archbishop of Imola he had been instructed by the Holy Office in Rome to have a nineteen-month-old Jewish child taken from his grandfather in the Lugo ghetto. The child's father, a young widower, had entered Rome's House of the Cathecumens and pledged his son. Extracting the boy from his family turned out not to be easy, and Mastai-Ferretti did not succeed in getting him out of the ghetto for several months. However, eventually he had the child sent off to Rome for baptism. ASVR, CC, n. 185, Libro di Battesimi, 1828–78, pp. 42, 47.

2. ASR, Ministero dell'Interno, tit. 66, 1847, vol. 486, pp. 135–45 (13 settembre 1846).

3. Martina 1967, p. 211.

4. ACDF, S.O., St.St., TT.3.f, fasc. 4.

5. Ibid., "I popolani di Roma e l'Università Israelitica."

6. "Indirizzo della Deputazione Israelitica di Roma a Nostro Signore Papa Pio IX. Nell'udienza sovrana accordatale il giorno 10 Gennaro 1848." ASCER, b.1 V b.

7. ACDF, S.O., St.St., TT 3.g.1.

8. ACDF, S.O., St.St., TT.2.n.17. Emphasis in original.

9. Ibid., Ferrara, 23 dicembre 1847.

10. "Gli ebrei si devono rispettare." *Il Povero*, 5 gennaio 1848 (Bologna).

11. Chadwick 1998, p. 77.

12. Letter dated December 23, 1849, quoted in Ferguson 1998, p. 476.

13. These events are described in Corti 1928, pp. 272–76, based largely on the original correspondence.

14. The initial Jewish petition, from the papal audience of January 5, 1851, along with the papal decision to create a commission, are found in ASR, Ministero dell'Interno, tit. 66, vol. 486, n. 39282; the Commission report is found there at n. 501781 (15 ottobre 1851). The efforts of both Carl Rothschild in Naples and James

Rothschild in Paris to enlist Austrian diplomatic support in 1851 for the efforts to get the Pope to relent and free the Jews of the Papal States of the restrictions they lived under are described in Corti 1928, pp. 275–76. See also Barbagallo 2001.

15. Martina 1967, p. 233.

16. Reproduced in Gennarelli 1862, pp. 78–81.

17. Martina 1967, p. 254.

18. ACDF, S.O., St.St., BB, 5, g.

19. Letter of 11 agosto 1852. Ibid. The archbishop of Bologna sent a similar letter to the cardinals of the Holy Office, dated 20 agosto 1852, pleading with them not to enforce these restrictions on the Jews.

20. This story is told in my book *The Kidnapping of Edgardo Mortara* (1997), and I tell it here only briefly. For the benefit of readers of my earlier book, my account here relies heavily on materials that I only got to consult after my earlier book. This is the correspondence between the French ambassador to the Holy See and the foreign minister in Paris.

21. On Antonelli, see Aubert 1961; Coppa 1990; Falconi 1983.

22. AMAE, Correspondance Politique Rome. Vol. 1008, pp. 343–348, Ambassade de France à Rome. Direction Politique n. 54 ; Rome 24 juillet 1858.

23. AMAE, Correspondance Politique Rome. Vol. 1008, pp. 432–34.

24. AMAE, Correspondance Politique Rome. Vol. 1009, pp. 8–16.

25. Two slightly different drafts of this letter by Count Walewski, both dated 22 September, 1858, Biarritz, are found in AMAE, Correspondance Politique Rome. Vol. 1008, pp. 443–44 and pp. 445–46.

26. AMAE, Correspondance Politique Rome. Vol. 1008, pp. 458, 459.

27. AMAE, Correspondance Politique Rome. Vol. 1009, pp. 18–19.

28. Letter of 9 October, 1858. Ibid., pp. 19–24.

29. On Rome in 1861, see Blustein (1921, p. 230). The Velletri case was the subject of an appeal to the newly formed Alliance Israélite Universelle, in Paris, by the Jews in Ferrara; AAIU, Italie, IC4, letter dated 15 août 1862.

30. "*Quanta cura*, December 8, 1864." *Catholic Encyclopedia*.

31. "Syllabus," *Catholic Encyclopedia*. Emphasis added.

32. Miccoli 1999, p. 226; Trachtenberg 1983, p. 20. On use of the term with respect to the Masons, and its identification with popular anti-Semitism later in the nineteenth century, see Mola 1992, p. 219.

33. On Lorenzino, see especially Volli 1968 and Caliò 1995.

34. The quote is from the 1896 edition of Gougenot (p. 120), which also has the preface alluded to above. Albert Monniot, author of *Le Crime rituel chez les Juifs* (1914, pp. 130–31), is but one of many authors who cite Pius IX's honoring of Gougenot for this purpose. On the Nazi edition of Gougenot's book, see Taradel and Raggi 2000, p. 197n64.

35. For a recent discussion of opposition within the Council to the proclamation of papal infallibility, see Wills 1999, pp. 248–56.

36. Chadwick 1998, pp. 217, 227.

37. Graetz 1992, p. 157.

38. Emphasis in original. The text of this speech is reproduced in De Franciscis 1872, p. 223, and was approved by the Pope before publication. Other, similar remarks made by Pius IX about the Jews in this period are quoted in Miccoli 1997a, p. 1404

Chapter Six: The Catholic Press

1. The count of Catholic periodicals is taken from Tagliaferri 1993, pp. 3–4.

2. On the history of *Civiltà cattolica,* see Dante 1990 and De Rosa 1999. A brief examination of the journal's anti-Semitic campaign in the last two decades of the century is found in Luzzatto 1987.

3. Oreglia, *Civiltà cattolica,* 10 febbraio 1881, p. 489.

4. As the special fiftieth-anniversary issue of the journal put it, "More than a simple journal, [*Civiltà cattolica*] is an institution desired and created by the Holy See and placed at its exclusive service for the defense of the Sacred doctrine and the rights of the Church" ("Per il cinquantesimo della Civiltà cattolica—ricordo storico," *Civiltà cattolica* series XVII, vol. VI, p. 21, quoted in Taradel and Raggi 2000, pp. 6–7).

5. De Rosa 1999 provides an authoritative, insider's view of the history of *Civiltà cattolica,* on which the above description of the relations of the journal to the Pope is based. The circulation figure is taken from the 1904 general index of the journal compiled by Giuseppe del Chiaro (1904), pp. iii–iv.

6. On Oreglia, see his necrology in *Civiltà cattolica,* 1895, IV, pp. 504–8.

7. Oreglia, *Civiltà cattolica,* 1880, IV, pp. 108–9.

8. Ibid., pp. 109–10, 112.

9. Oreglia, *Civiltà cattolica,* 1881, I, p. 225.

10. Ibid., I, p. 602.

11. Ginzburg 1990, pp. 63–74, offers an analysis of the spread of the theory that a Jewish conspiracy was behind the plague that ravaged Europe beginning in the fourteenth century.

12. Oreglia, *Civiltà cattolica,* 1881, IV, p. 477.

13. Steiman 1998, p. 35.

14. Stow 1977, p. 58. On the popes and the Talmud in the Middle Ages and early modern period, see Parente 1996, and Cohen 1999, pp. 317–63.

15. Oreglia, *Civiltà cattolica,* 1881, I, p. 727.

16. Katz 1961, pp. 158–59, 186.

17. See, for example, Frankel 1992; Rozenblit 1992; and Silber 1992.

18. Oreglia, *Civiltà cattolica,* 1882, (8 novembre).

19. It is worth noting that this new burst of long articles devoted to the denunciation of the Jews came shortly after the journal, which had moved to Florence following Italy's annexation of Rome in 1870, returned to Rome (1887) and was placed

under particularly close papal supervision (De Rosa 1999, p. 19; Taradel and Raggi 2000, p. 29).

20. Raffaele Ballerini, "Gli ebrei: perché restino ebrei." *Civiltà cattolica*, 1892, II, pp. 136–38.

21. Ballerini 1891. In the midst of the journal's renewed anti-Semitic crusade in 1890, the Jesuits were delighted to receive Leo XIII's blessings. *Civiltà cattolica's* authors, wrote the Pope, "have in their writings pursued the study of truth combined with the law of justice, and, having employed great intelligence in their works, have acquired great fame" (Del Chiaro 1904, p. vi).

22. F. Saverio Rondina, "La morale giudaica," *Civiltà cattolica* 1893, I, pp. 145–53.

23. "Cose straniere—Germania," *Civiltà cattolica*, 1893, I, pp. 374–78.

24. Ballerini, "La dispersione d'Israele pel mondo moderno," *Civiltà cattolica*, 1897, II, pp. 257–71.

25. Malgeri 1981, p. 278; Miccoli 1999, p. 243.

26. "L'antisemitismo in Francia," *L'Osservatore romano*, 1 luglio 1892, p. 1.

27. "L'antisemitismo in Francia," *L'Osservatore romano*, 2 luglio 1892, p. 1.

28. "Massoneria e giudaismo," *L'Osservatore romano*, 28 gennaio 1898, p. 1.

29. "Le solite frasi," *L'Osservatore romano*, 22 gennaio 1898, p. 1.

30. "L'emancipazione degli ebrei," *L'Osservatore romano*, 25 gennaio 1898, p. 1.

31. Lazzarini 1952, p. 423. In characterizing these journals as closely identified with the popes, I do not mean to suggest that there was never any friction between them and the pontiffs. In the early years of Leo XIII's papacy in particular, when some conservatives in the Church feared that Pius IX's strong conservative line might be weakened by the apparently more open-minded new pope, occasional tensions arose. Such was the case in 1885 when *L'Osservatore cattolico* published an article appearing to criticize Leo XIII for being too open to allowing Italians to participate in the Italian state, still branded illegitimate. However, in no case were the incessant denunciations of the Jews in these newspapers grounds for any papal displeasure. See Taradel and Raggi 2000, p. 28.

32. Canavero 1988.

33. Cardini 1948, p. 674. On Albertario, see Fonzi 1960a.

34. Davide Albertario, "Gli ebrei nel mondo," *L'Osservatore cattolico*, 12–13 novembre 1885. Emphasis in original.

35. "Trionfo degli Ebrei ossia il divorzio in Montecitorio," *L'Unità cattolica*, 15 marzo 1892, p. 249.

36. "L'antisemitismo in Francia," *L'Unità cattolica*, 26 giugno 1892, p. 589.

37. "Lo spavento degli ebrei per l'azione dei cattolici italiani," *L'Unità cattolica*, 13 ottobre 1892, pp. 919–920.

38. In an article two weeks later, titled "Few, but too many—or the overwhelming power of the Jews," the newspaper warned that although there were not many Jews in Italy, the Jews had a knack for always finding their niche "wherever there is

little or no work to be done and much money to make." "Pochi, ma troppi—ossia la strapotenza degli ebrei," *L'Unità cattolica,* 28 ottobre 1892, p. 1001.

39. "Gli ebrei nell'affare del Panama," *L'Unità cattolica,* 2 dicembre 1892, p. 1117. On the history of the Christian association of the Jews with worship of the golden calf, see Bori 1983.

Chapter Seven: Jewish Vampires

1. A great deal has been written about the early dissemination of the ritual murder charge. For a good recent example, focusing on England, see McCulloh 1997.

2. The literature on the early history of the ritual murder charge is large. Among the significant general works are Hsia (1988) and Trachtenberg (1983).

3. Cohen 1982, p. 13.

4. Grayzel 1989, pp. 13–14; Steiman 1998, p. 34.

5. On these orders and the Jews in this period, see Cohen 1982.

6. Quoted in Hsia 1992, p. 70.

7. Ibid., p. 72.

8. This account of the case of Simon of Trent is based primarily on Hsia (1992), Esposito (1990), Nardello (1972), and Quaglioni (1990).

9. This is a point also made by Miccoli 1997a, pp. 1525–26.

10. For an examination of the literary image of the vampire in the nineteenth century, see Twitchell 1981. A collection of extracts from nineteenth-century vampire literature can be found in Gladwell and Havoc 1992. It is worth mentioning that Bram Stoker's classic, *Dracula,* was first published in 1897.

11. Roth 1935, p. 16; Dagan 1903.

12. Hellwig 1971, pp. 81–88, 94–95. Rohling's *Talmud Jew* would go through seventeen editions and be read by hundreds of thousands.

13. I take this incident from a letter found in AAIU, Italie, I.C.5, correspondence n. 102 from the local AIU committee of Reggio Emilia to Adolphe Crémieux, Président du Comité Central de l'Alliance Israélite Universelle à Paris, Reggio li 24 Mai 1872. The quote from *L'Unità cattolica* (n. 112, 1872) is taken from Taradel and Raggi 2000, pp. 171n50.

14. Oreglia, *Civiltà cattolica,* 1881, III, pp. 96–103.

15. Oreglia, *Civiltà cattolica,* 1881, III, p. 477.

16. Oreglia, *Civiltà cattolica,* 1882, II, p. 473–82.

17. Oreglia, *Civiltà cattolica,* 1882, I, p. 739. The early 1880s case that most drew Oreglia's attention, and that of the Catholic press in general, was from Tiszaeszlar, in Hungary, which resulted in a dramatic trial. For a contemporaneous Jewish account of the trial, see Nathan 1892; for a more recent book-length analysis, see Handler 1980.

18. Katz 1961, p. 174.

19. Rondina, "La morale giudaica," *Civiltà cattolica,* 1893, I, pp. 145–60.

20. Rondina, "La morale giudaica e il mistero del sangue," *Civiltà cattolica,* 1893, I, pp. 269–81.

21. Oreglia, *Civiltà cattolica,* 1881, III, pp. 230–35; Oreglia, *Civiltà cattolica,* 1884, II, pp. 223–29.

22. "L'antisemitismo nel secolo decimonono," *L'Osservatore romano,* 10 luglio 1892.

23. "Per l'ebreo Buschoff," *L'Osservatore romano,* 21 luglio 1892, p. 2. The Catholic newspaper in Verona was so taken with the Buschoff case that, in an attempt to reach a broader audience, it published a small book on the subject, full of gory details (*Verona Fedele* 1892).

24. "Un nuovo assassinio rituale," *L'Osservatore romano,* 4 novembre 1899, p. 2.

25. "Omicidio rituale giudaico," *L'Osservatore romano,* 23 novembre 1899.

26. Lettere berlinesi," *L'Osservatore cattolico,* 8–9 marzo 1892, p. 2.

27. "L'Osservatore cattolico in Vaticano," *L'Osservatore cattolico,* 7–8 marzo 1892, pp. 1–2.

28. "Lettere berlinesi," *L'Osservatore cattolico* , 15–16 marzo 1892, p. 1.

29. "Lettere berlinesi," *L'Osservatore cattolico* , 28–29 marzo 1892, p. 2.

30. "Gli assassini rituali ebrei affermati nella Dieta dell'Austria Inferiore," *L'Osservatore cattolico,* 8–9 aprile 1892, p. 1. Emphasis in the original. The deputy's first name was not reported, but it appears to have been Ernst.

31 "L'Osservatore Cattolico nella Dieta Austriaca," *L'Osservatore cattolico,* 20–21 aprile 1892, p. 2.

32. "Un giornale antisemita," *L'Osservatore cattolico,* 22–23 aprile 1892.

33. Constant 1897, pp. 280–81. For the Italian translation of the Moldavian "ex-rabbi's" book, see Neofito ex rabbino 1883.

34. *Aceldama ossia processo celebre* 1896, p. 7.

Chapter Eight: France

1. Pius X is the only post-sixteenth-century pope to have been canonized. On the same day as Pius IX was beatified, Pope John XXIII was beatified as well.

2. According to Launay (1997, p. 15), twenty-three of the sixty cardinals at the time of the 1878 conclave were non-Italian.

3. The number of documents that Leo XIII produced in the course of his papacy attacking Freemasonry is staggering, said by Mola (1992, p. 217) to run well over a thousand.

4. Aubert 1990a, p. 71.

5. The above portrait of Leo XIII is primarily based on Aubert 1990a; Chadwick 1998, pp. 276–330; Martire 1951; and Launay 1997, pp. 15–20.

6. On Rampolla, see Malgeri 1982, Aubert 1990a, p. 92, and Civinini 1997.

7. Aubert 1990c, pp. 338–345.

8. Aubert 1990d, p. 56.

9. Hyman 1998; Malino 1999.

10. AAAR, B. 127. V. Bailly Lettres XII 1898–1900, pp. 97–8 n. 3283 au P. François Picard, Rome, 19 settembre 1899.

11. Sorlin 1967, p. 42.

12. "Une lettre du Pape relative à la presse," *La Croix*, v. 2, n. 22 (févier 1882), pp. 721–722.

13. In Verdès-Leroux 1969, p. 85.

14. "Qui gouverne la France?" *La Croix*, v. 2, n. 21 (janvier 1882), p. 711 (unsigned).

15. F. Picard, "Les Juifs," *La Croix*, v. 2, n. 22 (févier 1882), pp. 723–726. Emphasis in original.

16. Lindemann 1997, p. 115–16.

17. V. de P. Bailly, "L'ennemi," *La Croix*, 1882, n. 3, pp. 161–169. Emphasis in original. The Assumptionists' rallying cry quickly spread through France and even into Italy. In 1890 "Doctor" Martinez—identified as a professor of theology—published a book in France titled *Le Juif. Voilà l'ennemi!* In its review, *Civiltà cattolica* (4 ottobre 1890) sang the book's praises and called for an Italian writer "to do Italy a great service" by translating it. This a priest did the following year, publishing the Italian edition under the title *L'Ebreo. Ecco il nemico,* carrying the Church's imprimatur.

18. Katz 1970; Nicolaevsky 1966, pp. 37–39. The Italian case was somewhat different, for there some Masonic lodges were involved in organizing on behalf of the unification of Italy (although at the time Italy was unified, Jews played a minimal role in Italian Masonry) and for the separation of Church and state. For details, see Mola 1992.

19. P. F., "Mystères Talmudiques," *La Croix*, v. 3, n. 26, pp. 142–153 (1882).

20. This study was done by Delmaire 1991, p. 78.

21. Delmaire 1991, pp. 104, 110.

22. Delmaire 1991, pp. 191–92, 209–10. The population of the departments of northern France at the time incorporated well under one Jew per thousand Christians.

23. The first indication of the Pope's new instructions was given via the archbishop of Algiers who, at the Pope's request, enunciated the policy publicly in November 1890, stirring up a storm among the French clergy and conservative segments of the laity. See Civinini 1997, pp. 105–6.

24. It was in the wake of Leo XIII's call to the French Catholic Church to make its peace with the government that, in July 1892, he agreed to be interviewed by a secular female journalist for the French non-Catholic newspaper *Figaro*. The theme of the interview was the Church and anti-Semitism. In the interview, which was published on August 3, Leo XIII stressed that violence directed at anyone was contrary to the teachings of the Church, and also stressed the Church's vision that all people,

wherever they came from, were children of God, their souls made of the same essence. In general, he kept to a traditional Church outlook, stressing the role of the popes in protecting the Jews and inviting the Jews to accept baptism and convert. However, in warning of a new plague that was affecting modern society, which he termed "the kingdom of money," and insisting on the need to defend against it, the Pope—without naming the Jews—tapped in to one of the main themes of the Catholic anti-Semitic campaign of the time. On the *Figaro* interview, see Miccoli's (1996) account.

25. AAAR, Lettres du P. François Picard 1893–1895. VIII 1896–1899, n. 3515 au Père Vincent de Paul Bailly, Rome, 18 mars 1896.

26. AAAR, b. 127. V. Bailly, Lettres XII 1898–1900, n. 3285 au P. François Picard, Rome, 25 settembre 1899.

27. ASV, SS, EM, , a. 1902, r. 248, fasc.7 "Lamenti contro La Croix . . . diretta dai PP. Assunzionisti . . ." prot 51896, 30 agosto 1899, f. 3.

28. Quoted in Canepa 1978, p. 55.

29. Busi 1986, p. 59.

30. Ibid., p. 46.

31. Quoted in ibid., p. 76.

32. The article, from the 13 mai 1886 *L'Univers,* is quoted in Arnoulin 1902 :157–58.

33. Verdès-Leroux 1967, p. 147.

34. Jacquet and Rouyer 1897. See also Sternhell 1978, p. 237; Pierrard 1998, p. 27. For a look at Drumont's relations with the Jesuits, see Arnoulin 1902.

35. Drumont 1891, pp. 321–27.

36. ASV, SS, EM, a. 1895, r. 66, fasc. unico, Nonciature Apostolique en France, n. 453, Paris, 19 Marzo 1891, to Card. Rampolla, Roma.

37. Ibid., n. 1214. Reply from Card. Rampolla to Monig.ʳ Nunzio Ap.°, Parigi, 2 Aprile 1891; and n. 1660 Nunciature . . . France to Card. Rampolla, n. 457. Paris, 6 Aprile 1891. By 1900, in the wake of the police raid on the editorial offices of *La Croix,* and what Drumont took to be insufficient Church support of the Assumptionists, he launched an even fiercer attack. This time he aimed his fire not only at the papal nuncio but also at the secretary of state, Cardinal Rampolla, whom he charged with selling out France to please the Jews. Again, he sought to appeal to the mass of lower clergy by playing to their resentments toward the higher clergy. The papal nuncio reported this to the secretary of state in a letter dated 31 March 1900, to which he attached a February 1 article from *La Libre Parole.* ASV, S.S., E.M., 1902, rub. 248, fasc. 7 "Lamenti contro La Croix . . . diretta dai PP. Assunzionisti . . ." prot. 55850, Nunzio di Francia al Segretario di Stato, 31 marzo 1900, ff. 156–7.

38. "L'antisemitismo in Francia," *L'Osservatore romano,* 1 luglio 1892, p. 1. For an example of *Civiltà cattolica*'s praise of Drumont's writings, see Ballerini 1891, p. 38.

39. The congress program is found in ASV, SS, EM, a. 1900, r. 248, fasc. 9, ff. 27–30.

40. "Le Congrès de Lyon," *La Croix,* 28 november 1896, p. 2.

41. "Congrès de Lyon," *La Croix,* 1 décembre 1896, p. 2. For an examination of Drumont's role in the rise of modern anti-Semitism in France, see Winock 1982.

42. ASV, SS, EM, a. 1900, r. 248, fasc. 9, ff. 52–53 (15 novembre 1896).

43. The literature on the Dreyfus affair is immense, and continues to grow substantially each year. Useful collections of essays on the affair are edited by Birnbaum 1994 and Drouin 1994.

44. Cited in Holmes 1978, p. 234. The translation is his.

45. A similar point is made by Levillain 1994, pp. 435–36.

46. Wilson 1982, p. 526.

47. Wilson 1982, pp. 107–12. On anti-Jewish riots in France in 1898, see Birnbaum 1988 and 1998.

48. "Tradimento e traditori," *L'Osservatore romano,* 2–3 dicembre 1897, p. 2.

49. Quoted from "L'antisemitismo in Francia," in Miccoli 1997a, p. 1503.

50. In Brennan 1998, pp. 403, 450.

51. "Gli oppressori degl'Ebrei," *L'Osservatore romano,* 16 settembre 1899, p. 1.

52. "Un nuovo assassinio rituale," *L'Osservatore romano,* 4 novembre 1899, p. 2; "L'Omicidio rituale giudaico," *L'Osservatore romano,* 23 novembre 1899, p. 1.

Chapter Nine: Austria

1. Wistrich 1989, p. 34; Moro 1992, p. 323. For an excellent study of comparable developments in Bavaria, see Harris 1994.

2. Rozenblit 1992, p. 226.

3. Schorske 1980, pp. 120–30.

4. Among the works on Lueger and the Austrian political scene around the turn of the century, see Schorske 1980.

5. On Galimberti, see Mellano 1998; on Rampolla, see Malgeri 1982.

6. Miccoli 1997a, pp. 1426–27.

7. ASV, SS, EM, a. 1891, r. 247, fasc. 1, ff. 157–58.

8. The nuncio does not provide Rothschild's first name, but presumably it was Ferdinand Rothschild to whom he was referring.

9. ASV, SS, EM, a. 1891, r. 247, fasc. 1, ff. 174–76. Emphasis in original.

10. On Agliardi, see Fonzi 1960b.

11. My discussion of this incident is based on Miccoli's (1999, pp. 235–38) excellent account, which examines the relevant material in the Vatican archives.

12. Taradel and Raggi 2000, p. 36.

13. Quoted in Fumagalli 1993, p. 129.

14. Miccoli 1997a, p. 1455; Pulzer 1964, pp. 173–84.

15. ASV, SS, EM, a. 1895, r. 247, fasc. 2, prot. 27191 (31 maggio 1895), ff.66–68.

16. ASV, SS, EM, a. 1895, r. 247, fasc. 2, prot. 26831 (10 ottobre 1895). ff.47–50.

17. ASV, SS, EM, 1895, r. 247, fasc. 2, prot. 27788 (27 novembre 1895), ff.130–3.

18. Raffaele Ballerini, "La dispersione d'Israele pel mondo moderno," *Civiltà cattolica,* 1897, II, pp. 257–71.

19. ASV, SS, EM, a. 1902, r. 247, fasc. 10 prot. 16418 (2 febbraio 1894), ff.4–5.

20. ASV, SS, EM, a. 1902, r. 247, fasc. 10, prot. 16418 (5 febbraio 1894), f. 7.

21. ASV, SS, EM, a. 1902, r. 247, fasc. 10, prot. 44717 (23 giugno 1898), ff.182–3.

22. ASV, SS, EM, a. 1902, r. 247, fasc. 10, prot. 44717 (27 giugno 1898), f.184.

23. ASV, SS, EM, a. 1902, r. 247, fasc. 10, prot. 44731 (27 giugno 1898), ff.186–7.

24. ASV, SS, EM, a. 1902, r. 247, fasc. 10, prot. 44994 (30 giugno 1898), ff.50–51.

25. ASV, SS, EM, a. 1902, r. 247, fasc. 10, prot. 45120 (15 luglio 1898), ff.54–55. On the Holy Office investigation: ASV, SS, EM, a. 1902, r. 247, fasc. 10, prot. 44820. Suprema Congregazione del S.Uffizio. Cancelleria. Roma (5 luglio 1898 to Segreteria di Stato), f.194.

26. ASV, SS, EM, a. 1902, r. 247, fasc. 10, prot. 45342 (19 luglio 1898), ff.197–8; prot. 45353 (5 juillet 1898), ff.199–200.

27. ASV, SS, EM, a. 1902, r. 247, fasc. 10, prot. 58973 (24 sett 1900), ff.210–211.

28. ASV, EM, SS, a. 1899, r. 247, fasc. 5 (14 maggio 1899), prot. 50204, ff.147–8.

29. Taradel and Raggi 2000, p. 43.

30. ASV, EM, SS, a. 1899, r. 247, fasc. 3, prot. 51833 (27 agosto 1899), ff. 159–60.

31. ASV, EM, SS, a. 1899, r. 247, fasc. 3, prot. 51833 (31 agosto 1899), ff.161–62.

32. ASV, EE, EM, a. 1902, r. 247, fasc. 9, prot. 63124 (4 maggio 1901), ff.159–60.

Chapter Ten: Race

1. My discussion of the Spanish blood purity laws is based largely on Yerushalmi's (1993) excellent work. For a recent discussion of this history of racial thinking about the Jews by the Church, see Part Five ("The Inquisition: Enter Racism") of Carroll 2001.

2. Quoted in Kaplan 1988, p. 154.

3. Steiman 1998, p. 62. An Italian Fascist example is provided by Farinacci 1939, pp. 13–14.

4. Berkley 1988, p. 88.

5. Quoted in Salvadori 1999, p. 67.

6. Republished as Grégoire 1988. On Grégoire's life, see Ezran 1992.

7. Badinter 1988.

8. Lovsky 1970, p. 234; Trachtenberg 1983, p. 48.

9. Toaff 1988, pp. 103–4.

10. Busi 1986, p. 62; Delmaire 1991, p. 151; Modras 1994, pp. 151–52.

11. Pierrard 1998, pp. 59. For a discussion of the history of Catholic iconography of the Jew and its use in the twentieth century, see Pallottino 1994.

12. Chabouty 1880, pp. 669.

13. In Delmaire 1991, p. 111.

14. In Wilson 1982, p. 526.

15. On eliminationist anti-Semitism, see Goldhagen 1996.

16. Wistrich 1989, pp. 221–22.

17. "L'emancipazione degli ebrei," *L'Osservatore romano,* 24–25 gennaio 1898, p. 1.

18. Cited in Canepa 1978; from "Il Giudaismo nel mondo,"

Chapter Eleven: Ritual Murder and the Popes in the Twentieth Century

1. Machin 1999.

2. The correspondence is reproduced in "Une correspondance intéressante," *L'Univers Israélite,* 1 mars 1890, pp. 363–65.

3. Pierrard 1997, p. 128.

4. ASV, EM, SS, a. 1895, r. 66, fasc. unico, n. 82426, 26 juillet 1889.

5. ASV, EM, SS, a. 1895, r. 66, fasc. unico, n. 82426, 2 agosto 1889. The last phrase refers to the fact that Desportes sent a second copy for Rampolla to keep.

6. Desportes 1890, pp. 15–16. Emphasis in original.

7. ASV, EM, SS, a. 1895, r. 66, fasc. unico, n. 88675, 31 ottobre 1890.

8. ASV, EM, SS, a. 1900, r. 66, fasc. unico, n. 53476, 27 novembre 1899, f. 18.

9. In his cover note, the rector described Lord Russell's letter as a request from a humble son of the Church for the Holy Father to intervene "against the anti-Semitic propaganda in Hungary and France at a minimum by reissuing the censure of the ritual murder charge previously promulgated by Roman Pontiffs." ASV, EM, SS, a. 1900, r. 66, fasc. unico, n.53445, 4 dicembre 1899, ff. 15–16.

10. ASV, EM, SS, a. 1900, r. 66, fasc. unico, n.53441, 4 dicembre 1899, f. 17.

11. ASV, SS, a. 1900, r. 66, fasc. unico, n.53943, 21 dicembre 1899, f. 23; n.53943, 1 gennaio 1900, f. 25.

12. These have been examined for this case by Giovanni Miccoli (1997a, pp. 1532–38), whose work I rely on here.

13. In Miccoli 1997a, p. 1533.

14. Cenci 1933:5 and plate 1.

15. On the Polna ritual murder trial, see Nussbaum 1947.

16. ASV, SS, a. 1900, r. 66, fasc. unico, n.55196, 27 febbraio 1900, ff. 31–32.

17. ASV, SS, a. 1900, r. 66, fasc. unico, n.57936, Suprema Congregazione del S. Uffizio, Cancelleria, 31 luglio 1900, f. 41.

18. Found in ACDF, archive Rerum Variarum, 1901, n. 7 bis (Sul sacrifizio di sangue attribuito agli ebrei), as cited in Taradel and Raggi 2000, pp. 43–44.

19. For example, in a comparable period three centuries earlier (1550–1605), there had been eleven complete papal reigns.

20. This portrait of Giuseppe Sarto is based primarily on Aubert 1990b; Benigni 1911; Chadwick 1998; and Coppa 1998.

21. Herzl 1956, pp. 428, 430.

22. On Merry del Val, see Montini 1952 and Launay 1997.

23. Fumagalli 1993, p. 129.

24. Herzl 1956, pp. 427–30.

25. Appointment as prothonotary apostolic is one of the principal honors a pope can bestow, offering many ceremonial privileges to the recipient.

26. Miccoli 1997a, p. 1376.

27. Pius X was the first pope since Pius V, pontiff in the sixteenth century, to be made a saint.

28. In Pichetto 1983, p. 106.

29. This quote from the June 3, 1891 issue of *Piccolo Monitore* is reproduced in Taradel and Raggi 2000, p. 178n106.

30. See Poulat 1969. On Benigni and Pius X, also see Aubert 1990b; Pichetto 1983; and Coppa 1998, p. 147.

31. Documents reproduced in Szajkowski 1963, pp. 208–9.

32. Rothschild to Merry del Val: ASV, EM, SS, a. 1913, r. 66, fasc. unico, prot. 67162, Oggetto: Intorno all'asserto assassinio rituale nella nazione Giudaica, ff. 44–47; Rothschild to Norfolk: ff. 41–42.

33. ASV, EM, SS, a. 1913, r. 66, fasc. unico, prot. 67162, 18 October 1913, f.43.

34. Szajkowski 1963, p. 207. For details on the Beilis case, see Beilis 1992 and Leikin 1993.

35. These three documents are found in ASV, EM, SS, a. 1913, r. 66, fasc. unico, prot. 67162, ff. 30–31 (22 October 1913), f. 50 (3 November 1913), and f. 51 (4 November 1913).

36. Szajkowski 1963, p. 207.

37. Canepa 1992, p. 369.

38. "Notizie diverse—Italia," *Il Vessillo israelitico*, 15 novembre 1913, p. 620.

39. Quoted in "Notizie diverse—Italia—Firenze," *Il Vessillo israelitico*, 30 novembre 1913, pp. 656–58.

40. "Au jour le jour—Comment se défend Israël," *L'Univers*, 30 octobre 1913.

41. "Le Procès de Kiev—Une importante déposition," *L'Univers*, 2–3 novembre 1913, p. 2.

42. "Le Procès de Kiev," *L'Univers*, 9 novembre 1913, p. 2

43. "La lettre de Lord Rothschild au cardinal Merry del Val à propos du meurtre rituel," *L'Univers*, 12 novembre 1913, p. 3.

44. Pranaitis had, in 1892, published a book in Latin on how the Talmud viewed Christians in which the Talmud's demand that Jews murder Christian children for their blood was featured. He sent his book to the editors of the *Civiltà cattolica* with a personal dedication, and the following year, in 1893, it was cited approvingly by Father Rondina in the journal's pages as offering proof of ritual murder. It would take another forty-six years for an Italian edition of Father Pranaitis's book to appear, put out by *La difesa della razza*, the Fascist magazine dedicated to drumming up sup-

port for the regime's anti-Semitic campaign. See Taradel and Raggi 2000, pp. 33, 179n126. Indeed, as I write, an English version of the book can be found on anti-Semitic sites on the World Wide Web. Pranaitis has made it into cyberspace.

45. Paolo Silva, "Raggiri ebraici e documenti papali: a proposito d'un recente processo," *Civiltà cattolica*, 1914, II, pp. 196–215, 330–44.

Chapter Twelve: A Future Pope in Poland

1. On Benedetto XV, see De Rosa 1966 and Monticone 1990.

2. Tagliaferri 1993, p. 192.

3. McCormick 1957, pp. 14, 17. Her less-than-flattering view, however, seems to have had a wider following in the diplomatic community. John Duncan Gregory, the assistant to the British minister at the papal court, and a Catholic, described Pope Benedict XV as follows in a memo to his foreign secretary in late 1917: "The present Pope is a very decided mediocrity. He has the mentality of a little official, the inexperience of a parochial Italian who has hardly travelled at all and a tortuous method of conducting affairs which arises from years of office work connected with a fifth rate diplomacy [the Vatican's]. . . . He is without any particular charm or personality and he is obstinate and bad-tempered to a marked degree" (Hachey 1972). But note that after the Pope died, O'Hare began to alter her opinion, writing that Benedict XV, despite his unprepossessing appearance, had a record of significant diplomatic achievements on behalf of the Church in a difficult period.

4. AAIU, Angleterre. I. D. 13. Pologne. Letter to Louis Marshall, President, American Jewish Committee (carbon copy), from David L. Alexander, President, London Committee of Deputies of the British Jews, and Claude Montefiore, President, Anglo-Jewish Association, London, April 28, 1916, Jewish Conjoint Foreign Committee.

5. Rich documentation on this episode is found in AAIU, Angleterre. I. D. 13. Pologne. Many of these documents have been published, in French translation in the case of those written in English, in Korzec 1973, who analyzes these materials.

6. Castellan 1981.

7. A brief analysis of Ratti's Polish mission is provided by Morrozzo della Rocca 1996.

8. Periodically, the Vatican announces that archives covering another papal reign are now available for consultation by scholars. Exactly when permission to consult the papers from Pius XI's papacy (1922–1939) will be granted is not yet known.

9. Tollet 1992, p. 259; Watt 1979, pp. 357–58; Marcus 1983, pp. 4–8, 66–7, 100–20.

10. For a good overview of political developments in Poland in these years, including the role of Dmowski, see Watt 1979.

11. In Korzec 1980, p. 110n113. My description relies heavily on Korzec's work.

12. Astorri 1999; Aubert 1981.

13. In Wilk 1995, p. 37.

14. Letter of A. Ratti to Gasparri (17 August 1918), reproduced in Wilk, vol. 2, (1996) pp. 43–57.

15. These refer to the Austrian defeats connected to the Italian war of unification, the first in Lombardy and the second in Veneto.

16. Report from Count Jerzy Moszyński to A. Ratti (1 août 1918), reproduced in Wilk vol. 2 (1996), pp.107–27.

17. ASV, ANV, b. 192, Ratti to Gasparri (24 ottobre 1918), ff. 534–38.

18. ASV, ANV, b. 192, prot. 238, Ratti to Gasparri (2 novembre 1918), ff. 565–75.

19. ASV, ANV, b. 200, f. 16. "Appel au calme," Joseph Bilczewski, Archevêque Métropolitain, 25 novembre 1918.

20. ASV, ANV, b. 191, prot. 439 A 172, Encrypted telegram, Gasparri to Ratti (22 dicembre 1918), ff. 512–513.

21. Ratti to Gasparri (7 dicembre 1918), reproduced in Wilk, vol. 1 (1995), pp. 96–112.

22. Ratti to Gasparri (9 gennaio 1919), reproduced in Wilk, vol. 3 (1997), pp. 250–61.

23. ASV, ANV, b. 205 , "Notices sur les rapports polone-juifs" [undated], ff 322–27. In fact, a very visible part of the early Bolshevik leadership in Russia was of Jewish origin, derived from the small minority of Russian Jews who had left traditional community life and entered national society. Lindemann (1997, pp. 424–36) estimates that up to half of the top Bolshevik leadership in the years immediately following the Russian Revolution were of Jewish origin.

24. ASV, ANV, b. 200, ff. 22–23. Légation de Pologna à Vienne. Nota della Legazione Polacca a Vienna a tutte le Legazioni sui pretesi pogrom ebraici in Galizia da parte polacca (envoyé vers la fin de novembre [1918]).

25. ASV, ANV, b. 205, fasc. 3: "Gli Ebrei e la Questione Ebraica in Polonia (1915–19)." Protesta dei consiglieri ebrei di Kielce sul pogrom antigiudaico di Kielce dell'11 e 12 novembre 1918; e relativa discussione di essa al Consiglio Comunale della stessa città," ff.312–31.

26. Agostinus Łosiński, epus Kielcensis ad clerum diocesis Kielcensis, Kielce, 29 dicembre 1918, copia versio ex lingua Polonica (ms.), ASV, ANV, b. 206, ff.382–3; reproduced in Wilk, v. 3 (1997), pp. 368–70.

27. ASV, ANV, b. 200:"La vérité sur le 'Pogrom' de Lvov. Par un impartial. Versavie janvier 1919," ff.5–21.

28. ASV, ANV, b. 192, prot. 505, p 240. Ratti to Gasparri, Versavia 15 gennaio 1919; "Oggetto: La situazione in Polonia. I pogrom antisemiti." ff. 868–873r.

29. Reddaway 1951, pp. 507–8.

30. Kłoczowski 1990, pp. 452–53.

31. Zawadzki 1995, pp. 434–35. Estimates of the number of Polish Jews who died in the Holocaust can be found in Hilberg 1985, v. 3, pp. 1212–1213. An official census of the Jews of Poland in 1939 counted 3,351,000 Jews. Under 400,000 survived.

32. De Rosa 1966, p. 413. Upper Silesia is located at the point where Germany, Poland, and Czechoslovakia came together.

33. Pellegrinetti's diary covering this period has been published by Natalini 1994. The quotes here are from p. 250.

34. ASV, ANV, b. 193, "Relazione finale della Missione di Mons. Ratti in Polonia redatta da Mons. Pellegrinetti, Luglio 1921," ff. 426–498. Much of this report, but as we shall soon see, not all, has been published in Cavalleri 1990. This quote is from f. 462 of the archival copy.

35. Original is at ASV, ANV, b. 193, "Relazione finale della Missione di Mons. Ratti in Polonia redatta da Mons. Pellegrinetti, Luglio 1921," f. 431; the published version is in Cavalleri 1990, pp. 148–49.

36. ASV, ANV, b. 193, "Relazione finale della Missione di Mons. Ratti in Polonia redatta da Mons. Pellegrinetti, Luglio 1921," f. 433; Cavalleri 1990, p. 150.

37. ASV, ANV, b. 193, "Relazione finale della Missione di Mons. Ratti in Polonia redatta da Mons. Pellegrinetti, Luglio 1921," f. 451.

38. Levillain 1996, p. 8; Astorri 1999, p. 505.

39. Natalini 1994, p. 52–53.

40. Quoted in Moro 1988, p. 1118

Chapter Thirteen: Antechamber to the Holocaust

1. On the *Protocols of the Elders of Zion,* see especially Cohn 1981, but also Romano 1992 and Segel and Levy 1995.

2. Pichetto 1983, p. 119n33. Also see this source for other material on Benigni, Preziosi, and the *Protocols.*

3. "La Questione israelita e i cattolici francesi," *L'Osservatore romano,* 9 ottobre 1921, quoted in Moro 1988, pp. 1067–68.

4. Jouin 1920, p. 29.

5. The RISS subsequently sold the text of the speech as a pamphlet. Its cover consisted of a portrait of the clerically garbed Father Jouin (Jouin 1929).

6. Quoted in Sauvêtre 1936, pp. 177, 179.

7. Mgr. Jouin, "L'Impérialisme Juif. V. Conclusion," *Revue Internationale des Sociétés Secrètes,* 1925, pp. 81, 90. On Jouin's library, see Pichetto 1983, p. 114.

8. *Revue Internationale des Sociétés Secrètes* 1925.

9. Sauvêtre 1936, pp. 194–96, 223; De Felice 1993, pp. 42–43.

10. Quotes are reproduced in Miccoli 1997a, pp. 1565–66. My discussion is indebted to Miccoli's excellent analysis of this case. Additional material comes from Modras 1994, pp. 271–72. The text of the suppression of the Friends of Israel is found in *Acta apostolica sedis* 1928.

11. D. Mondrone, "Il padre Enrico Rosa D. C. D. G., 'In memoria Patris,' " *Civiltà cattolica,* 1938, IV, p. 485. Pius XI's view of the journal at the time can also be seen

from a letter he wrote in 1924 in which he expressed his appreciation for the fact that "from the journal's very beginning the authors set for themselves that sacred and immutable duty of defending the rights of the Apostolic See and the Catholic faith, and struggling against the poison that the doctrine of liberalism had injected into the very veins of States and societies. . . ." (*Civiltà cattolica*, 1924, III, p. 291).

12. Enrico Rosa, "Il pericolo giudaico e gli 'Amici d'Israele,' " *Civiltà cattolica*, 1928, II, pp. 335–44.

13. There was also a third article, which appeared between the two, in mid–1921 (III, p. 384), and which tells of the plan of the City of Vienna to raise property taxes to force the Catholic proprietors to sell their homes to the Jews.

14. "Austria," *Civiltà cattolica*, 1921, I, pp. 472–73.

15. "Austria," *Civiltà cattolica*, 1922, IV, pp. 369–71.

16. Martina 1998, pp. 348–49, 354; Miccoli 1997a, pp. 1547–48.

17. Pauley 1992, pp. 151–53. *Der Stürmer*'s motto, *Die Juden sind unser Unglueck*— The Jews Are Our Misfortune—could have been the motto of many Catholic organizations and publications over the fifty years preceding World War II.

18. Miccoli 1997a, pp. 1555–56.

19. Modras 1994, p. 226.

20. Heller 1977, pp. 110, 112.

21. Modras 1994, pp. 118–22, 151–52.

22. Modras 1994, pp. 247.

23. Modras 1994, pp. 284–85; Zawadzki 1995. Italians were kept informed of developments in Poland through the Italian Catholic press. In 1934, for example, in response to a wave of violent anti-Semitic demonstrations in Poland, a group of rabbis went to see the archbishop of Warsaw, Aleksander Kakowski, asking him to speak out against anti-Semitism. The archbhishop refused to do so, saying that while he condemned "all violence, whether the work of Jews or of Catholics," the Catholics had been provoked beyond all endurance by the Jews, who were the promulgators in Poland of anticlericalism, atheism, and pornography. "The anti-Semitic movement," the Polish cardinal concluded, "while producing excesses that are deplorable, has in large part been provoked by the Jews themselves."

The cardinal's remarks were reported in the major newspaper serving the priests of Italy, *L'Amico del clero,* which commented on the Polish Jews as follows: "So this is how it is with these good people, whining while trampling the freedom that has been conceded to them to their detriment, not even respecting the hospitality that they have received in Catholic countries and, when they can, taking the reins of power to drive [these countries] to their moral and material ruin out of the hatred they bear for Christ and for all that bears the marks of Christian civilization." After pausing to remind readers that the Church opposed any violence, the story concluded by arguing that the Jews themselves had "often brought on these reactions through their outrages and their provocations" (Miccoli 2000, pp. 300–1).

24. Cornwell 1999, pp. 184–86.

25. Mario Barbera, "La questione giudaica e il Sionismo," *Civiltà cattolica*, 1937, II, pp. 418–30; "La questione giudaica e le conversioni," *Civiltà cattolica*, 1937, II, pp. 497–502. Barbera was considered the country's preeminent expert on Catholic education (see Ghizzoni 1997). Blaming the Jews for communism was a major theme in the Catholic literature on the Jews on the eve of the Holocaust. Typical was the entry on "Marxism" in the authoritative German Catholic handbook on religion edited by the archbishop of Friburg in 1937: "materialistic socialism originally founded by the Jew Karl Marx." "Bolshevism" was similarly defined as "an Asiatic state despotism, in reality in service to a group of terrorists directed by Jews" (quoted in Miccoli 2000, pp. 291–2).

26. Mario Barbera, "La questione giudaica e l'apostolato cattolico," *Civiltà cattolica*, 1937, III, pp. 27–39.

27. 1938 marked an important turning point for the Jews of Europe, with legislation limiting the rights of Jews going into effect in Poland, Romania, Hungary, Austria, and Italy. Little if any objection was voiced by the Vatican to the passage of these laws and, indeed, in a number of these countries Catholic clergy were actively involved in the campaign to pass them. Germany's Nuremberg Laws, stripping Jews of civil rights, had been put into effect in 1935. On the "night of the Crystals" (November 9, 1938), Nazi sympathizers went on a rampage against the Jews, destroying large numbers of synagogues, Jewish-owned stores, and Jewish homes.

28. Mario Barbera, "Intorno alla questione del sionismo," *Civiltà cattolica*, 1938, II, pp. 76–82.

29. Mario Barbera, "La questione dei giudei in Ungheria," *Civiltà cattolica*, 1938, III, pp. 146–53. See Herczl (1993) for a sobering historical study of the central role played by the Catholic Church in the evolution of the modern anti-Semitic movement in Hungary.

30. "À propos de l'antisémitisme—Pèlerinage de la Radio catholique belge," *Documentation Catholique* 39 (1938), pp. 1459–62.

31. "Un discours du pape—L'antisémitisme est inadmissible. Nous sommes spirituellement des sémites," *La Croix*, 17 septembre 1938, p. 1.

32. Miccoli (2000, pp. 308–10) speculates that the decision of both *Civiltà cattolica* and *L'Osservatore romano* not to publish Pius XI's comments on the Jews reflects the changing center of Vatican power at this juncture. With Pius XI ailing, others in the Vatican—presumably the secretary of state, Eugenio Pacelli, who would soon succeed him as pope, above all—held sway, and they did not approve of Pius XI's remarks on behalf of the Jews. Although earlier the Pope had brooked no such internal opposition, by this point, just a few months before his death, he was no longer the powerful figure he had previously been. The German ambassador to the Holy See, Ernst von Weizsäcker, contrasting Pius XI with his successor, Pius XII, later wrote: "If Pius XI, so impulsive and energetic, had lived a little longer he would in all likelihood have brought about a rupture in the relations between the Reich and the Curia" (quoted in Miccoli 2000, p. 163).

33. For an analysis of Gundlach's encyclopedia entry on anti-Semitism, see Miccoli 1997b. An English-language translation of the complete entry is found in Passelecq and Suchecky 1997, pp. 47–49.

34. The complete text of the draft encyclical is repoduced in Passelecq and Suchecky 1997, pp. 176–275. The quotes here are from pages 249–257.

35. The story of the "hidden" encyclical is told by Passelecq and Suchecky 1995 (also see the preface by Emile Poulat), and by Miccoli 1997b and 2000, pp. 315–20. See also Cornwell's (1999, pp. 192–95) discussion. Because Pius XI never acted on the draft, there is no way to know whether he was—or would have been—pleased with it. It is significant, though, that he entrusted the task to Father LaFarge, who had no experience in working at this level of Vatican responsibility and who only happened to be in Rome by chance. It is hard to avoid the impression that the Pope, in taking such an unorthodox approach, was trying to circumvent normal channels, believing that his closest advisors would oppose preparation of such an encyclical.

36. Ghisalberti 1990, p. 86.

37. Farinacci 1938. Emphasis in original. Roberto Farinacci was among the most pro-Nazi of the Fascist leadership, and one of the minority in the Grand Council's historic meeting of July 25, 1943, to vote against deposing Mussolini. He later joined Mussolini in the Nazis' puppet Italian regime of Salò, and, just after Liberation, was executed by partisan forces. On the evolution of the Italian Fascist regime's anti-Semitism, see Sarfatti 2000.

38. Giani 1939, p. 24.

39. See Pichetto 1983, p. 89.

40. Archbishop Dalla Costa, quoted in Cavarocchi 1999, pp. 420–21.

41. On the Church's ambiguous position on the Fascist use of "race" against the Jews, especially as reflected in *Civiltà cattolica* from 1938 to 1943, see Taradel and Raggi 2000, pp. 98–123.

42. "Italia: 2. La posizione degli Ebrei.—3. La 'Civiltà cattolica' e la 'Questione ebraica,' " *Civiltà cattolica,* 1938, III, pp. 558–61. Emphasis in original.

43. De Felice 1993, p. 294.

44. The text of the Pope's note is found in De Felice 1993, p. 564. Also see Miccoli's (1989) analysis of the Holy See and the racial laws in Italy, as well as Spinosa 1952.

45. *L'Osservatore romano,* 14–15 novembre 1938; discussed in Marchi 1994, p. 838. The subject of the lack of public outcry in Italy over the 1938 racial laws remains practically taboo, for it goes against what Bidussa (1994) has labeled the "myth of the good Italian." According to this myth, while Germans, Austrians, Poles, French, Hungarians, Croats, and others collaborated gladly with the Nazis' campaign against the Jews, the good Italians did everything they could to help them. The study of Italian collaboration with the Fascist regime in general, much less with its racial laws, has barely begun.

46. For one particularly chilling description, sent to Pius XII at the end of August 1942, concerning the massacre of tens of thousands of Jewish men, women, and chil-

dren in Ukraine, see "Le métropolite de Léopol des Ruthènes Szeptyckyj au pape Pie XII," Léopol, 29–31 août 1942, document n. 406 in Blet et al. 1967, pp. 625–29.

47. Sarfatti 2000, pp. 224–25.

48. Letter of Father Tacchi Venturi to Cardinal Maglione, Rome, 10 August 1943. Document n. 289 in Blet et al. 1975, pp. 423–24.

49. Letter of Cardinal Maglione to Father Tacchi Venturi, 18 August 1943. Document n. 296 in Blet et al. 1975, pp. 433–34.

50. Letter of Father Tacchi Venturi to Cardinal Maglione, 29 August 1943. Document n. 317 in Blet et al. 1975, pp. 458–62. Tacchi Venturi included with this letter the petition he sent to Umberto Ricci, the new Italian Minister of Interior affairs. It began: "The Most Eminent secretary of state of His Holiness asks me to approach the competent authorities of the Royal Italian Government to obtain acceptance of the following three proposals regarding the existing racial law." After presenting each of the three proposals, he concluded his plea to the representative of the new government as follows: "This is an excellent means by which the government can repair the offence done to the Roman Pontiff by the violation of the Concordat. . . ."

51. Notes du cardinal Maglione, 16 October 1943. Document n. 368 in Blet et al. 1975, pp. 505–6.

52. In his discussion of this encounter, Miccoli (2000, p. 253) notes that it reflects the Vatican's deference to the Nazi view that the Jews were the enemy of the German people. In effect, the Vatican accepted the Nazi logic that any plea on behalf of the Jews who were then being sent to their death represented an act of hostility against the German people.

53. Notes du cardinal Maglione . . . p. 506.

REFERENCES CITED

The following list consists of those published works that have been cited in the text. It does not include any archival materials, nor any newspaper sources, nor articles from the Catholic press, all of which are cited in full in the notes.

Acta apostolicae sedis, XX (1928), pp. 103–4.

Aceldama ossia processo celebre istruito contro gli Ebrei di Damasco nell'anno 1840. 1896. Cagliari: G. Dessì.

Albert, Phyllis Cohen. 1992. "Israelite and Jew: How did nineteenth-century French Jews understand assimilation?" Pp. 88–109 in Jonathan Frankel and Stephen J. Zipperstein, eds., *Assimilation and Community: The Jews in Nineteenth-Century Europe.* Cambridge: Cambridge University Press.

Arnoulin, Stéphane. 1902. *M. Edouard Drumont et les jésuites.* Paris: Librairie des Deux-Mondes.

Astorri, R. 1999. "Gasparri, Pietro." *Dizionario biografico degli italiani* 52:500–7.

Aubert, Roger. 1961. "Antonelli, Giacomo." *Dizionario biografico degli italiani* 3:484–93.

———. 1981. "Gasparri." *Dictionnaire d'histoire et de géographie ecclésiastiques* 19:1365–75.

———. 1990a. "Leone XIII: Tradizione e progresso." Pp. 61–106 in Elio Guerriero and Annibale Zambarbieri, eds., *La Chiesa e la società industriale (1878–1922).* Storia della Chiesa vol. XXII/1. Turin: Edizioni Paoline.

———. 1990b. "Pio X tra restaurazione e riforma." Pp. 107–54 in Elio Guerriero and Annibale Zambarbieri, eds., *La Chiesa e la società industriale (1878–1922).* Storia della Chiesa vol. XXII/1. Turin: Edizioni Paoline.

———. 1990c. "Chiesa e stati europei." Pp. 337–424 in Elio Guerriero and Annibale Zambarbieri, eds., *La Chiesa e la società industriale (1878–1922).* Storia della Chiesa vol. XXII/1. Turin: Edizioni Paoline.

———. 1990d. "Introduzione: I cattolici alla morte di Pio IX." Pp. 35–58 in Elio Guerriero and Annibale Zambarbieri, eds., *La Chiesa e la società industriale (1878–1922).* Storia della Chiesa vol. XXII/1. Turin: Edizioni Paoline.

———. 1990e. *Il Pontificato di Pio IX (1846–1878)*. Translated by Giacomo Martina. *Storia della Chiesa*, vols. XXI/1 and XXI/2. 4th ed. Turin: San Paolo.

Badinter, Robert. 1988. "Introduction" to Henri Grégoire, *Essai sur la régéneration physique, morale et politique des Juifs*. Paris: Stock.

Ballerini, Raffaele. 1891. *Della questione giudaica in Europa*. Prato: Contrucci.

Barbagallo, Francesco. 2001. "The Rothschilds in Naples." *Journal of Modern Italian Studies* 5:294–309.

Beilis, Mendel. 1992. *Scapegoat on Trial: The Story of Mendel Beilis*. Introduced and edited by Shari Schwartz. New York: CIS Publishers.

Benedetto XIV. 1751. *Lettera della S. di N.S. Benedetto XIV a Monsignor Pier Girolamo Guglielmi Assessore del Sant'Officio Sopra l'offerta dell'Avia Neofita di alcuni suoi nipoti infanti ebrei alla fede Cristiano*. Rome.

Benigni, Umberto. 1911. "Pius X." *Catholic Encyclopedia* 12:137–39.

Berkley, George E. 1988. *Vienna and Its Jews: The Tragedy of Success, 1880s–1980s*. Cambridge, Mass.: Abt Books.

Berkovitz, Jay R. 1989. *The Shaping of Jewish Identity in Nineteenth-Century France*. Detroit: Wayne State University Press.

Berliner, Abraham. 1992. (German orig., 1893). *Storia degli ebrei di Roma*. Translated by Aldo Audisio. Milan: Rusconi.

Bidussa, D. 1994. *Il mito del bravo italiano*. Milan: Saggiatore.

Birnbaum, Pierre. 1988. *Un mythe politique: "la Republique Juive": da Leon Blum à Pierre Mendès France*. Paris: Fayard.

———. 1998. *Le moment antisémite: un tour de la France en 1898*. Paris: Fayard.

———, ed. 1994. *La France et l'affaire Dreyfus*. Paris: Gallimard.

Blet, Pierre, Robert A. Graham, Angelo Martini, and Burkhart Schneider, eds. 1967. *Actes et documents du Saint Siège relatifs à la Seconde Guerre Mondiale*, vol. 3: *Le Saint Siège et la situation religieuse en Pologne et dans les pays baltes, 1939–1945*. Vatican City: Libreria Editrice Vaticana.

———, eds. 1975. *Actes et documents du Saint Siège relatifs à la Seconde Guerre Mondiale*, vol. 9: *Le Saint Siège et les victimes de la guerre (janvier-décembre 1943)*. Vatican City: Libreria Editrice Vaticana.

Blouin, Francis X., Jr. 1998. *Vatican Archives: An Inventory and Guide to Historical Documents of the Holy See*. New York: Oxford University Press.

Blustein, Giacomo. 1921. *Storia degli Ebrei in Roma*. Rome: Maglione & Strini.

Boiteux, Martine. 1976. "Les Juifs dans le carnaval de la Rome moderne (XVe–XVIIIe siècles)." *Mélanges de l'École Française de Rome—moyen âge–temps modernes* 88:745–87.

Bori, Pier Cesare. 1983. *Il Vitello d'oro: Le radici della controversia antigiudaica*. Turin: Boringhieri.

Boutry, Philippe. 1997. "Une théologie de la visibilité: Le projet *zelante* de resacralisation de Rome et son échec (1823–1829)." Pp. 317–67 in Maria Visceglia and Catherine Brice, eds., *Cérémonial et rituel à Rome (XVIe–XIXe siècle)*. Rome: École Française de Rome.

Brennan, James F. 1998. *The Reflection of the Dreyfus Affair in the European Press, 1897–1899*. New York: P. Lang.

Breunig, Charles. 1970. *The Age of Revolution and Reaction 1789–1850*. New York: Norton.

Busi, Frederick. 1986. *The Pope of Antisemitism: The Career and Legacy of Edouard-Adolphe Drumont*. Lanham, Md: University Press of America.

Caffiero, Marina. 1991. *La nuova era: Miti e profezia dell'Italia in rivoluzione*. Genoa: Marietti.

———. 1993. " 'Le insidie de' perfidi giudei.' Antiebraismo e riconquista cattolica alla fine del Settecento." *Rivista storica italiana* 105:555–81.

———. 1997a. "Tra Chiesa e Stato. Gli ebrei italiani dall'età dei Lumi agli anni della Rivoluzione." Pp. 1089–1132 in Corrado Vivanti, ed., *Storia d'Italia, Annali 11, Gli ebrei in Italia, vol. 2, Dall'emancipazione a oggi*. Turin: Einaudi.

———. 1997b. "Tra repressione e conversioni: la 'restaurazione' degli ebrei." Pp. 373–95 in Anna L. Bonella, Augusto Pompeo, and Manola Venzo, eds., *Roma fra la Restaurazione e l'elezione di Pio IX*. Rome: Herder.

Caliò, Tommaso. 1995. "Un omicidio rituale tra storia e leggenda: Il caso del beato Lorenzino da Marostica." *Studi e materiali di storia delle religioni* 19:1:55–82.

Canavero, Alfredo. 1988. *Albertario e "L'Osservatore cattolico."* Rome: Stadium.

Canepa, Andrew M. 1978. "Cattolici ed ebrei nell'Italia liberale (1870–1915)." *Comunità* vol. 32, n. 179, pp. 43–109.

———. 1992. "Pius X and the Jews: a reappraisal." *Church History* 61:362–72.

Canonici, Claudio. 1999. "Condizioni ambientali e battesimo degli ebrei romani nel Seicento e Settecento." *Ricerche per la storia religiosa di Roma* 10:235–72.

Cardini, Luigi. 1948. "Albertario, don Davide." *Enciclopedia Cattolica* 1:674.

Carroll, James. 2001. *Constantine's Sword*. Boston: Houghton Mifflin.

Castellan, Georges. 1981. *"Dieu garde la Pologne!" Histoire du catholicisme polonais (1795–1980)*. Paris: Laffont.

Cavalleri, Ottavio. 1990. *L'Archivio di Mons. Achille Ratti visitatore apostolico e nunzio a Vasavia (1918–1921)*. Vatican City: Archivio Vaticano.

Cavarocchi, Francesca. 1999. "La stampa ecclesiastica di fronte alle leggi razziali."

Pp. 415–29 in Enzo Collotti, ed., *Razza e fascismo: La persecuzione contro gli ebrei in toscana (1938–1943)*. Rome: Carocci.

Cecchi, Dante. 1975. *L'amministrazione pontificia nella Prima Restaurazione (1800–1809)*. Macerata: Deputazione di storia patria per le Marche.

Cenci, Pio. 1933. *Il Cardinale Raffaele Merry del Val*. Preface by Card. Eugenio Pacelli. Rome: Berruti.

Chabouty, (abbé) E. H. [under pseudonymn C. C. de Saint André]. 1880. *Franc-Maçons et juifs, sixième âge de l'église d'après l'Apocalypse*. Paris: Société générale de Librairie Catholique.

Chadwick, Owen. 1998. *A History of the Popes 1830–1914*. Oxford: Clarendon Press.

Chazan, Robert. 1997. *Medieval Stereotypes and Modern Anti-Semitism*. Berkeley: University of California Press.

Civinini, Laura. 1997. "La nunziatura di Parigi. Politica e religione a fine Ottocento." *Nuova rivista storica* 81:1–30.

Clark, Christopher. 1999. "German Jews." Pp. 122–47 in Rainer Liedtke and Stephan Wendehorst, eds., *The Emancipation of Catholics, Jews and Protestants*. Manchester: Manchester University Press.

Cohen, Jeremy. 1982. *The Friars and the Jews: The Evolution of Medieval Antijudaism*. Ithaca: Cornell University Press.

———. 1999. *Living Letters of the Law: Ideas of the Jew in Medieval Christianity*. Berkeley: University of California Press.

Cohn, Norman R. 1981. *Warrant for Genocide. The Myth of the Jewish World-Conspiracy and the Protocols of the Elders of Zion*. Chico, Calif.: Scholars Press.

Colapietra, Raffaele. 1963. *La chiesa tra Lamennais e Metternich: il pontificato di Leone XII*. Brescia: Morcelliana.

Colzi, R. 1994. "L'ampliamento del ghetto disposta da papa Leone XII." *Archivio della Società Romana di Storia Patria* 117:215–30.

Consalvi, Ercole. 1950. *Memorie del Cardinal Ercole Consalvi*. Edited by Mons. Mario Nasalli Rocca di Corneliano. Rome: Angelo Signorelli.

Constant, R. P. 1897. *Les Juifs devant l'Église et l'histoire*. Paris. Gaume & Cie.

Convegno Internazionale di Storia del Risorgimento. 1981. *Atti del Convegno "Pio VII e il card Consalvi. Un tentativo di riformare nello Stato pontificio."* Viterbo: Auatrini Archimede.

Coppa, Frank J. 1990. *Cardinal Giacomo Antonelli and Papal Politics in European Affairs*. Albany: State University of New York Press.

———. 1998. *The Modern Papacy since 1789*. London: Longman.

Cornwell, John. 1999. *Hitler's Pope*. New York: Viking.

Corti, Egon. 1928. *The Reign of the House of Rothschild, 1830–1871.* Translated by Brian and Beatrix Lunn. New York: Cosmopolitan.

———. 1929. *La maison Rothschild. L'essor (1770–1830).* Paris. Payot.

Dagan, Henri. 1903. *L'Oppression des juifs dans l'Europe orientale.* Paris: Cahiers de la Quinzaine.

Dante, Francesco. 1990. *Storia della "Civiltà cattolica" (1850–1891): il laboratorio del Papa.* Rome: Studium.

De Felice, Renzo. 1993. *Storia degli ebrei italiani sotto il fascismo.* Revised edition. Turin: Einaudi.

De Franciscis, Pasquale. 1872. *Discorsi del sommo pontefice Pio IX pronunziati in Vaticano ai fedeli di Roma e dell'orbe dal principio della sua prigionia fino al presente.* vol. 1. Rome. G. Aurelj.

Del Chiaro, Giuseppe. 1904. *Indice generale della Civiltà cattolica.* Rome: La Civiltà Cattolica.

Del Monte, Anna. 1989. *Ratto della Signora Anna del Monte, trattenuta a' Catecumini tredici giorni dalli 6 fino alli 19 maggio anno 1749.* Edited by Giuseppe Sermonetta. Rome: Carucci.

Del Re, N. 1976. *Il vicegerente del vicariato di Roma.* Rome: Istituto di Studi Romani.

Delmaire, Danielle. 1991. *Antisémitisme et catholiques dans le Nord pendant l'affaire Dreyfus.* Lille: Presses universitaires de Lille.

Demarco, Domenico. 1949. *Il tramonto dello Stato pontificio. Il papato di Gregorio XVI.* Turin: Einaudi.

De Rosa, Giuseppe. 1966. "Benedetto XV." *Dizionario biografico degli italiani* 8:408–17.

———. 1999. *La Civiltà cattolica: 150 anni al servizio della Chiesa 1850–1999.* Rome: La Civiltà Cattolica.

Desportes, Henri. 1889. *Le Mystère du sang chez les Juifs.* Paris: A. Savine.

———. 1890. *Tué par les juifs, avril 1890: histoire d'un meurtre rituel.* Paris: A. Savine.

Drouin, Michel, ed. 1994. *L'Affaire Dreyfus de A à Z.* Paris: Flammarion.

Drumont, Edouard. 1887. *La France juive.* 2 vols. 115th ed. Paris: C. Marpon & E. Flammarion.

———. 1891. *Le testament d'un antisémite.* Paris: Dentu.

Église de France. 1997. *Le repentir: declaration de l'Église de France : 30 septembre 1997.* Paris: Desclée de Brouwer.

Esposito, Anna. 1990. "Lo stereotipo dell'omicidio rituale nei processi tridentini . . . Simone." Pp. 53–95 in Anna Esposito and Diego Quaglioni, eds., *Processi contro gli ebrei di Trento (1475–1478).* Padua: Antonio Milani.

Ezran, Maurice. 1992. *L'abbé Gregoire, défenseur des juifs et des noirs: révolution et tolérance.* Paris: Harmattan.

Falconi, Carlo. 1981. *Il giovane Mastai.* Milan: Rusconi.

———. 1983. *Il cardinale Antonelli.* Milan: Mondadori.

Farinacci, Roberto. 1938. *La Chiesa e gli ebrei.* Conferenza tenuta il 7 novembre xvii . . . a Milano per l'inaugurazione annuale dello Istituto di cultura fascista. Rome.

Ferguson, Niall. 1998. *The House of Rothschild.* New York: Viking.

Fiorani, Luigi. 1999. "Verso la nuova città: Conversione e conversionismo a Roma nel Cinque-Seicento." *Ricerche per la storia religiosa di Roma* 10:91–186.

Fischer, Lucia Frattarelli. 1998. "Ebrei a Pisa fra Cinquecento e Settecento." Pp. 89–115 in Michele Luzzati, ed., *Gli Ebrei di Pisa (secoli IX–XX).* Pisa: Pacini Editore.

Fleury, Alain. 1986. *"La Croix" et l'Allemagne 1930–1940.* Paris: Cerf.

Foa, Anna. 1997. *Ebrei in Europa: dalla peste nera all'emancipazione.* Rome: Editori Laterza.

Foa, Salvatore. 1965. *Gli Ebrei nel Monferrato nei secoli XVI e XVII.* Bologna: Forni.

Fonzi, Fausto. 1951. "Leone XII." *Enciclopedia Cattolica* 7:1156–8.

———. 1960a. "Albertario, Davide." *Dizionario biografico degli italiani* 1:669–71.

———. 1960b. "Agliardi, Antonio." *Dizionario biografico degli italiani* 1:405–6.

Frankel, Jonathan. 1992. "Assimilation and the Jews in Nineteenth-Century Europe." Pp. 1–37 in Jonathan Frankel and Stephen J. Zipperstein, eds., *Assimilation and Community: The Jews in Nineteenth-Century Europe.* Cambridge: Cambridge University Press.

———. 1997. *The Damascus Affair.* Cambridge: Cambridge University Press.

Freymond, Jacques, and Miklós Molnár. 1966. "The rise and fall of the First International." Pp. 3–35 in Milorad M. Drachkovitch, ed., *The Revolutionary Internationals, 1864–1943.* Stanford: Stanford University Press.

Fumagalli, Pier Francesco. 1993. "Ebrei e cristiani in Italia dopo il 1870: Antisemitismo e filosemitismo." Pp. 125–51 in *Italia Judaica, Gli ebrei nell'Italia unita 1870–1945.* Rome. Ministero per i beni culturali.

Gennarelli, Achille. 1862. *Le dottrine civili e religiose della Corte di Roma in ordine al dominio temporale.* Florence: Mariani.

Ghisalberti, Alberto M. 1990. *Il Parlamento italiano. Storia parlamentare e politica dell'Italia 1861–1992,* vol. 12. Milan: Nuova CEI.

Ghizzoni, Claudia. 1997. *Educazione e scuola all'indomani della Grande Guerra. Il contributo de "La Civiltà cattolica" (1918–1931).* Brescia: Editrice La Scuola.

Giampaolo, Maria Antonetta. 1931. "La preparazione politica del cardinale Lambruschini." *Rassegna storica del risorgimento* 18:81–163.

Giani, Niccolò. 1939. *Perchè siamo antisemiti*. n.p.: Quaderni della Scuola di Mistica fascista Sandro Italico Mussolini.

Gigot, Francis G. 1910. "Judaism." *Catholic Encyclopedia* 8:386–404.

Ginzburg, Carlo. 1990. *Ecstasies: Deciphering the Witches' Sabbath*. Translated by Raymond Rosenthal. London: Hutchinson Radius.

Gladwell, Adèle O., and James Havoc, eds. 1992. *Blood & Roses: The Vampire in 19th Century Literature*. London: Creation Press.

Goldhagen, Daniel. 1996. *Hitler's Willing Executioners*. New York: Knopf.

Gougenot, Henri Roger des Mousseaux. 1896 [1869]. *Le juif, le judaïsme et la judaïsation des peuples chrétiens*. Paris: Plon.

Graetz, Michael. 1992. "Jewry in the modern period: The role of the 'rising class' in the politicization of Jews in Europe." Pp. 156–76 in Jonathan Frankel and Stephen J. Zipperstein, eds., *Assimilation and Community: The Jews in Nineteenth-Century Europe*. Cambridge: Cambridge University Press.

Grayzel, Solomon. 1989. *The Church and the Jews in the XIIIth Century*, vol. 2, 1254–1314. New York: Jewish Theological Seminary.

Grégoire, Henri. 1988. *Essai sur la régéneration physique, morale et politique des Juifs*. Paris: Stock.

Gregorovius, Ferdinand. 1966. *The Ghetto and the Jews of Rome*. Translated by Moses Hadas. New York: Schocken.

Hachey, Thomas E., ed. 1972. *Anglo-Vatican Relations 1914–1939. Confidential Annual Reports of the British Ministers to the Holy See*. Boston: Hall.

Handler, Andrew. 1980. *Blood Libel at Tiszaeszlár*. New York: Columbia University Press.

Harris, James F. 1994. *The People Speak! Anti-Semitism and Emancipation in Nineteenth-Century Bavaria*. Ann Arbor: University of Michigan Press.

Heller, Celia S. 1977. *On the Edge of Destruction: Jews of Poland between the Two World Wars*. New York: Columbia University Press.

Hellwig, I. A. 1971. *Der konfessionelle Antisemitismus im 19. Jahrhundert in Österreich*. Vienna: Herder.

Herczl, Moshe Y. 1993. *Christianity and the Holocaust of Hungarian Jewry*. New York: New York University Press.

Herzl, Theodor. 1956. *Diaries*. Translated by Marvin Lowenthal. New York: Dial Press.

Hilberg, Raul. 1985. *The Destruction of the European Jews,* 3 vols. New York: Holmes and Meier.

Holmes, Jan Derek. 1978. *The Triumph of the Holy See. A Short History of the Papacy in the Nineteenth Century.* London: Burns & Oates.

Hsia, R. Po-Chia. 1988. *The Myth of Ritual Murder: Jews and Magic in Reformation Germany.* New Haven: Yale University Press.

―――. 1992. *Trent 1475: Stories of a Ritual Murder Trial.* New Haven: Yale University Press.

Hyman, Paula E. 1992. "The social contexts of assimilation: Village Jews and city Jews in Alsace." Pp. 110–29 in Jonathan Frankel and Stephen J. Zipperstein, eds., *Assimilation and Community: The Jews in Nineteenth-Century Europe.* Cambridge: Cambridge University Press.

―――. 1998. *The Jews of Modern France.* Berkeley: University of California Press.

Isaac, Jules. 1964. *The Teaching of Contempt: Christian Roots of Anti-Semitism.* Translated by Helen Weaver. New York: Holt, Rinehart and Winston..

Jabalot, Ferdinando. 1825. *Degli ebrei nel loro rapporto colle nazioni cristiane.* Rome: V. Poggioli.

Jacquet, A. J., and E. Rouyer. 1897. *Concours de la Libre Parole, sur les moyens pratiques d'arriver à l'anéantissement de la puissance juive en France.* Paris: Nouvelle Bibliothèque Nationale.

Jouin, Ernest. 1920. *Le péril judéo-maçonnique,* vol. 1, *Les "Protocoles" des Sages de Sion.* Paris: Revue Internationale des Sociétés Secrètes.

―――. 1929. *Discours de Monseigneur Jouin au Congrès de La Ligue anti-judéomaçonnique le lundi 26 novembre 1928.* Paris: Revue Internationale des Sociétés Secrètes.

Kaplan, Joseph. 1988. "Jews and Judaism in the political and social thought of Spain in the sixteenth and seventeenth centuries." Pp. 153–160 in Shmuel Almog, ed., *Antisemitism Through the Ages.* New York: Pergamon Press.

Kaplan, Marion. 1998. *Between Dignity and Despair: Jewish Life in Nazi Germany.* New York: Oxford University Press.

Katz, Jacob. 1961. *Exclusiveness and Tolerance: Studies in Jewish-Gentile Relations in Medieval and Modern Times.* New York: Schocken.

―――. 1970. *Jews and Freemasons in Europe 1723–1939.* Translated by Leonard Oschry. Cambridge: Harvard University Press.

―――. 1980. *From Prejudice to Destruction: Anti-Semitism, 1700–1933.* Cambridge: Harvard University Press.

Kertzer, David I. 1997. *The Kidnapping of Edgardo Mortara.* New York: Knopf.

Kertzer, Morris N., and Lawrence A. Hoffman. 1993. *What Is a Jew?* New York: Macmillan.

Kisch, Guido. 1957. "The yellow badge in history." *Historia Judaica* 19:89–146.

Kłoczowski, Jerzy. 1990. "I cattolici nell'Europa centro-orientale." Pp. 425–59 in Elio Guerriero and Annibale Zambarbieri, eds., *La Chiesa e la società industriale (1878–1922)*. Storia della Chiesa vol. XXII/1. Turin: Edizioni Paoline.

Korzec, Pawel. 1973. "Les relations entre le Vatican et les organisations juives pendant la première guerre mondiale." *Revue d'histoire moderne et contemporaine* 20:301–33.

———. 1980. *Juifs en Pologne. La question juive pendant l'entre-deux-guerres*. Paris: Presses de la Fondation Nationale des Sciences Politiques.

Landauer, Carl. 1959. *European Socialism*, vol. 1, *From the Industrial Revolution to the First World War and Its Aftermath*. Berkeley: University of California Press.

Launay, Marcel. 1997. *La papauté à l'aube du XXe siècle*. Paris: Cerf.

Laurent, Achille. 1846. *Relation historique des affaires de Syrie depuis 1840 jusqu'en 1842 . . .* vol. 2: *La procédure complète dirigée en 1840 contre les Juifs de Damas*. Paris: Gaume Frères.

Lazzarini, Andrea. 1952. "Osservatore Romano, L'," *Enciclopedia Cattolica* 9:422–3.

Leflon, Jean. 1977. *Restaurazione e crisi liberale (1815–1846)*. Translated by Carmelo Naselli. 2nd ed. Storia della Chiesa XX/2. Turin: Editrice Saie.

Leikin, Ezekiel. 1993. *The Beilis Transcripts: The Anti-Semitic Trial That Shook the World*. Northvale, N.J.: Jason Aronson.

Levillain, Philippe. 1994. "Les catholiques à l'épreuve: variations sur un verdict." Pp. 411–50 in Pierre Birnbaum, ed., *La France et l'affaire Dreyfus*. Paris: Gallimard.

———. 1996. "Achille Ratti Pape Pie XI (1857–1939)." Pp. 5–13 in *Achille Ratti Pape Pie XI*. Actes du colloque organisé par l'École française de Rome. Rome: École Française de Rome.

Lindemann, Albert S. 1997. *Esau's Tears: Modern Anti-Semitism and the Rise of the Jews*. New York: Cambridge University Press.

Lovsky, F., ed. 1970. *L'Antisémitisme chrétienne*. Paris: Cerf.

Luzzatto, Gadi. 1987. "Aspetti di antisemitismo nella 'Civiltà Cattolica' dal 1881 al 1903." *Bailamme* I/2, pp. 125–38.

Machin, Ian. 1999. "British Catholics." Pp. 11–32 in Rainer Liedtke and Stephan Wendehorst, eds., *The Emancipation of Catholics, Jews and Protestants*. Manchester: Manchester University Press.

Malgeri, Francesco. 1981. "La stampa quotidiana e periodica e l'editoria." *Dizionario storico del Movimento Cattolico in Italia 1860–1980*, vol. 3, pp. 273–295. Casale Monferrato: Marietti.

———. 1982. "Rampolla del Tindaro." *Dizionario storico del movimento cattolico in Italia 1860–1980*, vol. 2, pp. 532–4. Casale Monferrato: Marietti.

Malino, Frances. 1999. "French Jews." Pp. 83–99 in Rainer Liedtke and Stephan Wendehorst, eds., *The Emancipation of Catholics, Jews and Protestants*. Manchester: Manchester University Press.

Manzini, Luigi M. 1960. *Il cardinale Luigi Lambruschini*. Vatican City: Biblioteca Apostolica Vaticana.

Marchi, Valerio. 1994. " 'L'Italia' e la 'questione ebraica' negli anni Trenta." *Studi Storici* 35: 811–49.

Marcus, Joseph. 1983. *Social and Political History of the Jews in Poland, 1919–1939*. Berlin: Mouton.

Martano, Renata. 1987. "La missione inutile: La predicazione obbligatoria agli ebrei di Roma nella seconda metà del Cinquecento." Pp. 93–110 in M. Caffiero, A. Foa, and A. Morisi Guerra, eds., *Itinerari Ebraico-Cristiani: Società cultura mito*. Fasano: Schena editore.

Martina, Giacomo. 1967. *Pio IX e Leopoldo II*. Rome: Pontificia Università Gregoriana.

———. 1974. *Pio IX (1946–1850)*. Miscellanea Historiae Pontificiae 38. Rome: Editrice Pontificia Università Gregoriana.

———. 1986. *Pio IX (1851–1866)*. Miscellanea Historiae Pontificiae 51. Rome: Editrice Pontificia Università Gregoriana.

———. 1990. *Pio IX (1867–1878)*. Miscellanea Historiae Pontificiae 58. Rome: Editrice Pontificia Università Gregoriana.

———. 1998. *Storia della Chiesa da Lutero ai nostri giorni*, vol. 3, *L'età del liberalismo*. Brescia: Morcelliana.

Martinez (dott.). 1891. *L'Ebreo, ecco il nemico!* Prato: Giachetti.

Martini, Angelo. 1963. *Studi sulla questione romana e la Conciliazione*. Rome: Ed. Cinque Lune.

Martire, Egilberto. 1951. "Leone XIII." *Enciclopedia Cattolica* 7:1158–64.

McCormick, Anne O'Hare. 1957. *Vatican Journal, 1921–1954*. Edited by Marion T. Sheehan. New York: Farrar, Strauss and Cudahy.

McCulloh, J. M. 1997. "Jewish ritual murder: William of Norwich, Thomas of Monmouth, and the early dissemination of the myth." *Speculum* 72:698–740.

Mellano, M. F. 1998. "Galimberti, Luigi." *Dizionario biografico degli italiani* 51:492–4.

Metzler, J., ed. 1973. *Compendio di storia della Sacra Congregazione per l'evangelizzazione dei popoli o "De Propaganda Fide," 1622–1972*. Rome: Pontifica Università Urbana.

Miccoli, Giovanni. 1989. "Santa Sede e Chiesa italiana di fronte alle leggi antiebraiche del 1938." Pp. 163–274 in *La legislazione antiebraica in Italia e in Europa*. Rome: Camera dei Deputati.

———. 1996. "Un'intervista di Leone XIII sull'antisemitismo." Pp. 577–605 in *Cristianesimo nella storia. Saggi in onore di Giuseppe Alberigo*. Bologna: Il Mulino.

———. 1997a. "Santa sede, questione ebraica e antisemitismo fra Otto e Novecento." Pp. 1371–1577 in Corrado Vivanti, ed., *Storia d'Italia, Annali 11, Gli ebrei in Italia*, vol. 2, *Dall'emancipazione a oggi*. Turin: Einaudi.

———. 1997b. "L'enciclica mancata di Pio XI sul razzismo e l'antisemitismo." *Passato e presente* 15:35–54.

———. 1999. "Santa Sede, 'Questione ebraica' e antisemitismo alla fine dell'Ottocento." Pp. 215–46 in Alberto Burgio, ed., *Nel nome della razza. Il razzismo nella storia d'Italia 1870–1945*. Bologna: Il Mulino.

———. 2000. *I dilemmi e i silenzi di Pio XII*. Milan: Rizzoli.

Minerbi, Sergi I. 1990. *The Vatican and Zionism: Conflict in the Holy Land, 1895–1925*. Translated by Arnold Schwarts. New York: Oxford University Press.

Modras, Ronald E. 1994. *The Catholic Church and Anti-Semitism: Poland, 1933–1939*. Langhorne, Pa.: Harwood Academic Publishers.

Mola, Aldo A. 1992. *Storia della Massoneria italiana dalle origini ai nostri giorni*. Milan: Bompiani.

Montefiore, Moses. 1890. *Diaries of Sir Moses and Lady Montefiore*, ed. by L. Loewe. Chicago: Belford-Clarke.

Monticone, Alberto. 1990. "Il pontificato di Benedetto XV." Pp. 155–200 in Elio Guerriero and Annibale Zambarbieri, eds., *La Chiesa e la società industriale (1878–1922)*. Storia della Chiesa vol. XXII/1. Turin: Edizioni Paoline.

Montini, Renzo. 1952. "Merry del Val, Rafael." *Enciclopedia Cattolica* 8:743–5.

Moro, Renato. 1988. "Le premesse dell'atteggiamento cattolico di fronte alla legislazione razziale fascista. Cattolici ed ebrei nell'Italia degli anni venti (1919–1932). *Storia Contemporanea* 19:1013–1119.

———. 1992. "L'atteggiamento dei cattolici fra teologia e politica." Pp. 305–47 in Francesca Sofia and Mario Toscano, eds., *Stato nazionale ed emancipazione ebraica*. Rome: Bonacci.

Moroni, Gaetano. 1843. "Ebrei." Pp. 5–43, in Moroni, *Dizionario di erudizione storico-ecclesiastico*, vol. 47. Venice: Emiliana.

Morrozzo della Rocca, Roberto. 1996. "Achille Ratti e la Polonia (1918–1921)." Pp. 95–122 in *Achille Ratti: Pape Pie IX*. Actes du Colloque École Française de Rome. Rome: École Française de Rome.

Nada, Narciso. 1957. *Metternich e le riforme nello stato Pontificio*. Turin: Deputazione Subalpina di Storia Patria.

Nardello, Mariano. 1972. "Il presunto martirio del beato Lorenzino Sossio da Marostica." *Archivio Veneto* 103:25–45.

Natalini, Terzo. 1994. *I diari del Cardinal E. Pellegrinetti 1916–1922*. Vatican City: Archivio Vaticano.

Nathan, Paul. 1892. *Der Prozess von Tisza-Eszlár.* Berlin. Fontane.

Neofito ex rabbino. 1883. *Il sangue cristiano nei riti ebraici della moderna sinagoga: Rivelazioni di neofito ex rabbino monaco greco per la prima volta pubblicate in italiano.* Prato: Giachetti.

Nicholls, William. 1993. *Christian Antisemitism: A History of Hate.* Northvale, N.J.: J. Aronson.

Nicolaevsky, Boris I. 1966. "Secret societies and the First International." Pp. 36–56 in Milorad M. Drachkovitch, ed., *The Revolutionary Internationals, 1864–1943.* Stanford: Stanford University Press.

Niemeyer, Gerhart. 1966. "The Second International: 1889–1914." Pp. 95–127 in Milorad M. Drachkovitch, ed., *The Revolutionary Internationals, 1864–1943.* Stanford: Stanford University Press.

Niewyk, Donald. 1990. "Solving the 'Jewish problem': Continuity and change in German antisemitism, 1871–1945." *Leo Baeck Institute Yearbook* 35:335–70.

Nussbaum, Arthur. 1947. "The 'ritual-murder' trial of Polna." *Historia Judaica* 9:57–79.

Pallottino, Paola. 1994. "Origini dello stereotipo fisionomico dell' 'Ebreo' e sua permanenza nell'iconografia antisemita del novecento." Pp. 17–26 in Furio Jesi, ed., *La menzogna della razza: documenti e immagini del razzismo e dell'antisemismo fascista.* Bologna: Grafis.

Parente, Fausto. 1996. "La Chiesa e il 'Talmud.' " Pp. 521–643 in Corado Vivanti, ed., *Gli ebrei in Italia*, vol. 1, *Dall'alto Medioevo all'età dei ghetti*, Storia d'Italia, annali 11. Turin: Einaudi.

Passelecq, Georges, and Bernard Suchecky. 1995. *L'encyclique cachée de Pie XI.* Paris: Découverte. [English edition: 1997. *The Hidden Encyclical of Pius XI*, trans. Steven Rendall. New York: Harcourt, Brace.]

Pauley, Bruce F. 1992. *From Prejudice to Persecution: A History of Austrian Anti-Semitism.* Chapel Hill: University of North Carolina Press.

Pichetto, M. T. 1983. *Alle radici dell'odio. Preziosi e Benigni antisemiti.* Milan: Angeli.

Pierrard, Pierre. 1988. " 'La Croix' et les juifs de 1920 à 1940." Pp. 278–84 in René Rémond and Emile Poulat, eds., *Cent ans d'histoire de La Croix 1883–1983.* Paris: Le Centurion.

———. 1997. *Juifs et catholiques français: d'Edouard Drumont à Jacob Kaplan (1886–1994).* Paris: Editions du Cerf.

———. 1998. *Les Chrétiens et l'affaire Dreyfus.* Paris: Editions de l'Atelier.

Poliakov, Léon. 1975. *The History of Anti-Semitism,* vol. 3., *From Voltaire to Wagner.* Translated by Miriam Kochan. New York: Vanguard Press.

———. 1990. *Storia dell'antisemitismo,* vol. 4, *L'Europa suicida, 1870–1933.* Florence: La Nuova Italia.

Posener, S. 1940. *Adolphe Crémieux, A Biography.* Translated by Eugene Golob. Philadelphia: Jewish Publication Society.

Poulat, Emile. 1969. *Intégrisme et catholicisme intégral.* Paris: Casterman.

———. 1995. "Préface." Pp. 9–38 in Georges Passelecq and Bernard Suchecky, *L'encyclique cachée de Pie XI.* Paris: Découverte.

Prosperi, Adriano. 1998a. "Una esperienza di ricerca nell'archivio del Sant'Uffizio." *Belfagor* 53:309–45.

———. 1998b. "L'Inquisizione romana." Pp. 15–29 in *L'Apertura degli archivi del Sant'Uffizio Romano.* Rome: Accademia Nazionale dei Lincei.

Pulzer, Peter. 1964. *The Rise of Political Anti-Semitism in Germany and Austria.* New York: Wiley.

Quaglioni, Diego. 1990. "Il procedimento inquisitorio contro gli ebrei di Trento." Pp. 1–51 in Anna Esposito and Diego Quaglioni, eds., *Processi contro gli ebrei di Trento (1475–1478).* Padua: Antonio Milani.

Randall, A. 1956. *Vatican Assignment.* London: Heinemann.

Reddaway. W. F. 1951. "The Peace Conference, 1919." Pp. 490–511 in W. F. Reddaway, J. Penson, O. Halecki, and R. Dyboski, eds., *The Cambridge History of Poland: From Augustus II to Pilsudski (1697–1935).* Cambridge: Cambridge University Press.

Reinerman, Alan J. 1979. *Austria and the Papacy in the Age of Metternich,* vol. 1, *1809–30.* Washington, D.C.: Catholic University Press.

———. 1989. *Austria and the Papacy in the Age of Metternich,* vol. 2, *1830–1838.* Washington, D.C.: Catholic University Press.

Rocciolo, Domenico. 1999a. "Documenti sui catecumeni e neofiti a Roma nel Seicento e Settecento." *Ricerche per la storia religiosa di Roma* 10:391–452.

———. 1999b. "L'archivio della Pia casa dei catecumeni e neofiti di Roma." *Ricerche per la storia religiosa di Roma* 10:545–82.

Rodocanachi, Emmanuel. 1891. *Le Saint Siège et les Juifs. Le Ghetto à Rome.* Paris, Librairie de Firmin-Didot.

Rohling, August. 1872. *Der Talmudjude. Zur Beherzigung für Juden und Christen aller Stände.* Münster: Adolph Russels Verlag.

Romano, Sergio. 1992. *I falsi protocolli: il complotto ebraico dalla Russia di Nicola II ad oggi.* Milàn: Corbaccio.

Romeo, Antonio. 1948. "Antisemitismo." *Enciclopedia Cattolica* 1:1494–1505.

Rosa, Mario. 1982. "Clemente XIV." *Dizionario biografico degli italiani* 26:343–62.

———. 1997. "La Santa Sede e gli ebrei nel Settecento." Pp. 1067–87 in Corrado Vivanti, ed., *Storia d'Italia, Annali 11, Gli ebrei in Italia*, vol. 2, *Dall'emancipazione a oggi*. Turin: Einaudi.

Roth, Cecil, ed. 1935. *The ritual murder libel and the Jew: The Report by Cardinal Lorenzo Ganganelli (Pope Clement XIV)*. London: Woburn Press.

Roveri, Alessandro. 1974. *La Santa Sede tra rivoluzione francese e restaurazione. Il cardinale Consalvi 1813–1815*. Florence: La Nuova Italia.

———. 1983. "Ercole Consalvi." *Dizionario biografico degli italiani* 28:33–43.

Rovira Bonet, Francesco. 1775. *Ristretto della vita e martirio di S. Simone fanciullo di Trento*. Rome: G. Bartolomiceli.

———. 1794. *Armatura de' forti ovvero memorie spettanti agli infedeli ebrei*. Rome.

Rozenblit, Marsha L. 1992. "Jewish assimilation in Habsburg Vienna." Pp. 225–45 in Jonathan Frankel and Stephen J. Zipperstein, eds., *Assimilation and Community: The Jews in Nineteenth-Century Europe*. Cambridge: Cambridge University Press.

Rubin, Miri. 1999. *Gentile Tales. The Narrative Assault on Late Medieval Jews*. New Haven: Yale University Press.

Ruch, C. 1905. "Baptême des infidèles." *Dictionnaire de théologie catholique* 2:2:341–55. Paris: Letouzey et Ané.

Rudt de Collenberg, Wipertus. 1986. "Le baptême des juifs à Rome de 1614 à 1798 selon les registres de la 'Casa dei Catecumini.' Première partie 1614–1676." *Archivium Historiae Pontificiae* 24:9–231.

———. 1987. "Le baptême des juifs à Rome de 1614 à 1798 selon les registres de la 'Casa dei Catecumini.' Deuxième partie 1676–1730." *Archivium Historiae Pontificiae* 25:105–262.

———. 1988. "Le baptême des juifs à Rome de 1614 à 1798 selon les registres de la 'Casa dei Catecumini.' Troisième partie 1730–1798." *Archivium Historiae Pontificiae* 26:119–294.

Rüther, Rosemary. 1974. *Faith and Fratricide: The Theological Roots of Antisemitism*. New York: Seabury Press.

Salvadori, Roberto G. 1993. *Gli ebrei toscani nell'età della Restaurazione (1814–1848)*. Florence: Centro Editoriale Toscano.

———. 1999. *1799—Gli ebrei italiani nella bufera antigiacobina*. Florence: Giuntina.

Sarfatti, Michele. 2000. *Gli ebrei nell'Italia fascista*. Turin: Einaudi.

Satta, Fiamma. 1987. "Predicatori agli ebrei, catecumeni e neofiti a Roma nella prima metà del Seicento." Pp. 113–27 in M. Caffiero, A. Foa, and A. Morisi Guerra, eds., *Itinerari Ebraico-Cristiani: Società cultura mito.* Fasano: Schena Editore.

Sauvêtre, J. 1936. *Un bon serviteur de l'Église, mgr. Jouin protonotaire apostolique, curé de Saint-Augustin (1844–1932).* Paris: Maison Casterman, Ligue franc-catholique.

Schorske, Carl E. 1980. *Fin-de-Siècle Vienna: Politics and Culture.* New York: Knopf.

Segel, Benjamin W., and Richard S. Levy, eds. 1995. *A Lie and a Libel: The History of the Protocols of Zion.* Lincoln: University of Nebraska Press.

Silber, Michael K. 1992. "The entrance of Jews into Hungarian society in Vormärz." Pp. 284–323 in Jonathan Frankel and Stephen J. Zipperstein, eds., *Assimilation and Community: The Jews in Nineteenth-Century Europe.* Cambridge: Cambridge University Press.

Sorkin, David. 1992. "The impact of emancipation on German Jewry: A reconsideration." Pp. 177–98 in Jonathan Frankel and Stephen J. Zipperstein, eds., *Assimilation and Community: The Jews in Nineteenth-Century Europe.* Cambridge: Cambridge University Press.

Sorlin, Pierre. 1967. *"La Croix" et les juifs (1880–1899): Contribution à l'historie de l'antisémitisme contemporaine.* Paris: B. Grasset.

Spinosa, Antonio. 1952. "Le persecuzioni razziali in Italia—L'atteggiamento della Chiesa." *Il Ponte,* pp. 1078–96.

Steiman, Lionel B. 1998. *Paths to Genocide: Antisemitism in Western History.* New York: St. Martin's.

Steinsaltz, Adin. 1976. *The Essential Talmud.* Translated by Chaya Galai. New York: Basic.

Sternhell, Zeev. 1978. *La Droite révolutionnaire, 1885–1914: les origines françaises du fascisme.* Paris: Gallimard.

Stow, Kenneth R. 1977. *Catholic Thought and Papal Jewry Policy, 1555–1593.* New York: Jewish Theological Seminary of America.

Szajkowski, Zosa. 1963. "The impact of the Beilis case on Central and Western Europe." *American Academy for Jewish Research Proceedings* 31:197–218.

Tagliaferri, Maurizio. 1993. *L'Unità cattolica: Studio di una mentalità.* Dissertatio ad Doctoratum, Pontificia Universitas Gregoriana (Rome).

Talmon, J. L. 1967. *Romanticism and Revolt: Europe 1815–1848.* New York: Harcourt, Brace & World.

Taradel, Ruggero, and Barbara Raggi. 2000. *La segregazione amichevole: "La Civiltà Cattolica" e la questione ebraica 1850–1945.* Rome: Einaudi.

Toaff, Ariel. 1988. *Mostri giudaici: l'immaginario ebraico dal Medievo alla prima età moderna.* Bologna: Il Mulino.

Tollet, Daniel. 1992. *Histoire des Juifs en Pologne.* Paris: Presses Universitaires de France.

Trachtenberg, Joshua. 1983. *The Devil and the Jews: The Medieval Conception of the Jew and Its Relation to Modern Antisemitism.* Philadelphia: Jewish Publication Society.

Twitchell, James B. 1981. *The Living Dead: A Study of the Vampire in Romantic Literature.* Durham, N.C.: Duke University Press.

Verdès-Leroux, Jeannine. 1969. *Scandale financier et antisémitisme catholique.* Paris: Centurion.

Verona Fedele. 1892. *L'Infanticidio di Xanten e il processo . . . contro l'ebreo Wolf Buschoff.* Verona: Verona Fedele.

Volli, G. 1968. "Il beato Lorenzino da Marostica presunta vittima d'un omicidio rituale." *Rassegna mensile d'Israele* 34:513–26 and 564–9.

Watt, Richard M. 1979. *Bitter Glory: Poland and Its Fate 1918–1939.* New York: Simon and Schuster.

Weil, Henri. 1921. "Un précédent de l'affaire Mortara." *Revue historique* 137:49–66.

Wilk, Stanislaus, ed. 1995–99. *Achille Ratti (1918–1921). Acta Nuntiaturae Polonae.* Tomus 57, vols. 1, 2, 3, 5. Rome: Institutum Historicum Polonicum Romae.

Wills, Garry. 1999. *Papal Sin.* New York: Doubleday.

Wilson, Stephen. 1982. *Ideology and Experience: Anti-Semitism in France at the Time of the Dreyfus Affair.* East Brunswick, N.J.: Fairleigh Dickinson University Press.

Winock, Michel. 1982. *Edouard Drumont et Cie. Antisémitisme et fascisme en France.* Paris: Seuil.

Wiseman, Nicholas. 1858. *Recollections of the Last Four Popes and of Rome in Their Times.* London: Hurst and Blackett.

Wistrich, Robert S. 1989. *The Jews of Vienna in the Age of Franz Joseph.* Oxford: Oxford University Press.

Yerushalmi, Yosef H. 1993. "L'antisémitisme racial est-il apparu au XXe siècle? De la 'limpieza de sangre' espagnole au nazisme: continuités et ruptures." *Esprit* (mars–avril), n. 190, pp. 5–35.

Zawadzki, Paul. 1995. "Nation catholique et racisme culturel." *Sens* n. 11, pp. 430–45.

INDEX

Adler, Rabbi Hermann, 214–15
Affieh, Moses Abu el-, 87, 102–3
Agliardi, Msgr. Antonio, 192, 193–4, 195, 196–7, 198
Albani, Giuseppe Cardinal, 47, 61
Albertario, Fr. Davide, 149, 163
Alexander, David, 242–3
Ali, Mehemet, 88, 90, 97, 103–4
American Jewish Committee, 19–20, 242, 243
Amico del clero, L' (newspaper), 324n23
Ancona, 28, 36, 67, 76–8, 82–4, 109, 111
Antabi, Rabbi Jacob, 96, 102
Anticoli, Jeremiah, 38–9, 41
Anti-Jewish Alliance, The (journal), 215
anti-Judaism, 4, 6–9, 299n4
Anti-Judeomasonic League, 267
Anti-Semite's Legacy, An (Drumont), 179
anti-Semitism: of non-Catholics, 17, 187; Russian pogroms, 147, 157–8; *see also* Catholic anti-Semitism; modern anti-Semitic movement
Antonelli, Giacomo Cardinal, 120, 123, 124, 125, 167
Archives israélites (newspaper), 217
Asseldonk, Anthony van, 269
Assumptionists, 171, 176, 210, 218; *see also* Croix, La
Aubert, Roger, 167
Austria, 71, 103–4, 113, 222; Jews' history in, 186–7; Papal States' policy toward Jews and, 33–5, 78–9; and Tommaso murder case, 91, 96, 98–9, 104
Austrian anti-Semitism: Catholic Popular party, 195; Catholic press and, 186, 195–6, 200, 272–4; Christian Social party's role, 187–8; Church's political concerns and, 186, 188, 195; Church's relationship with Christian Social party, 188, 189–96, 202–3; Galimberti incident, 188–9;

Holocaust and, 10; "Jewish-liberal threat," Catholic response to, 201–2; modern anti-Semitic movement, Church's role in, 272–5; non-Catholic dimension, 187; priest-led pogroms in Galicia, 196–201; and ritual murder accusations, 158, 164, 219

Badeni, Count Casimir, 194, 195
badges for Jews, 28
Bailly, Fr. Vincent, 172–3, 176, 181
Ballerini, Fr. Raffaele, 8, 143–4, 146, 195–6, 286
banking industry, 79–80, 173
baptisms of Jews, 304n27; age and sex distribution of converts, 43, 303n10, 304n28; apostasy by converts, 44, 47–9; burial of the dead and, 52–3; children taken from parents, 41, 46–7, 49, 58, 59, 118–25, 304n28; dependents of converts, Church's focus on, 38–41, 53–5, 58–9, 303n22, 304n28; Easter eve ceremony, 42; House of Catechumens facility, 42–3; illicit baptisms, validity of, 44–7, 49–50; importance to Church, 41–2; Jews' resistance to conversion, 39–40, 41, 54–5, 304n28; Mortara abduction case, 5, 118–25, 214; mothers threatened with loss of children for refusing baptism, 55–6; motives of voluntary converts, 43–4; pregnancy situations, 56–8, 303n26; racial thinking about Jews and, 205, 209, 211; regulations governing, 302n3; validity issue, 50–2
Barbera, Fr. Mario, 277–9, 325n25
Beaudin, Jean-Baptiste, 95, 308n16
Beilis ritual murder case, 227–8, 230–6
Benedict XIII, Pope, 41–2
Benedict XIV, Pope, 42, 46, 50

345

Benedict XV, Pope, 242, 267; background, 239–40; death of, 262; election as pope, 239–40; Jews, policy toward, 241; Jouin and, 268–9; modernizing reforms, 240; personal qualities, 240–1, 321n3; Ratti mission to Poland, 244, 248, 250, 258; and World War I peace conference, 242

Benigni, Msgr. Umberto, 226–7, 266–7

Bernardino of Feltre, 153

Bernetti, Tommaso Cardinal, 33, 69–70, 75

Bises family, 50–2

Black Death, 138

Bleichröder, Gerson, 130, 173

Bloc Catholique, Le (newspaper), 211

blood libel, *see* ritual murder accusations against Jews

Bologna, 71, 112, 113, 125; restrictions imposed on Jews, 116–18

bolshevism charge against Jews, 246, 247, 252, 263, 322n23, 325n25

Bonet, Francesco Rovira, 43

Bressan, Msgr. Giambattista, 227

Brunner, Fr. Sebastian, 186

Bruno, Giordano, 101

burial of the dead, 52–3

Canepa, Andrew, 224, 231

Cardeli, Bernardo, 41

Carnival rites degrading Jews, 33, 74–5, 108, 109

Casimir the Great, king of Poland, 245

Cassidy, Edward Cardinal, 3

Castiglione family, 52

Catholic anti-Semitism: anti-Semitism/anti-Judaism distinction, 4, 6–9, 299n4; Church's defense of, 18–19, 269–72, 273, 281; Church's renunciation of anti-Semitism, 20–1; encyclical condemning racist anti-Semitism (not issued), 279, 280–2, 326n35; ideological offensive under Leo XII, 64–5, 77; "Jesus as a Jew" problem, 139; mendicant orders and, 153; modern anti-Semitic movement, central role in, 7, 9–10, 13, 205–6; opponents of anti-Semitism within Church, 269–71; Pius IX's

denunciations of Jews, 126–7, 129–30; popes' surreptitious involvement in, 213–14; racial laws of Fascist Italy and, 282–9, 327n50; Ratti mission's reports from Poland, 248–9, 250–1, 259–62; Talmud, campaigns against, 139–40; *see also* Austrian anti-Semitism; Catholic press; conspiracy theories regarding Jews; French anti-Semitism; Papal States' policy toward Jews; Polish anti-Semitism; racial thinking about Jews; ritual murder accusations against Jews

Catholic Church: Commission for Religious Relations with the Jews, 3–4, 6, 8, 10–11, 19, 205, 280; Congregation for Extraordinary Ecclesiastical Affairs, 192–3; Congregation of Propaganda Fide, 71, 88; espionage network, 226–7; fascism, support for, 15; First Vatican Council, 128–9; French government and, 176–7, 186, 239; Holocaust, denial of responsibility for, 3–4, 6, 8; Holocaust's exterminationist policies, opposition to, 9, 17; Holocaust's possibility and, 9–10, 15–18, 264–5, 300n6; Masons, hostility toward, 173–4; modernity, reaction against, 11; Nazi roundup of Rome's Jews, response to, 289–91; papal infallibility, doctrine of, 128, 129; popes portrayed as protectors of Jews, 18–19; Second Vatican Council, 11, 20, 156; socialist movement, opposition to, 14–15; Sodality of St. Pius V, 226–7; and World War I peace conference, 241–3, 285; *see also* Catholic anti-Semitism; Catholic press; Inquisition; *under* Papal States; Ratti mission to Poland; *and specific popes*

Catholic Popular party (Austria), 195

Catholic press, 13; assimilated Jews attacked by, 137–8, 151; Austrian anti-Semitism and, 186, 195–6, 200, 272–4; Benedict XV's suppression of anti-Semitic writings, 241; Catholic anti-Semitism defended by, 270–2; conspiracy theories regarding Jews, 135, 138–9, 143, 145, 146, 149–50, 151, 160–1,

233–4; criticism of popes, 312n31; denial of anti-Semitic intent, 145–6, 150, 165; on Dreyfus affair, 183, 184, 185; French anti-Semitism and, 171–3, 174–6, 177, 178, 183, 184, 185; ghettoization policy, proposed revival of, 134, 136, 138, 144; "good" and "bad" forms of anti-Semitism, as seen by, 147–8, 270–2; growth of, 133–4; Jewish morality attacked by, 139–40, 145; Judaism and Jews, distinction between, 148–9; love for Jews, claimed, 138; modern anti-Semitic movement and, 135–40, 142, 145, 146, 164, 172–3; Polish anti-Semitism and, 276; racial thinking about Jews, 137, 146, 210–11; ritual murder accusations, 156, 158–65, 185, 228, 232–6; secularization movement associated with Jews, 150–1; treasonous activities attributed to Jews, 144; violence against Jews attributed to themselves, 147; warnings to Jews, 148; *see also specific publications*
Cenci, Msgr. Pius, 220
Cento, 67
Cerruti, Pietro, 88, 89
Chabouty, Fr. E. H., 210
cholera, 72, 73
Christian Democratic movement, 180–2
Christian League of National Unity (Poland), 254
Christian Social party (Austria), 10, 187–8, 189–96, 192, 201–3, 211, 220, 222, 274
Citone family, 58–9, 304n27
Civiltà cattolica (journal), 147, 178, 213, 241, 277–9; anti-Jewish campaign, 134, 135–40, 143–6, 312n21; Austrian anti-Semitism and, 195–6, 272–3; Catholic anti-Semitism defended by, 270–2; denial of its anti-Semitic history, 7–9; on Dreyfus affair, 183; Fascists' admiration for, 283–4; founding of, 135; mission of, 135; modern anti-Semitic movement and, 142, 146; Pius XI's support for, 323n11; publication procedures, 135; on racial laws of Fascist Italy, 285–7; ritual murder accusations against Jews, 158–62, 217, 234–6

Clement VIII, Pope, 28, 108, 116
Clement IX, Pope, 74
Clement XII, Pope, 173
Clement XIV, Pope, 26–7, 156
Cohen, Isidore, 217
Colonna, Filippo, 38–9, 40, 44, 45–8, 51, 54–5, 56, 57, 58
Congress of Vienna, 31, 33
Consalvi, Ercole Cardinal, 62; background, 30; baptisms of Jews, 304n27; as candidate for papacy, 60–1; Church's adaptation to modern times, advocacy of, 30–1; and Leo XII, 61; and reinstatement of restrictions on Jews, 34, 35–7; and restoration of Papal States, 31; secretary of state appointment, 30
conspiracy theories regarding Jews, 13, 127; in Catholic press, 135, 138–9, 143, 145, 146, 149–50, 151, 160–1, 233–4; in French anti-Semitism, 173–4; Masons and, 173–4; modern anti-Semitic movement and, 265–9; in Ratti mission's report, 261; ritual murder accusations against Jews and, 233–4
Constant, R. P., 165, 218
Cornwell, John, 16
Corrispondenza romana (newspaper), 226
Crémieux, Adolphe, 103, 174
Croix, La (newspaper), 171–3, 174–6, 177, 178, 181, 182, 183, 209, 210–11

Dei Giudici, Bshp. Baptista, 155
Delassus, Henri, 225–6
della Genga, Annibale, *see* Leo XII, Pope
della Somaglia, Giulio Cardinal, 62, 68
Deloncle, François, 242, 243
De Paoli, Baron, 195
Deputy, The (Hochhuth), 3
De Rosa, Fr. Giuseppe, 7–9
Desbuquois, Fr. Gustave, 281
Desportes, Fr. Henri, 179, 214–18
De Töth, Fr. Paolo, 266
Dmowski, Roman, 246–7
Dominguito del Val, Saint, 220
Dominicans, 63, 139, 153, 165
Dreyfus affair, 148, 176, 182–5, 210

Drumont, Edouard, 164, 165, 177–80, 181, 182, 191, 209, 215, 217, 316*n*37

Ecclesiastical Journal, 64–5
employment of Christians by Jews, prohibition of, 29, 68–70, 76–7, 82–3, 118, 282
Enciclopedia cattolica, 18–19, 149
England, 103–4, 243; expulsion of Jews, 153; hostility toward Catholic Church, 214; ritual murder accusations, English Church objects to, 214–15, 218–21
Esterhazy, Marie Charles Count, 183
Eugenius IV, Pope, 101

Farinacci, Roberto, 283–4, 285, 326*n*37
fascism: Church's support for, 15; Italian regime, 15, 207, 282–9
Fede e Ragione (journal), 266
Feletti, Fr. Pier Gaetano, 116, 117, 118, 119, 125
Ferrara, 33, 34, 67, 84, 111–12
Foligno, 70
forced baptisms, *see* baptisms of Jews
France, 104, 113, 243; Church-government antagonism, 176–7, 186, 239; influence of French Church, 169–70; Jews' history in, 169, 170; and Mortara abduction case, 120–1, 122–3; occupation of Papal States, 29–30, 31; republican government, 169; *see also* French anti-Semitism
Franciscans, 139, 153
Francis Joseph, Emperor, 194, 195, 199
Fransoni, Giacomo Cardinal, 88, 89, 91, 92, 94, 103, 104–5
Frattini, Abshp., 39, 40, 54
Frederick II, Emperor, 152
Freemasons, *see* Masons
Freemasons and Jews (Chabouty), 210
French anti-Semitism: Catholic clergy's role, 170–1; Catholic press and, 171–3, 174–6, 177, 178, 183, 184, 185; Christian Democratic movement, 180–2; conspiracy theories regarding Jews, 173–4; Dreyfus affair, 148, 176, 182–5, 210;

Drumont's role, 177–80; expulsion of Jews, 153, 169; Holocaust, French Church's statement on, 299*n*3; modern anti-Semitic movement, Church's role in, 267–9; racial thinking about Jews, 210–11
French-Catholic League, 267
French Revolution, 13, 25, 143, 271, 283
Friends of Israel, 269–71
Frühwirth, Andreas Cardinal, 193
Funaro family, 56

Galicia, 196–202, 243, 249, 252–3
Galimberti, Msgr. Luigi, 188–9, 190–2
Ganganelli, Lorenzo Cardinal, 229, 230, 234
Garibaldi, Giuseppe, 113
Gasparri, Pietro Cardinal, 272, 277; as candidate for papacy, 262; Jouin and, 268–9; and Ratti mission to Poland, 247, 249, 250, 256, 258; secretary of state appointment, 247–8
Germany, 153, 164, 268; *see also* Nazi movement
Gföllner, Bshp. Johannes Maria, 274–5
ghettos, ghettoization policy, 41; anonymous denunciation of, 77–8; Catholic press's proposed revival of, 134, 136, 138, 144; Catholics' objections to, 67–70; economic effects on Christians, 70; ending of ghettoization, rumors about, 112–13; Gregory XVI's defense of, 81–3; Gregory XVI's re-ghettoization campaign, 75–8, 84; history of (1555–1775), 27–8; Jews' protests, 67; Leo XII's reinstatement of, 62–7; living conditions in ghettos, 72–4; Metternich's objections, 78–9, 80–1; Pius VI's reinstatement of, 27, 28
Giani, Niccolò, 284
Goluchowski, Count, 198–200, 201
Gougenot des Mousseaux, Henri Roger, 128, 174
Gramont, Duke de, 120–1, 122, 123, 124
Grégoire, Fr. Henri, 208–9
Gregorovius, Ferdinand, 42
Gregory, John Duncan, 321*n*3

Gregory IX, Pope, 139, 153, 158

Gregory X, Pope, 218

Gregory XIII, Pope, 63

Gregory XVI, Pope, 117; background, 71; and Carnival rites degrading Jews, 75; conservative outlook, 72, 106; death of, 106; election as pope, 70; employment of Christians by Jews prohibited by, 82–3; ghettoization policy, 75–6, 81–3, 84; personal qualities, 71–2; Rothschild family and, 80; sermons forced upon Jews, 84; and Tommaso murder case, 88, 89, 91, 95, 103, 105

Gruscha, Abshp., 189, 190, 191–2

Gundlach, Fr. Gustav, 281, 282

Harrari brothers, 86–7, 89, 90, 97, 102

Herzl, Theodore, 223, 225

Hillel, 141

Hinderbach, Prince, 154, 155, 156

Hitler, Adolf, 10, 275, 276, 290

Hitler's Pope (Cornwell), 16

Hlond, August Cardinal, 275–7

Hochhuth, Rolf, 3

Holocaust: Austrian involvement, 10; Church's denial of responsibility for, 3–4, 6, 8; Church's opposition to exterminationist policies, 9, 17; Church's role in making Holocaust possible, 9–10, 15–18, 264–5, 300n6; French Church's acceptance of responsibility regarding, 299n3; Polish involvement, 10

Holy Office of the Inquisition, *see* Inquisition

House of Catechumens, 41, 42–3; *see also* baptisms of Jews

Hungary, 185, 203–4, 271, 278–9

Industrial Revolution, 26, 143

Innocent III, Pope, 167, 185

Innocent IV, Pope, 152, 158, 161, 218, 229, 230, 233, 234, 235

Inquisition, 5, 12, 27, 33, 46, 125; and Austrian anti-Semitism, 198, 200; and

baptisms of Jews, 51–2, 54; Bologna Jews, restrictions on, 116–18; Friends of Israel and, 269–70; and ghettoization policy, 68–70, 77–8; history of, 153, 305n6; and Papal States' policy toward Jews, 63–4, 65–6; and ritual murder accusations against Jews, 219–20, 221

Italian unification, 13, 106, 113, 120, 125, 128, 129, 315n18

Italy, 243; Church's antinationalism, 168–9; Fascist regime, 15, 207, 282–9; modern anti-Semitic movement, Church's role in, 265–7; racial laws, 9, 282–9, 326n45, 327n50

Jabalot, Fr. Ferdinand, 64–5, 77

Jacur, Romanin, 224, 231

Jaspar, Msgr., 175

Jesuits, 26; Fascists' admiration for, 284; and racial laws, 207; *see also Civiltà cattolica*

Jewish France (Drumont), 178, 209

Jews: assimilated Jews, 137–8, 141–2, 151; Austria, history in, 186–7; banking industry and, 79–80, 173; Benedict XV's attitude toward, 241; France, history in, 169, 170; Pius X's attitude toward, 224–5; Pius XI's attitude toward, 249–50, 262–3; of Poland, 245–6; popes portrayed as protectors of, 18–19; and World War I peace conference and Church, 241–3, 285; *see also* anti-Semitism; Catholic anti-Semitism; Talmud

Jews Before the Church and History, The (Constant), 165, 218

John XXIII, Pope, 314n1

John Paul II, Pope, 3, 6, 10, 21, 166

Joly, Maurice, 265

Jouin, Fr. Ernest, 267–9, 284

Juif, Le (Gougenot), 128, 174

Julius III, Pope, 63, 101

Kakowski, Abshp. Aleksander, 324n23

Kertzer, David I., 5, 19–21

Kidnapping of Edgardo Mortara, The
    (Kertzer), 5
Kielce, 248, 253–4, 256
Kikiriki (magazine), 274
Killed by the Jews (Desportes), 179, 217–18
Kohn, Abshp. Theodor, 208
Kolb, Victor, 273
Kruszyński, Fr. Józef, 257

LaFarge, Fr. John, 280–1, 283, 326*n*35
Lambruschini, Luigi Cardinal: as
    candidate for papacy, 106; and
    ghettoization policy, 79, 80–1; and
    Tommaso murder case, 88, 89, 90, 94,
    95, 97, 98, 99–100, 102, 103, 104–5
Ledóchowski, Fr. Wladimir, 273–4, 281, 282
Leer, Francesca van, 269
Leniado, Joseph, 87
Lenin, V. I., 252
Leo XII, Pope (Annibale della Genga), 30,
    32, 57, 58, 71, 77, 108, 117; background,
    61–2; Consalvi's relationship with, 61;
    conservative outlook, 62; election as
    pope, 60–1; ghettoization policy, 62–3,
    66, 68; ideological offensive against
    Jews, 64, 65; sermons forced upon Jews,
    63
Leo XIII, Pope, 127, 134–5, 204, 224, 247;
    and Austrian anti-Semitism, 188, 189,
    190, 192, 193, 197, 198, 199, 200, 202, 203;
    background, 167; Catholic press, 133,
    163, 171, 312*nn*21, 31; Christian
    Democratic movement and, 181, 182;
    conservative outlook, 167; Dreyfus
    affair and, 176, 184; election as pope,
    166–7; French Church and, 176–7, 186;
    Jewish issues, approach to, 168, 315*n*24;
    legacy of his papacy, 222; personal
    qualities, 167, 223; "public relations,"
    sense of, 167–8; and ritual murder
    accusations, 163, 214, 215–19, 221–2
Leoni, Cardinal, 68–9
Leopold II, grand duke of Tuscany, 116
Libre Parole, La (newspaper), 164, 178
Liechtenstein, Louis Prince, 187, 190, 193,
    195

Livorno, 48–9, 116
Lorenzelli, Abshp. Benedetto, 177
Lorenzino of Marostica, 127–8
Łosiński, Bshp. Augustinus, 248
Louis, St., 139
Loyola, Ignatius, Saint, 207
Lueger, Karl, 10, 187–8, 189, 190, 191, 192,
    193, 195, 202
Lugo, 67
Luther, Martin, 17, 185
Lvov, 255–6

Maglione, Luigi Cardinal, 289, 290–1,
    327*n*50
Maimonides, 160
Maly Dziennik (newspaper), 276
Manning, Henry Cardinal, 214, 215
Marr, Wilhelm, 135–6
Martin V, Pope, 218
Martina, Fr. Giacomo, 108
Marx, Karl, 17, 277
Masons, 13, 126–7, 145, 148, 150, 167, 211,
    267–8, 315*n*18; Church's hostility toward,
    173–4
matzah, 93, 159
Mazzini, Giuseppe, 113
McCormick, Anne O'Hare, 240–1, 321*n*3
Merry del Val, Rafael Cardinal, 219, 220,
    247; background, 224; as candidate for
    papacy, 262; Pius X's relationship with,
    224; and ritual murder accusations
    against Jews, 229–31, 233, 234–5;
    secretary of state appointment, 223–4
Metternich, Prince Klemens von, 113, 186,
    301*n*18, 306*n*41; ghettoization policy,
    objections to, 78–9, 80–1; Leo XII's
    election as pope and, 61; Rothschild
    family and, 80; Tommaso murder case
    and, 96, 98
Miccoli, Giovanni, 15–16
Milan, 149
Mirari vos (encyclical), 72
Mit brennender Sorge (encyclical), 277
Modena, 95, 116
modern anti-Semitic movement, 79,
    264–5; Austrian movement, Church's

role in, 272–5; Catholic press and, 135–40, 142, 145, 146, 164, 172–3; Church's central role in, 7, 9–10, 13, 205–6; Church's defense of Catholic anti-Semitism and, 269–72, 273, 281; conspiracy theories regarding Jews, Church's promotion of, 265–9; economic sources, 141; first eruptions, 141; French movement, Church's role in, 267–9; Hungarian movement, Church's role in, 278–9; international congress of 1882, 142; Nazi roundup of Rome's Jews, Church's response to, 289–91; nazism, Church's approach to, 274, 275, 276–7, 282, 327n52; Polish movement, Church's role in, 275–6, 324n23; racial laws, Church's connection to, 282–9, 327n50; socialist movement and, 142–3; tenets of, 142, 206; voting rights and, 142; *see also* Holocaust

Moldavian monk, book on ritual murder, 91–4, 95, 105, 159, 165

Monastery of the Annunziatella, 42

Montefiore, Claude, 228, 242–3

Montefiore, Moses, 96, 103, 105

Montini, Msgr., 288

Morisi, Anna, 119

Mortara abduction case, 5, 118–25, 214

Moszyński, George Count, 249

Mussolini, Benito, 15, 263, 268, 277, 283, 287, 288–9

Mystery of the Blood Among the Jews, The (Desportes), 214–18

Nahmias, Samuel, 209

Naples, 153

Napoleon I, Emperor, 25, 29, 31

Napoleon III, Emperor, 114, 122, 174, 265

Nathan, Paul, 228, 230

Nazi movement, 15, 128, 207, 266; Church's approach to, 274, 275, 276–7, 282, 327n52; Nuremberg Laws, 9, 325n27; roundup of Rome's Jews, 289–91; *see also* Holocaust

Niewyk, Donald, 10

Norfolk, Duke of, 218, 219, 221, 228, 229, 230

Odescalchi, Prince Pietro, 72–3

Olivieri, Cardinal, 68–9

On the Jews and Their Lies (Luther), 17

Oreglia di Santo Stefano, Fr. Giuseppe, 136–40, 143, 159–60, 161–2, 178

Oreglia di Santo Stefano, Luigi Cardinal, 136

Osservatore cattolico, L' (newspaper), 149–50, 163–5, 312n31

Osservatore romano, L' (newspaper), 135, 211–12, 213, 267, 272, 284; anti-Semitic series of 1892, 147–9; on Dreyfus affair, 184, 185; Drumont, criticism of, 180; on racial laws of Fascist Italy, 288; and ritual murder accusations against Jews, 162–3, 217, 218; as Vatican's newspaper, 146–7

Pacca, Bartolomeo Cardinal, 31, 48, 49

Pacifici, Maddalena, 44–5, 46, 50

Papal States, 306n41; French occupation, 29–30, 31; history (1814–1870), 12–13; political collapse, 120, 125, 129; political unrest, 62, 71, 106, 113; restoration in 1814, 25, 31; Rothschild family's loans to, 80, 114–15

Papal States' policy toward Jews, 9, 11, 12, 19; Austrian attitude toward, 33–5, 78–9; badges for Jews, 28; Bologna's Jews, restrictions imposed on, 116–18; Carnival rites degrading Jews, 33, 74–5, 108, 109; Clement XIV's policies toward Jews, 26–7; employment of Christians by Jews prohibited, 29, 68–70, 76–7, 82–3, 118; enforcement of restrictions in time of political collapse, 125–6; Inquisition's report on, 63–4, 65–6; Jewish request for liberality, 33–6; Jews outside Papal States, efforts to impose restrictions on, 115–16; liberal conditions under the French, 29–30, 31; liberalization under Clement XIV, 26–7; Pius IX's policies, 107–9, 110–11, 113–15, 116; reinstatement of restrictions following restoration of 1814, 26, 27, 31–7; ritual murder accusations against

Papal States' policy toward Jews (*cont'd*)
Jews, *see* Tommaso murder case;
rituals, restrictions on, 29; sermons
forced upon Jews, 29, 63, 84–5, 108,
109, 307n43; social isolation of Jews,
28–9; social relations between
Catholics and Jews despite
restrictions, 109–10, 111–12; *see also*
baptisms of Jews; ghettos,
ghettoization policy
Pascendi (encyclical), 223
Passover holiday, 93, 159–60
Paul II, Pope, 74
Paul III, Pope, 42, 218
Paul IV, Pope, 27, 28, 207
Pavoncello, Sabato, 52–3
Pax super Israel (booklet), 269
Pèlerin, Le (newspaper), 210
Pellegrinetti, Msgr. Ermenegildo, 258–62
Perquel, Lucien, 242
Pesaro, 65–6, 67, 76
physical stereotypes of Jews, 210
Piatelli family, 56
Picard, Fr. François, 171–2, 176
Picciaccio, Pazienza, 39, 40–1
Piccolo Monitore (newspaper), 227
Picquart, Maj. Georges, 183
Piperno, Giuseppe, 73–4
Pisa, 74–5
Pius VI, Pope, 26, 27, 28, 29, 61, 75
Pius VII, Pope, 12, 31, 32, 34, 56–7, 61–2;
baptisms of Jews, 45–6, 47, 48; election
as pope, 30; reinstatement of
restrictions on Jews, 26, 35, 36, 37;
sermons forced upon Jews, 63
Pius VIII, Pope, 70, 117
Pius IX, Pope, 113, 167, 192; beatification of,
166, 314n1; Catholic press, 133, 134, 135,
149; conspiracy theories regarding Jews,
127; contact with Jews prior to election
as pope, 309n1; decision-making
process, 124; denunciations of Jews,
126–7, 129–30; election as pope, 106–7;
Jewish policies of liberalization and
then reaction, 107–9, 110–11, 113–15, 116;
Jews outside Papal States, efforts to
impose restrictions on, 115–16; legacy of

his papacy, 222; and Mortara abduction
case, 119, 120–1, 122, 123–5; papal
infallibility, doctrine of, 128, 129; and
Papal States' political collapse, 120, 125,
129; personal qualities, 107; and ritual
murder accusations, 127, 128; Rothschild
family, dealings with, 114–15; summary
view of his papacy, 166; Syllabus of
Errors, 126–7, 134
Pius X, Pope, 244; anti-Semitic figures,
dealings with, 225–7; background,
222–3; canonization of, 314n1;
conservative outlook, 223; death of, 239;
election as pope, 222; Jews, attitude
toward, 224–5; Merry del Val's
relationship with, 224; personal
qualities, 223; and ritual murder
accusations, 227, 230, 231–2
Pius XI, Pope (Achille Ratti), 16, 277;
background, 244; Belgian pilgrims,
comments on anti-Semitism to, 279–80,
325n32; *Civiltà cattolica*, support for,
323n11; death of, 282; election as pope,
244, 262; encyclical condemning racist
anti-Semitism (not issued), 279, 280–2,
326n35; Jews, attitude toward, 249–50,
262–3; Jouin and, 269; on racial laws of
Fascist Italy, 287–8; *see also* Ratti mission
to Poland
Pius XII, Pope, 15–16, 135, 220, 242, 277, 282,
287, 288, 289, 325n32
Pius Association, 273
Poland: borders controversy, 257–8; Jewish
population, 245–6; restoration of Polish
state following World War I, 243–4,
246–7, 256–7; socialist movement, 254–5;
see also Ratti mission to Poland
Polish anti-Semitism: bolshevism charge
against Jews, 246, 247, 252, 263, 322n23;
Catholic clergy's anti-Semitism, 257;
expulsion of Jews, demands for, 276;
Holocaust and, 10; Jews blamed for
Poland's problems, 248–9; Jews' Polish
identity, denial of, 258–9; modern anti-
Semitic movement, Church's role in,
275–6, 324n23; nationalism and, 246;
pogroms, 246, 247, 250, 251–4, 255–6,

261; ritual murder accusations, 156; World War I and, 246

Portugal, 153

Pranaitis, Fr. Justinus, 230, 235, 320n44

press, the, 133; *see also* Catholic press

Preziosi, Giovanni, 266–7

Pro Christo (periodical), 210

Protocols of the Elders of Zion, The, 265–8, 284

Proudhon, Pierre-Joseph, 17

Purim holiday, 93, 159

Quanta cura (encyclical), 126

racial laws, 9, 207, 325n27, 326n45; Church's connection to, 282–9, 327n50

racial thinking about Jews, 4; baptisms of Jews and, 205, 209, 211; in Catholic press, 137, 146, 210–11; Church's denial of involvement in, 205–6; Church's role in development of, 206–12; in French anti-Semitism, 210–11; physical stereotypes, 210; "scientific" arguments, 210; stench attributed to Jews, 209–10

Rampolla, Mariano Cardinal, 204, 239, 316n37; and Austrian anti-Semitism, 188, 189–90, 191, 192, 193, 194, 195, 197, 198, 199, 200, 201, 202, 203; background, 168; as candidate for papacy, 222; and French anti-Semitism, 176, 177, 179–80, 182; Galimberti incident, 189; and ritual murder accusations, 214, 215–19, 221; secretary of state appointment, 168

Ratti Menton, Count, 87, 95, 97, 308n16

Ratti mission to Poland: anti-Semitic orientation of reports, 248–9, 250–1, 259–62; Catholic political involvement, issue of, 248, 254–5; final report, 257–62; historical significance, 244; instructions for, 247–8; Jews' meeting with Ratti, 249–50, 262; pogroms, reports on, 251–4, 255–6, 261; recall to Rome, 257–8

Ratzinger, Joseph Cardinal, 5

Ravenna, 62

Regime fascista, Il (journal), 278, 286

Revue du Monde Catholique (journal), 178

Revue International des Sociétés Secrètes (journal), 267, 268, 269, 284

ritual murder accusations against Jews, 14, 20, 151; in Austria, 158, 164, 219; Beilis case, 227–8, 230–6; blood of Christians, Jews' alleged uses of, 92–3; Catholic campaign of late nineteenth century, 213–22; in Catholic press, 156, 158–65, 185, 228, 232–6; children allegedly preferred as victims, 93; conspiracy theories regarding Jews and, 233–4; Desportes, Vatican's support for, 214–18; Dominguito del Val case, 220; English Church's objections, 214–15, 218–21; executions resulting from, 154, 156; first instances of, 152; Franciscans and, 153; Inquisition investigation, 219–20, 221; Jewish organizations' objections, 227–31, 235; Lorenzino of Marostica cult, 127–8; Moldavian monk's book, 91–4, 95, 105, 159, 165; Muslims as alleged victims, 160; Pius IX's endorsement of, 127, 128; pogroms resulting from, 157–8; popes' identification with, 156; popes' protection of Jews, 152, 156, 161–2; Pranaitis's book, 320n44; refutation of the accusation, Vatican's refusals regarding, 218–22, 228–33, 234–5; Simon of Trent case, 152–6, 159, 161, 232–3, 234; Talmud and, 100–2, 160, 162; vampirism and, 156–7; *see also* Tommaso murder case

Rivarola, Agostino Cardinal, 62

Rohling, Fr. August, 136, 158

Rome, *see under* Papal States

Rome, Nazi roundup of Jews in, 289–91

Rondina, Fr. Saverio, 8, 144–5, 160–1

Rosa, Fr. Enrico, 270–2, 282

Rosenberg, Alfred, 128

Rosselli family, 54–5

Rossetti (Tuscan consul), 89, 97, 100, 102, 103

Rothschild, Alphonse de, 130

Rothschild, Leopold, Lord, 228, 229–30, 231, 234, 235

Rothschild, Baron Salomon, 79, 80, 98, 109

Rothschild family, 173, 186–7, 191; banking business, 79–80; Metternich's relationship with, 80; Papal States, loans to, 80, 114–15

Rovira Bonet, Francesco, 303n9

Russell, Lord, 218–19, 221

Russia, 104, 144, 243, 245, 247, 260, 263, 265; Beilis ritual murder case, 227–8, 230–6; pogroms, 147, 157–8

Russian Revolution, 14, 15, 271

Sacchetti, Fr. Giuseppe, 223

Sacconi, Cardinal, 124

Sala, Giuseppe Cardinal, 31–2, 208

Salonicli, Rabbi Moses, 87

Sardinia, 116, 165

Scheicher, Msgr., 202

Schindler, Msgr. Franz, 192–3

Schneider, Ernst, 202, 211

Schönerer, Georg von, 187

Schönere Zukunft (newspaper), 274

Schwarzenberg, Fürst Cardinal, 158

secularization movement, 150–1

Semaine religieuse de Cambrai, La (newspaper), 226

Senigaglia, 67, 68, 76

sermons forced upon Jews, 29, 63, 84–5, 108, 109, 307n43

Severoli, Antonio Cardinal, 61

Sherif Pasha, 88, 90, 96, 97, 100

Sicily, 153

Silva, Fr. Paolo, 234–6

Silveni, Col. Filippo, 58

Simon of Trent, St., 152–6, 159, 161, 232–3, 234

Sixtus IV, Pope, 155, 156

Sixtus V, Pope, 156

socialist movement, 142–3, 168, 180; anti-Semitism within, 17; Church's opposition to, 14–15; in Poland, 254–5

social-political changes of early 1800s, 25–6

Spain, 15, 153, 207

stench attributed to Jews, 209–10

Stoecker, Rev. Adolf, 142

Stojałowski, Msgr. Stanisław, 197–201, 246

Streicher, Julius, 274

Stürmer, Der (newspaper), 274

Syllabus of Errors, 126–7, 134, 167

Tacchi Venturi, Fr., 289, 327n50

Taliani, Abshp. Emidio, 198–200, 202–3

Talmud, 65, 93, 152, 234, 267, 284, 286; Catholic campaigns against, 139–40; contents of, 101; ritual murder accusations and, 100–2, 160, 162; on social contacts with Christians, 140–1

Talmud Jew, The (Rohling), 136, 158

Terni, Gioacchino, 78

Terracino family, 303n26

Testaferrata, Cardinal, 68

Thiers, Louis-Adolphe, 130

Thomas, Abshp., 179, 217

Tivoli, Salvatore, 47–9

Tommaso murder case, 159, 161, 233; alternative explanations for Tommaso's disappearance, 98–100; business dealings of accusers and suspects, 308n16; Capuchin account accusing Jews of murder, 86–8, 165; Church-orchestrated campaign to blame Jews, 94–5, 104–5; confessions of Jews, 87, 90, 96–7, 102–3; Jewish community's response, 91, 97, 103–4, 105; Jewish consuls' replacement, demands for, 91, 307n10; Moldavian monk's book on ritual murder and, 91–4, 95, 105; motives alleged to Jews, 90; release of Jewish suspects, 104; reports to Vatican officials accusing Jews, 88–91; skepticism about Jewish culpability in European press, 95–6; tortures of Jewish suspects, 96–7, 103; Vatican's certainty of Jews' guilt, 99–100, 103, 104–5

Toscano family, 57

treasonous activities attributed to Jews, 144

Treaty of London, 241

Tuscany, 115–16

Tzarphati, Joseph, 63